THE AUTOBIOGRAPHY OF A THIEF

Bruce Reynolds

4 6 8 10 9 7 5

First published in 1995 by Bantam Press

This edition published in 2013 by Virgin Books, an imprint of
Ebury Publishing

A Random House Group Company

Addresses for companies within The Random House Group Limited can be
found at: www.randomhouse.co.uk/offices.htm

The Random House Group Limited Reg. No. 954009

A CIP catalogue record for this book is
available from the British Library

The Random House Group Limited supports The Forest Stewardship
Council® (FSC®), the leading international forest-certification organisation.
Our books carrying the FSC label are printed on FSC®-certified paper.
FSC is the only forest-certification scheme supported by the leading
environmental organisations, including Greenpeace. Our
paper procurement policy can be found at
www.randomhouse.co.uk/environment

MIX
Paper from
responsible sources
FSC® C016897

Printed and bound in Great Britain by Clays Ltd, St Ives plc

ISBN: 9780753539170

To buy books by your favourite authors and register for offers, visit:
www.randomhouse.co.uk

Feb 20

ACKNOWLEDGEMENTS

I want to thank the following people, without whom this book would not have seen the light of day: Tom Benfield, for friendship and patronage; Tony Hoare, for inspiration and encouragement; Allen Dynes, for the same; Tony Thake (whose Transport flew me down to Rio); Norma Heyman, for lunch and the advice, 'Don't talk about it – do it'; and Max – sorry about the sacked city.

I also want to thank the following professionals: Rob Rohrer, for encouragement and for pointing me in the direction of Mark Lucas, the best literary agent in the world (until I can get hold of the Jackal); Martyn Forrester, and everybody at Transworld for having faith.

Last but not least, a special thanks to absent friends – Charlie (1932–1990), Buster (1932–1994) and most of all Harry (1931–1995) – for so many years of support and camaraderie.

Many of the names in this book have been changed to preserve anonymity. Where I have done so, any resemblance to real persons, living or dead, is an unintentional coincidence.

INTRODUCTION

In the eight years since this book was first published, time has exacted a severe but inevitable toll on many members of the cast. Some, like my boyhood cell-mate and fellow Great Train Robber Ronnie Biggs, have been ravaged by illness. Others, like Buster Edwards, Roy James, Harry and George 'Taters' Chatham, each a good and dear friend as well as a faithful partner-in-crime, have sadly left the stage for good.

When those diminishingly few of us who remain get together, the talk nearly always turns to one topic: the good old days. We mourn the passing of an age when stealth and finesse were king, not violence and guns. Don't get me wrong. As you're about to read, I wasn't always Raffles, the silk-gloved gentleman thief, relieving the super-rich of the odd well-insured bauble or two, and I was certainly no Robin Hood. I was a 'villain' – we all were – but none of us was *evil*. Somewhere along the line, crime became more brutal and violent, and many of us blame in no small way the sentences that were handed out to the Great Train Robbers in 1963. Thirty years per man for robbing a mail train was a disproportionate and Draconian tariff for a crime that was committed without firearms, and it should have come as no surprise to the authorities that, from that time onwards, criminals took the view that they might as well carry guns as not. After all, the sentencing couldn't get any tougher, yet carrying a lethal weapon might greatly improve one's chance of success.

Certainly such nostalgia was in the Rio de Janeiro air when a group of us arrived at Ronnie's home in Brazil in 1999 to celebrate the occasion of his seventieth birthday – and, coincidentally, the 37th anniversary to the day of the event that changed all of our lives forever: the Great Train Robbery. It had been seven years since I'd last seen the old reprobate. I knew that he'd had a stroke which had left him temporarily incapacitated and I'd been bracing myself for the worst, so I was delighted to find him alert, his mental faculties functioning and his sense of humour undamaged. As the Dom Pérignon was cracked and the Montecristos lit, the old stories were wheeled out once more and enjoyed to the full. 'Who'd have thought it,' Ron mused, 'that so much would have happened to those two teenage tearaways who sat hatching plots in Lewes Prison all those years ago?'

It was true, and especially for me of the previous six years. Writing this book seemed to have opened a great many doors for me, and, just for a change, all of them were legit. I found myself appearing on radio and television shows, reading at literary festivals, even addressing an audience of two hundred schoolboys at Eton College on the pitfalls of crime. I have reviewed cars for *Top Gear* magazine and films for the *Guardian*, been a consultant on two feature films and guested at the wheel of a Bentley in the Gumball Rally. At other times, it seemed I couldn't walk across my living room without tripping over documentary film crews from Germany, the UK, the USA, Brazil . . .

But for all that, I don't think I've changed. I think I'm the same person now as when I finished writing the book in 1995. Just a bit older, that's all.

'Whatever, there's only the two of us left now,' Ronnie said. 'Apart from the ones who got away.' He grinned.

I grinned back. 'Yeah,' I said, raising my glass. 'To those who got away.'

In the end, of course, not even Ronnie stayed uncaged.

On Friday 4 May 2001, I found myself aboard a private jet, chartered by the *Sun* newspaper, on a mission to bring my old cell-mate back to Britain. After 35 years on the run, Ronnie had finally decided it was time to face the music.

Aboard the plane with me were Mike Sullivan, crime editor of the *Sun*, and reporter Simon Hughes. My job was to ensure Ronnie kept his nerve as he boarded the return flight – and to help him face the moment of truth when he set foot on British soil. Scotland Yard had already told us they'd dusted off an arrest warrant from the vaults of Bow Street court, where it had been lying for years.

But first, Ronnie would sample three British treats I knew he had been longing for. We were flying out a curry, a six-pack of bitter and a jar of Marmite.

I became emotional as I pondered the task ahead. When Mike Sullivan asked me how I was feeling, I turned to him and said, 'I got him into it all those years ago when I persuaded him to join the gang and I feel a responsibility to be there for him now.'

Ronnie was a gambler and this was the final adventure for him. This was the final chapter in his life and it was the right way for it to end. Deep down, we all knew he was coming back to die, very likely behind bars.

I turned back and looked out of the window at the blanket of white cloud below. 'I don't want him dying a wanted man,' I said. 'We are locked together by our past and it's only right that I bring him home. It's what the Americans would call closure.'

PROLOGUE

The August moon was as white as a five-pound note.

Parking the Land-Rover off the road, close to the abutment of Bridego Bridge, I clambered up the embankment, slipping several times on the damp grass and loose rock. At the top, I paused to take a piss. It was more than just relief. Perhaps, subconsciously, I was establishing territorial boundaries like a tom-cat or a lion. This was my domain.

From the top pocket of my camouflage smock I took out a leather cigar case and selected a prepared Montecristo No. 2. Moistening the tapered end, I struck a match, carefully ensuring the flame burned the leaf evenly before I drew in the smoke. I exhaled into the night air; as it blended with the darkness, the thought ran through my mind: I have brought Cuba to Buckinghamshire.

I knew I wouldn't have time to finish it, but a Montecristo No. 2 is a fine companion to have whilst awaiting your destiny. I knew this would be my greatest moment, a night to remember. Whatever happened in the next few minutes, my life would never be the same again.

The waiting at Leatherslade Farm had been a trying time. Waiting always was; it was when people looked into themselves and questioned their motives. Were they dedicated and committed to the operation or had they been drawn in by the general enthusiasm and the lure of immense reward?

I had prowled around the various rooms. The scene had been reminiscent of all the war films I'd seen: the strung-up faces, the perpetual fag, the silent ones and the voluble, all going through their own personal routine for stressed-out times.

They had been over the plan again and again till they were sick of it. They'd respond automatically when their moment arrived.

Preparing to go, uniformed up, I had felt a great affection for all these guys; more, naturally, for those companions who'd shared in previous campaigns. I'd gone to school with Charlie when I returned from evacuation. Paddy and Biggsy I knew from my late teens; Gordon and some of the others from my twenties. It seemed inevitable that we were all in this together.

The atmosphere had radically changed with the prospect of moving, of getting the show on the road at last. No more waiting; here we go, boys! Filing out and merging into their various groups, they'd have to smarten up a bit before attempting to masquerade as a Guards company taking up duties at the Bank of England. They were a scruffy lot, no doubt about it; the uniforms had been left to individual choice and the lack of uniformity showed. It had exactly the effect that I wanted, however: they resembled old black-and-white photographs of irregulars – Popski's Private Army or the Long Range Desert Group. And their leader wore brown jump boots, olive drabs, the camouflage Airborne smock, the gold-rim glasses painted black, the close-cropped military haircut crowned by the sand-coloured beret of the Special Air Service. Yes, I'd thought, we could be David Stirling and his mob setting out from Jalo Oasis to hit Benghazi.

I looked up and down the track, first with the naked eye and then with the binoculars, not looking for anything specific, just settling in, accustoming my vision to the night and my surroundings. I took the walkie-talkie from my smock, checked Paddy at the dwarf signal, checked Roger and Roy on the gantry. Simple checks, no radio traffic to be interpreted. The next time I contacted them would be the last: identification of the target.

I looked at the glowing hands of my Omega stainless-steel watch. 2.45 a.m. Only fifteen more minutes to destiny. Visions of Drake and his motley crew at Panama, of Max my old cell-mate who had continually exhorted me: 'You've got to sack a city.' I hoped Max would not be disappointed that it was just a train.

I looked down at the tracks, at the illusion of the rails converging in the distance, where soft lights marked the outskirts of Leighton Buzzard. Ten minutes more and I should see the darkened mass of the train, picked out by side-lights.

I felt the cool night breeze against my face, bringing with it the scents of a country summer as well as the dank odour of diesel. Weeks of night recces had tuned my senses. I breathed in deeply, heard the scurrying in the undergrowth, the owl hoot, the constant myriad noises which pass for silence.

I knew I'd hear the buzz first. I'd heard it often enough before. Then I'd been closer, on the track itself, Lawrence on the Hejaz Railway, my ear to the ground picking up the minuscule vibrations while the train was still miles away. This time it was a gentle hum, that got louder and more urgent as the engine swept past Leighton Buzzard, before its roar filled the sky as it hurtled towards me. I stood up confidently, 'the youngest major in the British army', and felt my stomach turn.

1

The birth certificate states baldly that Bruce Richard Reynolds, son of Thomas Richard and Dorothy Margaret (née Keen), was born in London on 7 September 1931, at Charing Cross Hospital in the Strand. There's officialdom for you. No hint of romance – no mention of the fact that on a quiet day, if you leant out of a top window of the hospital with an ear trumpet, you could just about hear the sound of Bow Bells; in other words, that I was a cockney by the skin of my teeth.

The certificate also describes my father's occupation as 'porter', but it was Depression time and in reality Dad worked at anything he could find. Mother was a nurse at Putney Hospital for Incurables, and the two of them lived with her parents, Grandma and Grandad Keen, at 24 Florian Road, Putney.

Dad had part-time work waiting on tables at the Star & Garter. His pay depended solely on tips, so life must have been tough. Despite that, my memories, though clouded, suggest that this was a period in which I felt loved and secure.

We lived in a succession of flats in the Putney area until Dad came home one day with the news that he'd found work as a metal pourer in a zinc smelting works in the East End. We moved to Gant's Hill in Essex the next day.

The job was not everything Dad had hoped for. Labour conditions were bad; exploitation was the norm, dehydration was the danger. A large intake of liquid was necessary for health, and the longer my father spent at the grindstone, the more alcoholic the liquid became.

Our flat was above a tobacconist's-cum-sweet shop, owned by a Mr Kerr. He had been an engineer on several polar expeditions, primarily with Shackleton, and he'd often relive his experiences over a few beers with my father while I sat on Dad's knee.

Ford opened its Dagenham works in 1935 and Dad got a good job in the foundry. The economy was picking up and life was beginning to look good for us as well. Perhaps too good for Fate's liking. My mother went into hospital to give birth to my sister, and died a few days later.

'It was negligent care that killed her,' Dad said with bitter conviction.

This terrible blow was closely followed by the death of my infant sister – and then, still within the same year, of Dad's father. Poor Dad was bereft. He'd lost his entire family apart from his mother and son.

Granny Reynolds moved in with us, ostensibly to look after me, though it was probably as much to look after Dad. He was off the rails for a while, and quite understandably so; just how much sadness can one man bear?

When he settled again there was a new love in his life, a lady who was soon to become my stepmother. Amy and I got on well to start with but time revealed her lack of compatibility with Gran. Battle lines were drawn and domestic skirmishes occurred daily. I naturally sided with my gran, which must have made life difficult for Dad. When Gran eventually left to take up a live-in housekeeping job, I saw the upheaval as primarily my stepmother's fault. I rebelled, upsetting the family's stability; to ensure some sort of peace for them I was sent for weeks at a time to live with either Gran Keen or Gran Reynolds.

When I was allowed home, I made valiant attempts to fit in with the new family circle, but with little success. My dad gave me a scruffy little mongrel that he'd retrieved from Battersea Dogs' Home, but I loved it. I called the mutt Scotty and fell asleep each night dreaming of the adventures we'd have together when both of us were older. But one day I came home from school to find that my comrade-in-arms was missing. I spent two or three desperate hours searching for him in the streets before running home. It was then that Amy broke the news.

'The dog was taken ill,' she said. 'I had to have it destroyed.'

It was only much later that I learned the truth; that Amy was a cat lover, and Scotty had nipped one of them. She'd put my dog on its lead and dragged it straight to the vet's.

It was also during one of these periods, when I was still seven years old, that I decided to return to the Chase. I knew I shouldn't have gone. It was expressly forbidden; I'd been caught there once before with my pals and it had cost me a severe bollocking, a week's pocket money and, worst of all, no pictures on Saturday morning. I'd had to go through the whole of the next week not knowing how Flash Gordon was faring on his trip to Mars, or what had happened to the Claymen who metamorphosed from the earth.

The deep, flooded claypit had claimed the lives of several children over the years. We crawled as close as we could to the edge of the highest part and peered down into the grey, stagnant water. What were we looking for? For me, it was to unravel the mystery that lurked in the unfathomable depths. We knew that death was beneath the surface because of the kids who had drowned there, but what was death? Because of my mother, sister and Grandad, it wasn't exactly unfamiliar, yet I could never work out where they had gone. Had they gone to a different world? Maybe they were there in the depths of the Chase.

As we looked, each with his own thoughts, we exchanged tales of drownings, and of bodies found, until someone suddenly realized it was getting dark, and we should have been home hours ago.

As we crossed Valence Avenue, the last main road before home, we heard a faint whimpering. As we turned into Lindisfarne Road and hit home turf the sound grew in intensity. A few strides more and we realized where it was coming from. The whole street was out; a reception commit- tee of worried parents, concerned bystanders, Nosy Parkers and the police.

There was anger and relief as we were spotted.

Of my dad there was no sign, and in his absence the police began questioning me. 'Where have you been? The whole of the Dagenham force has been out looking for you.'

I confessed, only to get the dire warnings again of the Chase's potential dangers. They were talking about taking me to the station when a very irate Dad turned up and took charge with a clip around the ear and the threat of worse to come when he got me home. I knew what that meant. The belt was often threatened in our house but never used, but I knew that I was going to get it this time. Tears, sobs and pleas didn't help me; Dad was very very peeved. I had to lower my shorts and lie face down on the bed.

I heard Dad say, 'This is going to hurt me more than it hurts you.'

I yelped as the pain shot through me, but the second was close behind. And then the third and fourth. Through the tears I thought: Six of the best, that's the tariff. But Dad's heart wasn't in it and the last couple were perfunctory. He decided to withdraw pocket money, pictures and gate me for the weekend. That really was the punishment.

School the next morning saw my pals and me together talking of our respective punishment. Some had escaped more or less unscathed. Authority seemed to work in such arbitrary ways, I sort of knew already that I'd always have a problem with it.

There followed a few days of long faces between Dad and me before he had a serious talk. I responded because he was talking to me, he was my dad and I loved him. I promised to try harder in the future; the weekend curfew was lifted and pocket money restored. We were mates again.

He never used the belt again and I never revisited the Chase – not because it was forbidden but more that I'd already been there, I'd done it, and there were, anyway, other Chases, just as challenging, just as beckoning. For example, my stepmother's purse.

I'd often pinched money from her. Each time I would take a half-crown and buy a sheath knife, always the same brand, which cost about a shilling and had a bone handle and polished leather sheath. With the spare change, I'd get a couple of bottles of Tizer and a coconut ice and go down the park where I'd swig the pop and practise throwing the knife at trees.

This time, however, my stepmother had obviously had enough. She called the police and I was locked up for an hour in the station. Dad was not best pleased – particularly as his wife had involved Old Bill. They had a furious row which ended with me being further exiled to Granny Keen's – much to my delight.

I was now eight years old, and I think that as far as Dad was concerned I was pretty much uncontrollable. Then Hitler invaded Poland and the problem of what to do with me was taken out of his hands.

The outbreak of the Second World War was potentially an exciting time for me, steeped as I was in family tradition.

Great-grandfather Drake had been a Colour Sergeant in the Royal Marines and had gone down with the troopship *Birkenhead*; as family legend had it, he had received the VC for his bravery. Grandad Reynolds had served with the Royal Horse Artillery in Mesopotamia, had been at Gallipoli, and had somehow survived the whole bloody business.

I, too, became a war statistic when I was evacuated, along with a large number of other children, from Ford's Thameside jetty on to the *Golden Eagle*, one of three paddle steamers contracted to take us to safer rural havens. It was party time for us kids, gas masks dangling from shoulder strings in cardboard boxes, pockets full of sweets, bands playing as we sailed to our destination, Ipswich in Suffolk.

My stepmother was on board with my recently born half-brother, although I wasn't officially in her care. In fact, I saw her just once during the trip and she didn't even wave – maybe she didn't see me.

My first billet was with five other boys at a large farm near the village of Heveningham. It was early days in the war, everything was disorganized, no-one knew what was going to happen next. There were rumours of imminent invasion, not that we kids cared: the countryside had its own areas of new-found adventure to offer. I was at my original billet just a few weeks before moving close by to another farm with lots of kids. A good time was had by all.

Periodically we'd see squadrons of aircraft in the sky. We knew the types; aircraft recognition came naturally to us. Convoys of troops would pass through the village to our whoops and cheers. Guns and war: it was all very exciting.

There were, however, some very sad times – all the regular visiting days when other children's parents arrived by charabanc but there was no sign of my dad. Those days were very bleak for me, and in common with the handful of other kids whose parents never made it I spent the visiting hours in tears in the woods.

Dad always tried to explain his absence; he had responsibilities to his full-time Home Guard duties at Ford, and to my stepmother, who had returned to Dagenham with my half-brother only a few months after the initial evacuation. But I didn't understand. If it was safe enough for those two to be at home, then why not me? It only underlined the fact that I wasn't wanted, yet I never felt it was Dad's fault; the black and white of a child's reasoning saw it as directly due to my stepmother's influence. After all, Dad wrote to me every week, and his letters always contained a sixpenny postal order and a copy of the *Knockout*. They were constant reminders that I had a dad and that he cared for me.

Bombs fell on the east coast and Ipswich was badly affected. It was decided to move us to the safer area of Warwickshire. Nobody told me about this until one day, while playing in a burnt-out car on a rubbish dump, I was puzzled to hear my dad's familiar, three-noted whistle – the family call. Totally surprised, I stepped through the hedgerow and into his arms.

'They said you were going to Warwickshire,' he said. 'I took the rest of the day off work and caught the train to Ipswich, hiking the last ten or so miles.' I was so proud of my dad that day. It made up for all the times that I hadn't seen him, all the tearful days in the woods.

The move to Warwickshire was more organized, the billet an established one, everyone more accustomed by now to the exigencies of the war. I was put in with a couple by the name of Jackson, whose son was away at university in Birmingham. For a few happy months I was their substitute child, complete with hot-water bottles and cups of rationed cocoa. But then the Luftwaffe turned their attention to Birmingham and the Jacksons' son returned home to displace me.

A new billet was found with the Sparks family at Middle Rookery. They were a marvellous couple – they had no children of their own, but were looking after one other evacuee, a boy from Birmingham. We got on like a house on fire.

Mr Sparks loved his land and devoted his whole time to it. His feelings were shared by his wife and consequently they were very happy. Their happiness permeated the home. School was in the local village half a mile or so's walk away but the countryside offered so much stimulus it was never boring. The lessons were undemanding. All the male teachers had been called up for military service and the older female teachers could do little to curb the influx of rowdy strangers in the classroom.

I was reasonably good at anything to do with literature, but the teaching was so slipshod it rarely challenged us and we waited each afternoon for the bell to sound on the last class.

My pal Lester went back to Birmingham, and gradually the rest of the evacuees trickled back to London. Kids waited excitedly at the village hall for the charabanc to arrive and their parents to come to take them home. But as usual, nobody ever came for me. Dad never appeared for me to get a satisfactory reply to the question: 'Lester's gone home – why can't I?' There was only one thing worse than being told by your parents that you couldn't come home, and that was them not being there at all. Then you knew you were alone, truly alone.

The exodus of evacuees left the village hall school with just a handful of pupils, insufficient to justify its staffing levels. The school was closed. Those of us who were left were inducted to their nearest village school. I went to Rowington, a village a mile further away: all new faces, mostly locals. I was the solitary Londoner. At three-thirty each afternoon two things happened. The bell rang and the cry went up: 'Get the fucking Londoner!' The school was two miles from my billet; by the time I returned to London I was doing the distance in just over ten minutes.

The next day it would start all over again. But work on Sparks's farm had toughened me up, and though I was tall and skinny I was quite capable of holding my own. I was fortified, too, by Dad's dictum that if you have to fight, then fight to win – by whatever means necessary.

2

Even in the relative peace and quiet of the country, the war dominated our lives. We kids were caught up in the spirit of daring deeds and heroic battles, of dogfights and comradeship.

I was impressed, as were a lot of kids, with the efficiency of Germany as a fighting machine, picked up mostly from films and newsreels. I had quite a sneaking regard for the Hun, the SS and the U-boats, even to the extent of buying Teach-Yourself-language books and trying to learn the lingo.

Most of us were fascinated by stories of Hitler's evil empire – we had comic-book images of war created partly by the propaganda and by the vivid accounts of brothers, fathers or uncles who were fighting. As a result, German war souvenirs were especially prized and this gave me one of my first scams for making money.

I found a supply of the linen helmets that pre-war motor-racing drivers had used to wear. They were cheap to buy and looked almost like real flying helmets. Using my limited knowledge of German, a pal and I stencilled them with a name and unit: 'Hans Neubau, 45 Staffel, Mannheim'. We took them into school the next day and sold them in the playground as authentic gear from a downed Heinkel bomber. Thankfully, nobody wised up and asked why every helmet bore the name of the same airman. I guess they wanted to believe they had the genuine article.

Months went by and I saw my dad only periodically, though he always wrote. My stepmother visited me at Sparks's farm and brought Gran, who hadn't seen me since I'd been evacuated. It was great to see her, but soon after they arrived, an almighty row broke out when my stepmother told the Sparkses that I was a thief.

Gran jumped to my defence: 'It was his way of getting back at you!' she yelled. I'd never seen her so angry.

I thought to myself, That's right, I never stole anything from anybody in the country. Why didn't I, if I'm supposed to be a thief?

In truth, there was nothing to spend money on. Everything was on ration, including sweets, and my only objects of desire were penknives and elastic for catapults.

After the row, it should have been obvious to me that I wasn't going to be welcomed back by my stepmother. Yet when Dad broke the news to me, I felt crushed. I had missed the mythical place that was home – even though mine hadn't been a home for years. I didn't blame Dad – he was still my hero – but I could never forgive Amy.

I went to live with Gran Reynolds, which wasn't so bad. She loved me and I knew that a lot of kids had no-one at all.

The once-familiar skyline of Battersea was dominated by barrage balloons and pyramids of smouldering rubble, and tall, jagged shells of brickwork that had once been factories. Deep bomb craters had been flooded by water from the fractured mains and turned into ponds. Some of my old haunts now resembled a burnt-out film-set, with nothing but the façades of some shops and houses still standing. The dispossessed looked as bewildered and lost as the many cats and dogs that wandered in the areas they once knew as home. And yet, the spirit was one of defiance; amid the charred and smoking ruins the feeling that even I, as a young lad, could pick up was, 'Let Hitler do his worst: London can take it!'

Gran and Uncle Jack lived at 38 Buckmaster Road, Battersea, where you could have bought every house in the terrace for £400. Downstairs was a front room, bedroom, kitchen, scullery and outside toilet. These were Uncle Jack's quarters; Gran and I had two bedrooms, a kitchen and lavatory on the first floor. She made a real fuss of my homecoming, vacating her real feather bed for the first night to make a special occasion of it. The house backed on to a cemetery, which was good for me, because it meant I could sneak in and out without going down the street. I'd just cross over the gravestones, jump a back wall and climb into my bedroom without anyone knowing I'd been out.

Gran was quite devoted to the Catholic Church so we always had a piece of fish on Friday. She also cooked bits of mixed grill, boiled bacon, stews and pease-pudding. I was never hungry. When pals came to supper, they used to say, 'Your gran should have an arm as big as that,' while they exaggerated her muscles. I was always reading at meal-times, and she'd ask, 'Do you want a bit of bread and jam?' and I'd just sit there, nose in the latest adventure of Leslie Charteris's The Saint, and say, 'Yeah,' and she'd be sawing away at the loaf, building up her biceps.

My father used to come and see me every couple of weeks from Dagenham. It became a routine: he'd come over on Saturday at lunch-time and have a meal, then we'd go and watch Chelsea play. I wasn't that interested in soccer because I wasn't any good at it, but the ritual was important to me because it meant that I was with my dad. Sometimes we'd go on local outings, or he'd bring gifts, like a model aeroplane kit. When I was older we started going to town, sitting together on the 77 bus from Battersea to Charing Cross and talking about grown-up things. Dad told me stories that exemplified the basics of life as he saw them – that if you want a friend you have to be a friend, that you have to put in if you want to take out. He taught me that there was a balance in everything; maintaining that balance was the art of living.

Dad told me tales of his working life, each story illustrating some particular quality that he thought I might benefit from, some pearl of wisdom wrapped up in homespun philosophy. In the thirties, he had worked Saturdays in his girlfriend's father's bike shop. One day, a customer came in and wanted to buy 'the most expensive inner tube you've got'. Dad told him they sold three different manufacturers' tubes. Running through the price range, he demonstrated each in turn. The customer was not impressed.

'I don't need to know any of that,' he said. 'Just give me the most expensive.'

Dad showed him the cheapo, the one he hadn't shown became of its basic price, and said that it was the most expensive.

'That's more like it,' said the customer, admiring the tube and paying the exorbitant price without a murmur. The moral, my dad said, was that the most expensive is not always the best – and also that you cannot be honest with some people; that's not what they want.

Dad was always drawing my attention to signs, seeking my interpretation of their message before giving me his. 'Give your eyes a chance,' he'd say. 'The eye doesn't always reveal what it sees; the familiar can pass almost unnoticed because of its very familiarity. You see that sign?' He nodded at a NO SMOKING notice. 'What does that say?'

'It means you're not allowed to smoke,' I said.

'Yes, that's right – but it's also the name of a comedian.'

'A comedian?'

'Yes, the guy was going for his first audition and he wanted a name that was unique, something a bit different. He looked at the sign of NO SMOKING written across a pair of doors and "Eureka! That's it!" NOSMO KING became his stage name. You see, the moral is that things are not all they appear, and what you think you see may not be what you get. Look at everything with open eyes, Bruce. There are many interpretations on any given theme.'

I'd nod attentively, absorbing the wisdom of my old man. Later, I'd catch the bus back home on my own.

School was never a problem, although I laughed too much in class. I was hopeless with figures but quite good with words and anything to do with history and geography. My only serious bollocking was when the Moscow Dynamos came to play Chelsea, and me and about ten mates skipped school to go and watch. It was a once-in-a-lifetime thing.

My real heroes were motor-racing drivers – the old Bentley boys like Woolf Barnato, who was super-rich and connected with De Beers, and Sammy Davies who was a journalist as well as a driver. Dick Seaman, a British guy, drove for Mercedes before the war, which was quite ironic. He even won a Grand Prix.

During the war, when flying aces became glamorous figures, I read a lot about First World War aces like Von Richthofen and the American squadron, Esquadrille Lafayette. I got more of a buzz looking at a Sopwith Camel than I did from a Spitfire – there was something more basic and adventurous about them. Von Richthofen wasn't my cup of tea. He always seemed to be flying high and picking off stragglers; my favourite was a guy called Voss, who had almost as many kills but was much more of a character. He was killed at the end, flying straight into six SE5s. I really wanted to be the guy that drove into all of them – fuck the danger, just get amongst them and do some damage! It was the grand gesture more than anything else that excited me.

I joined the Scouts when I was thirteen. In theory I should have joined the troop at the end of my street but I joined the one up Lavender Hill, which was a good ten minutes' walk away. Maybe it was because they wore a navy-blue shirt and shorts instead of plain khaki.

I stayed with them a couple of years on and off and got interested in climbing. A friend of mine, Pete, and I found an old chalk quarry in Box Hill; we'd heard that chalk was the nearest equivalent to ice for climbing. It was probably only twenty feet off the ground but it seemed more like sixty. I went first and Pete followed. Without ropes and pegs, we managed to get about halfway when Pete got stuck below me and froze.

'I can't come down and get you, so I'll go to the top,' I said.

But a few feet further I got to the point where I couldn't see any way up and I panicked. I made a flurried grab for a handhold and didn't make it and came tumbling down, landing on the scree and rolling. I wasn't hurt badly, just bruised, and was quite proud when I told people I'd been 'injured in a climbing accident at the weekend'.

I had become aware of reading when I was evacuated and I read a lot of G. A. Henty – always with a historical background: with Marlborough at Malplaquet, with Nelson on the Nile. And always the same story – the young boy gets involved with the squire and he goes to fight at Crecy or somewhere and makes good. I liked naval histories best of all – 'Boy' Cornwall who'd got the VC for staying at his post at Jutland, and Mountbatten on the *Kelly*. Each night, we'd listen to the World Service on the wireless. The Lillibullero theme music was very stirring and so were the tales of heroism; like the motor torpedo boat that got back to England because a sailor lay in the water for 48 hours holding the rudder; and the pilot who crawled out on the wing of an aircraft to put out a fire. I thought: That's it, do something famous like that and you're made for life.

It was the same when I saw Eric Portman in *The 49th Parallel*, the film about a German U-boat which gets damaged and runs aground on the coast of Canada. The crew manage to get ashore and make their way to America, being pursued all the way. Afterwards, I would walk across Wimbledon Common with three or four mates and I'd imagine we were on the run. I'd lead the way with my British army officer's holster at my side, highly polished and empty, ready to blast us out of danger.

Everyone of my age was interested in guns. I had a pistol, a really old one with a brass blunderbuss end. It had belonged to an uncle of mine on my stepmother's side. He'd been in submarines and overstayed his leave only once in his lifetime and that was when the ill-fated *Thetis* went down in Liverpool Bay. He should have been on it.

1944, and the war dragged on. To most of us kids it was what we'd always known. Memories of evacuation and country pleasures paled before life in the city. We'd had the nightly air raids, the barrage of anti-aircraft fire, the shrapnel that cascaded from the sky on to the communal street shelter's roof while women knitted and babies cried, and old boys in their private corners talked of Mons, the Somme, or Vimy Ridge. We kids just sat and listened, drank our tea and cocoa, living for the moment; we were up all night and in the grown-ups' world.

In the mornings we'd look for shrapnel – the larger pieces being the most prized, having great value in the swapping market. We all collected badges and any sort of militaria; they all had their value, but the most prized of all were weapons – bayonets, commando knives and occasionally a chamberless revolver from another war. This would be prize of the week, with everyone desperate to get their hands on it. The wheeling and the dealing that went on would not have looked out of place at the Stock Exchange: a week's pocket money, the stamp collection, the Hornby train set, anything and everything would be swapped for the revolver frame – generally to have it confiscated at once by parents.

Bernard Polly, one of my pals, had access to his uncle's Lee Enfield .303 rifle. Rumour had it that he'd brought it back with him from Dunkirk. Bernard would let us cock it and fire it cold; it had these great sights which lifted up, calibrated for hundreds of yards. We'd hold off the whole of the Waffen SS in his back garden, taking it in turns to fire before the final 'Fix bayonets!' and charge. We always ceremoniously wiped the blood off the bayonet afterwards.

We all wanted that rifle: we wanted any rifle, any gun. 'If you want to get ahead get a gun,' we used to mutter like a mantra, and, 'A gun, a gun, my kingdom for a gun.' But all that were legally available were air pistols and air rifles, and then you had to be fourteen – and proof of age was necessary before you could buy one. A few kids, those that had everything, had them; I plotted to get one. My daily morning paper round wages, saved up for a month, would get me the funds I needed, but who could I get to buy it for me? I was only thirteen, a year short of qualification.

Good old Gran. I worked on her, knowing that she had no bias against firearms: a country girl, she was used to farmers having shotguns around. More than that, Gran was an avid Western fan. Didn't I know it – I had to cycle to the private lending library for her every week to take out her books. Gran was into Zane Grey and Clarence E. Mulford's Hopalong Cassidy sagas. She was also a once-a-week filmgoer, Westerns her favourite. She knew about 'the law of the gun', at least in fictional form. I was sure that she would respond to my blandishments – and she did.

I gave her the £3 one Saturday morning and watched from the gate as she set off for the shops. I was still at my post an hour later when she returned with the parcel in her shopping bag, wrapped in brown paper and string: a push-in, cylindrical-barrelled, Diana .117 calibre air pistol. With that blue-black metallic sheen it looked fantastic; in the half-light, with your eyes half-closed squintingly, it could have been a Luger or the big Mauser. I was infatuated.

However, my new love was hopelessly inaccurate, as endless afternoons pot-shotting at tins in the back garden proved.

Boredom led me from potting tins in the back garden to potting bigger tins on the back garden wall, and then to potting at gravestones in the cemetery beyond. Inevitably there were complaints from people who objected to being harassed by ricochets off the stonework, but no-one knew the identity of the phantom shooter. No-one, except Uncle Jack and Aunt Tiny who lived downstairs, and my dear old Gran. They laid it on me that the police would be calling soon, that I'd be nicked and the air pistol confiscated.

I cooled it for a bit, concentrating on fashioning a holster to facilitate the fast draw, then practising that interminably in front of the mirror. I called in Gran one afternoon for a demonstration. It all went well until the fourth draw when overeagerness to impress caused me to pull the trigger on the draw and I shot her in the arm.

'Oh!' was her startled reaction – this accompanied by a vigorous rubbing of the injured arm. A close inspection revealed a blotch the size of a mosquito bite. I was relieved and happy that she wasn't hurt, but niggling deep down was a terrible disappointment: there wasn't much power in this gun. I lost most of my interest now; quick draws were out, it was back to desultory pot shots at the gravestones, which led inevitably to more complaints.

It was Uncle Jack who answered the door to the PC who called investigating.

'No, Officer, there's no-one here with an air gun.'

Satisfied, the PC left to continue his enquiries. Uncle Jack gave me some verbal stick and threatened to tell Dad the next time that he visited. This was serious, and attempts to recruit Gran as an ally failed.

'Get rid of it before your dad comes,' she said.

The gun was causing problems but I was reluctant to part with it. I preferred to wait and see what Dad said; after all, I hadn't shot anyone. Well, I'd shot Gran, but that didn't count – that was an accident.

Dad was due on the Saturday. He usually arrived around midday and I made sure I wasn't about. I knew I'd have to face him but I preferred later rather than sooner. It was tea-time when I got home, cautiously entering the kitchen. Gran was lovingly crimping the edges of a steak-and-kidney pie, my dad's favourite.

'Where is he?' I asked.

'He's having a lie down in your room, Bruce.'

'What did he say about the police and my air pistol? Is he mad with me?'

'He's not happy with you, Bruce, but he's not mad. He seems more upset with me that I bought it for you,' she replied. 'He wants to talk to you, he said to wake him up when you come in. Take him a cup of tea in.'

I recognized it as a good move – sweeten him up – so with a bold front and a quickening heartbeat I took his tea into my bedroom. He was awake, propped up on the pillows, his boots on the floor. He was a big man, my dad; six foot plus and fifteen stone, and he dwarfed my single iron bed. He looked rested and relaxed as I gave him a kiss with his tea, but he had that quirk of a grin on his face that presaged every serious enquiry.

'What have you been up to now, son?'

Sitting at the foot end of the bed I told him everything – and that involved shooting Gran. I expected an explosion. Not so, though the quirky grin had gone. His tone was serious as he said, 'It has got to go, son, no messing about, no arguments, the air gun has got to go.'

My plaintive 'But . . .' met with cold, firm resolve. Still I persisted. In the face of Dad's rising irritation, I took it to the brink. 'But, Dad . . .'

He cut me off curtly: 'You'll do as I say, I don't want any messing about. Get rid of it, and no lip, you're not too big for a good hiding.'

The memory of the belt gave fuel to my fears; his involuntary movement off the pillows was construed as prelude to an attack, and my immediate response was to grasp his left foot with both hands and with all my strength I applied a footlock. I gave it a twist; he responded with a grunt. I'd got him, I thought, now what did I do with him? I was appalled.

Straightfaced, Dad looked at me. We held glances, eyes locked for a moment before he said, 'Stop messing about, son, let go of my foot. I am warning you now, let go.'

There was no way that I could win; I'd have to let go at some time.

'Promise me that you won't whack me, Dad, promise and I'll let go.'

'Just let go,' was his response.

'Promise, Dad,' remained my obdurate plea.

'Let go now then, son, I promise,' was the finale of the finesse.

Still feeling apprehensive – you don't catch a tiger by the tail every day – I resorted to tried and tested panaceas. 'Another cup of tea, Dad?'

He assented with a nod and I scurried back to the kitchen and Gran.

'Are you all right?' she asked. 'Is your dad all right?'

'I think so.' The truth was that I didn't know what Dad's reaction would be, it was the first direct challenge that I'd ever made, and it was as much a surprise to me as it had been to him. In our periodic sparring sessions he'd stand there while I threw punches but not for long, his arms and muscles were so hard that I ended up with bruised knuckles. He'd laugh then, and giving me a dig in the biceps would say, 'You'll have to get a bit bigger and a bit stronger before you can fancy your chances with your old man.'

In a way it was reassuring to have a tough dad. Street credibility played its part and though Dad didn't live with us he was about with me every couple of weeks. I was always proud to be out with the 'old man', especially if he was in uniform.

I was still subdued when Dad joined us a little while later for tea.

'The matter's settled,' he said to Gran. 'Bruce will be getting rid of the gun and there will be no more pot-shots into the cemetery.'

I nodded my affirmative, thankful that the episode was over.

Dad never held grudges; when the aggro was over that was the end of it. I accompanied him on his way home, the number 77 taking us to Charing Cross, where he caught his bus back to Dagenham. The bus journey was always where Dad and I talked of the more 'serious' aspects of life. This night it appeared that he realized that I was growing up and I sensed that he was trying to instil some sort of responsibility. He obviously found it trying that my sense of 'honour' was not up to his standards.

He told me of his relationship with his own father. 'When I started cycling, he neither encouraged me nor discouraged me. There was no interest from him at all. Yet on the morning of my first real race, the Bath Road 100, my father turned up at the start at five o'clock in the morning to wish me well.'

With that example having been set for him, I thought, no wonder he'd hitched from Ipswich to Heveningham during my evacuation.

We were sitting on the top of the bus as usual, as near the front as we could get. Dad was a smoker, and this particular night he offered me a cigarette. I declined; I'd done my experiments with Charlie Wilson years before and decided it wasn't for me. I appreciated the gesture, though; I was too young then to read its meaning, but I worked out later that his psychology was to dispel the attraction of the forbidden.

When I got home Gran said, 'He worries about you, you know. He's a good father.'

'I know that, Gran, and I'm sorry. I didn't mean to cause trouble. I'll get rid of the gun next week – at school, probably.'

I wasn't really sorry to part with the gun; the novelty had worn off. It took me most of the week to find the right swap – the new spike-design British Army bayonet, scabbardless but unique. No-one else had got one. With that bayonet I was sure that I could conquer the world.

3

I left the Scouts and joined the Sea Cadets, and everything seemed to point to me eventually going to the naval training school at Exmouth. I certainly didn't have any other ambitions.

I was fourteen and a half when I finally applied, and Dad came with me to County Hall for the medical. My eyesight had never been good and in the years before Michael Caine made wearing spectacles *de rigueur*, it was considered swottish for a kid to need them. The Navy certainly didn't approve.

Dad consoled me on the pavement after I had failed.

'What are you going to do now?' he asked.

I'd been reading a bit of Dennis Wheatley and fancied the notion of being a foreign correspondent in dangerous lands.

'I'm going to be a reporter,' I replied.

I had a rough idea where Fleet Street was and Dad confirmed it. Dad went home and I walked over Westminster Bridge and along the Embankment until I reached Bouverie Street and cut up towards Fleet Street. The first newspaper office that I saw was Northcliffe House, the imposing, white stone edifice that housed the *Daily Mail*, *Sunday Despatch* and *Evening News*.

'I want to be a reporter,' I said to the hall porter, and he pointed me to the personnel department. 'You could start as a messenger boy,' he said. 'That's the way to get on.'

I started the next day. It was a marvellous job. I liked the late shift best and weekends, when there wasn't much to do. There were a lot of ex-servicemen and the two lift men, Dick and Harry, had both lost arms in the war. When we sat down and drank tea they'd tell tales of derring-do in the western desert and Italy. Dick had lost his arm at Anzio and because they'd heard of the battle everyone used to talk to him about it. Poor Harry had lost his arm somewhere like Belcon Pays in Belgium, so the only topic open to him was the weather.

Most of my job was delivering letters, but occasionally I would escort VIPs around the place. Douglas Bader, the flying ace, used to come in quite regularly, and I got his autograph. Frank Robinson was the racing correspondent. In '46 he tipped Airborne to win the Derby. I liked the sound of the name and although I was only on 32 bob a week I decided to risk sixpence on it each way. It won at 66/1.

Some of my weekly wages went to Gran for board, but most went on my bike. I was really into cycling and had joined a London club. My dad had given me his old racing bike, a Bates, which had a novel fork system and was recognized by all the cycling *cognoscenti*. The De Laune Club was a really pukka men-only affair and we'd go on club runs, forty of us, into the country. The hard riders, the men, would meet us for lunch somewhere – they'd done eighty miles while the rest of us had done about fifty.

While on the paper, I got this idea of going into the fight game and joined the Northcliffe amateur boxing club. I was six foot two, but weighed only nine stone six. I trained really hard and the coach said he thought I had potential.

My dad's advice was doggereled into, 'Head up, chin in; straight left will always win.'

I only had one fight. My dad's excellent advice certainly worked – for the other guy. The bloke knocked the shit out of me with his straight left for three one-minute rounds. I came home and said to Gran, 'I've decided not to become a boxer.'

'I don't blame you,' she said. 'Bloody silly.'

At least it taught me a lesson. I was never as good as I thought I was going to be, even at that age, so I had to learn to get by on diplomacy. If you can't smash your way through, you've got to talk your way out.

About this time, I was going out with a girl who lived at the top of our road and was madly in love with her. I wasn't having sex with her, but it wasn't from lack of trying. It was coming out of my ears at that age but intercourse was unknown territory.

It all changed one night in Battersea Park when I was initiated by a woman in uniform. I was about sixteen and I had a cycling pal called Teddy Briggs, who was big, good looking and a really great rider – everything that I wasn't. We met two Wrens who were stationed on the Embankment, just over from Battersea Park where we used to ride. We were in shorts, and I suppose quite sun-tanned, and they were absolutely fascinated. They would have been 25. The one I ended up with wasn't the best-looking girl in the world, but my eyesight wasn't great and, after all, she was a Wren with black stockings that went all the way to the top.

Up until then, I had thought that it was solely a male prerogative to want and enjoy sex. I discovered the truth that night in Battersea Park, although when I got home, I had to give Gran an explanation for staying out.

'I met this Wren,' I said, opting for honesty.

'How old is she?' Gran asked.

'She's twenty-five and from Scotland. Her name is Annie.'

Gran was about to launch into her lecture when I said, 'I want to marry her, Gran.'

That took her aback. Gran fell silent, shaking her head.

I only saw Annie once more. She got posted away from London and we lost touch but I never forgot her. The image of her black stockings and uniform was imprinted on my mind, and for years afterwards I only had to hear the word 'Wren' for my periscope to start rising.

To become a reporter I had to move into the press room, but before a position came up, there was an opening in the accounts department. The father of the chapel told me to take it. 'Once you're in there, you're there for life,' he said.

My dad was impressed. For someone who'd been unemployed a 'job for life' sounded pretty attractive.

I thought it was going to be a step up, but I found myself in this enormous office on the first floor overlooking the Thames, with maybe a hundred other people. There were ten rows of desks which ascended in seniority, and from left to right, up to Mr Hutchins, the chief accountant.

I sat at a desk all day classifying invoices alphabetically. Next to me, on my right and therefore one rung higher up the ladder, was a young guy who'd been a sub-lieutenant in the RNVR. He'd had his own motor torpedo boat towards the end of the war and spoke fluent Arabic. I couldn't understand why he was working in such a dead-end position.

'I've got a wife and two children, it's a good job,' he told me, but it didn't seem right. This guy had seen plenty of action; he'd been in the thick of it and now his head was buried in stacks of paper.

Where was the romance? I thought, as I sat at my desk or wandered along the Embankment each lunch-time and stood on the foredeck of the *Discovery*. If I closed my eyes I could imagine myself standing there alongside Shackleton, feeling the wind sting my face and tug at my shirt.

Going back to the office, I would look at the repressed faces and realize that it was no sort of life. Maybe one day I'd be like Mr Hutchins up there, but I wouldn't be happy. When I voiced my misgivings to Dad, he said, 'All jobs are like that, son. I advise you to stay.'

Sometimes in my lunch hour I would go and window-shop at Gamage's department store. One day, in a temporary car park that had been built on a bomb site in Leather Lane, I spotted the most beautiful car I had ever seen, a 4½-litre Bentley. The racing history engraved on the bonnet stated that it had won Le Mans. I spent an entire hour just staring at this gleaming machine and thinking, I could never buy a car like this.

I had an old scouting friend who worked at the Middlesex Hospital as a laboratory technician. Listening to him talk, it sounded a far more exciting choice of career and I imagined actually achieving something and ending up like Alexander Fleming discovering penicillin. When he offered to wangle me a job, I jumped at the chance.

I told my dad that I was leaving the *Mail*, and he wasn't too upset. I guess he reckoned I was moving from one position where I had a great future to another where I also might have one. They couldn't believe it at the *Mail*, although the fact I was moving into a hospital made it more respectable. There was a whip-round and they gave me a couple of little presents and a card which said, 'Gone on to better things.' I was touched.

Work at the hospital wasn't what I expected, and it didn't take me long to realize that in my lowly position I wasn't going to discover any new wonder drugs. Part of my job was to kill twelve guinea-pigs a day so that their blood could be used for culture growth. I wasn't comfortable with it. When I'd lived in the country, I accepted things like pigs being slaughtered. Every day something died, because there was plenty of vermin. At harvest time we used to surround the last square to be cut and everyone would wade in, battering the rats and mice. In the country, death's just another part of life – but it didn't seem right in the city.

'I don't like the killing,' I said to Gran, and I could tell by the look on Dad's face that he could see the writing on the wall.

At that time there was no professional cyclist in Britain but road racing was becoming very popular. Paris Cycles had an independent team that rode in the Milk Race and other events; their arch rivals were a team sponsored by a firm called Dayton.

I got a job with Paris Cycles in Stoke Newington, working under a guy called Harry Gretsch. He'd started off making cycles and because the whole ethics of road racing was a continental thing, anything from across the Channel was in great demand. So instead of calling his bikes 'Gretsch' he called them 'Paris' and painted them flamboyant colours. His Tour de France model really took off and did tremendous business.

I started as a trainee, assembling frames and cutting up tubes to required lengths. The place was full of ex-servicemen who had been abroad, and who had all been cyclists. I soon realized that I was never going to be good enough to make the team. I had the talent, which was probably only an extension of my shape and the fact I was pretty fit, but what good is potential when you don't have the application? It wasn't even a case of training hard for six months – the top rank was years away. And it was a bloody hard life. An independent cyclist got maybe half a normal wage per week and then there was the travelling.

At the end of the season there was a big run called the Kingston Closure, from Kingston to Bognor. All the London clubs were invited which, of course, was an open invitation to everyone who fancied themselves. About five hundred riders assembled in Kingston and the youngsters – the lunatics – started first. We had got to just about the other side of Esher when twenty or so guys were brought down and strewn all over the road and I managed to get away alongside four lads from the Dayton team. A coach went by, and it was a regular ploy of ours to sprint behind big vehicles and use the slipstream.

Suddenly I was in front. There was a lot of jostling but it didn't really get heavy because the riders beside me could see I was just a kid. For me it was a victory – I had all these great riders around me. Of course, it couldn't last. When we came to the Devil's Punchbowl I couldn't stay with the coach and, going up the hill, power told and I was dropped. When I got to the top of the Punchbowl and the coast down into Hindhead I was on my own; the field was behind me, the professionals in front, and I was absolutely shattered because I'd given it my all. I pulled in at a café and had a nice cup of tea and a sandwich, watching them all go streaming through – including all my little gang who were riding like lunatics to catch me up.

I'd had my victory. When I finished my tea, I got back on my bike and rode home.

I left Paris Cycles under a bit of a cloud. When the Tour of Britain was coming up, I took a few days off and one of the guys who worked for Dayton said, 'Come to Birmingham in our van.' Unfortunately I bumped into Harry Gretsch, who wasn't best pleased that one of his employees was fraternizing with the opposition. He was a big powerful guy and a bit of a bully.

When I got back, he gave me a chance. He asked me to do a particular job at piecework rates. I had to cut a concave section out of the tube that went into the bottom bracket. I worked more or less all day with these, working out what I was getting – a penny a piece – thinking to myself, There's a good day's work there. And then, half an hour before I finished, an awful realization hit me. The tubes were double-butted at one end, and single-butted at the other. I'd been cutting the concave in the wrong end.

No way could I face Harry, so I just left. I told my dad that I couldn't go back and he became quite bolshie.

'Have you had your holiday money?'

'No.'

'Well, ring them up and see about it.'

'No, leave it out, Dad.'

'If you don't ring them, I will. I'm not having this. Every man has an inalienable right to be treated as a human being, son. Always stand up for yourself and what you believe in.'

So my dad rang Harry Gretsch.

'Yes, you can have your boy's holiday money,' he was told. 'But he owes us £25 for the tubes he's fucked up . . . and £40 for the bike.'

Which was why I didn't want my dad to phone him up – because Dad had given me £40 for my bike, and I had pocketed it and written Harry an IOU. I got one hell of a bollocking for not telling the truth and that was the end of Paris Cycles.

I wasn't out of work for long. I went to Claude Butler's on Clapham High Street, hoping they would teach me about bike frame building. It turned out they didn't want anyone in the cycle division, but they had a contract for building radar towers out of alloy and took me on as a trainee fitter. I was still only an impressionable seventeen-year-old and found myself surrounded again by ex-servicemen.

I was working as part of a team with two men, cutting up sections of metal. It was my job to cut it from the straight alloy, angle it and chamfer it, so it was all ready to be set in and riveted. You had to work as a team to keep the fabricators supplied – something I understood from my time on Sparks's farm: like it or not, the job had to be done. The money was quite good and I felt I was learning something.

It was at Butler's that I met my Nemesis in the shape of Cobby, an archetypal wide boy who was a year older than me and doing a more senior job. Cobby was one of those guys who argued with everyone. The foreman was 45 years old and built like a brick khazi, but Cobby would tell him to fuck off. I'd never met anybody like that before. Normally, when you worked at a place and spoke to the governor, it was, 'Yes sir, no sir.' Cobby said what he liked and got away with it, and I admired him for it.

When Cobby said, 'Do you fancy going to the pictures?' one evening after work I told him I had no money.

'You don't need any money, I'll show you.'

So Cobby began showing me all the train stations in London where you could jib without paying, and how to get into a cinema through the emergency exit. He could even get into the Albert Hall for the Proms. We lived ten minutes apart and started to meet at the Junction most evenings and go into the West End.

It was a simple matter of going round the back of the cinema and finding a door that had been left open. We slipped inside and made our way to the Gents. The correct way was to wait until somebody came into the toilet, then go out just before them in case the usherettes were looking for people coming out.

I was amazed. Afterwards, Cobby said, 'Come on, we'll go home by tube.'

He took me the wrong way through an exit and at the Clapham Common end he knew ways of slipping out unnoticed.

In fact, Cobby knew all the moves. I'd never been in a dance hall but Cobby got me interested. He was really into music, particularly the new bebop stuff that was just coming in and the progressive jazz of the big bands like Stan Kenton's. Cobby was a pretty good dancer, with plenty of chat for the girls – everything that I wasn't.

Cobby was only about five foot nine and looked like a smaller version of Robert Mitchum, with heavy acne scars. He might have been only a year older than me, but he was far more worldly and a born rebel. Suddenly I started to see an alternative way of life which was quite exciting. He used to talk about robberies and sounded experienced, although he'd probably just picked up stories from older people we met at the dance halls.

Sunday afternoons we would go to the pictures. The main one was the Granada at Clapham Junction and we'd wait outside in our little groups for an hour before it opened. Suits were the big thing then, with bird's-eye the favourite material, or sometimes brown hopsack. I didn't have the money to buy one, but I could see that all the guys who did had girlfriends – and that during the film they got lots of groping done.

The same little groups would be at the Wimbledon Palais, the Hammersmith Palais and the Lyceum. Of course, when you went there you stayed with your own group. Inevitably there were rows, which sometimes got a bit nasty. Quite a few guys used to carry knives. One of our group was a porter at Smithfield meat market and it was said that he used the joints of meat to practise stabbing people and cutting them up. He was an unusual character, very quiet and unassuming, yet he had a jack-knife with which he used to cut whole rows of people's faces. I never got involved, I just made the numbers up; I knew my capabilities.

I suppose we were a gang. There was always a pecking order, which was usually topped by the biggest guy and the one who had the brains to go with it. Then there'd be various lieutenants. We had a meeting spot at a café on the Wandsworth Road called Herbie's. I just seemed to become part of them, which meant proving myself – and the task in hand was never going to be helping old ladies across the road.

The first real job was in the City when we smashed the window of a tobacconist's kiosk and got about ten lighters, which were a good selling article at the time. Cobby was keen to branch out. We made a few attempts to break into phone boxes and over the next couple of months drifted into smash and grabs. We never broke into people's houses – it was usually just a shop window. I never expected to get caught; it didn't enter my head.

Up until then, my relationship with the police was strictly limited, but I'd had my first real brush with them when I was fifteen. I often used to meet mates at a coffee stall near Battersea Bridge, particularly on summer evenings. This particular night I left there at about ten o'clock and was heading down Queenstown Road when a policeman with his bicycle called out, 'Oi, where's your lights?'

I yelled 'Bollocks!' and rode on, chuckling to myself, but the next thing I knew a squad car screamed up and forced me into the kerb. Three policemen jumped out.

'What are you up to?' one of them demanded.

'You nearly knocked me off my bike,' I said.

He accused me of abusing a police officer.

'What? Where? Who?' I protested and then saw the bobby pedalling towards us, puffing hard. The first thing he did was poke me in the chest, and then he kicked my bike into the kerb. I saw red and kicked his in retaliation.

I was really pissed off. Maybe my reaction was partly political. I'd done a bit of reading of people like Karl Marx – not really understanding them but they definitely left me with an adversarial attitude to the police. What really made me angry was that this elderly copper said, quite kindly, 'Come on, son, get into the car, you'll be all right,' but as soon as I did he pinned my arms behind my back and said, 'Right, I've got the little shit – let him have it!'

I was bleeding and bruised and I kept thinking, They can't do stuff like this.

When we got to the police station at Nine Elms the governor came in and I could see him thinking, What's this skinny kid in shorts doing here with bloodstains all over him?

He looked at the arresting officer as if to say, 'Haven't you got anything fucking better to do with your time?'

I was still fuming about getting slapped around and the red mist descended. I picked up a chair and tried to throw it at the old boy who had held me down. It missed but ended up hitting the inspector. Things got a touch nasty again and I knew I was in the cells for the night unless I could get bail.

The only person likely to help was Gran, and they went round in a squad car and told her I was in trouble. They wouldn't give her a lift to the station, however. Even though she was in her seventies she had to walk the 3 miles from Battersea at midnight.

In fairness to the police, I suppose they had a job to do. They didn't need some saucy young whippersnapper giving them lip. Maybe they wanted to teach me a lesson but it got way out of hand. Getting so knocked about really shocked me. I was naïve enough to think that that sort of thing didn't happen; that the police were somehow above that. I just couldn't conceive how three adults would start wading into a teenager. And as for their treatment of my gran, that was just despicable.

The next morning I had to appear in court and was fined a pound or two, although I didn't understand most of what happened. Why on earth were they making such a big deal about it?

It was the first time that the name Bruce Richard Reynolds appeared on a charge sheet, but it didn't fill me with remorse or a sense of shame. Just loathing and contempt. Justice didn't triumph.

4

I disappointed a lot of people but not quite as much as I imagined. Gran had taken one look at my face and bloody nose and realized that nothing I'd done could have justified such a beating. Having spent her entire life working for a pittance, knowing that if she voiced any objections she'd be slung off the job, she realized that life was rarely painted black and white. She'd spent years listening to my grandfather and father talking about trade union law and ranting about Peterloo and Winston Churchill shooting the miners.

Later on, when she obviously knew I was doing things that weren't exactly within the letter of the law, she seemed to shut her eyes and ears. She didn't want to know.

There was a chemist at the bottom of my road at Battersea and one night we smashed the window and grabbed some cameras. I brought them home and Gran spotted them. Next day, she went shopping and saw the chemist's broken window.

'You shouldn't be doing it,' she said angrily. 'You're mixing with bad company.'

I didn't like upsetting Gran. She was about the only person I'd listen to. Eventually she stopped berating me because she was one of those souls who decided that if you couldn't do anything about something it was best forgotten.

My dad tried to pull me into line but I was growing up and he had ceased to be the hero I once thought. He told me: 'Bruce, if you're going to go this way, where are you going to end up? What are you doing it for? You're not getting anything out of it. It's just stupid.'

Cobby and I started getting more ambitious. We went out one night with the intention of breaking into a pub, mainly because we'd heard another couple of blokes boasting, 'Yeah, we done a pub last night.' We were somewhere out Cheam way, it was about two o'clock in the morning, and we decided to try our hand. We had a couple of tools with us – a chisel and a jemmy, plus pocket torches, which made us feel good, like the pros that we aspired to be.

Of course, saying that you're going to do a pub is easy; actually to do one is entirely another matter. We didn't have a clue what we were about. In fact, we were about to call it a night when a totally different opportunity seemed to present itself. A woman appeared out of the shadows, blonde and buxom, wearing nothing but a pink Milanese nightdress.

'Wonder if she's looking for a bit of young rough,' Cobby said.

'She's come to the right address,' I said. But my hopes were dashed when I saw the anxious expression on her face.

'I thought someone had knocked on the front door,' she said. 'I came downstairs, but there was no-one there. So I went out into the street, and the door closed behind me. I'm locked out, what am I going to do?'

The hunter became the Good Samaritan as I put a comforting arm around her. My only thought now was to get the poor woman home, get in through a window for her, put the kettle on, then give the house a quick spin while she was distracted and see if we could make the evening pay.

'I'll climb up to there,' I said, nodding at a partly opened upstairs window. 'Then I'll come down and open the door.'

She watched as I climbed up the pipe and levered the window open. Then, straddling the frame, I was about to

drop into what looked like a kitchen area leading to the
hallway when some sixth sense caused me to look a bit
harder. As my eyes adjusted to the darkness my sphincter
tightened. Four slavering, silent Dobermanns were awaiting
my next movement. One of tentative withdrawal was the
signal for all hell to break loose; deprived of their prey they
barked and howled their bitter disappointment, leaping up
and down in desperation.

I was shocked. I wasn't afraid of dogs, not ordinary dogs,
anyway – but these Dobermanns were something else.

The woman called out, 'They're all right, don't take any
notice of them.'

I wasn't going to have any of that. 'Stand by the door and
call them to you, and make sure that you keep talking to them.'

Mustering all my reserves of bottle I moved through the
window and waited for their mistress's voice to summon them
to the door. When the clamour of barking ceased, I dropped
down to face them apprehensively. Malevolent eyes devoured
me, then turned back to the door and their mistress's voice.
It was now or never: I sauntered nonchalantly to the door,
slipped the Yale, and opened up.

The dogs were the first out, slobbering around their
mistress. Then I saw Cobby and two policemen.

Fucking hell, I thought, are we nicked? The guts and
scrotum were already tightening up, but I got the wink from
Cobby in reassurance: it's sweet. Whatever he'd told them
they appeared to have accepted it.

Feeling now more like mine host I opened the door wide
for all to enter – the woman, the dogs, Cobby and the two
policemen. After donning a dressing-gown the woman made
us all tea. The boys in blue were quite jovial, it was a pleasant
diversion for them and would look good on their occurrence
sheet – maintaining their good relationship with the public.

Cobby was prattling about the girls we'd met at the Locarno,
about us dropping them home and then walking home to
Battersea. It was our standard story when getting a pull early
in the morning from Old Bill. What else could you say?

The woman was profuse in her thanks to us and to the
police, who had happened to pass by and see her on the
doorstep with Cobby. They, too, were pleased with our

public-spirited attitude – so much so that they offered to drive us home. Now that was an offer we couldn't refuse.

There was a linoleum firm on Wandsworth Road and we got it in our heads to break open the safe even though we knew nothing about safe-cracking. Eventually, Cobby, his brother and I broke into the canteen and stole some cigarettes. Afterwards we walked along Wandsworth Road to Battersea Park and hid the spoils in a rubbish bin. Someone saw us and the next day we were nicked.

I was given probation and didn't lose my job, but it damaged my prospects. I had to work on my own at a mechanical press, feeding a band of thin metal, about a sixteenth of an inch thick, into the press, which dropped down and punched out the Claude Butler badge. It was great for the arms but boring as hell.

Eventually I resigned. I was six months short of my eighteenth birthday and, as a result, virtually unemployable: conscription was in force and employers were bound by law to re-employ workers after their stint of National Service. Nobody wanted to take on a lad who was about to disappear into the Army in six months' time.

Cobby tried to sell me a sun-lamp one day, swearing blind that it wasn't nicked. I thought it would be great for Gran's arthritis, and paid him a fiver. The next day, I got a visit from a Detective Constable Drury.

'Bought any sun-lamps recently?' he asked.

'Yeah.'

'Who from?'

'A bloke in a pub.'

He stared at me for what felt like eternity, and then said, 'Are you sure you can't do anything to help me with my enquiries?'

I denied everything, but got charged with receiving stolen goods and was fined £20. The day after the hearing, Drury called at the house again.

'You're not very clever, are you, Reynolds?' he said.

'What do you mean?'

'Well, you've just paid a twenty-quid fine, but I gave you the chance to do something about it. Silly fucker, I could have straightened the whole thing out for a tenner.'

That was more or less the last I heard about Drury until 1977 when, as a Commander at Scotland Yard, he was sentenced to eight years' imprisonment after he had been found guilty of corruption.

Cobby and I expanded our theatre of operations to areas where the privileged lived and shopped, like St James's, Pall Mall and Mayfair.

One night we did a gun shop in Bury Street, opposite Pall Mall. There was nothing technical about our entry, although we had advanced enough to modify our methods and keep down the noise. Brown paper liberally coated with treacle applied to the window ensured that glass did not cascade on to the pavement.

Cobby gave me the all-clear and I unrolled the paper. With treacle running over my gloves and arms, I felt like an insect stuck to fly paper as I wrestled with the window. Finally it was in place and I gave a heave with the iron bar. The method was so effective that Cobby, just fifty yards down the road, didn't hear a thing. Raking away the remaining shards, we helped ourselves to four air pistols, which our juvenile minds imagined we could use to do hold-ups.

Unfortunately, our euphoria was short-lived. Cobby's father spotted two of the guns under his son's bed and called the police. Under questioning, Cobby spilled the beans and we were both nicked and charged with theft. I pleaded guilty to everything. My dock brief (*lawyer supplied by the court*) was a young lady who launched into this amazing speech about my background and how much shame I'd brought to my respectable family. She eulogized me for being a patrol leader in the Scouts, and produced a certificate from the Scouting Association for money earned on Bob a Job Day. Unfortunately, it didn't cut much ice with the judge. Instead of further probation, he sent us to the Allocation Centre at Wormwood Scrubs, where Borstal boys awaited their fate.

I had no idea what it would be like in prison. Of course, I'd heard stories – bits and pieces from people who'd been inside. My Uncle Jack once showed me a cat o' nine tails which he said was from Wandsworth prison. He was one of those guys who collected bits and pieces like that; he also had two ostrich eggs that he'd got from God knows where.

Nothing Jack told me could prepare me for Wormwood Scrubs. When Cobby and I were allowed into the exercise yard for the first time, we looked out across the yard where the inmates were shuffling in two circles, one inside the other. There were three hundred people but only twenty guys in the centre. They were the escapees or potential escapees and wore different uniforms with a yellow stripe on the trousers like the 5th Cavalry. I turned to Cobby and said, 'That's the cream, Cobby. That's where we've got to be.'

The Allocation Centre took up one wing of the Scrubs and was run along the lines of a prep school. We were still regarded as boys and at certain times in the day there were parades and marching. We gave the screws plenty of cheek. I knew how to sneer at them because I'd seen Humphrey Bogart do it in *Passage to Marseilles*.

Everyone had a nine-month to three-year Borstal sentence and I suppose the aim of the Allocation Centre was to place people where they thought they belonged. The severe cases went to high-security prisons and the open centres were for those offenders who showed some degree of intelligence.

I got friendly with a guy named Trevor who'd done Borstal before and he educated me about the possibilities. He knew which prisons were easier and how to swing a placement by applying to learn a particular trade. Both of us got Gaynes Hall, which was good, Trevor said – he'd been there before. Cobby and his brother went to Hollosey Bay, a big farm in Suffolk.

My new home was a rambling old country house in Huntingdonshire which had been used during the war as an SOE training facility. The governor was a former running Blue and was still madly into the sport. Apart from the main house, there was a collection of army huts and Trevor and I would jog round the place. We'd be running and the governor would appear out of nowhere and run with us for a mile and chat to us about various things like the chain of command. I thought he was a good fellow but soon discovered that he wasn't really in charge. The Borstal was run by the boys.

Each hut had a leader who was responsible for his charges. Not surprisingly, these guys tended to be the biggest and strongest inmates. Trevor and I were separated and I had a

Scouse geezer in charge of my hut. Within a couple of days I began talking about escaping. Eventually Trev and I came up with two plans. Plan A was to go to Sicily and connect up with Salvatore Giuliano, the celebrated bandit of the time, who was capturing all the headlines. I rather fancied that, but if we couldn't get that far, Plan B was to join the Foreign Legion.

Somehow, my hut leader got wind of the escape plans and came down very heavy on me. He announced in front of everybody, 'You will not escape while I'm in charge of this hut.' I was a new boy and there weren't many Londoners about. This Scouser was throwing down the gauntlet.

I accepted the challenge.

Unfortunately, the Scouser had a pal called Harry who had a reputation as being the second hardest guy in the Borstal. When I walked outside the hut, Harry grabbed me and suddenly I realized they were going to do me two-handed, which I discovered was a Borstal tradition.

I held my own for a while, much to my surprise, but then Harry kicked me from behind, right in the coccyx. I collapsed on to the floor. At least the Scouser didn't have an honourable victory; he had to have a mate help him.

The whole incident made me sick and I knew I couldn't stay. The system was crazy. I'd grown up reading all the escape books like *The Wooden Horse* and I had this image of a dramatic flight avoiding a nationwide dragnet. Every hero in history had escaped from somewhere or other. The very word 'escape' had a magic ring.

I found Trevor and said, 'Are you coming?'

We pulled another guy in with us and did a lot of planning. The idea was to go across country, following the electricity pylons which hopefully would lead to a main road. From there we would hitchhike to London. We had compasses and had been collecting iron rations – mainly cooking chocolate – from the kitchens.

Three days after the fight, on a cold, wet and windy night, we made our move.

5

The lights were turned off at ten o'clock and I heard the night watchman making his rounds. I waited half an hour and slipped out of bed. The guys were waiting for me. We'd managed to get a couple of civilian overcoats which at least covered our uniforms.

It was a dark night and we stayed in the deeper shadows until we got our night sight adjusted. It wasn't unknown for the governor or the security to be snooping around, and we wanted to avoid any confrontation. With luck it would be reveille before we were missed, by which time we hoped to be back home in 'the Smoke'.

We followed the electricity pylons, which headed south, but it was only after two or three hours of crossing rough country that we discovered that the pylons ran in an elongated circle; we found ourselves more or less back where we had started. It was then that we decided to head in the direction of the river, which was perhaps the only true landmark that we knew in the area.

Our escape plan worked perfectly until we began to feel the effects of all the cooking chocolate we'd eaten. At about three o'clock in the morning, as we lay pressed into the furrows of a ploughed field to escape the wind, we all got the shits and had to get up periodically and squat. It was bitterly cold.

We should have headed for the nearest railway station, caught a train and been home within a few hours, but I had visions of patrols combing the countryside and watching the trains. So we pushed across country until we came to the river. Obviously, we couldn't cross at a bridge because the whole of England was out looking for us, so the only alternative was to swim. Suddenly there was dissent in the ranks. The guy with us said he couldn't swim and refused to even look at the water. We started arguing and I suggested we split up. I said I was going to swim the river further downstream but was really looking for another way across because I didn't fancy taking the plunge either. I gave them my overcoat and went off on my own and left the two of them together. I discovered later that they were nicked the same day.

Just before dawn I reached the main road and hitched a lift with this old colonel type who saw the grey flannel trousers and navy socks and asked me what I was doing. It didn't look like a uniform but I told him I was in the Army and had to get to London as part of an initiative test.

'I'll give you a lift,' the colonel said, 'but not any money. Too much like cheating, what?'

He dropped me at Newport in Essex and from there I caught a train to Liverpool Street and did a Cobby through the ticket barrier. I only had a few pennies in my pocket but at Sloane Square I bumped into a vending machine and five bob popped out. I made my way to the coffee stall at Battersea and the guys had a whip-round for me. They treated me like an all-conquering hero.

I went home to Gran but three days later I was nicked walking across Clapham Common by a policeman who recognized me. I was pretty well known around Lavender Hill police station by then. He was helped by a Dick Barton – the name we used for members of the public who went to the assistance of police. By next morning I was back in Wandsworth Prison in the Borstal punishment centre where they sent the trouble-makers.

The regime at Wandsworth was designed to punish and indoctrinate. No radios were allowed, or newspapers, and we were limited to three books a week with a strictly non-interchange policy. There was virtually no communication allowed between prisoners except for an hour on Saturday and Sunday afternoons during exercise. On other days there was no talking – that was a nickable offence – even in the workshop or exercise yard. Instead they bullied us through a PT routine of press-ups and leg lifts.

Nothing could prepare me for the unrelenting attempts to break the human spirit. You had to fight against it and find ways of communication even though it was punishable by bread and water or the forfeiture of privileges. A 'privilege' was having a bed in your cell all day.

Bread and water was called the Number One Diet. You could only be on it for three days and it was three days on a normal diet and another three days on bread and water until the punishment was finished. As a show of solidarity, it was our policy not to eat the bread. We'd sip the water and leave the rest, just to let the screws know they weren't going to break us. It wasn't so hard really. Your stomach gets used to being empty.

The Number Two Diet could be dished up for weeks on end. Basically, it was porridge for breakfast with no milk or sugar, lunch was porridge and potatoes, and dinner was porridge.

You had to laugh or go crazy. The screws were all ex-army types and to a man they treated us as if we were beneath contempt. But they never broke my spirit. If anything they made me more determined.

After three months, they deemed that I was ready to be sent back to a Borstal and the governor of Gaynes Hall agreed to give me another try.

The Scouser had gone, along with his mate Harry. Instead, there were a couple of Londoners in my hut and for the first time we were in the ascendency. There was an inverted snobbery about where you came from, but it had the same importance as going to the right school in 'high society'. For instance, it was infinitely preferable to have originated in the Elephant, the Angel or Hoxton rather than in Hampstead or Belgravia. Guys questioned about their background would sometimes shame-facedly reply 'Southend', which would lead to general derision and piss taking. The more slum-ridden the better. Battersea was OK, and so were Bermondsey, Deptford and King's Cross.

I should have learned my lesson the first time and done my Borstal quietly. Instead, I raided the camp kitchen, stealing sugar, chocolates and cake for our hut. Someone informed on me and I spent a week on the Burma Road, which was the name for the punishment regime at every Borstal. In my case, it was fatigue duty, which meant doing double the work.

'I'm not staying here. I'm away tonight,' I muttered to a guy called Bowl, whom everyone called Bowler. I'm sure he was the role model for George Cole in the St Trinian's films. His Cockney rhyming slang was almost incomprehensible although I did try to learn. I was under the impression that all the top thieves talked in rhymes and if I wanted to be one I would have to learn their language.

Bowler was a good storyteller and very fond of giving public recitals of the prison epic 'Drummer Bill':

Now I was in the pub with my china Drummer Bill
As it was his nature he had one eye on the till
Now things were very dodgy and funds were getting low
We sips our mild and bitter and decide to have a go.

We had talked a lot about stealing cars and I was impressed that he could drive. But when we left in the middle of the night and tried to steal a car, Bowler, the so-called expert, was bloody hopeless and I quickly began doubting all his stories.

We made our way to a railway station, which was deserted at that hour, and jemmied the slots off the public toilets. We got a grand total of twenty pennies. At about two in the morning a goods train came through and we ran alongside, jumping into a coal truck. It was full of big lumps of coke and we had to dig a hole in one corner so we could sit down and try to sleep.

Two or three hours later, I poked my head out the side and saw we were in Wood Green. It was time to bail out. There was a coffee stall near the station and we each bought a pie and cup of tea. It was one of the best meals I'd ever eaten. Afterwards, we brushed off the coal dust and cleaned up before catching a train to Hammersmith. We were still in Borstal uniforms – rough grey flannel trousers, a battle-dress shirt with a windjammer-style top – so we stole clothes from a back garden.

Bowler had friends in Hammersmith – two brothers who were both good fighters. I'd heard about Dickie, the eldest, from the dance hall circuit. His brother Donnie had been at Hollosey Bay with Cobby so he knew about me.

Donnie was basically a walk-in thief who concentrated on the big old Victorian houses with basements. There was no subtlety about the bloke. When the place was empty, he'd break in whichever way he could and smash open the gas meter with a poker or chisel. Often he'd pick up thirty quid or so, which wasn't a bad score.

Bowler and I split up after a few days and I stayed with Donnie. I was still wearing someone else's trousers, jacket and shirt – none of which fitted.

A week went by and I was getting my bearings when Donnie said, 'Come on, let's go out. My brother-in-law is a window cleaner and he's given me a steer on how we can get some money. It's only a walk.'

It was a big house and Donnie rang the doorbell to make sure it was empty. We broke through a window and hadn't been inside more than ten minutes when we found five hundred quid. I'd never seen so much money. Apparently the house owner had some restaurants and didn't trust the bank.

Donnie and I couldn't believe our luck and I went straight into the West End. American clothes were the fashion and there was a shop called Smart Bros, which was challenging Cecil Gee. Just like in the movies, I walked in and said, 'Fit me out with a suit,' and flashed a few notes. Suddenly shop assistants were scurrying about. They even sent somebody to get me a pair of big brothel creepers in brown leather with a suede insert and a Crombie overcoat.

I bought a hat – a big grey number which probably looked a bit ridiculous on me but what the hell, how many eighteen-year-olds could afford one? In total, I spent about fifty quid, which still left me with two hundred. Even though I didn't drink, I went into a nearby pub and ordered a half of brown ale with a whiskey chaser, along with a cigar. This was a celebration.

Being in the West End, it wasn't long before I was sniffing round the painted ladies. One in particular caught my eye and after a delicate financial negotiation a deal was struck and we jumped in a cab. The fare was about two quid and I was panting before the wheels were in motion. There were then more negotiations. For a pound she would take off all her clothes in the back of the cab. For another quid she'd go further. Meanwhile, the cabbie was driving around as if nothing was happening in the back. He knew he'd get his cut. Pretty soon I was so hot it was running out my ears and she suggested we go to a hotel.

'Can you pay?' she asked.

'Not a worry,' I assured her.

We found a place up Bloomsbury way and I paid for a room. Once inside, she gave me a quick taster of what I could expect and then said, 'Why don't we have a bath?'

I thought, What a life – I'm gonna be bathed by this lovely creature, it can't get any better. We went down the hall to the bathroom and she turned the taps.

'Shouldn't we have a bottle of Scotch?' she said as I was getting undressed. I didn't drink in those sort of quantities but right then she could have had anything she wanted.

'It's a fiver,' she said, volunteering to go down and get it. I went back to the bedroom and got the money and then she saw me into the bath.

I must have had some sort of premonition because I had taken the precaution of putting the bulk of the money I had left under the wardrobe, lifting it and wedging the notes under one corner. Anyway, I'm soaking in the bath imagining all the things we're going to do and five minutes becomes ten and then twenty. The water was getting cold. Then it hit me. I got up, dried myself off and went back into the bedroom. Yep, she'd gone. Thankfully, she hadn't found my stash; she'd just taken off with the fiver, plus the money I'd given her for our little rendezvous in the cab.

It was the sort of incident that could get me quite unbalanced and I went down to the desk clerk and demanded that he give my money back for the room. If we weren't staying, why should I pay?

I accused him of being in cahoots with the girl and things began to look quite nasty. It wasn't worthwhile having a real row because the police would be called and that was the last thing I wanted. Discretion got the better of valour and I decided to write it off as a lesson.

As I was walking away from the desk, an American came into the lobby with his girl and asked for a room. The manager told him they were fully booked, and I piped up, 'You can have mine – I'm vacating it.' This caused another row because apparently that wasn't allowed, and the upshot was that we all left and I walked out of the hotel with the Yank and his girl.

We began talking and decided to share a cab down to Leicester Square. Then the strangest thing happened. As we were driving along, the Yank said, 'Do you mind if you drop me here? Here's something towards the fare.'

He got out and left me with this girl, who looked at me and said: 'Where are you going?'

I shrugged and she said: 'Well, I'm going to have a drink.'

It was late, so I suggested we go to a hotel. We found one near Paddington Station and spent the rest of the night together – and most of the next day. I guess she was just on the fringes of the game – not a full-time professional, although I did give her a twenty because she was on her uppers. The money didn't make any difference to me. It didn't have any great value, and she really needed it.

Oddly enough, I bumped into her a week or two later when the fortunes had changed a bit and I hadn't got any cash. She gave me a tenner and her phone number.

6

I was unlucky to get caught again. I was on a tube with Donnie and his mate Gus when a policeman stepped into the carriage and recognized me. You would have thought my face was plastered on every shop-front, the way Old Bill kept picking me out of the crowd. I wasn't even in my territory.

'You're on the run from Borstal,' he said.

I looked at Gus and Donnie but it was clear they weren't about to get involved.

I was marched off the Metropolitan line to a police station, but on the way the whole vision of the Wandsworth punishment centre flashed up before me.

The sergeant had me by the coat but suddenly I wrenched myself free. I jumped over a fence and dashed into the middle of Hammersmith Broadway. I was dodging traffic and figured, quite rightly, there was no way he would risk his life running after me. About five hundred yards down the road I slipped into a pub and ordered myself a pint. I was standing there, looking about, and as I glanced at the door my heart sank. There he was. He pointed his finger and said: 'I want you.'

This time he twisted my arm behind me and muttered in my ear: 'Wait till I get you alone. Your feet won't touch the ground. I'll teach you to make me look like a fool.'

If he aimed to frighten me, he did a good job. So much so, I figured there was no way I was going to let him get me back to the cells. I decided to lunge for the nearest window and put my fist through it. If I cut myself, he'd have to take me to hospital, which was preferable to a kicking at the station.

So with all the force that I could muster I slung the two of us at one of the shop-fronts on the corner of the Broadway. He let go and I hit the window and bounced off. The rebound gave me a head start. I vaulted the fence and dashed into the traffic, and this time I kept running through the backstreets until I got to a bus garage on the Broadway. I found an empty bus and crouched down upstairs – a good move unless he did a search.

I was frightened of moving but even more frightened of staying there, so eventually I went to the entrance of the garage and looked around. I looked left and it was all clear, then I looked right. There he was – on the corner, doing exactly the same thing as me. Our eyes met and it was like a scene from a Keystone Cops movie. I took off again and found myself jumping into back gardens alongside the tube lines. He was closing in on me so I crossed the tracks, leaving him stranded on the other side. He wasn't game to cross after me.

I didn't feel smug, just frightened, and I didn't stop looking over my shoulder until I got home to Gran's and picked up my bike.

'I've got to get out of town,' I told her, sounding every inch the fugitive. By then I saw myself very much as a Jesse James figure.

I rode a hundred miles that day, all the way to Warwickshire.

I didn't want to go straight to the Jacksons' farm, so I booked into a bed and breakfast not far away. There was an American woman staying there and we struck up a conversation. Maybe she was lonely, or an older woman looking to seduce a young man, but the upshot was that we spent a pleasant night together in her room, cementing the Atlantic alliance.

The next day I went to the farm and told the Jacksons that I was touring around. I stayed a couple of days and then moved on. Eventually, having run out of money, I decided to go home, even though it was fraught with danger. I rode back and crossed over the cemetery to get into the back of the house without being seen. That night I slipped out again and went to see an old cycling pal who was working on the Wandsworth Road. I didn't stay long with him and his mates, but five minutes after leaving two policemen charged me off my bike and I was nicked. Somebody had rung the police station, having heard the gossip that I was on the trot from Borstal.

So back I went to Wandsworth Prison, the Hate Factory.

In the punishment centre, awaiting allocation, I met a very engaging bloke called Ronnie Biggs. Like me, he'd been there before. He had gone to Usk in Monmouthshire, a grim old Borstal miles from anywhere. It wasn't his cup of tea and subsequently he left without permission.

Ronnie was nearly my height but bigger built and always seemed to have a smile on his face. His background was similar to mine – the broken home, the wartime evacuation and the burning ambition to do something with his life, something that was out of the ordinary.

We were both South London boys, which drew us closer. Ronnie had been in the Air Force, qualifying as a chef.

'Not quite the image that I aspired to,' he said. 'I'd been looking to be another Douglas Bader, only with legs.'

I empathized with him, recounting my early ambitions to join the Navy. It seemed that our romantic notions of adventure had run parallel.

We worked together in the woodshop, where old tarry blocks would be sawn up to suitable lengths before being handed out to be further chopped up and bundled as kindling for the various Government Department fires. It was during the loading of one of the Government vans that Ronnie and I were co-opted by another ex-RAF boy who had the notion that he would escape by hiding underneath the van, clinging on to whatever he could.

We thought he was crazy blitzing it in this fashion and a certainty to get nicked, but he was adamant about giving it a go. At a nod from us, out of the screw's eyes, he slipped underneath whilst we completed the loading.

Back in the woodshop the discipline screw called the roll. He was puzzled that he couldn't balance his book and concluded that he must have made a mistake. We were watching him intently. He was restless. He called the other screws over, then the instructors, showing them his roll. There was an animated dialogue before the order was given to down tools and the roll was called again. No mistake this time. The alarm bell was rung and in charged the heavy mob. Lined up, we had our names ticked off the roll and then we filed back to our cells, the cry echoing around the wing: One away, sir.' It was music to our ears – we'd got one away!

Ted Blair clung on to the underparts of the van and dropped off directly outside the Home Office. It was a nice touch. Of course, he was nicked within a few days, lying asleep at home, but Ted didn't care. In spite of the belting he received on his return to Wandsworth, he'd done his thing and beaten the system. It was a victory for all of us.

Soon afterwards I switched on to the coal party, a highly privileged position. I managed to get Ronnie a job as well, so we could talk when not working – although that wasn't often. We were boys doing a man's job, yet we competed amongst ourselves as to who could shift the most coal, who was the toughest, who could truly endure.

Having twice gone on the run from Gaynes Hall there was no chance of being sent back there. They allocated me to Rochester, a senior Borstal with a grim reputation. The assistant governor was a guy called Wheeler, who had been an officer in the Gurkhas and lost an arm. He gave me a big pep talk on my first day, saying things like, 'You've gone about it all the wrong way, son.'

Finally, he asked: 'So, are you going to try and escape from here?'

'Yes,' I said.

He tried to strike a deal with me, hoping I'd promise to give it a month.

'Well, I can't promise anything,' I said. 'Look, there's probably nothing wrong with this place, I just don't want to be here.'

Within days I was planning how to get out. A couple of guys I'd met in Wandsworth also fancied having a run so we looked at our options. This time our wing was enclosed within a prison surrounded by high walls. I figured that from the fourth landing I could stand on the rails and smash a skylight which led on to the roof. From there we could crawl along to a point about two yards from the wall. With a run-up of a few steps, we could launch ourselves across the gap and hopefully hang on when we hit the wall.

I smashed the window, cutting my ear as we crawled through. When we reached the corner, the others went first. The smallest guy launched himself into the wall, stuck tight and then climbed over until he dropped down the other side. The second guy also got over. The alarm had sounded by the time I threw myself across the gap, hitting the wall with my stomach, knocking all the breath out of me. I couldn't get a hold and slipped down the inside, realizing I was up shit creek without a canoe. There was no way back into the wing and within minutes the place would be crawling with screws. The only way out was through the main gate, which would have to be opened if they were sending people out to look for the others.

When I got to the gate the staff were mooning about, waiting for orders. An estate car was ready to leave. I took a deep breath and started running. Suddenly I was sprinting past them and they were so surprised it took them a few seconds to react. It was another Keystone Cops routine as they gave chase across open fields.

I heard someone close behind me – so close he called out to his mates, 'It's all right, I've got him.'

Fear added wings to my heels and I reached a mass of brambles which I tried to leap over but didn't quite make it. I managed to roll under and crawl deeper into the shadows. I lay there for four hours, waiting for darkness. When night fell, I crawled out and found the nearest road. I tried to steal a motor bike but couldn't get it started – not that I knew how to ride, but it was a good time to learn. What most preyed on my mind was the knowledge that I would probably have to swim the Medway if I wanted to reach the main road to London. Screws were normally posted on the Medway Bridge when anyone escaped because nobody ever thought of heading south, cutting across and coming back. Every escapee went straight for the river.

When I reached the river, I started having doubts. I really wanted to swim it because it would look great on my CV –

but at two in the morning the water didn't look very inviting. I decided to check out the bridge first.

Watching it for a while, I saw nobody on patrol, but, just in case, I waited until a young couple started walking across and I slipped in between them.

'How is old Phil?' I said. 'I haven't seen him in ages – we used to be at school together . . .' I was jabbering away like an old friend while they smiled nervously and shrugged at each other.

On the far side of Rochester there was a steep incline that the lorries crawled up in second gear. I picked one with a roped-down load and dragged myself up. It was freezing on top in my blazer, flannels and a bloodstained shirt. While I was trying to get comfortable without losing my grip, the driver caught sight of a silhouette and must have thought one of the ropes had come loose. He pulled off the road and began yanking on the ropes, lifting himself up to check the load.

'What the fuck are you doing there?' he asked.

Thinking quickly, I invented a story about being at school in Rochester and having been beaten up by some nasty boys, which accounted for the blood. I had no money and I was trying to get home.

'I can drop you off at Blackwall Tunnel,' he said, feeling sorry for me.

Home by this time was Hammersmith, not Battersea. I had connections with Ronnie and his brother, who would give me a place to stay. Eventually, the driver dropped me near Mile End and gave me a shilling. 'That should get you a bus to Hammersmith,' he said kindly.

Early in the morning, as I waited for the first bus, a young guy in his mid-twenties sidled up to me.

'What Borstal are you from?' he asked.

'You've made a mistake – I'm at a public school in Rochester.'

'Don't fuck me about,' he said, 'my brother's in fucking Portland so I know.'

I figured him for a policeman so I coughed up. 'OK. I've just had it away from Rochester.'

He nodded and said, 'Do you want something to eat?'

He gave me a couple of quid and his address. I promised to repay him, but with a brother in the trade he probably knew that he'd never see his money. Lending money had a way of balancing itself out. I'd been ripped off myself by so many implausible hard-luck yarns, and giving and taking money is all about swings and roundabouts.

I spent six weeks on the run, living in Hammersmith and doing nightly crimes, mainly breaking and entering. Generally, we didn't need a lot of tools: just a two-inch wood chisel which had the width and thickness to open most windows, while the sharp edge was useful for chiselling things off a wall or floor.

7

When I was nicked six weeks later and got eighteen months – a year with good behaviour – Dad turned to me sadly and said, 'Son, you've made your own bed, you'll have to lie in it.'

After two stints of Borstal training, and being over eighteen, they sent me to Lewes Prison, which wasn't a bad nick although it bore the legacy of Judge Jeffreys, the hanging judge, who once presided there. It housed mainly young cons because they didn't want us mixing with the old lags who would lead us astray or set a bad example. Most of the guys were my age and I was delighted later on to meet some old acquaintances like Biggsy and some new ones like Jimmy Humphreys and Mad Dog Cohen.

Ronnie had been grassed up for a robbery on a bookmaker in London and got three and a half years. I hadn't expected to see him again; but then, I didn't realize at the time that most of the people I had met in the Scrubs would be crossing my path all through my life. Prison does that: you've shared a common experience that is always there, it is an integral part of your life, never to be forgotten.

Biggsy was doing a carpentry course and again I joined him. Sadly, soon afterwards I fell victim to the typical power struggles that dominate prison life. I had an argument with a guy called Grover in the carpentry shop and things got out of hand before the screws pulled us apart. We were marched up before the governor in a military-style ceremony. The man sat behind his desk with his chief officer standing at his side like an adjutant.

When a con gets nicked for fighting, the form is to say you are sorry and that it was simply a spur-of-the-moment flare-up of tempers – nobody's fault and not to be repeated. I told this to the governor who then ordered me outside while he interviewed Grover.

I was called back and the governor accused me of attacking Grover with a hammer.

'Is that what he said?'

'Yes.'

I couldn't believe it. Grover had committed a cardinal sin in prison culture. He broke the code and grassed me up. As they led me out, I snapped and took a swing at him. Shame I missed him, particularly when I realized what was coming. I had to be taught a lesson for taking the law into my own hands.

They slung me into the punishment cells where I had to wait for my medicine. My landing screw, who didn't talk much but was quite a nice guy, was in charge of the beating.

Normally, if they really wanted to hurt you, it was the spread-eagle job, where they'd pin you down and take turns kicking you up the bollocks. This time, they held me down and flayed away with their sticks, smashing me across the shin bones and chest. I was beaten systematically, dispassionately, calmly and rationally, as if following step-by-step diagrams in the prison officers' instruction book. They weren't even angry – just six screws doing their duty with the maximum of efficiency. All the while, I was screaming like crazy because that's what they wanted to hear. If you didn't scream, they just kept beating until you got the message that authority is the one that hits the hardest.

They left me in the darkness, bruised and battered, and I lay there through the night, listening for the door and wondering if they were coming back. It wasn't unknown for the bastards to wait an hour and then repeat the treatment. Lying there, scared out of my wits, I realized that I was never going to be an outright rebel.

Everyone had a different defence to an institutionalized beating. Some advocate fighting back. They reason that if you lash out, you are liable to be clubbed unconscious and then you won't feel the pain or remember what happens to you. But I knew they could kill me if they wanted. People die in prison all the time; bones are broken and heads are split.

I was lying on the cell floor, cold and hungry, when I heard my name called from outside. Going to the window, I heard the voice say, 'Coming down!'

I put out both hands to receive the hot tin that had been lowered on a string from two landings above. I broke my fingernail trying to prise the lid off, but it was worth it. Inside was half a pint of steaming-hot cocoa, liberally laced with sweetened condensed milk. It was the best drink I'd ever had; I glowed from within, less from the cocoa itself than from the sentiments of solidarity that it expressed.

Ronnie had arranged for a whole group of the lads to act in concert, swinging the line with its precious contents from cell to cell overhand until it was directly above me, and then lowering it down to me. They were all risking severe punishment but they didn't care. You can never forget things like that or the people who are responsible.

From the Grover incident on, I was blacklisted and on every screw's potential hit list. My conduct was 'prejudicial to the good running of the prison' and the safest place I could be was on punishment, confined to a tiny cell in the block.

In fairness, Lewes was a reasonably good nick, tough but fair. The authorities regarded it as a showcase prison and, being Sussex, a monied county, all the JPs and magistrates would regularly visit to see a nice jail, full of nice prisoners who got plenty of food and exercise. It was a blot on the governor's record if there were too many of us on punishment.

Whenever the VIPs visited, the place was spruced up and cells from which privileges such as the wash stand and mirror had been removed were refurnished. One bitterly cold day when I was sitting in my cell, swaddled in mailbags, eating porridge and boiled, unpeeled potatoes from a dinner tin, the door was slung open by a screw and a woman in a tweed skirt peered inside.

'Visiting magistrate – any complaints?' she brayed.

Her incredulity was hard to disguise as she saw me sitting there, draped in sacks, looking more like an animal than a human being.

'One or two,' I said, and commenced to list them.

The governor didn't appreciate her adverse reports on this. He decided that he didn't need a bad egg like me and arranged my transfer, along with another 'trouble-maker', a Battersea Boy called Les. Both of us saw ourselves as the intransigent, unbroken élite who had been rewarded by being sent to a less liberal nick.

Winchester was a regular prison but there was a particular wing for YPs (*young prisoners*), of which there were about twenty at any one time. We basically had the place to ourselves, which was brilliant, and the two regular screws were pretty good guys. One, Francis, was of the old school, and Jim was an ex-Para who adopted the policy that if we didn't rock the boat, neither would he. Even so, Jim wasn't averse to using his elbow if he thought you were stepping out of line, but he wasn't sadistic and he'd sometimes bring us any leftover cakes from the kitchen.

I seemed to have learned my lesson from Lewes that you don't challenge authority head on, but one night someone outside my cell was coughing incessantly, driving me mad. Eventually, I called out, 'Go away and fucking die somewhere else.'

The flap over the spyhole lifted and I suddenly realized I'd made a big mistake. When the door didn't open I figured the warder had gone to get his mates. I lay there, reading the noises, and then heard the key in the door.

A con came in carrying cocoa, which was delivered at seven every morning. I breathed a little easier and took my mug, but suddenly a fist sent me sprawling across the bed. The con jumped on me, trying to get his fingers around my throat. I hooked his legs from under him, and tried to flatten his head on the floor, all the time wondering why the hell this adult prisoner was mad with me.

After we were pulled apart I sat in my cell trying to work things out. Suddenly it all made sense. The con belonged to a working party that used to go down and dredge parts of the river. It was a privileged job, normally given to guys who are pretty close to the screws. Obviously, this guy was acting as a mercenary for one of his masters.

The whole affair lacked class and I knew I wouldn't feel better until I'd obtained some form of retribution. My mate

Les was all for springing the fucker two-handed but I wanted to handle it alone. When this con came walking through the wing on his way to the bathroom a day or two later, I stood up, threw a bag in his face and punched him low in the guts, doubling him over helplessly. A well-aimed kick followed and he collapsed on the floor writhing in pain.

Jim was furious. I'd rocked the boat and I expected another beating in the punishment cells.

I tried to appeal to his macho instinct. 'Jim,' I reasoned, 'you would do the same thing if it happened to you. It's a matter of honour.'

While he couldn't argue with that. Jim also sensed that feelings in the block were running high. A revolt was on the cards and eventually everyone was locked up except for Les and me.

Jim said: 'Right, you straighten up your lot and I'll straighten up mine, no-one gets nicked – that's a promise.'

Honour was satisfied all round – well, maybe not all round – but at least the boat was steady again.

Shortly afterwards, I was told that instead of being discharged from Winchester when my sentence had finished I would have to finish my Borstal. It was only much later that I discovered that this was illegal; in the meantime, it was back to the Hate Factory for relocation and another six months.

The old chief at Wandsworth, a sergeant-major-type who had an annoying habit of jabbing his keys into your ribs, just painfully enough to irritate, told me: 'You got another six, do you want to do it easy or do you want to do it hard?' These guys always ask questions to which there is only one answer.

As it turned out, the Wandsworth Borstal wing was being closed and everybody transferred to Reading. Saying farewell to the Hate Factory was pure joy and the two coachloads of boys behaved as if they were on the annual treat of a charabanc to the coast.

We were all allotted various jobs and I took over as No. 1 Baker. A member of a well-respected boxing family from Clapham was my No. 2. In the next six months we spent all our spare time together, practising our combination punches on sacks of flour in the kitchen.

My last night at Reading was the longest of my life, with the hours punctuated by regular chimes of a nearby clock. I tried to put my life so far into some sort of perspective and remembered the words of Mr Honeywell, my first Borstal governor.

'You've caused your family a lot of grief and yourself a lot of unhappiness,' he had said.

I couldn't argue with that.

8

I was twenty-one years old when I left Reading gaol. As I passed through the main gate in my prison-made discharge suit, I turned on my heels and glanced back, silently saying farewell and taking stock of the memories.

My dad was waiting for me when I stepped off the train at Paddington Station. I hadn't seen him since I'd been away, but we'd exchanged letters. He was quite emotional when we met, caught up by a desire to make up for what was irretrievably lost. I guess we both needed to sustain the illusion that there was some semblance of a relationship but I had gone away a boy and come back a young man steeped in the prison culture and we now had very little in common.

Later, as I walked across Hyde Park in brilliant sunshine, the trees looked greener and the air smelt fresher than I ever remembered. Yet even then I was living on borrowed time. In my pocket I had call-up papers for National Service instructing me to report to the local induction centre for an Army medical. Dad was optimistic about my future in the Army. It wasn't quite the Last Chance Saloon, but he figured I might find a niche somewhere which would satisfy my appetite and ease his conscience.

There were about ten other Borstal conscripts and the medical officer asked each of us if we really wanted to be soldiers. At least my poor eyesight was no longer considered a handicap. I'd grown less self-conscious about needing glasses, although I never wore them on romantic assignations. On the trot from Borstal, I splashed out on a pair of rimless glasses which were very fashionable at the time. They cost £40

– which was bloody expensive – but guys like Glenn Miller, the band leader, were wearing them, and in the nick, Billy Hill, the self-styled king of the underworld, wore a rimless pair. If it was all right for Bill, it was all right for me.

I was assigned to the Royal Army Medical Corps at Ash Vale Barracks in Aldershot. The posting had great potential because it allowed a back-door entry into the élite groups of the Army Physical Training Corps and the Paras.

In the meantime I had a few days of freedom and was determined to enjoy every minute. Home in Battersea, Gran welcomed me with a hug. She hadn't changed. From the careful cut-outs on her shoes to accommodate her bunions to the crowning grey plaits of her hair, she was just as I remembered. Her smile told me that all transgressions were accepted. I was still her little boy.

Gran's response to most things in life was to have a cup of tea. It was a deep-rooted ceremony of hospitality, accompanied by the personal quirk of a bowl of rice pudding. She cooked a rice pudding every day just in case I dropped in.

It was great to be home. My room with its view of the cemetery was unchanged; my battered bugle was hanging from the gas bracket, beside the water colour of a Bugatti at speed, a print of a Wellington taking off for Berlin, a photograph of me at fifteen riding my first bike race, and the model of the *Golden Hind* that was still uncompleted yet occupied pride of place on the mantel.

In the attic, my bike rested upside down. Gran had oiled it once a week and demonstrated its free running by spinning the wheels. She knew it was my only real possession of value and had lavished care on it as if it represented her absent surrogate son.

That night she asked about my future. She was a wise old lady and didn't want me going back to prison.

'I'm not a criminal, Gran,' I said. 'It's not a career.'

But even as I spoke the words I should have realized that there is no such thing as an ex-convict – once you've been inside you are stigmatized, in the same way that all policemen and prison officers are stigmatized. Once anyone knows you're a former convict, the reaction is immediate – you're an outsider.

Cobby had done his Borstal at Hollosey Bay in Suffolk with his brother Peter, serving eighteen months to my three years. That first night we went into the West End, drawn to the brightness and cosmopolitan air of Soho. We didn't drink or smoke, so sat over tea at Lyons Corner House in Piccadilly, an all-night Mecca for the low-life and transients, and let our imaginations run wild.

For hours we watched the action, our eyes and everybody else's looking for 'mysteries' – the girls who for one reason or another had sought refuge there – and listening to the rituals of the chat-up and seduction. Our own efforts were pitiful compared to the older guys with reputations or money, often both. They made their entrance usually three- or four-handed, swaggering between tables and tipping their broad-brimmed hats which were almost mandatory for aspiring 'heavies'.

'If you can't fight wear a big hat,' was a popular London saying, but none of us wanted to test its truthfulness, especially when the headwear was complemented with a nine-inch razor scar.

I envied them. In the naïvety of my youth, these men were my heroes. They had money, girls and power. They were somebody.

On my first day I was late reporting to Aldershot – not a good way to start. The sergeant took me aside and explained that he knew about my past but it would go no further. When the adjutant gave me the same story, it was obvious that every man and his dog knew I'd done Borstal.

The fact that I was a convicted felon meant that I was respected by some, but there were a few public-school types with officer aspirations who let it be known that I was beneath contempt. The feeling was mutual. One night I got a bollocking from the sergeant in front of the billet and he said, 'It might be the Borstal way, son, but it's not the Army way.'

That was enough. I thought, Fuck the Army, they're a load of wankers; and decided to go back to London to the real life.

At midnight I slipped out of my billet, crossed country till I hit the railway lines and followed them until early morning. Walking on sleepers, you have to adopt an odd sort of gait, almost a hop, skip and jump; but railway lines make great escape routes because they always lead somewhere.

I got to Gran's at about eight in the morning after catching an early train from Weybridge. For once there was no rice pudding but dear old Gran fried up bacon and eggs for breakfast. I warned her to expect a visit from the police and left the house soon afterwards, dumping my Army gear with Uncle Jack, who could flog it for a few quid.

That night I went back to the Corner House to watch my heroes and revel in my new-found status as a deserter from the Army. I was John Mills in *Waterloo Road* come to life. It wasn't a wise choice of venue. Deserters and runners of every description seemed to congregate there and the police regularly swept up all-comers. I chose the wrong night and got caught in the net.

Within hours my identity was established – 'Bruce Reynolds, absent without leave' – and a military escort took me back to Aldershot. Some form of military adjudication had to be made – not quite a court-martial but along those lines. In the guardroom there were about a dozen other misfits including a betowelled Jehovah's Witness who refused to wear a uniform so they'd taken his own clothes away. He was an example to me; they had taken his dignity but they couldn't take his faith and he was doing things his own way. If I wanted to be free, I had to take the initiative.

That night in my cell I tentatively slashed my arm and then continued more desperately until the flow of blood was gushing. Lying back on my bunk I waited for the routine patrol. It took longer than I expected but finally I was discovered and rushed to hospital for a blood transfusion.

Afterwards I was transferred to Queen Elizabeth Military Hospital at Woolwich. There was an armed guard outside the locked ward and twenty or so prisoners/patients inside. As we entered the room, they struck up a rousing rendering of 'Roll Out The Barrel', played on imaginary instruments. They were all misfits or deserters who were trying to work their ticket on the grounds of mental instability. But it was obvious, in some cases, that the years of acting the role had totally taken over and they truly were mad.

Their obsessions were contagious and they were not the influence that I needed. Sure I wanted out of the Army, but not in a strait-jacket. I didn't see that as a way of winning.

Having thought hard about it, I told the visiting psychiatrist that I felt my past conduct had been a minor aberration caused by my going directly into the Army from prison and that I was now ready to return to unit and to soldiering. Back I went to Ash Vale Barracks.

My interrupted career in the Army lasted precisely two days. The sergeant gave me endless grief; it was clear that I'd been labelled a trouble-maker — a bad apple who had to be reminded of the fact constantly.

Part of my punishment was to clean the head office and there I noticed a list of the conscripts, including a name that I recognized. There couldn't be many Schmidts, I thought, remembering an old Borstal acquaintance. I found his billet and discovered that he was indeed another lost soul.

'I'm getting out of here,' I said. Schmidt thought about this for a while and decided that he, too, fancied a midnight flit.

That night we made our way to the railway tracks, retracing the path that I'd followed on my previous departure. We walked till early morning then caught the first train into Waterloo. Schmidt lived down Peckham way, so we said our goodbyes after arranging to meet in two days' time. I didn't turn up: I sensed that Schmidt wasn't really dedicated to a life of crime, he just wanted out of the Army. I couldn't see him as a partner in crime, nice guy that he was. I never saw him again.

Finding somewhere to stay was never a problem. There were always friends who'd let me crash for the night, or I'd climb the embankment by Wandsworth Bridge Road and sleep in one of the railway carriages. Generally this was OK as long as I was out by six o'clock. Then I'd find an early-morning café, buy a cup of tea and contemplate the new day.

Pretty soon it was like the pre-Borstal days. I linked up with Cobby and a few old pals like Paddy Ryan and Bob Lucas, and we were going out every night breaking into houses and shops. There wasn't much money involved but it kept things ticking over.

None of us had a driving licence, but Bob had picked up just enough knowledge to be able to steal a car. We used to take the last tube to somewhere like Cockfosters, arriving at about half-past twelve, and then we'd stay out of sight for another hour. Then we'd pick a street and go from garage to garage until we found a car with the keys in the ignition. We'd push it silently down the driveway and when we were out of sight we'd practise our driving. It was hilarious. Bob would be coming up a rise to a red light and realize that he couldn't do hill starts, so he'd have to do a U-turn and go round in circles until the lights changed.

Our first real coup came when we smashed the front window of Burberrys in the Haymarket. We only got a half-dozen coats, but in publicity terms it was huge because Burberrys was such a famous store.

I had already earned a reputation amongst our little gang for my various techniques for smashing windows, although I'd dispensed with treacle and brown paper. With some windows, particularly the big ones, you had to be careful about loose pieces, which could suddenly come down and cause a nasty injury. My technique was to rake the window diagonally from corner to corner with a six-foot iron bar, similar to those used by railwaymen.

When we made the headlines next day, I suddenly thought: If we can nick ordinary coats, why not fur coats?

The lean post-war years had passed and the consumer society had emerged. What every woman seemed to want was a fur coat. The retail price of a mink ranged from as much as £1,500 to three or four grand, which meant that not many women were going to get what they wanted. A crooked one could be had for as little as £250, which was much more within their means.

We started small, targeting suburban furriers. Bob would drive, I smashed the windows and Cobby – or one of the others – would help grab the gear. We got very cocky about our success and began staking out showrooms and manufacturers, hoping to steal an entire shipment. Eventually, a Daimler excited our interest. The driver was obviously a major agent or buyer who drove between the showrooms in the West End.

Obviously, we wanted to hit him in the morning when he was loaded up for his rounds. We picked a location in Bond Street where he regularly delivered two large plastic bags into a major furrier's. Meanwhile, there were three bags left in the boot.

We had an ignition key made and simply stole the Daimler when the driver disappeared inside. Changing to another vehicle, we sped home to examine our prize, flushed with success. Just imagine – minks? Chinchillas? Sables? We had hit pay dirt.

Brewing a pot of tea to heighten the anticipation, we finally unzipped the bags and spilled the contents on to the floor. The silence was absolute. We were the stunned recipients of eight hundred pairs of children's elasticized swimsuits.

I felt like I'd just sent a winning Pools coupon to the laundromat. Where did we go wrong?

A few days later I was stopped above St John's Hill on my way to Wandsworth. Two plain-clothes policemen recognized me but after a struggle I broke free and took off in the direction of Battersea Rise. I dropped down on to the railway and crossed the lines at Clapham Junction, hoping they wouldn't follow. Laying low for a while, I lost them and reasoned it was best to stay away from the area.

Unfortunately, the policemen took my escape personally. They put a bit of pressure on people and, after a tip-off, caught me one night as I left a café in Tooting with a couple of mates. I was bundled into a blue police box while they went chasing after the others.

I wasn't about to give up so easily. I threw my back against the door, broke it open and went sprinting along the street with my knees pumping. I was leaping back fences, gaining valuable ground, until a garden wall collapsed beneath me and Old Bill picked me up with typical gentleness.

There was no escape this time. Just a few weeks after fleeing the Army I was bruised, dazed and well and truly nicked.

9

Three years was a heavy sentence for half a dozen charges of breaking and entering. My prep-school days were over. At 21, I had graduated to university and was enrolled with the mainstream criminal élite at Wandsworth.

The dons in Wandsworth are more persuasive than any of the dons in Oxbridge or Palermo. All the big names were there – people like Alfie Hines, Fraser, Kiley, Steel and Stanton. These guys really knew about life. They were famous for their exploits and, listening to them, I was in awe of their experiences. They talked about getting ten grand for their whack when the most I'd ever had in my life was £250. I'd been wasting my time on boyish pranks. It wasn't a career, it was a bit of excitement, but suddenly I was thinking that I'd missed the big picture. Crime, it appeared, could be very well paid.

At times, Wandsworth was like an old boy reunion of the élite criminals in the land. There was a camaraderie which made me feel at home, even though I was in the presence of my elders and betters. I realized that I liked these people. They weren't layabout and goons – they were professionals who took their work very seriously.

In those three years I made my contacts for the future. I listened well, storing information away, just as years earlier I had immersed myself in the heroic tales of fighter pilots, mini-submarine captains and Dick and Harry, the one-armed ex-servicemen at the *Mail*.

I knew various screws, some of whom were OK. Others were barking mad. There was one called Taffy Thomas who used to enjoy ordering people to have haircuts. It didn't matter if you'd only just had it cut – Taffy wouldn't take any lip. As a result, I once got shorn five times in a week.

One particular con, Billy G, who was one of our icons, shaved all his hair off on his last day so that when Taffy went to say, 'Get your hair cut,' he looked up and saw this totally smooth head.

Taffy's face turned an ugly shade of purple; he glared at the bare skull and then back at the con, and then he nicked him for being bald without permission.

When I came home, in 1954, my dad pulled me aside and we had a long talk about the future. He was basically saying that it wasn't fair on Gran if I was going to continue leading the same sort of life.

My own ideas on my future career were starting to form and they conflicted in almost every sense from Dad's. Although I linked up with Paddy again and we did a bit of hoisting (*shoplifting*) I was more interested in branching out and making some serious money.

Paddy had always been a gambler and knew a lot of the dog-racing crowd. I wasn't interested in the dogs but through an acquaintance of his we heard about a bookmaker who always carried his money home with him. That night we broke in and crept his trousers out of the bedroom; there was five or six hundred pounds in the pockets. Paddy's mate got a whack for the information and we split the rest between us.

I had money again and a new avenue for making more of the same. We did a few more creeps, often based on hope rather than firm information, but there was very little chance of getting nicked.

I had been home about six months and was still looking for the bigger opportunity when Paddy and I began to venture further afield. Country houses were ripe for the picking and 'climbing' was the crime of the moment. We began hitting the Home Counties.

Paddy had a mate called Ernie Watts who was a climber and about five years older than me. He was certainly more intelligent than your average con and he had all sorts of good ideas about crime. Ernie was working with a partner called Harry who was by far the most experienced among us. He had been involved in the Eastcastle mailbag job, the first major post-war theft, when £287,000 was stolen from a post office van on 21 May 1952.

The robbery had been executed with immaculate precision. The van was followed every night for months as it left on its journey to Oxford Street. Cars had been stolen specifically for the raid. In the early hours of Wednesday morning one of the team had disconnected the alarm system on the van whilst the staff were on their tea-break. As the van left Paddington, a call was made to a West End flat and four men climbed into one of the stolen cars, a green Standard Vanguard, and the four others into a 2½-litre Riley. As the van turned into Eastcastle Street, off Oxford Street, the two cars blocked the driver's path. Six men attacked the three post office workers and then drove off in the van, leaving them on the pavement.

Rewards totalling £25,000 were put up by the insurance companies but despite intense police activity for over a year there were no charges.

I was in awe of Harry. He had been into battle and emerged unscathed. No matter what else happened in his life, he would always be remembered for the Eastcastle job. I, too, wanted to make my mark.

Paddy and I teamed up with Harry and Ernie, specializing in the climb.

The *modus operandi* was pretty standard. Normally we went three-handed – the driver, the minder and the goer. The driver would drop us off at the entrance or the best route inside. Depending on the house, we would arrange the first pick-up for three-quarters of an hour later. If we pulled out for any reason, we could come back and put a newspaper or some other sign by the side of the road which signalled that we wanted to be picked up.

If the first rendezvous passed, the driver would return every half-hour. He couldn't do it too often because there could be the local policeman or a concerned citizen who would become suspicious.

The best time for a climb was invariably just as the rich home-owners were sitting down to dinner. Nobody would be upstairs because the staff would be serving table and generally there was the background of noise of scraping plates and cutlery to muffle the sound of a window sliding open.

We would normally find a ladder in one of the outbuildings, or use the drainpipes to scale the walls. I was always amazed at how careless people were, particularly with jewellery and furs. They would leave them on the dressing-table, or draped over the bed. I could be in and out within ten minutes, searching just the bedrooms and scooping up the spoils. However, none of us knew the value of things. I would take the tom (*jewellery*) and furs, not realizing that a piece of furniture nearby was probably worth eighty grand.

Ernie was quite well read and saw himself as a master planner rather than a man of action. Unfortunately, there can be too much planning. After a month plotting a raid on a horse trainer at Epsom, we knew how many people were in the house, what time they had dinner, when they retired – the works. It was going to be a classic climb.

On the night, I was sitting in a tree beside the house, waiting for the right moment, when I saw someone climb a drainpipe and enter through an upstairs window: the same way we were planning to go in. Ten minutes later, he left and the alarm was raised. Suddenly we were in the same position as the burglar – except we were escaping from the scene of a crime that we didn't commit. Afterwards, I decided that the opportunist approach was often the best.

The gang relationship developed very subtly, and increasingly I was paired with Harry rather than Paddy. Harry was more gung-ho, whereas Paddy was inclined to follow Ernie's 'let's-wait-and-see' approach. Harry and I worked well together. When we wanted money, we stalked the houses of the great and good; and when we wanted girls, we hunted in the dance halls.

On one of these expeditions, we met up with Bridget and Rita, two Irish girls who were barely sixteen. Ah, what a wonderful age! No phoney saccharine maturity, only eager naïvety and innocence waiting to be sullied.

Bridget and Rita were new to Streatham's Locarno, one of the fleshpots of suburbia, yet they knew the routine. 'See you home, darling,' was a means of introduction which could lead to – at the very worst – a good-night kiss.

A successful relationship was greatly enhanced if you had transport – a motor bike or better still a car. Not many of us did, so Harry and I opted to take the girls home by cab. They had never been in a taxi before and their sense of awe was impressive. We indulged the impression by taking them on a sight-seeing tour of the West End. It was amazing because they had never seen the sights before. They lived in East Dulwich – not the residential part, more the residual overflow of council flats that towered over Dog Kennel Hill.

We got our kisses that night, but nothing more, although I recognized something of myself in Rita Allen. Intelligent and well read, she realized that there was more to life than East Dulwich. She wanted to go places and do things.

Rita's father had died when she was seven, leaving Mum with the prospect of bringing up four children – three girls and a boy. Money was short yet the kids were well cared for. The girls were sent to the local convent school and, as the saying goes, 'Catholic girls are either saints or sinners.' Rita was no saint and I loved her for it.

From that first chaste kiss our relationship grew. Soon I knew all the family, including her stepfather who periodically appeared on the scene to act out the ascribed role. It wasn't the home he stayed in; it was the home that he got away from.

Meanwhile, business was flourishing, so much so that Paddy went out and bought a British racing-green MG TC, a nice little car, not great in the power division but with bags of appeal where women were concerned. Naturally, I couldn't go out and buy the same car. What I really wanted was a Ferrari, then I could truly see myself as following in the tyre tracks of Woolf Barnato and the Bentley boys. Unfortunately, I didn't have the money for a Ferrari, but I did have enough for a Norton Dominator 88, the best motor bike on the market and a guaranteed two-wheeled adrenalin rush.

My first attempt to ride it was disastrous when I confused the brake with the throttle and laid it down before hitting a wall. I gave myself two days to recuperate before walking the bike up to Spencer Park, a quiet area that I knew from my paper round, and there I set about mastering the machine. All day I rode, turning and changing gears until my confidence was soaring. Geoff Duke move over!

Rita was certainly impressed. We got on well together and I thought that, in some distant future, we'd get married. Gran and Dad both liked her and I loved her family, which seemed more secure and whole than my own. It was great visiting her house, particularly with the bike, because all the kids would want a ride. I had a favourite among them: Franny was the youngest girl and she was always the most excited when I arrived.

Rita and I were in love and we discussed setting up home together. We rented a three-roomed flat in Streatham and moved in. It was sad leaving Gran in Battersea, although it was too much to expect her to cope with my activities and all the attendant worries of police raids. She probably thought that if I settled down with Rita I would change my ways. Gran never gave up hope.

For the first few months I enjoyed the comfort and security of having Rita waiting for me at home. She cooked me great meals and occasionally we went out to a club – a nightclub at that. The first time I visited one, the Celebrity off Bond Street, I walked in the plush entrance and down the sumptuously carpeted stairs, admiring my image in the mirrored walls and I thought to myself, 'Bruce, you've arrived.' I saw myself as Burt Lancaster carrying a torch for Yvonne de Carlo, who was dancing to a hot Latin number while the men undressed her with their eyes.

Rita loved the night-life. Being young and very attractive in her fresh-faced way, she was always being paid compliments by the clientele and I had to establish proprietorship at an early stage. From her point of view she didn't see enough of me because I was working, but at the time the validity of that complaint was lost on me. The male was the breadwinner and the woman attended to his needs and the home.

Of course, no relationship is perfect. One night when Rita came home late from the cinema – or so she said – I became irrationally jealous. My anger simmered for two days until finally I stormed out of the flat, I slammed the front door, mounted my Norton and roared off down the road at maximum revs.

Stretched out on the bike, bombing down the Kingston bypass, I had no idea where I was going. Suddenly it began to rain. I didn't care. Then it dawned on me that I was being drawn somewhere. The firm had an old bit of work that was on the books – an American lady with a young consort who entertained in great style at a big old ranch house in West Sussex. It was rumoured to contain a magnificent collection of jewellery and furs.

As I approached Guildford, the possibility of doing the job on my own captured my imagination. Switching to the A3100 and then to the A283 I roared on through Petworth, the rain still bucketing down and chilling me to the bone. Closing down the throttle to legal speed, I swept through Arundel. I had only a few miles to go now but it was largely unfamiliar territory. On a previous visit we had come in from a different direction and the rain made it difficult to get my bearings.

Finally I cruised between the gardens of an estate and identified the house. There was no sign of life anywhere and not a light to be seen.

For a moment I considered going home and coming back with the team, fully prepared. No, I would have a closer look. The rain was on my side now. Finding a small lane at the back of the house, I stowed the bike in a mass of brambles and crossed open fields for a quarter of a mile before I came to the walled enclosure. I saw a faint glimmer of light showing through a back window, though I couldn't be sure.

Circling the house, I slid over the wall and crossed the lawn. The light was shining through a chink in the curtains and the window was partly open. It had been raining all evening. Would they have gone out and left the window open? Not likely. And what about the dogs? – I knew she had four poodles.

Cautiously, I slipped away from the window, retracing my footsteps back to the wall. How could I establish if they were home? By telephone. It was a risky option because owners are wary of strange unspeaking callers.

I found a forlorn-looking call box in the nearby village and, fumbling in my drenched jacket, took out some pennies. There was no answer. I waited a minute before redialling and then tried a third time, just to be sure.

Making my way back to the house, I was still caught in a dilemma about waiting for the team or doing it alone. When I peered into the kitchen, there was still no sign of life. I slipped open the window, drew the curtains to one side and crawled through. Almost without thinking, the decision had been made.

There were four dishes containing water. Hmm, so the dogs are here. But where? Two doors led out of the kitchen and one was ajar. There was a growl and a yap before a doggy chorus started up and the poodles came scampering into the kitchen, licking my hands and wanting a game. 'At least I didn't have to waste time finding them titbits in the fridge.

They followed me around as I slipped from room to room and then settled into a routine search. I knew what I was looking for – jewellery and furs – most likely kept in the main bedroom or a separate dressing-room. A blue mink and a sable were easy to find. My luck was in. But where was the 'tom'?

A cupboard in the dressing-room provided the answer. Inside was a small safe about two foot high and a foot wide.

I had no tools, or the expertise to open it, but I managed to manoeuvre the safe on to a small rug and drag it across the floor to the kitchen, accompanied by a pack of playful poodles. When I opened the kitchen door they thought it was time for 'walkies' but I had a more weighty problem. What to do with the safe?

Should I come back for it with the bike? Could I hide it somewhere and retrieve it later? Could I take it with me?

You've got it now, hang on to it, I told myself. Take it with you – it could be the prize of a lifetime. This could be *it*.

Draping the furs over my shoulders, I cradled the safe in my arms and started humping it over a quarter of a mile of muddy ground. When I reached the wall, I couldn't lift it high enough to push it over and had to build a platform of bricks and boxes.

The bike was in the brambles and I pondered again the possibility of hiding the safe and coming back. You don't know what you can do until you try, I thought.

Maybe if I could get the safe on the fuel tank, I could ride home with it perched between my arms. Kick-starting the Norton, I attempted to lift the safe on to it but the weight and angle of the muddy ground sent it toppling over on top of me. Frustrated and angry, I tried again with the same result. Propping the bike against a derelict wall, I placed the safe on the tank, draped the furs on top and slid on behind it. I held the bike vertical and kicked the starter pedal. I fell three times before the engine fired.

Clutch in, gear selected, clutch out, I moved slowly away, cradling the safe between my arms. Everything appeared OK for a distance until there was a slight movement of the safe on the tank and the whole bike nearly toppled. I couldn't control it completely with the pressure of my inner arms.

On the twisting, turning back roads, the weight would swing from one arm to the other, threatening to tip the bike or tear out my shoulders. Worse still, my night vision was impaired by the constant rain and, each time I brushed my goggles, the balance of the bike went haywire. I was so exhausted that there was no way I could lift the safe back on to the bike if I lost hold of it.

Finally, I cleared the unlit back roads and diverted to the main route, despite the possibility of road blocks. If the

American woman had come home, the police would already be looking, so I decided to see how I felt when I hit the A24; not far to go now.

When I reached the smooth, straight road, I could cruise along with the minimum of discomfort and I began thinking about the prize again – visions of what I might have and what difference it could make to my life. The argument with Rita had been forgotten. I was looking forward to the welcome when I got home.

It never paid to be complacent, so I concentrated on riding, switching roads at Dorking to the A25 through Reigate. I was on the last leg now, nearly home.

This would be the most dangerous time as I entered built-up areas. What would a police car crew make of this bedraggled figure on a high-powered motor bike, nursing a large box? The reflections from shop windows as I approached the centre of Redhill gave the answer: I was just a goggle-faced, amorphous blob on a motor bike.

I throttled down at a red light and suddenly saw Mr Plod sheltering from the rain in a shop doorway parallel to the traffic lights. If I ran the light, I would surely be caught, so I coasted to a smooth stop and kept the throttle open so the engine wouldn't stall.

The lights took an eternity to change and my eyes never left the road. Yet I caught a sign of movement as the policeman took several steps across the pavement to take a closer look. Don't panic, concentrate on the revs, eyes on the lights; thank God it's amber, don't rush, wait for the green, that's it – go.

It was a smooth take-off and I rode sedately until out of sight, then opened the throttle wide and felt the surge of confidence begin to flow. I'm going to make it.

I had no tools to open the safe, so I decided to drop in on Harry and use his garage overnight. We could open it in the morning. I was bringing home the bacon to Rita.

I picked up the Kingston bypass and rode on to Harry's place in New Malden. Harry recognized the throb of the Dominator, and opened the door just as I'd cut the engine and dropped the safe on the ground.

'What's up, mate? Are you all right?' he asked solicitously.

'Yeah, I'm all right. I've just obliged the Yank. Got a peter here,' I said laconically, fully aware of the effect of my words.

'Fucking hell, get it in the garage! Here, out of the way, I'll do it.'

Harry could see I was totally shattered. Over a cup of tea I told him the details of the night, explaining the row with Rita and my wild drive south. He gave me the benefit of his marital experience and we talked about relationships. Harry felt that a factor in my relationship with Rita was the absence of role models in both of our lives. Neither of us had lived a normal childhood, Rita without a father and me without a mother. We didn't know what we were supposed to do in a relationship, we hadn't had the experience of growing up in a normal family. What he said made sense and, flushed with a sense of achievement, I resolved to be more patient and more considerate towards Rita.

I telephoned her, hoping that she was at home. Our first words were almost identical apologies. We were in love again. Crashing on a sofa, I dreamed of the vast spoils that lay locked in Harry's garage.

After a victory breakfast of bacon and eggs, we prepared to open the safe. It was an old Milner with a riveted back. A hammered chisel lifted the back edge and we clamped in the jaws of the big bolt cutters, working in unison to turn the handles and roll back the rear plate like opening a can of sardines. Fifteen minutes later, the rear plate was off, the asbestos fireproofing had been removed and we hammered and chiselled open the inner box of sheet metal.

Sadly it was not the prize of a lifetime but a very nice touch just the same.

Harry took the jewellery over to Ernie and explained what I'd done. Ernie got his whack and there was something for the contact who'd provided the information.

Afterwards I went home to Rita, awarding myself a couple of days off to recuperate, in bed of course. I needed it. After humping that half-hundredweight safe across fields and on to a motor bike and bringing it home, my arms were badly bruised and felt long enough to belong to an orang-utan.

Rita fell into my arms. She had thought that I was never coming back, but all was sweet again. 'Journeys end in lovers meeting.'

* * *

If things were quiet, Harry and I would have a looky-looky day trying to drum up future business. On one such outing in the West End we spotted a Daimler tucked behind the Dorchester and the back seat nicely accommodated two pristine pigskin suitcases. Alas there was no sign of a woman – an important criterion when deciding whether it was a 'goer' because it signalled the presence of jewellery – but it was too good a chance to miss.

The car had a security cut-out so we couldn't drive it away. We took the cases and hailed a cab to Victoria Station. Then we walked through the terminal building and picked up another cab.

Getting home, we checked our prize and discovered only a man's luggage, with the consolation of a diamond set of cuff-links and studs, all from Asprey. At least it would more than pay expenses. Going through the cases, we also discovered a portfolio of purchases in the property market and, intriguingly, an order for a Mulliner-bodied Rolls-Royce. This guy had dough, big dough.

An address label listed his home as by the Wrekin, in Shropshire – worth a day-trip. We were not disappointed. The grand Georgian house was hidden from the road by a wooded copse and was accessible only by a long drive. At dusk, Harry dropped me off and I strolled up the gravel past well-kept shrubbery and rolling acres of gardens. Lights through the trees indicated strong drainpipes and easy access to the main bedrooms. The dining-room was lit up brightly and gave a clear view of dinner in progress. We were in business.

I fancied having a go there and then, but Harry was expecting me within the hour. Reporting back, we decided to mark it down for a later date – it was always good to have a full engagement book: it created the excitement of future spoils.

Tentatively, we pencilled it in for 29 March, Grand National Day, knowing that a trip to the track would provide us with a cover story in case we were picked up and questioned by the local police.

We needed a third hand and I suggested we invite 'Chad the Shad, the Lurker in the Long Grass', otherwise known as

'George the Jolly Gypsy'. His real name was George Cheatt – quite something to live with.

Chad was about fifteen years older than me and looked a lot like Cesar Romero, with a moustache and a selection of expensive suits. Along the way he'd acquired many more possessions than anyone else I knew, including a Jaguar XK120, but his main claim to fame was that years earlier, before the war, he had been caught in the coal cellars of Buckingham Palace, having found a way in. He didn't talk about how he managed it, but always said he could do it again.

Chad was one of those larger-than-life characters who inspired countless stories – not all of them true. What couldn't be denied was that George lived life to the hilt and no matter how messy the situation he always came up smelling of eau-de-Cologne.

He'd tell his wife, 'I'm just popping down the betting shop, luv,' and then turn up two weeks later, looking sun-tanned and relaxed.

'I had a bit of work to do,' was all George would say, when in reality he had taken a girl from one of the clubs to the South of France, rented a scooter, gone up into the hills, found himself a nice little hotel and rattled her bones for a fortnight. On one such sojourn, he claimed they spent a week in a very cosy foursome with the hotel owner and his wife. It may have been true – you just didn't know with George.

His climbing expertise was second to none and he was always good company. In many ways, I wanted to impress the old lion; to demonstrate my prowess in the hope that it might lead to some invitations from him.

Chad was all in favour. He liked the circumstances of the plot and also the idea of a day at the races. We would drive up on the Friday, do the climb, stay that night in a hotel and drive on to Aintree for the National on the Saturday.

We took the minimum of tools: a torch, a William Rogers big blade sheathknife, gloves and cheap Bata creepers that could be slung away afterwards so that nobody could match footprints left in the gardens. None of us relished getting pulled by the country cops, who had a natural antipathy to London firms invading their turf.

Harry dropped us off parallel to the drive, and hugging its edge we made our way towards the copse. Everything was the same and there was the lovely Georgian house, lit up and welcoming. There were quite a few cars in the driveway, indicating they had company, and pride of place went to the royal-blue Mulliner Rolls. It was nice to see that his order had been fulfilled.

Dinner was underway and we counted ten people at the table, with servants hovering around them. It was the classic set-up of the climb.

There were two possible main bedrooms – they are nearly always the ones with the best view – and I chose the left, mainly through habit, but possibly too as a throwback to my one-time political leanings. Chad approved and gave me a leg up to the first joint of the drainpipe system. I climbed to the flat surround of the window, surprised to find it unlocked but, then, fortune favours the brave.

The room was enormous, and sweeping the space with my eyes, I immediately recognized it as a female's room. The dressing-table yielded an assortment of rings which I scooped into a pocket, and then I continued searching for a jewel case which would hold the main articles. All the possible hidey holes were explored and then I opened the door to the landing, hoping to reach the other bedroom.

For some reason, a coat was hanging from the door. With so much wardrobe space, why would anyone leave a coat there? It had a Hardy Amies label as well as a sunburst diamond brooch that was too big to be genuine.

From the landing I could see the sweeping staircase descending to the ground floor and hear the dinner-table banter. I walked past the stairs, pausing to look down the banister and spied two fur coats laid out on a table together with a prominent jewel box. Momentarily it threw me out of my stride. Should I risk going down and collecting the loot?

It wasn't a sound move, I decided. The servants were using the hallway and could easily discover me. Instead, I searched the other main bedroom. The wardrobes had security locks and opening them would create too much noise. I quickly scanned for the keys and opened a door that I thought led to a dressing-room. It was a walk-in shoe repository, with his and hers sections, but pride of place was occupied by a large Chubb safe.

I tried the handle, wishing it unlocked, and wistfully searched for the key near by. No such luck.

Slipping on to the landing again, I retraced my footsteps but was strangely drawn to the top of the staircase. I looked longingly at the two coats and the jewel box, sorely tempted.

What would Chad do in the circumstance? Or 'Taters' – George 'Taters' Chatham, the legendary climber who was reckoned to have stolen and spent several million pounds in the forties and fifties?

A chance was a chance, I decided, and began sauntering down the stairs. Hopefully, if the servants spotted me, they would assume that I was one of the guests. The tension increased as I drew nearer, but I never took my eyes off the prize. I scooped up the two coats, closed my hand on the jewel box and calmly walked back upstairs. At any moment I expected to hear somebody shout for me to stop.

When I got to the woman's room I breathed a brief sigh of relief, threw the coats on the bed and tipped up the jewel box. It turned out to be a vanity case but at least I had the fur coats. Almost as an after-thought, I took the snide brooch on the Hardy Amies jacket behind the door, thinking it might fetch a few quid. Even fakes have a value and maybe 'Red Face Tommy' could find a home for it.

Chad was waiting for me outside. I clucked my tongue to signal him and threw the coats out the window.

'Nice one, son,' he said, guiding me to firm ground.

'I got a bit of tom as well,' I told him as we crept away from the house towards the drive. The party was still in full swing behind us.

Harry was on a thirty-minute pick-up but periodically sweeping through the area in case we had problems. I put a newspaper at the side of the road to tell him that we were ready. When the headlights picked up the paper, he reduced speed and we leapt from the hedgerow and bundled ourselves inside.

'We got a good earner,' said Chad.

Harry turned from the wheel, seeking confirmation from me, and I smiled.

Sitting in the back, I ran through the whole story, giving them a playback of the highlights. The coats were zipped in a holdall and the rest was in my pockets.

'Wait till we get to the hotel, we can see it at our leisure then,' said Chad with a wink. It was all part of the game – the delayed gratification of that wonderful feeling of success as we sorted through the spoils.

I couldn't resist flashing the snide sunburst brooch to Chad. 'What about that then?' I said. 'Imagine if it's right.'

'Show me,' said Chad, turning from the front passenger seat.

'Fucking hell,' said Harry.

Chad held it up to the eye, but the light was poor and he could only speculate.

'It's a very nice piece, snide or not, it's an article of value.'

Pulling into a country pub about fifty miles from Aintree, we were lucky to get rooms. The clientele were all going to the Grand National and the atmosphere was celebratory. We met in Chad's room and I turned out my pockets on the bed. There were three good-quality rings – diamond, emerald and aquamarine stones – an odd Victorian rose diamond brooch and the two mink coats which would fetch about a grand.

Then we all examined the snide piece.

'It looks right to me,' I said tentatively, knowing I had the least experience. Harry concurred with me but we were both waiting for Chad's verdict.

'Well,' he said, 'it's either the best snide I've ever seen or it's as right as Lord Chief Justice Goddard.'

We celebrated over a nice meal and a couple of bottles of wine, joining in the pre-race party crowd. Harry and Chad were bigger gamblers than drinkers and were already planning to shorten the odds on a few favourites at Aintree. I'd never been to the National although I'd read about it and seen the race on cinema newsreels.

The day dawned brightly and we shared a bottle of Moët as a pre-race aperitif, toasting further success before we joined the crowd to study the form and prices. I didn't see much of Chad and Harry throughout the day. This was their territory and they knew most of the trainers, jockeys and big-time bookies by name. They were group-hopping, hoping to pick up a winning tip whispered in confidence.

Meanwhile, I wandered around the paddock, marvelling at the beauty of the horses and the ladies. For the big race I put a tenner on a rangy old plodder called The Crofter, which was priced at 100/1. I figured that if I was going to bet, why not get value for your money?

Chad and Harry laughed at my choice. To them I was a typical mug punter but I'd seen hundreds of their racing 'certainties' finish way down the field. And I still remembered how Airborne had turned my sixpence into a whole week's wages. They backed the well-fancied Sundew, ridden by Fred Winter. He'd never won the National, but a lot of people thought that this could be his day. The field galloped around the first circuit and Chad, looking through his Zeiss bins, gave us a commentary until they appeared in view for the run to the line. Four fences out and in the lead, going very strongly, was the old plodder The Crofter. I was jubilant and let them know it. A grand beckoned.

Harry's face was grim. Chad was imperturbable. We joined the Aintree roar, a Kop-like wall of sound, and I was probably the lone voice bellowing for The Crofter. But the finishing line couldn't come soon enough and the old plodder was swept up by the fast finishers and came home fourth.

Only afterwards did I realize that Sundew had won. Chad and Harry were celebrating. My tenner was nothing compared to the serious amounts they had put on the race. There is a smugness about all big winners after collecting their winnings, and Chad and Harry were no exception. They prattled on about never having any doubts; Sundew was always going to win; without question.

As an expression of solidarity, they gave me a handsome share of their winnings and we supped on more Moët, toasting everyone who had made the weekend so successful, including The Crofter who had given me the best tenner's worth of fun in my life.

The sunburst brooch was indeed genuine. It made us four grand, while the other baubles fetched two and the furs six hundred quid. With Chad and Harry winning over a grand apiece on the National, it was a profitable weekend and a sign of things to come.

10

The climbing business was booming and I was often earning more than a thousand pounds a week, the equivalent of £15,000 in today's money.

Still I didn't splash out on a car. I realized it was a lot easier to hide a motor bike than a car. Harry showed a lot of courage riding pillion – given my dodgy eyes and the fact that I quickly had a couple of bad accidents. I broke a leg riding down the coast and had another bad one on the Southend road in an accident.

Just as I began questioning the wisdom of motor bikes, my Norton burst into flames one night at the Robin Hood garage on the Kingston bypass. A few drops of petrol from the filler nozzle leaked on to the hot cylinder head and suddenly the bike was alight. It was the end of a two-wheeled love affair.

Shortly afterwards, Harry and I bought our first business car together, a Ford Zodiac. For my own personal transport I bought a Triumph TR2, just under a year old. It had once belonged to Don Cockell, the British heavyweight champion, who was silly enough to fancy his chances against Marciano, and needless to say he lost.

I had always had a fascination with cars, ever since I hero-worshipped racing drivers as a kid. To me, a sports car was the ultimate status symbol.

Although I already knew the basics from joyriding in Cockfosters on a Friday night, Cobby undertook to teach me the finer points, like clutching and changing gears. Once I had mastered them, it made dragging (*stealing from cars*) a whole lot easier.

All the old cars had a Lucas ignition which operated on a simple rectangular key that could be replaced by virtually any strip of metal. Without any pressure, a screwdriver could be pushed in or even a stiff piece of foil. This made the cars ridiculously easy to steal. Later they introduced a coded key system as a security measure. This, too, was ludicrously easy because the key details were often printed on the dashboard or the ignition and you could actually read them from outside the car. You spotted a load, got the key number, and trotted round to your nearest garage and said, 'Can you please give me FA No. 38?' No proof of ownership or ID was necessary. You got the key and away you'd drive.

If you did this often enough, you could build up an entire set or, better still, buy the complete series of keys from a mechanic looking to make a few extra quid. Unfortunately, this created its own problems. It was bloody hair-raising sitting in a driver's seat testing a few hundred keys when you were never sure when the owner was coming back, or if he'd look out a window and call the police. The only way to handle the pressure was to shut yourself totally off from the outside world. If you act suspiciously, people are going to think it is suspicious, so you carried on as if it was the most normal thing in the world for someone to be sitting in a car, running through a set of keys big enough to choke a horse.

It always amazed me that the car manufacturers didn't do more to stop auto-thefts. Maybe vested interests were at work. It was the same with number plates. Hills, the number plate people, didn't turn a hair when you said, 'I need a set for a 3/4 Jaguar, XYZ 303.' They wanted a name and address but there was no checking. A lot of crime could have been stopped if the politicians had made it mandatory for the car's log book to be produced before any new set of number plates was printed.

After my lessons from Cobby, I was floating around on my own one day and decided that I was going to get a ringer (*a stolen car with plates*) for myself. Behind Leicester Square there was a club called Ciro's. There were always quite a few cars parked up there and I knew exactly what I wanted, a Vauxhall Velox, because that's the car I'd driven with Cobby. I got the key number by sticking my face up against the window and bootled around the corner to a nearby garage. Fifteen minutes later I slid the key into the lock, opened up and nestled in the driver's seat. It was lunch hour and there were quite a few people moving around, but I kept my cool, adjusting the mirror – yes, that's me – and reacquainting myself with the gear shift.

Everything checked out so I started the ignition, scared shitless, but feeling good. I was actually doing it all by myself; I was stealing a car.

Right, I thought. Clutch in. Easy on the accelerator. Clutch out very very slowly. I knew the drill, but for some reason the car didn't move. I checked everything and tried again. The same thing happened. The engine was screaming, my foot was off the clutch and the car was going nowhere. I looked down. The handbrake! Christ!

I eased it off and put my foot down, giving it the same amount of power, but instead of pulling away, the car shot forward and smashed into the car in front.

Within seconds people were crowded around me, looking at the damage. I got out, rubbed my head and said to the commissionaire who'd arrived, 'Would you keep an eye on this? I'll just go and get a policeman.'

And I tootled off, round the corner and away.

I couldn't believe it when the incident was reported in the *Evening Standard* that afternoon. Harry rang me up and asked, 'Was you down at Leicester Square today?'

'Yeah, as a matter of fact I was.'

'I knew it was you when I read it in the paper.' He was laughing.

I suppose I should have learned my lesson, but on the first day I had the TR, I drove from Battersea to a pub at the Elephant and all the way I could smell something burning. Finally, someone pulled alongside me.

'Have you been driving with your handbrake on?' he shouted.

'Course I haven't,' I said, too embarrassed to admit it.

11

Socially, I was moving upmarket and entering a whole new world. Harry and I began drinking in a pub called the Star in Belgravia. The owner, Paddy Kennedy, was one of those hosts who believed that insulting people was the best way to attract customers, and people used to find it very amusing when he ranted, 'What you fucking doing here? Why don't you fuck off?'

The Star was a hang-out for a strange mix of people. There were moody film stars, clapped-out directors, would-be starlets, petty thieves, aspiring gangsters and the real thing. Among this odd congregation, there was a group I regarded as the inner circle – the cream of London's crooks.

Harry was my entrée; he was an established figure and, through him, I was slowly made aware of a whole other life that I'd never experienced. Everyone at the Star seemed so sophisticated; the women made the girls from the Streatham Locarno look like a different species. Diana Dors was a regular, with Dennis Hamilton, her current old man, and an entourage of film people. Bonar Colleano, Susan Shaw, Samantha Eggar, Harry Fowler were also regulars, as were Richard Harris and Bobby McKew, one of the Chelsea 'entrepreneurs'.

There was a motor-racing crowd that used to get in there as well, like Mike Hawthorne and his pal Peter Collins, always with their own large crowd. And then there was Billy Hill and his entourage who, when lined up along the bar, looked like a walking *Who's Who* of the underworld.

All in all, I met a lot of people at the Star who were to influence my lifestyle and career. Because they were older and wiser, I had respect for them, but what most impressed was their style. They were driving Railtons and Alvises and dining at the best restaurants.

Up until then, fine food never used to figure in my thinking. If I wanted a meal, I'd go to a pub. Similarly, I had never had a bottle of wine with a meal. The first bottle I ordered was recommended by the waiter, who suggested La Flora Blanche, which was a Sauternes. I was eating a steak and I thought this dessert wine was really nice. As with so much of my knowledge, I began reading books to discover what people should drink with particular foods.

Another regular at the Star was 'Dandy Kim' Cabul-Waterfield, who specialized in escorting rich heiresses and always drove a Bentley. It wasn't pretentious or boastful, he honestly looked as if he was born to have one. Another new friend was a bloke nicknamed 'Roller' Reg because of his taste in cars. He'd also been in on the Eastcastle job.

I was a novice compared to these guys. They knew I was a

thief, but I was a junior on the edge of the inner circle. Yet, by being around them, my horizons began to expand.

A business deal with Bobby McKew helped entrench me further. He was friendly with an Indian prince who was into motor racing in quite a big way and wanted to drive in the Monte Carlo rally. He bought an Aston Martin, had it modified and got a top production car driver called Les Leston to be his co-driver. Unfortunately, the prince struck trouble because he had to pay tax on the Aston Martin if it was going to stay in this country. He didn't want to take the car back to India and he didn't want to pay the tax so they decided to sell. It was 1956, at the height of the Suez Crisis, and you couldn't sell cars – particularly a gaz guzzler like an Aston Martin – because petrol was on rationing.

Bobby arranged the sale and I got an amazing deal. It was a DB24, British racing green and just under a year old, yet I paid only £1,100.

'You should never have a green car,' people used to say to me, pointing out the overtones of bad luck. Yet the contrary was true for me; although I had a couple of accidents, mainly due to my ineptness at the wheel, the Aston represented an amazing period of luck for me where everything went right. It reminded me of the marvellous quote by Napoleon: 'I don't care if he's a good general, is he a lucky general?'

There were two particular regulars at the Star who became my role models – Jimmy Fox and Little Freddy. Jimmy looked like Curt Jurgens and dressed the same, so that one of his nicknames was Lord Jim, from the Conrad novel. Little Freddy was perhaps the smartest man I ever met. I remember seeing Lawrence Harvey one day up by the Burlington Arcade and thinking how unbelievably elegant he looked, as if he'd just stepped out of a shop window. But Freddy had his own style. He used to wear handmade shoes from MacLarens in Albemarle Street, and his tie would always be slightly to one side, as if he had forgotten that he was about to take it off.

Jimmy and Freddy were both established faces and were then concentrating on the dog-doping business. There were various other scams around in the mid-fifties, but gambling attracted a lot of criminal interest, not just racing but also illegal card games.

London didn't have a legal casino. Instead there were house parties, most of them arranged by Billy Hill, and by rigging the games he ensured that no-one except him finished with a profit. The scam was pretty simple. Patsy 'Golden Hands' Murphy, one of Billy's associates, suffered terribly from arthritis and had gradually moved into the nether world of professional thieving and then into gambling. Patsy was a very good card player with the ability to lure people into a game and build up their confidence before taking them to the cleaners. It was like the classic story of the gambler hitting town and asking the bell hop if there is any action. The bell hop warns him that the only game is crooked, but the gambler goes anyway. The next day the bell hop asks him how he fared.

'I lost. It was crooked.'

'I told you so.'

'Yeah, I know, but it was the only game in town.'

I never understood gamblers. Even the whole logistics of betting: whether 11/8 was better than 4/1 was a struggle for me, although I had friends who made a good living at it for years.

Freddy and Jimmy had been doping dogs for ages when I met them. There was no real science attached to it, although they were more scientific than most. Basically you gave a dog a shot of phenobarbitone and it would usually run as if it had downed half a bottle of Scotch. Trouble was that not all dogs were affected in the same way, which meant that, after working all your bets, the dog occasionally came storming home in front and upset the scam.

Freddy and Jimmy were both so experienced that, over time, they had dismantled many of the kennels and rebuilt them with a sliding section that could be removed by taking out a screw. This made it ridiculously easy for them to get inside and do the business.

I was loosely a part of this set and proved useful because I wasn't a well-known face in gambling circles. If Fred wanted to put a sizeable bet on a particular dog, he obviously didn't want to use people who were regularly putting money on because the bookies could get wise and slash the odds. I was unknown and could lay a couple of monkeys with various people without any of them suspecting that Freddy was involved.

But it was a mug's game. Maybe one in every twenty people I saw at race meetings was involved in some form of illegal enterprise. They all knew the dogs were crooked; some were actively involved in doping, yet they would still clutch their race guides and insist that a particular dog couldn't get beaten on its form. It was crazy.

Doping had become so popular that people like Freddy had to make sure they didn't hook up a dog that had already been done by somebody else. Otherwise some poor mutt would leave the box too wired up to put one paw in front of the next.

This is pretty much what happened at New Cross one night when the syndicate arranged a mammoth coup.

'We cannot lose,' he said and indeed they couldn't. When the traps opened, the two favourites came out and ran fifty yards before going backwards. They didn't drop dead but might just as well have done – they were walking at the end and the crowd were shouting, 'Rigged! Rigged!'

They tried to have the race rendered null and void but, of course, no-one could prove anything and the organizers weren't really concerned.

To me the whole affair seemed very shortsighted. Jimmy and Freddy were discreet and never too greedy, but the other crowd were aiming to get as much money as they could regardless of the consequences to the animals and ordinary punters.

Afterwards, Freddy turned to me and said, with a straight face, 'It's fucking bringing the game into disrespect, mate, innit?'

For some reason, thieves are naturally drawn to gambling. It was a folly that ranked alongside wine, women and song, but, unlike my contemporaries, I indulged in all except gambling. I had my own folly. The Aston probably cost me, pro rata, almost as much as my peers lost at the tables and the track, but it suited me because when you're working with partners you can't hoard money when the others have none. It's no use saying, 'I can't loan you any because you'll only go and blow it.'

What's yours is theirs – and vice versa – so it suited me to be spending my share on the car.

Jimmy Fox had an Alvis at the time and Little Freddy had a Jaguar. We became friends, mainly on a drinking basis but occasionally we'd have a meal together and talk about possibilities. I was still very much a junior, but was privvy to information from the inner circle.

One night, a highly respected figure from Fulham called George, alias Little Caesar, was drinking with Harry and I overheard them talking.

'Who's the tall thin fellow you're hanging around with?' asked George.

'You mean Bruce?'

'Yeah. He seems to have plenty of money, can we put a bit of rope round him?'

George was contemplating tying me up.

Harry laughed. 'No, no. He's at it.'

'Yeah, well, who is he?'

'Oh,' said Harry, 'he used to be the youngest major in the British Army.'

It was one of those off-the-cuff remarks that seemed to stick because I was obviously tall and straight-backed. Often after that, people would say to me, 'So you were in the Army?'

Usually I'd reply, 'Yeah, I was in the Army – for two fucking days.' But other times, I'd play up to them and let them believe I'd been an officer.

Little Caesar's big claim to fame was having once worked with Taters Chatham and later with Nobby Clarke. He was called Little Caesar because he looked the part – a small man with a Roman nose and an unpredictable temper. He was forever getting nicked and the most famous story about him involved a supposed verbal the police produced when trying to implicate Nobby in a crime.

They claimed that Little Caesar had been seen running from the scene shouting, 'Wait for me, Nobby Clarke of Number 18 Garven Road, Fulham, wait for me!'

The Star was an amazing place, full of strange and familiar faces. Lucky Lucan drank there before he allegedly offed the nanny and did a runner. He had a pal who was maybe twelfth in line for the throne. I met this guy and thought that if some catastrophe befell the royals and everyone was wiped out, this guy would be king. He was without doubt the biggest nincompoop I'd ever met.

Another character was the aforesaid Nobby Clarke – who looked like a 'Nobby' because he had one of those rough faces, like a house that had been lived in and then trashed. Nobby's big buzz was dog racing but, for entertainment, he and his wife used to lie in bed at night listening to police messages on a radio scanner.

Somewhere along the line, Nobby had become a key-man. He could do things with keys that people said couldn't be done. Nobody was ever able to explain it, but Nobby had some sort of Yuri Geller-type ability of mind over matter. It wasn't scientific, more a natural talent, and it meant that he could take a supposedly unpickable Chubb lock and it would fall apart in his hands.

Nobby could have made a fortune but he was quite content to go out every couple of weeks with a few mates, open somewhere up, and receive his whack. He was totally garrulous, talking absolute nonsense most of the time. He'd say something like, 'I've got to go to White City tonight, there's a dog I've gotta back in the sixth race, number 3, Dancing Delight.'

'Oh yeah, Nobby, where d'you get that from?' we'd ask, taking the piss.

'Oh, a geezer told me that works selling flowers at the cemetery.'

'He's a good judge then, is he, Nobby?'

'No, no, he's not a good judge, but his sister knows the bloke who's shagging the kennel girl and she says it's gonna win.'

You couldn't get a more tenuous tip, but Nobby would go to the track and bet everything he had on it. He had all sorts of strange ways. He claimed he was Montgomery's driver during the war, but he was the worst driver I'd ever met. He used to have an ex-police car because he had this vague idea that he would be mistaken for a policeman, but there was absolutely no chance. He lived in Fulham all his life and every policeman in the area knew him and knew he was driving an ex-police car, but Nobby still went through with the charade.

Whenever I saw him and asked how he was getting on, he would complain about his partners, saying that all they wanted to do was drink beer and fart in nurses' faces. And he had other particular stock sayings that would get repeated three or four times in the course of a conversation, such as, 'Fucking nightclubs! They're just highly decorated coal cellars, selling inferior liquor at exorbitant prices.'

Eventually, Harry and I decided to have a trial run with Nobby. We went out without anything specific in mind but I was so impressed with his expertise with keys that I wanted to continue the association. Up until then we'd done jobs the hard way with six-foot bolt cutters, sawing bars and breaking through brick walls. It was hard work and yet Nobby would come along with his pocketful of keys and the locks would dissolve.

Unfortunately, Nobby was hopelessly disorganized and habitually clumsy. He would have one pocket bulging with keys and the rest empty. The idea was that each time he unsuccessfully tested a key he'd put it into another pocket. That was the theory. In practice he'd sometimes get halfway through the business, then forget which pocket was which.

We gradually evolved a technique with him which was like something from the Theatre of the Absurd. First we'd find a prospect which could be a clothes shop, a record shop, a chemist or a jeweller's.

Harry and I would go in on spec, select the target and make sure the street was relatively clear. Then we'd walk Nobby up to the door.

'All right, all right, everything all right,' he'd be muttering. 'Sweet, Nobby, sweet – remember, you are the manager locking up.'

As he started trying keys in the lock, we would keep reminding him. 'You are the manager locking up.' And he would reply, 'I am the manager locking up – click, click, click – I'm the manager locking up.'

Meanwhile, we kept look-out and if we saw someone coming we'd raise the alarm. 'Nitto (*look out*), Nobby – there's a cozzer coming down the street.'

He'd look up, pause for a minute, and say, 'No, bugger it, I went to fucking Borstal with him.' And he'd continue trying the keys as if nothing was wrong. It was absolutely hair-raising watching the policeman walking along the other side of the street while Nobby kept fiddling with the keys.

Yet, at other times, we'd be going through the litany of 'You are the manager locking up', 'Yes, I am the manager locking up', and Nobby would see something suspicious and just march away, without saying a word. We'd have to follow him and eventually he'd say, 'I'm moving because of so and so,' and he'd give us a bollocking. 'Didn't you see him? Fucking hell! You'll get us all nicked.'

Nobby was totally uncontrollable. One time, an innocent punter came up and asked, 'Is the shop open?'

Nobby turned and said, 'No, but it fucking soon will be.'

One day he was fiddling with a door and a man and his wife came up.

The guy said, 'Excuse me, what do you want?'

'What do you mean, what do I fucking want?' said Nobby.

'Who are you?' asked the woman.

'Who do I look like?' asked Nobby. 'I'm the fucking manager locking up, that's who I am.'

'That's strange,' said the man. 'Because I happen to be the manager and I'm not locking up.'

'Are you?' said Nobby. 'Are you, indeed? Well, we'll fucking see about that.'

And then we just walked away.

Nobby really only wanted racing money. He would work until he had a large chunk, maybe a grand, and then didn't want to pick any more locks until he'd lost his money. He worked on a weekly basis and, by rights, should never have done jobs alone because he was capable of fucking so many things up. That's why a lot of people found him very very difficult to work with.

Nobby could open up almost anything, but his speciality was doing shops that shut in the lunch hour. We did a couple with him but generally we chose to hit them on early-closing days and at weekends, particularly in the City of London and the West End.

Nobby made the mistake of tackling little shops which maybe had twenty or thirty quid in the till. Sometimes, he'd be inside and a customer would knock on the door.

'What do you want?' he'd ask.

'I want half a pound of ham.'

So Nobby would carve off a great lump and say, 'There you are, pay me next week.'

We added a whole new dimension to Nobby's talents because in the past he had been working with two guys who were basically dead bodies, just labourers for him. Harry and I did much more. If we found a place that was belled up, Nobby would get us in next door and we'd cut through the wall upstairs and come down, bypassing the alarms. Or we'd use an electric saw to come up through the floor boards from the cellar. It was exciting and frightening, lying on your back with the blade spinning a few inches from your face.

We were making regular money and were possibly the best-dressed guys around. We began hitting country towns like Bath which had nice jeweller's, smart men's shops and branches of companies like Jaeger and Burberry. With historic towns, they try to preserve the façades of the past, and old premises were better for us; modern buildings tended to have plenty of reinforcement in the walls. Often with old buildings you could push a plasterboard down and suddenly you were in the back of a jeweller's. It was as easy as that.

With money and an unlimited choice of menswear, Harry and I were always dressed to kill, but Nobby looked like something the cat dragged in. We tried to spruce him up but he was one of those guys who you could dress up and within five minutes he'd look a scarecrow again.

Nobby had certain shops that he visited – after hours, of course. He had them all over England – places where he got his favourite shoes, trousers and jackets and his wife's underwear. He was adamant that we shouldn't 'spoil' these shops by knocking them over in a substantial way.

'That's one of my regulars,' he'd say, pointing out a shoe shop. 'I took the missis there on Sunday.' And I could picture Mrs Nobby sitting in a chair being fitted out with two or three pairs while her husband kept one eye on the unlocked door.

Nobby might not have been flash, but he was the last of the great romantics. He'd always want to do chemist shops so he could get some 'Charnel' for his wife. She had gallons of the stuff but Nobby would still keep bringing it home. And no matter how many hundred times we told him it was Chanel, he still called it Charnel.

Harry and I steered Nobby in the right direction and the association became very profitable. I built up quite a sizeable tank – about three grand, most of it in white fivers. Gran was my banker.

'Is it safe, Gran?' I used to ask her.

'Oh yes, very very safe, Bruce.'

'Where is it?'

'Under my mattress.'

Good old Gran, she didn't trust banks.

Nobby started having a few winners at the dogs, which wasn't good news for Harry and me because it meant that he was less inclined to work. He was particularly unhappy about going out of London and would get physically sick on long car drives. The only way you could cheer him up when he lapsed into a homesick silence was to point things out to him. We'd be in Barnet, on our way home, and say, 'Nobby, look! There's a red bus – a double-decker,' and he would visibly perk up like one of Columbus's sailors spotting a seagull.

Thankfully, Nobby's luck at the track would never last and he'd come round, swearing like a trooper at bookies and eagerly enquiring about the next job. After one run when he blew six grand he was keen to get his hands on money quickly. We'd seen a jeweller's on a previous trip to Birmingham – one of the old-fashioned shops with a gate outside and then an inner door and Nobby had said at the time, 'I can do that.'

For some reason we'd never got round to it, but eventually decided to make the journey. It was a perfect set-up, with the jeweller's shop in a crescent with only a few shops near by. It was a Saturday afternoon and all nicely locked up.

The first job was to take the padlock off the outer door. We had bolt cutters but Nobby shrugged us aside and went to work with his keys, in broad daylight, with people wandering past. Harry and I put a strong block on, moving to shield him with our bodies and coats. Of course, it only took a minute and we gambled on the fact that people don't notice things when they don't expect them.

The outer gate was opened and then Nobby concentrated on the shop door. Within two minutes we were inside. Harry replaced the padlock with one of our own, just in case we wanted to come back, and then we started cleaning out the showcases. I found a safe in the back room, an old John Tann double door.

'Do you think we could do anything about this?' I asked Nobby.

'Na, not a John Tann – you can't do anything.'

Although I'd never actually blown a safe, I had enough basic knowledge to know that you put a bit of gelignite in the keyhole, shoved in the detonator, attached a battery and stood well back.

A few years earlier, at Winchester prison, I'd promised a mate that I'd learn the art of safe blowing. When my mate was released, we rented a car via Cobby and drove down to Mousehole in Cornwall and broke in to a quarry to get gelignite and detonators. On the way home, we pulled off the road into some fields near Stonehenge. I was eager to see the magic of alchemy at work. Ted demonstrated the basics, using an old petrol can as a substitute safe, placing a lump of gelly inside the can and plugging in the electric detonator. The cap of the can was replaced and screwed down with just the detonator wires running from it; then Ted joined these wires up to extra leads which we ran for some fifty yards before settling down behind some earthworks and connecting up a nine-volt battery.

Ted looked at me and said, 'Here goes,' and promptly probed the other contact in place completing the circuit and *bingo* – the blast erupted all around us. There was no trace of the petrol can, just a depression in the ground – testament to the power that had been unleashed.

'That's good gear,' Ted said. 'We'll be able to do anything with this.'

I was overjoyed. To me it appeared that I'd received the keys of the kingdom; there would be no stopping us now.

We even got as far as picking out a bank, Lloyds in Hartley Witney, and decided to break in on the following weekend. Unfortunately, two days before the job, I got a telegram saying that Cobby had been nicked. He'd taken the motor back to the car-hire firm unaware that the boot was full of gelignite. Ted also vanished from the scene when his wife surfaced and gave him an ear-bashing about parental responsibility.

My safe-blowing career was put on hold, but as Nobby and I discussed the jeweller's John Tann, I fancied a crack at it. Then again, it was a nice day's work and there was no point in getting greedy. We locked up and Harry tested the new padlock for good measure, before we drove back to London.

Typical of Nobby, when we got back to his house, he suddenly mentioned the safe again. 'Oh, yeah, it'd be fucking easy to blow that. I could blow that with my hands tied behind my fucking arse.'

Up until then, I'd always assumed Nobby was just a key-man, but he assured me that he'd been with guys who'd blown safes and knew the ropes.

I turned to Harry. 'OK,' I said, 'we'll go back in. How about it, Nobby? I'll get some gelly and the gear. We'll go up there tomorrow and do the safe.'

'No, no, no, the jeweller might have come back. Not a good idea,' Nobby complained fiercely, shaking his head.

For the next few hours we kept on at him until he finally agreed and I disappeared to get the explosives from our lock-up.

We drove to Birmingham the next morning, a Sunday, and I had a quick scout round. The burglary hadn't been discovered yet, so the shop was just as we'd left it. We had the key to our own padlock and were straight in.

During the drive, Nobby had done a typical about-face and began whinging about John Tann being impossible to blow.

'I don't know what the fucking hell I've come up here for, this is all bollocks. You can't do John Tanns.'

I was humouring him. 'Come on, Nobby, how do you know unless you try?'

He went through the motions and I watched him put some gelly in the keyhole, press the detonator in and wind it around the handle. We moved well away, shielding ourselves behind a counter, and then touched it off.

The explosion made remarkably little noise and when we looked at the safe, it looked unscathed.

'I fucking told you! I fucking told you!' screamed Nobby. 'You can't do a John Tann.'

I walked up, turned the handle and the door opened. Nobby had popped the safe perfectly – the way people say it should be done, but rarely succeed in doing.

Inside was all the cream jewellery and a nice chunk of money, about five grand. Then, of course, the crowing started with Nobby dancing around singing, 'I done a fucking John Tann. Fucking knew I could.'

I couldn't believe the buzz blowing a safe gave me. It was the ultimate power trip. Unless you've been there, you can't understand how a little block of gelly and a handful of detonators can make you feel almost omnipotent. I couldn't wait to try again.

12

Getting rid of stolen gear was often more dangerous than the actual theft. The first step was to find a reliable fence, which is almost a contradiction in terms. By their very nature, fences are untrustworthy and the one thing you can rely on is their greed. To stay in business they often have to work with the police – occasionally 'giving them a body' to protect themselves by grassing on a smaller thief to safeguard their more valued 'suppliers'.

Whenever we wanted to get shot of furs we had a fence called Baggy Eyed Bagel the Bayswater Buyer. He was pretty typical of the breed. If you took coats to Baggy in the summer he'd say, 'Who wants furs in the summer?' And if you took them in the winter he'd say, 'Everyone's got them already.' You couldn't win with Baggy.

Our regular fence for tom was Stan, who'd been taking our stuff for years. After blowing the safe in Birmingham we arranged to meet in a flat in Leyton.

There's a science to dealing with guys like Stan – a delicate bartering process involving much shaking of the head in disgust and outrageous sob stories about destitution, cash-flow shortages, marriage problems and sick pets.

Stan was a small-time operator so we only showed him the chains and rings that we'd taken from the display cases. The really nice stuff from the safe was kept under wraps. Stan looked at the dross and figured the pads sold for about two hundred quid in the shop but were worth only about fifteen on the street. This is where the real bargaining started and you learned something about greed. Stan was shaking his head.

'What sort of money were you looking at?' he asked.

I let Harry do the talking. 'Well, going by their mark up . . .' he said, laying on three layers of gloss, 'we were thinking about three grand.'

Stan looked as if we had insulted his family. 'For this? Is this all you got?'

'Well, no, we got some other gear but it's all cream, Stan. To be honest, mate, it's a bit beyond you,' said Harry, baiting the trap. 'And the problem is we don't really know how much we've got so we don't know what to charge.'

Stan showed no emotion whatsoever as he suggested that perhaps we should let him have a look. We laid the jewellery out before him and his eyes lit up momentarily. There wasn't a piece worth less than five hundred quid.

'It's got to come to ten grand, Stan,' said Harry.

'How do you make it come to that? I can't see ten grand there.'

So I said: 'What can you see there?'

'Well, maybe seven and a half.'

This was more than we expected, but we continued the charade until finally the price was agreed. Stan paid seven and a half grand for the cream and there could be no crying afterwards if he'd made a mistake – that was the crucial thing. He was the expert, he knew what he was buying.

Of course Stan tried it on about two weeks later. He called up, screaming foul and saying he couldn't make his money back. He wanted a bit of leeway, but a deal is a deal. Stan was just being greedy. He saw an opportunity and couldn't resist it.

Nobby's availability was subject to the dog racing calendar, what favourites were running at Stamford Bridge – 'the Bridge' – or White City. This didn't suit us, it made it too difficult to plan anything in advance, so Harry and I began working with others. One of them was an old side-kick of Little Freddy who went by the name of Champagne. This guy was the real McCoy – totally efficient, calm, dispassionate and cool under pressure – everything that Nobby wasn't.

He'd say things like, 'I think there's four cozzers coming down here,' but he wouldn't take off immediately. He would wait until the last moment, just in case the police turned round or walked down a side-road.

Nobby, on the other hand, was totally unpredictable and would say, 'I'll handle the first one,' and start shaping for a fight. Although Nobby was quite renowned as a fighter in his youthful days, I saw him twice get hold of someone, swing a punch and miss completely, finishing up on the pavement.

Champagne had an old friend in the scrap-metal business in York and on a visit to the yard this friend showed him around, pointing out his new house, his Lagonda and the new safe in his office.

'What was wrong with the old one?' asked Champagne.

'Well, with the dough I got now, I wanted a new one.' His friend then opened the safe which was chock-a-block with cash.

'How much do you think there was?' I asked, as Champagne related the story to us.

'Dunno. Fifty grand at least and God knows what else.'

The guy obviously had more money than sense, flashing his wad like that. Apparently, he had left his wife and was living in the house on his own, but he was rarely there, spending most of his time with a girlfriend. We went up to York to check out the house, which was next to his scrap yard. I rang the bell at ten o'clock at night but there was no sign of life so we scouted around.

Exactly as Champagne described it, there were two safes in the basement, one of them a brand-new Chubb and the other an old Milner. What to do now? We decided to wait for the guy to come home and get the keys off him.

This decision to directly confront people – to look them in the eye, rather than steal from them secretly, involved a new level of bottle.

It was an option that became increasingly attractive because the new safes on the market were being made to withstand gelignite. The logic was simple – what concern were alarms, pressure pads or armed guards if you already had the key? The trick, of course, was to find the man with said piece of metal in his jacket pocket.

It was a psychological game – even if you didn't want to hurt anybody, they had to believe that you were serious. Face to face with your victim, you wanted them to be scared – so scared they would jump, sit, lie still, do anything you wanted. But all the time, deep inside, you too, were just as frightened.

We spent all night in the house and packed it in at 6 a.m. when there was no sign of him.

The next night the same thing happened. He didn't come home and we finished up driving back to London and then going up again in the evening. This went on for a week, which meant we were covering a lot of miles for nothing. It's not a good idea to stay locally, in hotels, because you run the risk of raising suspicion, and we had a parallel job in the offing in London. It was another solid piece of information, this time about an Indian prince with an estate down Sunningdale way, who had a treasure room packed with steamer trunks. According to our introduction, who had seen a few of the trunks opened, one was full of crisp, white fivers, another had trays of stones, and another was bulging with sovereigns. It was a veritable Aladdin's cave and we had difficulty imagining how much it was worth.

After the partition of India, quite a few of the maharajas moved to England. Like the Arabs years later, these guys were almost unbelievably wealthy and I even read about one who had solid gold taps in his bathrooms. According to our introduction, the maharaja had recently died and the estate was going to be moved to a safe-deposit vault. He was friendly with the secretary and would be able to get us details of where, when and how the stuff would be moved. We could waylay the convoy on the road and do the business.

So while we were in York each night, we would periodically call and ask, 'Any movement yet?'

'No. Could be tomorrow, could be next week, I'll let you know as soon as I know.'

We did a lot of humming and hahing over which job should have priority. Although the maharaja's jewels were obviously more valuable, the York affair would be relatively simple if the guy actually came home one night instead of getting his leg over.

Off we went to York again and this time the Lagonda was parked out front.

Right! We're in business, I thought. We had a hurried kick around of our options and decided to nab him as soon as he comes out of the house. Anyway, he comes out quicker than we expected and catches us unprepared. He drove off and we followed him in our Wolseley 690, which was quite fast.

Eventually, after a drive through the backstreets, we cut him off at a corner and I leapt out, slung open his door and pulled him out. He was bundled into the back seat of the Wolseley, while I drove the Lagonda round the corner and gave it a search.

The target was wrapped up on the back seat and we found the keys in his pocket, but he kept saying, 'What's it all about? What are you doing?'

'Be quiet, it's nothing to do with you.'

'No, you've made a mistake. You don't want me. You want my uncle, not me.'

The guy sounded pretty convincing, but we tried the house anyway. The others went inside and I drove around the streets with the guy lying under a blanket on the floor. I kept telling him everything would be OK. Just as I got back to the house, the others were coming out.

'Did you get it?'

'Get it! Fucking hell, we got about eight grand out of both safes.'

It was a decent score and we were all in high spirits on the drive back to London. Meanwhile, our hostage was sitting in the corner of the car looking more and more depressed. When we stopped for a bite to eat, he kept prattling away: 'What am I going to do? This is the first time my uncle's left the keys with me. He's going to think it was me. What am I going to do?'

'You're going to shut up and eat your fish and chips,' I said.

'But what are you going to do with me?'

'You'll be all right, we'll put you on a train.'

We got to an industrial estate in Ealing, took him out of the car, walked him into the estate, and said, 'Wait there a minute.' Then we drove off and left him.

It should have been a day to celebrate, but the festivities were tempered when we got back home and discovered that our introduction had been ringing us from the moment we left. All the maharaja's treasure had been transferred to the vault. That one had got away.

According to Harry, we didn't 'funk' it enough. 'Funk' is a strange skill which is connected with the power of positive thought. The whole idea is that if you wish for something to come true, it will come true.

I was never a believer in 'funk' – it sounded more like blind hope than any mental skill. The power of thought to effect any positive action requires the faith to move mountains which, of course, Harry had.

One morning we spied a van delivering to a shop. The driver had gone inside and Harry and I were standing on the pavement and he said to me, 'Funk the keys are in it.'

How the hell can my thoughts make any difference? I thought, but sure enough, the keys were in the ignition. Before we could climb in and disappear, the driver came back out and got behind the wheel.

Harry was furious. He turned to me accusingly, his face bright red, and said, 'You didn't funk, mate. That's why we haven't got it.'

Meanwhile, the driver was in the van and Harry said: 'OK, fucking funk that he's forgotten something.' He was standing beside me, with a look of absolute concentration on his face as he projected his thoughts.

What a total waste of time, I thought – the guy was going to drive off any second and nothing we did would make a difference. But, lo and behold, I saw the driver pause and begin thinking. He got out of the van and walked into the shop. He'd barely disappeared and we were in the van, driving away and when we got round the corner Harry said, 'Y'see! Y'see! You fucking funk and you get it.'

Harry had a gambler's mentality and was positive that he could control events by his thoughts; he could funk things to happen which, of course, they regularly did. I still think there was no great secret – Murphy's law is just as prevalent in the criminal world as it is in any other world. Things can go disastrously wrong for you but, just as equally, the pendulum swings and everything goes absolutely right.

* * *

Often, when we had no inside information and nothing in the diary, Harry and I would trawl the 'trade' publications. In our line of work these were magazines like *Tatler* and *Harper's* which listed social engagements, along with photographs of rich socialites and occasional features about their splendid houses. What better way to smell out potential hits?

I clipped a small story about Mrs Dodge of Dodge Motors fame arriving in England and attending a première in the West End. Horace Dodge was almost as famous as Henry Ford and I figured that his missis would have plenty of gear. It was almost obligatory for the jewellery to be flaunted at public occasions; it must be half the fun of being rich, letting the Joneses see what they are competing against.

The article mentioned that the Dodges were staying in Surrey and it wasn't difficult to find the estate agent who was renting them the property. We took a drive down to Englefield Green to look at the house. It was a day out more than anything else; we found a nice place for lunch, cracked a few bottles of wine and felt very civilized.

Over the meal, I glanced up and noticed a familiar face. Looking closer, there was another, and then another – we weren't the only people interested in Mrs Dodge. There must have been four firms who'd come down from London: a rogue's gallery of thieves all interested in the American socialite.

One of them was Peter Scott, known to the media as 'The Human Fly', an Irishman who had been burgling since he was a teenager and would eventually become a legendary figure in the underworld. They even made a film about him, *He Who Rides a Tiger*, starring Tom Bell and Judi Dench.

Using informants, like chauffeurs from Knightsbridge and maids from Mayfair, Peter persecuted the rich and opulent to fund his lifestyle. He lived in Belgravia, drove a royal blue Jaguar 3.8 fixed-head coupé, the XK140, and was always with lovely ladies. He squired a millionaire's daughter, but apparently the millionaire viewed this liaison with suspicion, warning Peter that association with his daughter did not give access to the family fortune. He didn't care, Peter, he wasn't looking to marry a fortune – he wanted to go out and nick one, and then go out and nick another one . . . and he did.

Perhaps his most celebrated coup was robbing Sophia Loren after hearing that she was being paid in jewellery for the film she was making in England. Pretending to be a journalist, he was tipped off as to her whereabouts by a petrol pump attendant, broke into the house and took a briefcase containing cash and jewels. At the time it was listed as the largest jewel theft in the world, worth around £200,000. He also rifled through her lingerie, and the speculation was that he got more for her drawers than he did for the gear.

Peter eventually married the face of the sixties, the beautiful Jacqui Bowyer, and they were always around the best places, at home and abroad.

Although I can't be sure, I'm pretty certain that he managed to get inside the Dodges' house. He got rumbled but managed to escape, though empty-handed. The Americans were wise to the risk and the next day they transferred to a suite at Claridge's for the duration of their stay.

That was the whole essence of the climb – you could never be sure what you'd find when you slid open the sash window and rifled the dressing-table. Sure we had information, but it was rarely reliable. For a number of years there was a guy working for a top insurance company who would provide detailed house plans, along with an inventory of what was inside. Even then, it was never a sure thing. Someone might have twenty thousand pounds' worth of jewellery but if they are at the theatre on the night you call, nineteen grand is probably hanging from their ears and neck. That's just bad luck.

13

I saw myself as very much an up-and-coming member of the underworld, which led to a certain amount of unspoken rivalry with more established faces. Although I'd finished my apprenticeship, so to speak, I was still trying to make my mark and was prone to rushes of blood to the head.

In the Star one night I was drinking with Peter Scott and I mentioned Alexander Korda, the Hungarian-born film director who was once married to Merle Oberon. He lived off Cheyne Walk and I'd heard that he had a built-in safe in the bedroom concealed in a wardrobe. As one bottle of wine followed the next, the talk grew bolder and bolder until I suddenly heard myself saying, 'Let's go and have a look at it now.'

We were fairly merry as we walked around the quiet streets of Chelsea, giggling and larking about. I was totally unprepared, wearing heavy brogues and a suit, but I figured Peter was testing me, seeing if I had the bottle. Of course, it could have been the other way round. I was too pissed to remember.

We stumbled through back gardens, looking for a ladder and making so much noise that the neighbourhood dogs were howling in chorus. The houses around there are particularly well protected and Securicor had regular patrols. This made it especially dangerous but we carried on until we found a Jacob's (*ladder*). By then, the safe was almost a secondary consideration. The object of the exercise was to test each other's nerve and see who would cry uncle first and say, 'Let's leave it out.'

Eventually, we called a truce and both of us adjourned to the Star for another drink. 'We'll look at it another night,' I suggested.

'When we're sober,' added Peter.

Then we both fell over.

We never did work together again. I realized we would always be challenging each other and finish up getting nicked for the sake of pride or a foolish dare. It was OK for the newer guys to take outrageous risks. They wanted to get noticed, just as I wanted to be noticed, but I'd done my articles, let them do theirs.

Inevitably, as my reputation grew, invitations began to arrive and Harry and I began working with some legendary names.

Eddie Chapman was cast in the heroic mould. His story was larger than life, far eclipsing the fiction of Charteris and Fleming. One of the leading safe-breakers of pre-war days, having been initiated into the art by Lord Jim, he'd been captured while on the run in Jersey after blowing a cinema safe and nicking £1,200. He got two years for that. The sentence started in 1939, the year before the Germans invaded the Channel Islands.

The astute Eddie did a deal with the occupying forces and was flown to Germany for training in espionage and sabotage. He was landed in England, where he immediately contacted MI5. Working for the British under the codename Zigzag, Eddie then did enough to convince his Nazi paymasters of his loyalty before returning to Germany. He met all the high-ranking Nazis, and was sent back to England on another mission. At the end of the war, the authorities granted him a full pardon for all his previous crimes and in later years his story became a film, *Triple Cross*, starring Christopher Plummer.

When I met him in the Star, Eddie had just returned from the legendary voyage of the *Flamingo*, Billy Hill's yacht. In the company of Franny Daniels, Patsy Murphy and some other very interesting characters, he had been involved in – what? Speculation was rife. Was it gun running, a plot to corner the highly profitable spice market, an early essay into the drugs field, or a plot to break the Sultan of Morocco out of his prison in Madagascar? No-one would ever know. After travelling to Tangier, Corsica and Toulon, the *Flamingo* mysteriously caught fire and sank in the harbour.

Patsy 'Golden Hands' Murphy was also a slick operator before his joints began to seize up and he retired to the card tables. He invited Harry and me to his place in St John's Wood. His black Rover 75 was ostentatiously parked out front, alongside a '49 Roller belonging to Roller Reg. After the greetings and a mandatory cup of tea we got down to the business in hand. Patsy had two targets in mind, twenty miles apart, near the Wirral.

Our introduction for the first job was a successful dealer in antique silver, who had been doing business with the target for years and between them they had buried a few bodies. Our Deep Throat knew all about him, down to how much cash was in the safe, but the big prize was in the garage and protected by security alarms: antique silver, a collection amassed over the years. The market for antiques of any sort had rocketed, but especially for silver. At last, could this be my Eldorado?

The second job was equally promising but the provenance of the original information was not as good. It came from an Irish builder who was working as a manager for the owner of a construction company. He knew all about the target's business dealings – the honest and the corrupt – including deals with council officials who were enticed into making green belt land available for housing developments. According to our informant, there was a six foot by three foot filing cabinet crammed with money. His precise words were, 'You'll shit yourselves when you see how much is inside.'

We discussed the range of equipment we should take – difficult in the circumstances, but when in doubt I always followed good old Baden Powell's motto, 'Be prepared.' Patsy took the Rover and we drove our current ringer, a Jaguar Mark Seven, that had plenty of boot space to accommodate the prize.

We had a full range of gear, most of it acquired over the years thanks to Nobby's expertise with keys. Apart from the normal tools there were two electric saws, hammers and drills plus two sticks of polar ammonite and seven electric detonators. Seven was considered a lucky number and despite the best planning and total application, luck was still the magic ingredient of success.

I was the junior with the firm. Patsy and Harry had been part of Billy Hill's firm involved in major robberies, and Reg had also spent time working with Nobby. Yet I was the only one among us that had a criminal record. The others had pristine characters – officially at least – but unofficially, the Criminal Records Office at Scotland Yard must have had reams of reports on their alleged activities.

This made it safer to work outside London. The local constabulary would put the burglaries in their incident book, have a nose round, take a few prints if they could find any, and then write them off as unsolved. This was how most police investigations went, unless matters were complicated by a violent act which rocked the boat and raised the ire of the chief constable, who would then kick arse all the way down through the ranks.

Patsy and Reg went ahead in the Rover while Harry and I followed, keeping them in sight. We had a couple of hundred miles to drive and didn't stop. Good rest spots for car men are equally good pull-ups for the Old Bill, and a London accent was enough reason for them to start asking questions.

We rendezvoused in Chester on the Saturday afternoon when it was full of shoppers. Pairing off to different hotels, we arranged to meet later that evening. Harry and I were relegated to the three-star hotel while Patsy and Reg had four-star accommodation – the privilege of rank!

Meeting later, we took the Rover to check the targets, which were supposedly empty for the weekend. The general consensus favoured the antique collector, but when we saw the rambling Victorian house with its unkempt gardens and tawdry paintwork it looked deserted.

'What do you think?' asked Patsy.

'Let me out and I'll slip around and have a look,' I said.

I walked back, passing the house before sliding into the alley at the side. Glancing up at the house I saw a familiar burglar alarm box. It was supposed to be a warning but to me it was an invitation. People don't pay insurance premiums when they have nothing to insure and alarms are mandatory for insurance.

I retraced my footsteps, skirting through the garden to the front of the house where the heavy main door was barred by inset double Chubb locks. We couldn't go through without raising a racket, so I kept looking. The double garage door had similar locks. This guy was so well protected, there had to be something inside.

'I really fancy it,' I said, getting back in the car.

The others weren't so keen. They had built up a mental image of an 'Aladdin's Cave' and the run-down house didn't fit the picture. Even Harry, who normally took my side, was reluctant, and I was out-voted.

It was frustrating. Maybe they doubted my professional opinion or wanted to curb my natural impetuosity. I had a reputation for being game for anything, whereas Patsy and Reg were more circumspect. Perhaps that was why they had never been caught.

By the time we got to Delamere I began to feel optimistic again. This was a much classier area, with the requisite Rollers in the driveways and burglar alarms just as prominently displayed. It screamed 'nouveau riche' – music to my ears because these people had to advertise that they had bundles and ape the old money classes with their swank balls and dinner dances.

At the entrance to the driveway, a large slab of oak proclaimed in seared rustic capitals that this was 'Dunedin'. A single light had been left on to give the impression that somebody was home. I scouted around and decided to make an entry via the back through what appeared to be a bathroom window. I criss-crossed the window with sellotape and smashed it with my fist.

Crawling inside, I couldn't tell if the door was belled and didn't want to take a chance. I called for the toolbag and began drilling a sequence of holes about two feet from the floor running parallel across the door, connecting them up with a keysaw until I had cut a hole.

I crawled through on to the landing and looked back to find the door had been wired with contact points on the extreme right-hand corner. The first hurdle gave me confidence as I examined the landings and found all the doors were similarly belled. The others followed me inside and we located our target room – the home of the filing cabinet. There was a security lock on the door but I used the same technique of cutting a hole through the bottom panel.

Inside was an office with a large rosewood desk and leather chair. Near by was the filing cabinet, squatting like the Buddha of the Bucks.

Patsy was allowed the privilege of opening it – after all, it was his bit of business – but when he levered the top drawer it was empty. It was the same with those below and we glumly looked at each other. Patsy was not amused. Our information was either incorrect or out of date – either way we came up empty and could only make a quick sweep, looking for a consolation prize.

Harry found two minks in the bedroom and Patsy found the main jewel box, but it looked as if most of the best pieces were with the lady of the house. I couldn't stop thinking about the filing cabinet. Where was the money? I wandered through the house, pretending I was the owner. Where would I hide the money?

Generally people who hoard money like to have it close by. They like to see it, count it, gloat over it, feel it running through their hands; no bank statement of assets can give you the same feeling. There's nothing to match the thrill of cold, hard cash.

In the bathroom, I opened the heated linen cupboard and noticed a floorboard was loose. I levered it up and explored below with a groping hand. My fingers were walking in the crevices and touched a sharp metal edge. Hooking my fingers behind it I dragged out a steel, olive-green, ammunition box, about 16 inches by 8 inches.

'I've fucking got it,' I cried, clutching it to my chest.

The firm gathered around and I was given the privilege of opening the box. As the lid flipped open, it revealed five packets of banknotes, each containing a grand. There were smiles all round and pats on back, although no-one was going overboard about five grand. But whatever else happened, the weekend had paid its way and anything else would be icing on the cake.

We drove back into town to our respective hotels and met up the next day, Sunday. Everyone was in high spirits and the post-mortem on the previous night's events reached the consensus that our information had been correct but out of date. It gave us a better feeling about ourselves.

I was particularly happy. Finding the money had elevated my status, and reputation was the all-important thing to me. There has always been a mythological aura surrounding lucky faces in the 'crim' world. Some privileged people have possessed it, Patsy being one of them. They didn't call him "Golden Hands' for nothing. I, too, was lucky.

We went back to the rambling house at Hope and too a quick spin around the area. Confirming nobody was home, we parked up and approached on foot, carrying our toolbags down the alley to the back garden.

I knew exactly where I wanted to enter and nobody questioned the decision. They were paying tribute to my lucky nature. I climbed a ladder of drainpipes and smashed through the bathroom window. With such a rambling old place, it was difficult to know which doors and windows had alarm connections, so I regarded them all as suspect. A hole had to be cut in every door, which meant it took a long time getting downstairs to the garage.

The firm was close behind me, waiting for the good news. They weren't to get any. When I found the light switch in the garage, it lit up an immaculately clean interior. In the words of George Gershwin, 'I got plenty of nothing'. There were lacquered showroom shelves and velvet panels but no sign of the antique silver that they had once displayed. We viewed the emptiness in disbelief.

Patsy and Reg wanted to call it a day, reasoning that there was no point in being greedy and taking a risk when our information had proved incorrect. However, this time Harry was with me. He wanted to search the rest of the house. Being gamblers by nature, the others finally agreed, unable to ignore the fact that I was feeling lucky and might just do it again.

We started searching room to room, concentrating on doors that were locked. The first two were empty but the third proved to be the office and squatting in one corner was a medium-size Milner. While Patsy primed the keyhole with gelly, we retired to the landing, waiting for the dull thud and pungent scent of burnt chemicals.

The charge blew and we scurried back inside, reaching for the handle of the safe. It turned, clicked and opened. Inside were bundles and bundles of banknotes in varying currencies. There were no markings to say how much we'd uncovered but the sheer number of bills was thrilling. I was on a roll, and while the others sorted through the cash I kept looking.

There was another locked door. I went to work. Cutting a final hole, I kicked the severed part of the woodwork through into the room and poked my head through. The torch bean picked up a random clutter of clothes, suitcases, cardboard boxes and tea chests. It was a junk room, but in the 'crim' world junk rooms are legendary. There are countless stories, not all of them apocryphal, of them holding vast wealth.

'Got anything, mate?' Harry asked, poking his head through the bottom of the door. I was rummaging through piles of overcoats, breaking open battered suitcases, upending chests full of books and tearing the string binding on cardboard boxes. The dust and stench was everywhere.

'I think so,' I said, coughing and spluttering. I had kicked aside a painter's dustsheet and hit something solid. It was an old iron chest with a side handle at one end. It appeared to be some primitive safe of a kind I'd never seen before. Although only about two foot square, it was monstrously heavy – the way gold is heavy – and I started dragging it towards the door. With Harry pulling and me pushing, we got the box to the landing, where Patsy recognized it as an old-fashioned strong-box.

'It's bloody heavy,' I said.

'Yeah, that's 'cos it has a cast-iron shell.'

'Could be full of gold,' I suggested, which made Patsy laugh.

'Listen, it's dreck. Leave it behind.'

Reg was in favour of giving it a shot and we dragged it to the window and dropped it into the garden below. I was rather hoping it might smash open, but it simply embedded itself in the soft turf. Harry went for the car while Reg and I man-handled the box into the boot. Harry and I elected to drive it back to London with the rest of the incriminating evidence. The risk was justified by the buzz of physically bringing home the spoils; we were hunters bringing home the kill.

We rendezvoused at Patsy's, smothing the box in an overcoat as we carried it into his garden shed. It was a shame to use explosives on such an antiquity but we were all dog-tired. A quick shot blew the box into several pieces and scattered small bags across the floor. Each was tied with string and sealed with wax. We cleared a table and began opening them one at a time.

Each bag had a piece of paper listing the contents and a date. It was obviously a pawnbroker's collection of un-redeemed pledges – rings, brooches, sovereigns and chunks of old gold. We'd hit the jackpot again: lucky Bruce!

Although the 'ladder gangs' were making all the headlines in the early fifties, the climb had become so popular and spawned so many copycats that the pickings became leaner. Home owners were tightening security and the Establishment put the squeeze on judges to up the sentences for burglary.

The new movers and shakers were gelignite gangs who preferred blowing safes to climbing ladders; and I was all for the change – having developed quite a taste for explosives. By 1957 I was older and wiser and the piss and vinegar of my younger days had disappeared. People like Patsy had taught me that doing jobs on spec was dangerous. It was far safer to work with inside knowledge and do some planning.

It was Patsy who came up with the coup at Dodge Motors at Kew, an independent company that was eventually absorbed into the General Motors Group. A brand-new Chubb safe had just been installed which apparently held a sizeable chunk – about five grand. Unfortunately safes were getting more sophisticated, so we sought the advice of a friendly locksmith.

The normal method of poking gelignite into the keyhole was out of the question because the new model had an anti-explosive locking bar. The guaranteed method was to drill a hole at an angle about 6 inches from the top and another 6 inches from the bottom. The locksmith even gave us a template of the door, showing us how to avoid four bolts hidden from view. After the drill had punched through, we had to pack the holes with explosives and, with any luck, the door should rip open.

Dodge Motors was patrolled by security guards so we spent several days timing their routine until we figured that we had an hour between their sweeps. Reg kept watch, while Patsy, Harry and I went in through a side door. We'd earlier changed the lock so we could use our own key and lock it behind us. The brand-new Chubb was exactly as described, although there was a second safe, much older, and it raised the possibility of the money being divided.

We used standard steel drills powered by an electric motor which made a racket, so I had fabricated a box with glass fibre to muffle the noise, although the motor needed air to cool it down and was going to be difficult to silence.

The technique worked a treat. We packed a normal amount of gelignite in the holes, went behind the door, popped it and the whole front plate swung back on its hinges. The bars weren't sheared, but twisted with such a force that it threw the door open.

What a buzz! We scored about three grand, which was a little disappointing because we didn't have time to blow the old safe and later we found out that the rest of the money was inside.

Obviously, not every job went so smoothly. Good information is always the key but no amount of planning can prepare you for the unpredictable foibles of human nature, whether it be a lovers' tiff that brings a couple home early from an evening out, or PC Plod changing the route of his nightly stroll.

There was a jeweller's in Piccadilly that I quite fancied the look of. Next to it was a tobacconist's, and then, on the corner, the headquarters of the Greyhound Racing Association. Nobby took one look at the building and said, 'I can get in there.' We scouted the location on a Sunday afternoon and considered breaking in through the Greyhound Racing place, then bricking through to the tobacconist's shop next door. From there, we could tackle the jeweller's.

Nobby got us in, and we started off in typical fashion, attacking the wall to the tobacconist's with pickaxes and sledge-hammers. After an hour of hammering, we barely dented the brickwork and realized it was going to take all day. At the back of the place I discovered that a lift shaft took in space immediately behind the two shops. Crawling inside I managed to plant some gelly and blow a hole directly into the basement of the jeweller's.

Upstairs in the main shop I found the safe, clocked the layout and then crawled back outside, waiting to see if I'd triggered any alarms. We disappeared for an hour, returning to find no sign of Old Bill. Harry, Patsy, Reg and I went in, leaving Nobby as the outside man. We couldn't have made a worse choice. Any policeman would pull Nobby immediately if they saw him mooching about. By his very nature he looked suspicious.

When I took a good look at the safe, I discovered a wire looped around the handle and across the front of the door. This was obviously belled-up, which meant that any attempt to open the door would break a connection and set the alarm off. But whoever rigged up the device had used too much wire; by unscrewing the handle we could remove it gently with the wire attached and lay it at the front of the safe beneath a piece of tacked-down carpet. The connection was intact and we were free to work on the safe.

We drilled two holes in the top but exactly the same thing happened when we tried to drill through the bottom; the metal refused to yield. There was no alternative but to let rip with a charge, which blew a small twisted hole. Crouched at the back of the jeweller's, within view of the front window, we held a war council. We were tantalizingly close to a right touch with diamonds, rubies and emeralds, all the cream, but the hole wasn't big enough to reach inside.

'We're fucked,' said Harry.

'So close and yet so far,' I lamented.

Patsy was having no such talk. 'Let's bomb it open!'

I watched him pack a French letter full of gelly and lower it through the twisted hole at the top of the door. He was going to detonate the blast inside and hopefully blow the door open. The big question was whether the explosive would simply blast out through the gap rather than against the metal.

It didn't make a distinctive sound; not so specific that someone would say, 'That's a safe being blown.' Although it was rather a dull thud, we felt the entire building shudder, but the door didn't give.

We had scattered to keep a lookout. Nobby was patrolling Piccadilly, looking as obtrusive as only he could and making all sorts of hand signals that nobody could understand. Harry was on the other side of the lift shaft, keeping an eye on the Greyhound Association, while Reg went upstairs.

Harry poked his head through the hole and said, 'I'm going to have a shit, would you mind the front?'

'Yeah, sure,' I said.

Patsy was working on the safe, preparing another charge. All of a sudden I heard an emergency whistle and dived through the hole. Harry was lying on a guy on the stairs.

'I caught him coming in through the door,' he said, breathing heavily.

A frightened old age pensioner was struggling beneath him.

'What are you doing here?' I asked, trying to calm him down.

He seemed a nice old guy, who said he occasionally came in on weekends to do a bit of work. I sat him on a chair, tied a loose blindfold and made him a cup of tea.

'How long are you boys going to be?' he asked, taking a sip. 'Not that I mind. Good luck to you. I'm on your side.'

Harry kept an eye on him while we set another charge. We were just about to set it off when Reg appeared on the stairs.

'There's something wrong.'

We crept upstairs and through a window saw Nobby walking up and down the road. Further along a police car was parked on the corner.

Under pressure you learn about a person's character. Patsy, supposedly the real professional, suddenly panicked. 'We're fucking nicked!' he cried, almost ready to sit down and wait for Old Bill to tap him on the shoulder.

'Bollocks to that,' said Harry. 'We get out over the rooves.'

He led the way, taking us across the sloping slate and between chimney pots. When he reached an open window, we dived through and found ourselves in a bedroom.

'Who are you?' asked a startled old queen, clutching what at first appeared to be a teddy bear. The small dog gave an uncertain growl.

'Police officers!' I said. 'Where's the key to the door?'

'Where's your authority?' he asked.

'Where's the key to the bloody door? We're in a hurry, there's someone in the building.'

The key was on the side and we slipped out the door and down the stairs to the street. It was about five o'clock in the afternoon and we could see the police car parked up at the top of the road. We split up. Harry and I crossed the road and kept walking. The police saw us but I was wearing a British Army officer's 'warm' – an overcoat – and didn't fit the bill. If we'd looked scruffy or started to run, they would have been on us in a flash.

When we reached Berkeley Square, in an alleyway by the old Astor, we took off like greased lightning and caught a cab in Curzon Street to Victoria, where we bailed out and caught another cab.

The next day, the headlines described us as 'The Four Thin Men' who escaped over the rooftops and missed out on a £100,000 fortune. A well-known theatre producer, the poof we have encountered, described how four men had dropped into his bedroom on a Sunday afternoon. He must have thought it was Christmas.

My Dad rang me up.

'I see you made the news,' he said.

'Oh yeah?'

'Yeah – you bastard.'

It was the closest thing you could get to a compliment coming from the old man.

14

Despite their reputation as the 'artisans' of the criminal world, there is no such thing as an expert safe blower. I certainly never met one. After talking to lots of different people who truly knew about explosives, I discovered that it was far more technical than most people imagine. So many things can affect it – the atmosphere, the temperature, the positioning and the vagaries of metal. When Nobby blew the John Tann in Birmingham, it had been more a case of good luck than good management.

Even so, public imagination was captured by the 'gelignite gangs' and it soon became a serious criminal offence simply to be caught in possession of explosives.

I was shopping one afternoon at Burberrys with Chad the Shad. We had just popped a few bits and pieces in the boot of the Aston, which was parked around the corner, and decided to stroll up the Haymarket.

Chad whispered, 'It's on us.'

'Where?'

'There's two cozzers over there and they know me double well. If they say anything, we've got nothing to worry about, leave it to me – but if they ask, you don't know me too well, that sort of thing.'

The policemen crossed the road and approached us. Among the local constabulary this pair were notorious for picking on people who had some form.

Chad acted really cool, but then, he didn't realize that I had a cigar box full of gelly under the front seat of the car.

'Excuse me,' one officer said. 'Hello, George.'

'Hello, Mr Twyford, Mr O'Reilly. Are you both well?'

Neither officer recognized me and they very politely called me 'sir'.

'We've been observing you in the shops and putting packages in the car.'

I said, 'That's right. We've been to Burberrys and bought some clothes.'

'Is that your car then, sir?'

'Yes,' I replied.

'Do you mind if we have a look?'

'Certainly not,' I said, knowing I could hardly say no.

I was sweating blood. Twyford was talking to Chad while O'Reilly began the search.

'This friend of yours, do you know him very well?' he asked me.

'Yes, very very well, marvellous chap, George – very droll, met him at the club.'

'Oh well, I should tell you that this man is a notorious criminal.'

'Is that so? How jolly interesting.'

He looked at me a big strange and began opening the doors, giving the car a good spin over. I eyed Chad who looked totally unconcerned. If only he knew what was under the front seat. We were facing five to seven and he was smiling and joking.

If he finds it I'm away, I thought. I'll just keep running.

O'Reilly bent down and pushed his hand under the seat. His fingers touched the side of the cigar box and he ran his hand along it. I'm nicked, I thought, waiting for him to pull it clear. His hand reappeared, empty. He must have thought that he'd been touching the end of the seat.

Getting to his feet, O'Reilly looked at his partner and shook his head.

'He's not good company for you to keep, sir,' said Twyford, motioning towards Chad. 'I advise you to stay away from him. Obviously we wouldn't have searched your car if we didn't have suspicions about your friend.'

With that, they let us go and we drove away, leaving the two policemen on the pavement. About a quarter of a mile down the road, I turned to Chad and said, 'Lucky one there, George.'

'Fucking lucky! We were clean – the fucking animals.'

'No, I've got half a pound of gelly under the front seat.'

Chad's face turned white and he gave me this pained look that said, 'Let me out at the next corner.'

Old Chad had a lot of bottle and we ended up taking the gelly out to a small place he had in the country, a piece of land that he'd bought, in the hopes of getting building permission, and we buried it there.

About three weeks later, I was at the races at Sandown with Harry, and as we walked round the paddock I spotted two familiar faces.

'It's Twyford and O'Reilly,' I said.

As we passed them, the two policemen lifted their hats. 'Hello, Harry,' they chorused and then looked directly at me. 'And hello, Bruce.'

Bloody hell! The game was up. They knew me. I wasn't a playboy who'd befriended George Cheatt in the clubs any more. I was Bruce Reynolds, former Borstal boy and suspected burglar.

Of course, that was only the half of it. Already I was branching out and each mission became more daring. The newest coup was a throwback to the outlaw heroes of my youth – highway robbery.

We had information about a market trader on the south coast who always carried a float of two or three grand, which was supplemented by another few if he'd had a good day on the stalls. We didn't know exactly where he lived, so a decision was made to waylay him on his way home.

At any one time we had two or three stolen cars parked up in various streets around the West End and every few days we would move them to make it look as if they were being used and not abandoned. One of them was a 2.4 Jaguar, sleek and black, which looked the sort of vehicle that a chauffeur might be driving – perhaps the chauffeur of a senior policeman.

'Right. That'll be the police car,' I said. 'Nobby will drive.'

'And who's going to be the inspector?' asked Harry.

I volunteered. With a black raincoat, white shirt, black tie and just a normal dark blue cap decorated with a bit of braid and a Boy Scout badge, I vaguely resembled a member of the Dorset Constabulary.

It was a risky plan. Impersonating a police officer – IPO they called it – was a serious offence, punishable by six or seven years in gaol.

Late on a Saturday afternoon in October, we parked up in a layby on the outskirts of Bridport, knowing that within an hour our quarry would be on his way home along this same road. As he drove by, we eased in behind his van and sat on his tail until we reached a nice stretch of road. Flashing the headlights, we pulled alongside and waved him over.

'What's up, guv'nor? What've I done? I was only doing thirty mile an hour,' he wailed.

Immediately I knew the type of guy we were dealing with. His whinging attitude was typical of some market trader when confronted by the law. It felt good to be temporarily on the other side, the man with the power.

'Stand there! Show me your licence! Where do you live?' By firing orders and getting him moving, I immediately took control. 'Right, what you got in the back of the van?'

'Nothing, guv'nor, nothing.'

'Let me have a look then!'

As he turned his back, Harry whacked him across the shoulder and he went down. He wasn't hurt, just stunned, and we helped him into the back of the Jag.

'You're not policemen. Who are you . . .?' he mumbled.

'Be quiet, you'll be all right.'

Harry kept him busy while I retrieved his wad of cash from under the driver's seat. There was more money in a belt around his waist but when Harry spied his ring he gave us a sob story about his grandfather having given it to him on his death bed. At most it was going to fetch us fifty quid, so we let him keep it. As a rule I was not superstitious but the guy could have been an old traveller or a gypsy and he might have put a curse on us. For fifty quid it wasn't worth the risk.

I locked up the van to protect his stock, and left it parked beside the road. Then, laying him on the back seat of the Jag, we drove back towards London. There was no talk in the car – we were wary about using names or mentioning anything that could identify us. It was dark by the time we got to Esher Common and we bundled him outside and walked him a little way into the woods.

'Just lay down, don't move for ten minutes, we'll be here.'

He didn't say anything as I left and walked back to the car.

The script had gone like clockwork. We were all-stars and well rewarded, but, unknown to us, a final act was still to be played out. A few days later, when I went to pick up the Jag from the parking space for our next job, it was missing, along with a bootful of hand tools, drills and a circular saw.

There was no question about what these were for, and if the police had found the car they would have sat on it, waiting for us to come back. But the Jaguar was missing and the only logical explanation was that another firm had nicked it for villainy. It was like playing pass the parcel with a stolen car.

I didn't think any more about it until the police called Nobby, asking about the Jaguar. They said that a car had been found with various equipment in the boot, and in one of the holdalls they had found a dry-cleaning ticket that was issued to his brother-in-law.

'Fancy that,' said Nobby. 'I can't think how that could have happened.'

The police then interviewed me, since I was an associate of Nobby's, and I pleaded total ignorance. 'Well, I borrowed a bag from a mate and I lost it a few months back and I haven't seen it since.'

Of course, Old Bill wasn't convinced. They continued to put out feelers and call people in until eventually I got the hint and someone friendly at the station accepted a few quid to make sure the case was closed.

But there was a lesson to be learned. The police had found the car because the van driver I left lying in the bushes at Esher Common had got to his feet and followed me, and clocked the registration number as we drove away. The only thing that saved us from being nicked was the fact that the police for some inexplicable reason decided not to stake out the parking spot and wait for our return.

15

Every member of a gang has a job to do and success depends upon each one playing his part. Not everybody can work with a team. Some people can't trust enough and are driven crazy by doubts. Others are incapable of spending six or seven hours locked inside a building doing a safe, not knowing what's going on outside; and worrying that the look-out will go to pieces and run.

It always starts with the question, 'Do you think we're all right?'

'Relax, we're fine. Nothing to worry about.'

Then they start fidgeting, trying to find something to do while you're drilling the safe, but you can see them being eaten up inside.

'Do you think we'll hear the whistle? I mean, if there's a problem, will we hear the whistle?'

'Yes, we'll hear the whistle.'

'Maybe we should have tested it out.'

'Believe me, we'll hear the whistle. Relax.'

Some people are good at the long drawn-out jobs; others are brilliant at the in-and-out system. Whatever the case, you choose carefully and learn quickly that even people with gleaming reputations can lose their bottle. It was like Patsy, an old pro, being ready to curl up and be nicked when we were rumbled in Piccadilly. It was worth remembering.

The lesson was reinforced when we plotted to nick a payroll being delivered to Shepperton Film Studios. On Thursday afternoons a van would leave the studios and go into Shepperton to collect the money from the bank. On its way back we planned to ambush it at a bridge where the road narrowed and, on a pre-arranged signal, a wheel man in a parked car would drive on to the road and ram the van.

Harry and I were waiting on the bridge suitably covered up and I had a 14lb axe ready to smash the windscreen. It was a shock tactic. When the glass caved in they would be frightened and disorientated for long enough for us to get the upper hand.

We nicked a car for the ramming – a Ford, because they were easy to steal. In the boot we found three cases of champagne, with the bottles lovingly nestled in straw. It seemed a shame to waste them, but we couldn't carry these crates around while doing a bit of business. Eventually we started drinking champagne as if it was lemonade and spraying it over the car for good luck.

I figured it was a good omen, finding the fizz, and we were all in high spirits as we waited for the van. Harry and I were on the bridge wearing floppy old hats and scarves and I was trying unsuccessfully to hide this whopping great axe. We were encouraging each other and rehearsing the details. There has to be a momentum established in a robbery. Nobody can be cold. They have to be gee'd up so that important decisions are made in a split second and there is no time for negative thoughts to creep in.

We saw the car drive by and park up in the layby, so we knew the van was about a minute behind. This was it.

The van arrived, turning over the bridge, and we waited for Patsy to come accelerating out in the Ford and ram the sucker. But the van just drives straight on by. Harry and I were looking at each other in disbelief and we spied Patsy driving off in the opposite direction. Our own getaway car was a couple of hundred yards away so we had to abandon dignity and start running. What had happened? Where the hell was Patsy?

When we got back to London we held a post-mortem and everybody felt sick, including Patsy, who claimed the clutch had slipped but it was pretty obvious that he was lying. At the last moment his bottle went, or he changed his mind. Whatever the reason, it stuck in my mind because he left Harry and me hanging out to dry. If a police car had been close we would have been nicked without a shadow of a doubt.

A few hours afterwards, Harry was still raving. 'How could he?' he asked me. 'How could he not do it?'

Of course I didn't have the answer. I tried to take his mind off it. 'What do you fancy doing now?'

'Fucking nothing.'

'Well, let's go round and see Nobby and see if we can save the day.'

'Fuck you, and fuck Nobby. I just want to sulk.'

I got fed up with him. 'Well, fuck you as well, I'm going round to see Nobby, I'm hungry.'

'You're always hungry, you always want to go out.'

He was right, of course, but we were both in very different situations. Harry had a wife and kids to support and a family to embrace him, whereas I had a girlfriend and a burning desire to establish myself. I was one of a gang with a reputation, but I had no real power; that hadn't come yet. I wasn't even sure of my own potential.

I went to see Nobby and he prattled on in his usual manner, talking about various pieces of work.

'I got a jeweller's in Harrogate. Let's go have a look and see if you think it's a goer.'

Nobby wasn't normally prepared to travel out of London but he knew I'd go anywhere.

Then Nobby started talking about another bit of information. He looked from side to side in his own sitting-room, as if Old Bill was crouched behind the sofa. Normally, Nobby's information – like his dog tips – was very, very suspect and not to be taken seriously, but for once he had an amazing amount of detail. The possible target was a dealer in dirty pictures who had a safe in his house that weighed perhaps a hundredweight and was said to hold about fifteen grand.

While he was talking, Chad the Shad arrived.

'Nobby's just told me about a coup up in Harrogate – and perhaps while we're up there we can have a look at this other place and do the two?'

Chad said: 'Great, let's go!'

I was quite surprised by the eagerness. He was hungry, George. 'You've got a car?' he asked.

'I've got the working ringer, we can take that.'

The ringer was a Riley Pathfinder and we piled in for the drive from Fulham. Before we left, I rang Harry. 'Nobby's got something and I'm going to have a look at it with Chad – do you want to come?'

'No, I do not want to fucking come.'

'All right. It's up to you.' I knew Harry's moods.

'We'll go to Harrogate first then, George,' I suggested.

'Fuck Harrogate,' he said, 'We'll have a look at this private residence with the fifteen grand.'

We found the place in a dingy little backstreet of Doncaster and did a drive past.

'I don't fancy it,' I said.

'Don't fancy it?' Chad said. 'Didn't you see them minky curtains?'

'No.'

Any curtains with ruffles on them he called 'minky' – obviously inferring there were minks inside.

'You're a better judge than I am, Chad.'

To kill some time, we drove up to Scotch Corner and had dinner in a nice restaurant. It was all very civilized and, like the eager acolyte, I listened to Chad's stories about his past exploits. In his youth he was a very good creeper – getting into houses while people slept and taking jewels from the dressing-table and wallets from trouser pockets. It's a nerve-racking occupation because people can wake at any time.

I was trying to add to the conversation, bringing all the worldly wisdom of my twenty or so years, when I said, 'Chad, it's been my experience in life that all people with moustaches are snides.'

I saw him look at me and then the awful realization dawned that he had a moustache.

'Present company included,' I blurted, and he started laughing.

After a meal and a bottle of wine, we stowed up for a few hours and hit the house at about half-past two. Scientifically, three o'clock in the morning is when the body is at its lowest ebb; this is the time when most people die in their sleep.

The plan was literally to carry the safe out while they were asleep upstairs, so we parked up about five minutes' walk from the terrace house and climbed over a wall into the back garden. It could not have been simpler. After jemmying a straightforward window, we were in the kitchen. None of the downstairs doors was locked, so we walked straight into the room and the safe was sitting in the corner covered with a cloth with an aspidistra on top. Lovely, we'd got it.

Each taking a corner, we bent down in unison and lifted, but the safe refused to budge. It was built into a cradle which was bolted through the floor boards.

'Hang on, we're fucked,' said Chad.

'Maybe not,' I said.

I popped down to the cellar, hoping to reach the bolts and undo them, but discovered the place packed full of coal.

'Looks like we'll have to creep them for the keys,' said Chad.

As the junior on the firm, I naturally expected that this was my job. I was quite adept but was the first to admit that it wasn't my field. Some people are always better than others at doing certain things, and if Paddy had been there he would have been up the stairs in a flash while I minded him from just outside the bedroom door.

Chad and I crept up the stairs, with me leading the way, but as we got to the door he tugged at my jacket and said, 'Hold on, I'll go in.'

He pushed open the door and we could hear gentle snoring. Chad was on his belly, slithering into the darkness, and for a few minutes I could hear faint movements. When he reappeared on the landing, he was clutching a pair of men's trousers. We tipped out the pockets. No key.

So Chad went back inside, replaced the trousers and returned with a jacket. We tipped out the pockets and again found nothing.

'OK, I'll see if I can find her handbag,' he said, disappearing again. This time he came out with a leather handbag under his arm and we expectantly tipped the contents on to the floor. Out falls a little Chubb key. Chad looked at me; I looked at him. Maybe, maybe not – we weren't celebrating yet.

Downstairs I gave the key a kiss for luck and slid it into the lock. It turned in the well-oiled chamber and the door opened to reveal a stamp collection in a display box and four packages done up in brown paper. The stamp collection was supposedly worth five grand, but the real score came when we tore open the packages. It's money – all money.

Cramming it into a bag, we locked up the safe, put the key in the handbag and the bag on the dining table. We figured that the next morning the lady of the house would ask, 'Now, where's my handbag? Did I leave it downstairs?' And when she found it there was no reason for them to look in the safe; no reason to think anything had gone wrong.

Back in the car, we were over the moon. I'd never seen so much money. I kept saying, 'Chad, how much do you think we got? Do you think there's fifteen thousand? It looks a lot more – if it's all right can I have a look?' And I leaned over the back seat, opening the suitcase, just to see all this money and think, Fucking hell, suppose we got fifty grand?

It took us quite a while to get home. Chad had worked up north and knew lots of side-roads and backstreets. He was a very careful guy in this respect. We had the count-up back at his place, sitting around the kitchen table. It was more or less £15,000 in cash plus the stamp collection.

Then came the business side of things – how much were we going to give Nobby?

'It was a great bit of information, Chad,' I said. 'The guy who stuck it up is entitled to his whack.'

Chad was cunning. 'Yeah,' he says, 'but we're not dealing with the guy who stuck it up – we're only dealing with the guy who stuck it up to us.'

So I said, 'Well the whole point of giving people their fair share is that you've got a satisfied customer and they'll come back again.'

'What was you thinking then?' he asked.

'Well, it's up to you.' I deferred to his greater experience, also knowing that if he decided on a low figure it was more money for me.

'OK, I think we should give Nobby a grand.'

'A fucking grand? That's a bit strong – we made fifteen grand.'

'Bruce,' he said, 'I know Nobby's psychology. Whatever you give him, he'll think you've ripped him off.'

Chad was the man, so I said, 'OK, we'll give him a grand.'

'Right, I'm going home to get some sleep and I'll meet you tomorrow morning and we'll go round and see Nobby. He's going to ask us about the jeweller's at Harrogate.'

'We'll tell him we had a look at it and it was a no go. Anyway, he won't be complaining. He'll be only too happy with his grand.'

I was living with Rita and when I got home from George's at eleven o'clock in the morning she was still in bed. I stripped off my clothes, slung the money on the bed and grabbed hold of her. We were rolling around on pound notes and white fivers and I was thinking, This is really good, this is a ten-grand fuck this one.

Later that day, when we gave Nobby his money he was delighted. And so he should have been – it was a thousand pounds for nothing. I asked him, 'What are you going to give the geezer who stuck it up?'

'I'll give him a hundred pound,' he said.

'You're better off not giving him anything than giving him a hundred pound!'

'I fucking know him,' Nobby says. 'Fucking parasites, that's fucking all they are, poncing off of us.'

This was strange logic, but Nobby was full of strange logic. A couple of weeks afterwards I was talking to someone who knew all of us, and he said, 'I was talking to Nobby the other day, he reckons you fucked him.'

'How did we fuck him?'

'He says he put you on to some work and you gave him a grand, and if you gave him a grand it meant you must have got an awful lot more.'

I realized that Chad was right. It wouldn't have mattered if we'd given Nobby three, four or even five grand; he would simply have assumed that we'd nicked· sixty. In truth, there was no point in being honest because you were never going to win.

Harry was even more pissed off when he heard about our good fortune, but he still got a share. We had a loose arrangement that if we went on jobs separately, we would give each other a certain percentage of the takings. Loosely, the split was two thirds and one third, and over time it balanced itself out.

Because of my success with Chad, we started seeing a little more of him. There was a driver working for a hire-car company who told us about a jeweller who he chauffeured once a week, on a Friday evening. He would pick up the guy's girlfriend from her flat, take them out for the evening, then drop them home, usually at about two or three in the morning. The driver said the girlfriend had a couple of nice coats and loads of tom.

Harry and I debated whether we should break into the flat while she was out, or wait and tie her up, to make sure we got the jewellery she was wearing. These decisions can never be taken lightly. It was a serious charge, roping someone up, so we had to be sure it was worth the risk.

When it came to business, Chad the Shad was totally non-violent and refused to be involved if we were planning to tie up the jeweller's girlfriend.

'Let's do it the right way,' he said. 'Why run the risk?'

Eventually we all agreed, even though it meant we might well miss the really prize pieces of jewellery because she was probably going to be wearing them – along with her best mink.

I went in through the back and got to the second floor. Straightaway I found a couple of mink coats which I threw out the window. I crammed jewellery into my pockets and began searching the rest of the flat. In a wardrobe, I found a briefcase with about a grand in it, along with bundles of tissue folders which were probably holding gems.

I thought I'd scored in a big way but when we got home, we found the tissues were empty. Unlucky. At least we had the money. George was looking at the jewellery and I saw him frown.

'What's up?'

'These don't look right,' he said.

'What do you mean?'

'There's something wrong with the stones.'

He was right. When we put the jewellery through the market, we discovered they were fakes, made up with zircons and glass. It was the same with the coats. They were made up to look like minks and you had to be a good judge to tell the difference. The jeweller had obviously been giving his girlfriend little presents that she thought were expensive tokens of love while in reality they were cheap imitations. You learn a lot about human nature doing the climb.

Insurance scams were also pretty common in the late fifties, although I myself had never been asked to burgle to order. It was easy money because, in theory, there was no chance of getting nicked. The owner wanted you to steal the stuff, or at least pretend to steal the stuff, so he wasn't likely to start hollering and raise the alarm.

When a friend in the jewellery business finally asked me to do an insurance burglary, I jumped at the chance.

'What sort of money are we talking about?' I asked.

'Two grand,' he said. 'He's going out for the night and all you have to do is break in and make it look as good as you can.'

'OK, but I want something in advance.'

'All right. There's the address and I'll talk to the guy.'

Eventually, he put up a grand and I staked out the house, trying to get an idea of the daily movements. I wanted to know more about my 'employer' because there was always a possibility that I was being set up. A mate in the legal profession had told me how certain members of the public had virtually been seconded on special duty by the police. Some were retired officers who'd been given funds to buy pubs, supermarkets and hardware stores – places where they would be in contact with people. These were apparently used to collect information on criminal activity and organize set-ups. My insurance coup seemed legit, but, but, but . . .

Harry and I situated ourselves up in the large back garden of the house, timing the routine inside. At about eleven o'clock one night the lights went off downstairs and went on upstairs. We figured they were going to bed, but suddenly the back door opened and the man of the house walked outside. We could see his silhouette as he went along the path and disappeared into the greenhouse.

'What the fucking hell's he doing in there at this time of night?' I whispered to Harry.

'Obviously his plants need watering.'

'Well, it's a funny old time to be watering your plants.'

When he came out, he locked up the greenhouse and went back into the house.

'Let's just have a look-see in the greenhouse,' I suggested. 'Just a little look-see.'

Getting inside was easy and we wandered through the neat rows of plants, all of them freshly watered – all except one. How strange, I thought, picking up the pot. I gave it a shake, removed the plant and underneath was a chamois leather bag rattling with diamonds.

'What shall we do?' I asked, fingering the rocks.

'We're contracted,' Harry said.

'Yeah, I know, but we're going to get a couple of grand for breaking into this guy's house. We've got a touch here anyway.'

He looked at me. 'Fuck it. Strike now. They're not going to know it's anything to do with us anyway.'

We took the diamonds, put them through and got about four grand. When I next saw the jeweller, he asked about the insurance coup and I explained that I was too busy.

Oddly enough, we didn't hear a scream about the theft. The guy probably thought it was too much of a coincidence that someone had smelt out the diamonds. Perhaps he figured that his wife was involved and had put her lover up to the theft. Whatever the case, we heard nothing more and I generously returned his grand.

I was riding my luck gloriously, banking money with Gran and spending up big on clothes and restaurants. In crim circles, the right clothes are as important as the right car and being seen in the right place. The spin-off is that you are then able to mix with the right people. Social occasions – dining, drinking, racing – all doubled as fishing expeditions. You never knew what you'd come up with in the trawl – an overheard conversation, a glimpse of fabulous jewellery, contacts who have larceny in mind. The height of earlier sophistication – dinner at a Scotch Steak House – had become dinner at the Caprice. Dressing for the occasion was all part of the excitement.

Bondy and Buzz, two of the more advanced thieves of the time, were typical of the new breed of crim. They drove MGs and dressed in Donegal tweeds, cavalry twills and suede chukka boots. Golf bags or tennis rackets were strewn on the back seat, proclaiming to the world that they were above suspicion. It made sense to me not to look like a thief, although this was a lesson that was lost for years on the young up-and-comings who wanted to look like crims as well as be crims.

My own wardrobe was ever-changing – not least because of the wear and tear of brambles and drainpipes, and because shoes and suits had to be discarded as possible evidence.

Whenever the oportunity arose for pleasure I was heavily indulgent and never regretted it afterwards. My mate Max typified the feeling when he told me, 'Know what I reckon would be your perfect night out, Bruce?'

'What?'

'Chartering a boat with a cargo of money, and shovelling it overboard as fast as you can.'

The fifties and sixties were a crazy time; lunacy was in the air and swanking was the order of the day. Stoned, drunk and rampant, that was me – wallowing in Lautrec's dictum, 'In excess or not at all.'

Some nights we'd go to Esmeralda's Barn, a club in Knightsbridge for the famous, titled and/or rich. The photographer Anthony Armstrong-Jones was a member, and would often appear with his royal fiancée. A character named Sidney Cane was also a regular there, although he always announced himself to strangers as 'Sir Sidney Rawlinson-Cane, Bart'. We, *sotto voce*, would then always add: 'Two laggings, one bound-over and a probation.'

Sir Sidney had made money during the war, quite legitimately I was sure, and drove around town in a canary yellow Rolls-Royce. At one time he was engaged to the heiress to the Wills tobacco fortune, but rumour had it that the engagement was broken off when the family gave the Bart £20,000 to leave her alone.

Sir Sidney was astonishingly successful with women, which on the face of it was odd given his lack of height and looks. But what he lacked in inches in one respect, he more than made up for in another. His party piece when drunk and standing at the bar, was to expose his mammoth member and engage himself in a bout of oral sex. I only ever saw this exhibition once, and it was the same evening that a certain aristo was also on site. Nobody could be sure if she had witnessed the event, but when I looked around the room the table her party had been sitting at was empty and a half-finished glass of Scotch had most uncharacteristically been left behind.

I reached the zenith of this conspicuous consumption in '57, when I was paying £10 a week for the flat in Streatham with three cars parked outside: a Ford Zodiac convertible, an Aston DB2/4, and a Porsche Super 75.

It was all part of the swanking, of making out that I was someone. Being a thief, a successful thief, you can be almost any person you want to be, for as long as the money lasts. It's the freedom to switch roles that really counts; it's the movement, the zest that gives excitement to life in the new role.

Even though I had Rita, I spent a lot of money on other women, out of curiosity as much as anything else. I wanted variety. I wanted to sleep with them all – good girls, bad girls, tall ones, short ones. Bond Street and Curzon Street seemed to be entirely populated by elegant French working girls who never failed to produce that frisson. Harry and I picked up a girl once in Hyde Park who looked like an absolute film star, about seventeen, leggy and doe-eyed. She was absolutely unbelievable at her stuff. Harry took her away somewhere and did what he was going to do, and then it was my turn. After that, we'd often go and visit her. She was so beautiful, in fact, that Harry and I agreed to get her a flat and keep her to ourselves. We went to look for her one night to put the proposition to her, but she'd gone missing and we never saw her again.

They were great days when everything seemed to work and I became a sought-after member of the criminal fraternity. Even when things didn't go to plan, Lady Luck was on my side.

We had a tip-off from an informant about a large building company with offices facing Paddington Station which was sending money out by post to all its various construction sites. Someone who worked there had given us the information and described how the Post Office would pick up the registered packages and send them out to the various depots. A Post Office van would pull up at five o'clock of a Wednesday afternoon and two postmen would go inside and collect the parcels in two sacks.

Having given it the once over, we came up with a plan. We would have men inside and as the posties walked along the corridors we would sandwich them between two of us coming one way and two going the other. With four against two, we might not even have to whack them.

On Wednesday afternoon, we were all in position. There were five of us, in three cars, and we were waiting for the van to pull up. Then, out of nowhere, a local Putney boy who knew all of us double-well, walked along the street. This guy had been at it over the years, but what was he doing there? Something was definitely wrong.

Harry whispered to me, 'Have a look at the fucking newspaper seller.'

I recognized the type immediately. He was a great big old boy in plain clothes except for his big black boots. Giving our eyes a further chance, the entire scene changed.

'There they are – there's about three of them on the roof spotting,' I said.

'And there's a funny van down there with just the one man in it,' said Harry.

The job was obviously off but we played it cool and waited for the van to arrive. When the guys got out, you could see they weren't postmen. These two poor cozzers went in and came out, carrying the bags and were looking round as if to say, 'When are we going to be attacked?'

When nothing happened, they stood there like lost sheep, wondering what to do next.

I never did find out who set us up. The local Putney guy wasn't involved; that was a total coincidence. From then on we never listened to anything else this informant offered. He pleaded ignorance, but in this profession, if people get compromised and fall into the hands of the police, they are never safe again. The police sew them up one hundred per cent.

If someone is pally with Inspector So-and-so, it doesn't necessarily mean that he's a grass. He could be getting favours done for him, but then, that normally means doing favours back.

At various times, different policemen have said to me, 'Bruce, you'd be surprised who are informers.'

I replied, 'Well?' – looking for some examples.

'Anyone you care to name that's got a name in the underworld.'

Naturally, I thought it was simply police dialogue – their way of saying that I wouldn't be out of order if I gave them some information.

I'd never been very involved with policemen, never had the desire; although I used to drink with a few of them when the Star in Belgravia lost favour and we began frequenting a pub called the Marlborough, which was in the same street in Chelsea as the local police section house.

The Marlborough was Ben Slennet's pub and was probably the closest I ever got to having a 'local' in my life. We used to drop in there for a few after-timers and sidle up to the bar next to Bob Huntley, who was then a chief detective inspector before becoming head of the bomb squad, and Maurice Ray, the Yard's top fingerprint expert. They all knew we were at it, but as long as we didn't do anything on their patch they weren't too concerned. Life was about not rocking the boat.

Huntley was one of the old-school cozzers. He was unsophisticated and very down to earth. One night he said to me, 'We got a bit of a problem, Bruce, I don't know if you can give us any help?'

'Don't go talking business, we're having a drink,' I said.

'I know and I wouldn't normally ask but we're up shit creek. We're getting all sorts of pressure and in this particular area I think you could help without any worries.'

The term 'serial killer' hadn't been invented then, but there was a nutter on the loose who'd done about six homosexual guys in odd situations; some of the bodies had been found in cupboards.

'If you hear anything in the course of your travels,' said Huntley, 'anything you think could be connected, I would appreciate it if you gave us a word.'

'Of course,' I said.

If I had heard anything, I would have called him. My war wasn't with all parts of society. I was leading a life where the police were my adversaries but they were also my pals. When I saw them outside my house supervising the traffic, it was always, 'Good morning, officer. How are you going? Fucking job you got!'

One evening a few of us were in the Marlborough and started talking about a new club that was opening in Chelsea. The first drinks were free on opening night, so Harry, myself and Roller Reg decided to check the place out. When we got there I recognized four very tasty customers sitting near the bar. Roy Kent was one of them, a hard-nosed detective sergeant who knew all the angles, and his companions were of a similar ilk.

Normally I'd have steered well clear, but weighing things up, I figured that it was not a wise move to ignore them. Obviously they knew who we were and perhaps it would be best to say hello and play the diplomat.

I went over. 'Gentlemen, fancy seeing you here.'

'Well, we could say the same,' said Kentie, eyeing me suspiciously.

After some good-natured banter, I went to the bar to buy them all a round. Reg sidled up to me, most upset.

'Christ! What are you doing?' he whispered, smiling weakly at the policemen. 'I'm not sitting with them. Are you off your head?'

'Look, mate, you know they're the opposition, what's the point of giving them the hump?'

'I'm not going to give them the hump, but fuck them, I'm not buying them a drink.'

'Well, that's fucking up to you.'

Realizing he was embarrassing himself, Reg finally sat down, nursing his drink in silence. Having drained our glasses, Roy Kent rose to his feet.

'What you drinking, Bruce? How about you, Harry?' Then he turned to Reg.

'Ah. Nothing. I'm going now, I don't want a drink,' he said, getting to his feet and making a quickish exit.

'What's his problem?' said Kentie, a little put out.

'Don't ask me, you'd better ask him yourself,' I replied.

'Fuck 'im.'

Nothing more was said and we had a couple more drinks before making our excuses and leaving.

The next morning, Reg was arrested. A police search found silly bits and pieces worth no more than thirty quid, but far more seriously, he was driving a stolen car. Reg had nicked it two days earlier – the first he'd stolen in his life – and it got him busted. He did a deal before going to court, pulling some important strings. It kept him out of jail but Reg had learned his lesson.

Afterwards, Harry and I contemplated whether Roller had been the architect of his own arrest. Did Roy Kent and his mates decide to work him over? Of course, we'd never know, but from my point of view there was no mileage in making enemies of the police. After all, they had a job to do. And if someone broke into my house and stole my stuff, they'd be the first people I'd call.

16

On the morning of 6 June 1957, I got a phone call from Uncle Jack to say that Gran had been taken ill; it was serious, and the doctor had been called. I went round to Buckmaster Road straightaway.

'How is she?' I asked the doctor.

He shook his head sadly. Gran had suffered a stroke, he said; she was conscious but confused, and wherever her mind was it was manifestly not in the here and now. His prognosis was that she might relapse into a coma; there was only a slim chance that she might recover. She was eighty-seven.

'I'll monitor her condition,' he said. 'We can only hope for the best.'

I stayed that day. Dad and my half-brother Mac came over later. We all felt empty; we all recognized the inevitable, that Gran was slipping away. I stayed the night, trying to make contact, but she was somewhere else, and when she tried to speak the words didn't make sense. By the morning I knew that, but for a miracle, Gran was gone.

When the doctor came around he said that whatever chance she had, she would be better off in hospital. I shot Dad a glance. He knew as well as I did that she would have fiercely opposed the move; she belonged to the generation and the class that believed you only went to hospital to die.

Gran was admitted to Bolingbroke Hospital, where she lingered semi-conscious in her own world for five days. I went there every day and it was killing me. At times, seemingly conscious that she couldn't talk sense, she'd gesture for pen and paper, but the written scrawl was as illegible as her speech. I'd write a reply and hold it up for her to read, but there'd be no flicker of the eyes to say that she understood. Occasionally there'd be a smile, like a baby's smile, perhaps in response to a childhood memory that I'd recounted or maybe it was her own wanderings down memory lane. I'd never know.

After five days and nights of it I could take no more. I said to Dad, 'I can't handle this,' kissed Gran good night and, with a whispered 'God bless' in her ear, I left.

When Dad phoned me the next morning from the hospital he spoke with the flat tones of the grieving.

'Gran died last night, son.'

I felt my throat tighten and tears well in my eyes.

There was a long pause – as if Dad was trying to come to terms with the finality of it – before he added, 'Peacefully.'

I went to the hospital. He was holding it together, but with great difficulty. As I put my arms around him, he let it go, and I had my cry too. Gran had gone, and the sense of loss was greater than any that I had ever felt. Gran had always been there, she had always been the heart that beat for me.

The funeral took place a week later, the diminutive two-car cortège that pulled away from Buckmaster Road consisting of family in one car, friends and neighbours in the other. I looked at our meagre gathering and thought, Is this the way to say goodbye to someone so well loved? Was this how it all ended?

Coming to terms with the first death in my adult life revealed the guilt I felt at not having done more for Gran when she was alive. I remembered a Scout camp when I was fourteen, two glorious weeks of freewheeling activities in Devon, roaming the countryside, swimming in cool streams. The pleasure was only broken on the penultimate day by a letter from Gran remonstrating with me for my selfishness in not sending her a postcard.

I was upset; Gran was on my side – why was she mad at me? I sent off a card immediately, knowing that I'd be home before she received it. As a further sweetener I scraped together the remainder of my spending money and bought her a Chinese back scratcher.

She loved her present and brushed aside my muttered apologies. My selfishness was not referred to again, and I concluded that it had been one of Gran's bleak periods when she'd felt unloved. I knew all about that.

Now, standing by her grave, I contemplated how she would never again chide me when I asked for the sixth slice of bread and jam; she'd never moan when her pastry board had been used for my models, or when I got her to hold them for me while I pinned and glued them. I would never again bring her the Vaseline Hair Tonic, that she believed was so good for her hair; or the occasional bottle of Mann and Crossman's brown ale to complement the dinner.

I preferred Schweppes Indian tonic water, something Gran never understood.

'Why you drink that stuff I don't know,' she'd say. 'It doesn't even taste nice.'

'That's because of the quinine in it, Gran. It's bitter because it's like medicine. It keeps the malaria away.'

'But there's no malaria in Battersea.'

'I know, Gran – good stuff, innit?'

And then she'd laugh.

As the coffin was lowered into the ground, I took a handful of earth, crumbled it in my hand, and sprinkled it over the box. Gran was not there; she lived on in memory and always would.

As the hearse pulled away, it reminded me of when I'd taken Gran for a spin down to the coast when I bought my first car. Initially, she had been reluctant: cars were unfamiliar to her, as they were to most of her generation and class. No-one in the street owned one; her expectation was that the only time she'd be driven would be in an ambulance or a hearse.

Eventually, she was quite pleased to be driven about by her grandson in his big posh car – especially when she saw the neighbours. Ownership of a motor was a symbol of achievement and respectability; it somehow negated my reputation as the black sheep of the family.

As we wandered away from the graveside, the priest shook my hand. He spoke of Gran's faith and the sustenance it had provided her. 'She always wanted to visit Rome and see the Holy Father,' he said.

'I know,' I said, and turned my head away. It was a reminder of promises made and not fulfilled.

It had been on that same drive to the coast that I had first asked Gran, 'What is the one thing that you would like to do in your life?'

'I'd like to visit Rome and see the Pope,' she replied.

'That's OK. I'll take you – we'll fly to Rome.'

'Oh no, I couldn't fly. I wouldn't feel safe.'

'We'll drive then,' I said. 'Catch a ferry over the Channel and we'll be there in a few days. How about that, Gran?'

'Let me think about it, Bruce.'

I had found her dearest wish and wanted to make it come true. I also knew that for the right amount of money – a contribution to the Vatican City coffers – an audience with the Pope himself was possible. Periodically I'd raise the subject of Rome and I always got the same reply: 'I'm thinking about it, Bruce. Maybe later in the year.'

We went back to Buckmaster Road for the symbolic wake. Aunt Tiny had prepared some tinned salmon sandwiches that no-one touched. We drank our tea with muted, stolid comments before going our separate ways home. I was the last to leave.

I made a final tour of the house, and in every room I saw Gran. She was cutting bread at the table, she was standing by our old gas cooker with a bowl of rice pudding in her hands, and she was oiling the wheels of my beloved bike in the attic.

Why hadn't I taken her to Rome for an audience with the Pope? I should have insisted.

As I closed the front door behind me, my only consoling thought was that she might not have met the Pope, but if all the religous dogma meant anything, then at least she'd be meeting with the Guv'nor very soon.

17

I was never involved in the heavy side of crime – the dark side inhabited by the likes of the Krays – but occasionally I brushed shoulders with one or two of the heavy boys.

I first met Reg and Ronnie years before when I was doing Borstal, and even then they were itching to fight and make a name for themselves. Now, years later, our paths still crossed. One of our principal buyers when we were shoplifting was an associate of Charlie Kray's, the elder brother. Charlie wasn't a heavy as such, although he'd done a bit of professional boxing and had a reputation for being able to handle himself. Through another buyer I was reintroduced to Reg and Ronnie, who in 1954 were just emerging from the obscurity of the East End and developing a reputation for mixing it with the bigger boys – one of whom was Jack Comer, better known as Jack Spot or simply 'Spot'.

From my earliest inception into the crim world the names of Billy Hill and Jack Spot signified power. They were the names; a close second was Frank Fraser, the icon of the prison culture. I'd heard of their exploits; I was just a bit player, they were the stars. They were an inspiration, especially Bill and Frank: they were thieves, and good thieves, whereas Spot was a gangster and a moody (*fake*) one at that.

In the late forties, Spot and Billy Hill were the two most powerful crime figures in the country. Hill grew up in Camden, north London, and was one of 21 children in a family that had countless links with crime. His gang specialized in safe-breaking, smash and grabs and sophisticated shoplifting. Spot, a Polish Jew, ran an illegal gambling club out of the Aldgate Fruit Exchange and controlled most of the local rackets. He liked to say he profited because he was 'tougher than the other toughs'. London was carved up between them and a lot of villains were eager to join their firms. Billy Hill later exposed Spot as an informer: he had given evidence in a criminal court against a group of his own kind, which literally destroyed him, his reputation and thus his power.

On one trip to take gear up to a buyer for Spot, who had a place just off Leather Lane, I met Reggie and Ronnie again. They were there because Spot had some connection with 'Italian Albert' Dimes, who controlled all the bookies' pitches at the racing. Reggie had a bayonet in the back of his belt and Ronnie had a gun. They were tooled up, ready for action.

'How you going, Bruce?'

'Fine. And you?'

Reggie nodded. There wasn't much else said between us; they were clearly a bit tense and not in the mood for a chat. I learned later that it was all to do with a power struggle, and

Ronnie and Reggie wanted the buyer to act as some sort of referee.

Two of the few true heavies I ever worked with were Big Bill Smith and Dan Lee, who had been mixed up in the Soho Gang Wars. Big Bill had been associated with Billy Hill since his youth, when he was nicked for a raid on a jeweller's in O'Connell Street. He was a straight-up guy, never said a word, did a couple of years and then came home. He'd earned the respect that he got. Whilst doing his own things he would always be available if a call came from Billy Hill, the reverse being equally true. Dan got a five for an attack on Spot, but neither of these two guys fitted the stereotype image of the heavy. Both of them were intelligent and well spoken, and serious about whatever they were doing. That gave them the weight.

They rang me up one day and asked me to meet them.

'We've got a great bit of work: we want you to come along and blow this safe for us.'

I didn't consider myself an expert – there was no such thing – but obviously word had spread and that's the way legends start building. I had some gear so I said, 'What have we got to do?'

I guess you could call it a domestic dispute. The target was a successful businessman from Essex who owned several pubs and did a lot of travelling. The guy was loaded but his estranged wife felt she wasn't getting her fair share, so she passed on the information that there was a nice chunk of money in the house.

'He's very well protected,' she said. 'He's got a very good dog and when he's away from the house, it's loose in the place and dangerous.'

Now I hate dogs, they are the bane of a burglar's life, but it is part of my nature to say yes to everything until I hear all the details and make up my mind.

'I'm all right with dogs, don't worry about it,' I said and we arranged to go down and have a look at the place.

There were just the three of us and we had no problem in parking up and getting into the grounds of the house. The windows weren't belled up, but as soon as I pushed one open, there was the dog. The other guys were looking at me and I was looking at the dog. I didn't fancy this fucker at all, but they were standing there, as if saying, 'Well, what are you waiting for? Ain't you going in?'

'OK, all right, I know what I'm doing, I'm just getting his eyes used to my face.'

I climbed through the window, waiting for the dog to take a piece out of my leg, but instead he started rubbing himself against me, being double friendly.

'It's all right, come on in,' I whispered.

Bill started through the window but the dog wouldn't have a bar of it. I knew the owner's name was Jack, so I started trying to distract the dog. 'Where's Jack? Come on, boy, where's Jack?' The dog was looking around, but when Bill put his head through the window the dog started growling.

'I'll take him into another room and shut him in,' I suggested.

That solved the problem and we finally got downstairs to where the safe was bricked into a wall. This makes blowing them difficult because the safe can't expand, or can only expand a certain amount.

I only had four dets because we'd been told it was an old safe, but after four blasts the box was still very much intact. The problem called for a much more scientific solution. We took our shirts off, grabbed a pickaxe and sledgehammers and began thumping it out of the wall.

Every now and then the dog started whining and I had to go and play around with him or feed him bits of steak from the fridge. Meanwhile, I had a mooch around upstairs to work out our best escape if anyone should come. The dog was beside me and I kept saying, 'Where's Jack?'

Suddenly a chill went through me. I was in the bedroom and there was a loaded shotgun by the side of the bed and a duty roster which gave the impression that every hour a policeman called there and ticked it off. Surely he wouldn't go to all this trouble just to frighten burglars off, I thought. Or would he?

Scenarios were racing through my mind as I stared out the window, wondering if a policeman was already roaming through the gardens.

Finally, I took the dog down to the front door. He jumped up on me with his front paws and I said, 'Where's Jack? Wait for Jack.'

When I rejoined the guys, I told them, 'It's such a lovely dog, he's going to let us know when Jack comes back.'

And that's exactly what he did. We had just carried the safe outside and were loading it in the car when the dog started barking like crazy. As we drove off towards London, I looked back over my shoulder and said, 'I should have given him another biscuit. He was such a good boy.'

We took the safe to the Putney workshops of an old friend of mine who had a little engineering business. He was an expert at cutting open a safe but the final score was hardly worth the effort. Our blistered hands, sweaty clothes and session of dog-sitting had earned us barely five hundred quid.

It wasn't my first or last experience with dogs and I learned quickly never to underestimate them. They're unpredictable and I've got the scars to prove it. One or two narrow escapes made me think how difficult it would be to handle the really big dogs that were well trained.

I had read somewhere that dogs were particularly suscep-tible to the smell of tigers or lions because they could scent the potential threat of a predator. This seemed logical, so I made a few enquiries at London Zoo and arranged to meet one of the keepers for a drink after work. Over a quiet couple of beers, I asked him if he could get me a bag or two of tiger shit.

'Yeah. I've got this new bird, see, and she's a bit, er, you know . . .'

The keeper spluttered on his pint as he pondered the possibilities. Then he said, 'Sure, mate, that shouldn't be a problem.'

I thanked him, and as I left I warned, 'It's got to be fresh mind – I don't want any of yesterday's.'

The next day, I met him when he finished work at half-past six and he solemnly handed over a decent-sized bag of the stuff, weighing a couple of pounds. We negotiated a price and decided that the going rate for tiger shit was three quid a pound.

I already had a job in mind and took off down south to a house patrolled by six Dobermanns. Putting the ladder against the outer wall, I climbed to the top. All was quiet, but as soon as I stuck my head over the top all hell was let loose. The dogs snarled and yelped, their eyes crazed with hatred. I gestured down to my mate and smugly called for him to pass me up the bag. I flung it over the wall and listened.

Silence.

I grinned as I stuck my head over the top, expecting to see the arses of six Dobermanns as they ran for their lives. Instead, I froze.

'What's happening?' my pal called up. 'What are they doing? Are they frightened?'

'Fucking frightened?' I said as I struggled to take in the scene. 'Fucking frightened? They're fucking eating it!'

Of course, I thought afterwards, it might be all right in India or those places where dogs know about tigers but a domestic dog in this country just wouldn't know it was eating tiger shit; he wouldn't know a tiger if it bit him.

You met some remarkable characters in my line of work; to call them colourful hardly did them justice. The names are part of the charm; wonderful monikers like Rubber-Faced Mary, Dordie the Jook, Shooting Brake Bill, Murray the Head, Brian the Swan and Waiting-for-the-Big-One Bill.

One of my favourites was Red-Faced Tommy, and if ever a name summed up an individual, this was it. Tommy was fat, with glasses and a conversational patter that rivalled a Bren gun. He also had a face with the pigmentation of a baboon's bollocks.

He asked me to drive for him one day, to take him to an address in Surrey and pick him up after he'd done the call. The target was apparently a big wheel in the timber business on the south coast who, according to Tommy, 'was fucking made of money'. It was the usual story, however: Tommy had no inside information on the safe and only a vague idea that the cash was kept in a room off the main bedroom. It didn't smell good at all to me, but when we arrived Tommy was raring to go.

'Well, this is it – you can just see the outbuildings and the main house, it's got a courtyard. Now leave it to me, do whatever I say, don't panic, I've got it under control.'

'Fine. It's your party.'

Tommy instructed me to drive into the courtyard – an unusual ploy but I followed his lead. The tyres had barely stopped turning when all of a sudden a shutter opened and a shotgun was pointed through the window.

'Fuck off, you! Who do you think you fucking are, you fucking bastard? Wait there, I'll be fucking out in a minute!'

The front door flung open and out strode an elderly gent, with the shotgun pressed to his shoulder and aimed at the windscreen. I was shitting myself.

'John, me old mate,' said Red-Faced Tommy, 'there's no need for all this . . . come on now.'

'No need? No need? You're fucking dead!'

Tommy is spluttering apologies trying to save himself. 'Now, John, I know exactly how you feel, and if you want to you're entitled to shoot me – I know that, John, but it wasn't my fault.'

'Wasn't your fault? You fucking jarred me up with them tractor tyres.'

Tractor tyres? What the hell was going on here?

Apparently, Tommy had sold him a set of tractor tyres which he promised were brand new but, in fact, were cheap retreads.

'That's why I'm here,' Tommy told him. 'I've come down to give you the money back. Isn't that right, Bruce?'

After many apologies, the old geezer finally lowered the barrel of the shotgun and invited us inside. Tommy pulled out a bottle of Scotch that he'd brought with him and both of them sat down and started drinking like old friends. Soon they had mellowed and were swapping stories.

'What you doing down this way, Tommy?' he asked.

'I told you, I'm down here to give you your money back.'

'Tell me, I know you, you cunning old rascal, you wouldn't drive down from London – you've got something in mind, you ain't having me over again, are you?'

'I didn't have you over. Honestly, I've just come down to give you your dough back.'

After a while, Tommy breaks down and says, 'Well, as a matter of fact, John, I got a customer to see down at Portsmouth.'

'Really?'

The old guy pressed for more information and finally Tommy relented. He pulled out a newspaper cutting about a jewellery robbery.

'I got these jewels,' Tommy says, 'and the buyer's down there.'

'Can I have a look?' asks the old geezer.

'No, you shouldn't look, that's not your sort of game, is it?'

'Well, I'd just like to have a look, I ain't seen that sort of jewellery.'

Out come two rings, displayed on the table.

'I'd like to have a go at this, Tom,' he said.

'It's not up your street, is it?'

'Sure it is. Come on. Let's do some business.'

Eventually a deal is struck and Tommy collected a couple of grand for the gear. We said our goodbyes and started the drive back to London.

Throughout all this, I was totally bamboozled. We were supposed to rob this guy and Tommy ends up shaking hands and strolling away with two big ones.

'What about the guy in Portsmouth?' I asked. 'Isn't he going to be sore about the tom?'

'There ain't no guy in Portsmouth.'

'Well, where's the gear come from?'

'I bought it off Toby, he does all my jars for me.'

(*Jar* = snide – moody: ie, not right, false, phony. Jar is generally used in the trade when describing something which is not a diamond but purports to be. The origin may be from glass from the bottom of a jam jar. Guys at the trick talk about 'jarring someone up'. He who buys the jar is said to have been jarred up. There is a nice little business going on manufacturing jars, ostensibly legal. Tommy would have his man somewhere making up anything that Tommy required. He'd have his selection of shanks – rings – and stones. Prevalent then were rutiles and cubic zircons, very impressive: it is difficult for the layman to tell the difference from the real thing. They can and do make up anything – I've seen large emeralds which under spectrograph reveal their construction layered like a sandwich.)

'But you know this guy?'

'John's all right. I'll go back down there in three months' time, he'll fucking moan, but where's his life without me? He's there working all the time, he loves it when I come down; he knows he's being had over, but he don't care, he's got so much money and he likes the company. He likes hearing the next story I'm gonna tell him and that's all he's waiting for. I'm his whole life. He'll always pull up the money because one of these days, he thinks to himself, I really might have something.'

That's how Tommy lived his life – conning people unmercifully. But because he did it with charm and never got too greedy, he got away with it.

18

Things were going so well for me. I was riding my luck and living on champagne and pure adrenalin. Each new caper was a revelation and an education, so much so that I barely considered the possibility that I would be caught. Of course, all our planning was designed to remove the threat yet strangely it seemed out of the question.

Every week I searched for my Eldorado – more for the adventure than the financial rewards. I was beginning to see the thief as an artist, writing the scenario, choosing the cast, deciding the location, acting and directing the action. Nothing could match the tension, excitement and sense of fulfilment.

There were nights when we would be celebrating at the Astor or the Embassy and we would spy another group of crims supping magnums of champagne. Bottles would be exchanged as we would toast each other's success amid much ribaldry. It was exciting. This was the recognition I had always craved.

My lifestyle complemented my ambition. I would wine and dine at the finest restaurants, take the Aston to Monaco for the Grand Prix, or to Le Mans and then on down to the Côte d'Azur. I was living a fantasy life that I had created for myself. I think that I was in love with the Riviera before I saw it, much as you could be in love with a romantic pen-friend you'd never met. I knew all about it from books; everybody who was anybody either lived there or had lived there; there was magic in the very words 'Riviera', 'Côte d'Azur', 'South of France'.

My first visit had been in '55. Rita and I flew to Paris and caught the *Mistral* express that took us to Nice. We stayed at the Hotel Westminster on the Promenade des Anglais, revelling in the luxury surrounding us, discovering authentic French cuisine, a revelation to our untutored tastes. I loved the open expanse of the boulevards, the palm trees swaying in the offshore breeze and the warm inviting water of the Mediterranean. To lie on the beach all day, with a walk to get a drink or snack somewhere, seemed to be about the highest form of pleasure one could imagine; this was how I wanted to spend my life.

Then, just when I thought that Nice was the place for me, we went to Cannes, driving along the Croisette, past the great hotels – the Majestic, the Carlton, the Martinez. The sea was the bluest blue that you could ever see and the air had that clear, clean tang that you could taste as you breathed it greedily in. Fuck Nice, I thought, this is the place: if I can get it all together then this is where I'll retire to.

Lord Jim and Little Freddy were both regular visitors to the South of France in the summer. Harry and I called in on them at the Carlton in Cannes and they wined and dined us at all the acclaimed restaurants – always with the requisite lovely lady in attendance. Ah, the good life – I was constantly drunk with the atmosphere, this was what it was all about.

Harry and I had travelled extensively in Europe, always by car. Most of the time we justified it as business, following up a clue. Really, though, it was an excuse to get on the road, follow our noses and see what we could find. It enabled us to pursue our interests: Harry being a gambling man followed the classic horse races, whilst I was equally involved in the motor-racing scene.

Visiting most of the major museums, we even concocted a plot to remove Marie Antoinette's necklace from the Louvre. It was a bit hairy but I recokoned it could be done. 'Who cares if we're caught?' I said. 'How many people can say they got nicked stealing Marie Antoinette's jewellery?' The romance escaped them and it went on the books for later referral.

Harry played along with my enthusiasm; to dampen it would have signified a lack of confidence. Besides, telling me that it couldn't be done would be regarded as a challenge.

I was in Nice in 1956 with Harry and Stan the fence, looking to buy a piece of beach with a friend of Charlie Kray's. There was a square off the Place Massena with a whore every twenty yards – and of course, with the Mediterranean sun, every one of them was an absolute film star and no exaggeration. We had a competition to see how many we could have in one day. Stan had thirteen, Harry twelve, and I lost. I only had ten.

We also had a night in Toulon when we started about nine o'clock and ended up at half-past five in the morning, having exhausted the possibilities and gone back to see who was left from the whores we'd ignored earlier. We ended up with two charwomen going to work. It was so sordid, we were in this hotel and for some reason or other I was doing this bird on the floor on the cold lino. Just because you'd been chasing it all night long, you had to see the job through.

On one trip to the South of France, I met up with Chad the Shad in Cannes. He'd heard I was abroad and came looking for me. He didn't have a car or my address so he booked into the Majestic in Cannes and got a bus along the coast to St Raphael, planning to ask around and sit in a few bars until I showed up. By chance, he saw the Aston parked up outside a café and found me polishing off a decent bottle of Gevrey Chambertin. Of course, he had seen To Catch a Thief and he arrived in the old rope-soled espadrilles, with a scarf round his neck and a beret on his head.

Chad fancied a little French thieving and had already done his homework. The place was littered with wealthy notables, including the Aga Khan, whose spectacular villa, Château d'Horizon, could be seen for miles up and down the coast. His first job, a planned heist from a suite at the Majestic using the ventilation shafts for entry, came to nothing when the target failed to keep his booking. Then we began looking around for alternatives.

We were sharing a bottle in a café one night when I spied a stunning girl who looked the spitting image of a young Ingrid Bergman. I'd never really fancied sophisticated ladies, but this one was gorgeous. I went over to her table. 'I was just commenting to my friend on how beautiful you are,' I said. 'Ingrid' and I shared a few drinks – just enough to encourage me to dance – and when the party was over, I offered to drive her home. It was only when I dropped her off outside one of the biggest villas ever built that I realized that I'd been romancing one of the Dubonnets. My mind did some serious gymnastics as I weighed my obvious lust with the thought that the parents of this stunning creature were obviously loaded. Could I turn this to my advantage?

We made a date for the following night, but she failed to show and I never saw her again. Several times Chad and I drove down the private road on to the beach, to survey the house and contemplate turning it over. But security was likely to be very tight and we had lost our unwitting source of inside information.

Chad wanted to hang around until mid-August when there was a major society ball in Monte Carlo and it would be crawling with the rich and famous. He talked a good robbery, did Chad, but I sensed that he was really looking for an excuse to spend another month in the sun.

One of the essences of being a thief is that you can justify what you're doing at any time. It is perceived as planning. 'We'll give it another three days,' you can say, or 'We'll have a look at that tomorrow,' when all you're really doing is lying on the Martinez beach drinking champagne cocktails. Naturally we were looking at all the main jewellers – Van Cleef & Arpels, Cartier, Chaumet – whose plush shops lined the corsos done out in white marble and slate. Every thief in the world must have looked in these windows and wondered, How can you do this?

Cartier's in Monte Carlo, adjacent to the Hotel de Paris, preoccupied our attention. We noticed that on some days the staff went out to lunch leaving the stock unattended: was there a way that we could effect an entry? We couldn't turn off the front door, which in all probability was belled, but there was a fanlight above the door that might be accessible. Chad thought that by fronting it out, approaching the door dressed as workmen with a small ladder, we could make an entry – or rather, we could make the entry for me to go through and collect the window display from the inside as well as collecting up the many items on display in the showcases inside. It was a nice thought and one that tempted me for its audacity but it wasn't really on. There was too much left to chance and I didn't fancy doing hard time in the Bastille.

We'd trawled through the names and addresses of the rich and famous, and went to view all their villas. One of them was Jack Warner of Warner Bros, who had a villa, 'Aujourd'hui'. Chad was reluctant, which was good enough for me; he survived on gut instinct and was rarely wrong. A year or two later, someone relieved Warner of £20,000 in cash from his safe as well as a large quantity of jewellery, but it wasn't me!

Then I read that Lady Docker had her jewellery stolen in circumstances remarkably similar to our possible target at the Majestic hotel. One never knows for sure in this game – was it you, Chad?

In those days my priorities were pretty simple – crime, cars and crumpet – though not always in that order. I still had the Aston, which gave me a buzz, but in 1957 there was a new sports car making the running. Porsche had become trendy and I decided to splash out and buy German. I went over to the factory in Stuttgart to pick it up, opening the throttle on the autobahns and marvelling at the acceleration and the way it hugged the corners and made you feel as if your arse was only inches from the asphalt.

About three weeks later, I decided to take Rita across in it to Le Mans. I was telling her about my driving prowess and explaining the fundamentals. 'You can see from the line of trees that the road is about to curve into quite a long, fast, right-hand bend,' I explained.

I hit the corner at speed and lost control totally. The rear of the Porsche slid away and we skidded into a pile of gravel at the side of the road. Luckily, there was only minor damage to the car. But another half hour down the road, the rain began teeming down. All of a sudden I was in a small hamlet that appeared out of nowhere, coming down a hill on a steeply cambered road. It turned to cobblestones just as I crested the next rise and confronted a lorry coming up the other side. I had to brake hard but got it all wrong again. This time the Porsche slewed off the road into undergrowth, which unfortunately concealed a brick wall.

Rita and I were both quite shaken, with one or two cuts and bruises, but my pride and joy, my James Dean special, was a wreck. I felt sick enough to cry for being such an idiot. We limped across country at forty miles an hour in the twisted Porsche, heading for Germany.

It took us a week to reach Stuttgart. The customer service manager looked at me as if I had just deflowered his youngest daughter. They repaired it as good as new, which is exactly how it looked when a few weeks later, in the backstreets around St John's Hill, an articulated lorry hit me from the side and mangled it beyond recognition. More than my pride was hurt this time but I counted myself lucky to survive.

Of course, I had a right hassle with the insurance company, which tried all the tricks to avoid paying out, but the lorry driver got nicked for dangerous driving and eventually the claim was settled.

I still had the Aston, but my love for sports cars was beginning to wane – tempered perhaps by thoughts of self-preservation. Either I could put it down to bad luck, or realize that I was a danger to myself. Whatever the case, I decided to live longer and bought myself a Ford Zodiac convertible, brand new from the showrooms. I hated it. There was nothing wrong with it whatsoever but after you've been handling an Aston Martin and a Porsche, it felt like driving a fruit barrow.

19

It had been a great few years. Harry and I were established as partners and our combined talents recognized. We were getting top-notch information as well as receiving invites from other groups anxious to combine and share in our success.

To be known, however, had its downside. My name was being bandied around Scotland Yard – not surprising really, considering my rapid progress through the ranks and my string of flash sports cars. The policemen who drank at the Marlborough had a reasonable idea I was up to no good, but there was an unspoken understanding that we didn't operate in their territory. Similarly, pals would see me having a quiet drink with a superintendent or sergeant and realize that it was no conspiracy. I was simply collecting information and making contacts.

Getting pulled in the Haymarket with Chad, when they searched the Aston and failed to find the gelignite, exposed me as a major player, and within days my name and description would have been mentioned in dispatches between stations.

To a degree I was ambivalent about such attention. On the one hand I wanted the recognition and notoriety; on the other hand it wasn't good business to have a high profile. I relied on the belief that there would always be crims who would self-destruct and make themselves an easy target for police. The more the better, because it kept Old Bill busy and allowed me to get on with my trade.

Rumour had it that there was a network of chosen policemen operating in London who had been seconded from the force and established in small businesses. The undercover operation was designed to bring them into contact with their local crims and was the beginning of what became a criminal intelligence programme. It was well known amongst our intimates that Harry and I were regulars at Battersea Park running track, and soon it became obvious that the police would occasionally slip someone down there to have a look and perhaps get a clue about what we were up to.

Our 'bloodhound' was a guy called Ginger who said he was a postman and a runner, although he always arrived just as we were leaving or having a shower. He was a nice guy, but there was no way he was a postman. I knew more about the Post Office than he did.

There were probably more like Ginger, secretly sporting Met badges, and it was best to take precautions. I'd never forgotten the wartime poster which proclaimed 'Careless talk costs lives'.

We had a lot of rules and one of the most important involved firearms. We didn't touch guns and avoided anyone who did. The younger element, brought up after the war and influenced by Hollywood's gangster films, thought that guns were glamorous instead of just dangerous. They made armed robbery fashionable but shut themselves off from the mainstream of criminals. It was a different mentality. All our early role models had been found in the crime classics, books which 'floated' around the nick, such as *I, Willy Sutton* – alias Willy the Actor on account of his masterful performances to gain admittance to banks; and *Anatomy of a Crime* – the post mortem on the original Brink's Boston robbery, then the biggest cash haul in history.

Sure, some of these villains carried guns, but only a few, and my generation remained against them. Ironically, though, this reluctance did not extend to using firearms for personal vendettas. Somehow, this was deemed to be socially and politically correct.

From my point of view, I could never believe that guns were efficient devices in the hands of criminals. Guns being so foreign to our culture, people were inclined to panic when confronted with a firearm and the results were occasionally tragic. Yet secretly, I was smitten by the mystique of Smith and Wessons, Walthers and Brownings. Most of my Borstal pals had seen Richard Widmark selecting his personal Luger from the rack in *The Street with No Name*. We all saw ourselves in that role. Mind you, we also watched the French classic *Rififi* and saw ourselves drilling through the ceiling of Mappin & Webb's Paris branch and overcoming all the sophisticated alarms with our ingenuity. We seemed to forget the last section of the film when the gang fell out and most of them wound up getting killed – somehow it destroyed the illusion.

Our security was bound up in the concept of the cell. We rarely worked with anyone outside the circle and it had kept us safe while many other crims had gone to the wall, back to the Hate Factory. The circle included people like Harry, Chad, Nobby, Ernie, Little Freddy and Lord Jim – basically my role models and mentors from the past.

Sometimes we linked up with outsiders but first they needed to show impeccable references and have an introduction from someone in the circle. One was Steak (*Steak and*

Kidney: Sidney) who was a former partner of Fred's. They had started off together as kids and each found their own level. Later he paired up with Nobby and proved to be a good influence. Technically clever, physically strong and with plenty of courage, he made sure Nobby was less erratic.

Steak preferred the low-profile approach. A devoted family man, he eschewed the flamboyant way of life that most of us were leading. Together we did a few Co-ops, stores and dairies, initially blowing the safes and later switching tactics and confronting the cashiers for the keys.

On one such job on a Saturday night, we were there waiting to go when one of the dairy vans was towed into the yard by a breakdown truck. All the staff were out in force and we reluctantly abandoned the job, feeling cheated and scouting around for an alternative. Steak knew of a big-time smuggler, a wealthy guy and lunatic gambler, who was certain to be at White City dogs that night. We made a unanimous decision to cop for him and, gearing up with a ringer and one of our own cars, we headed off to the track.

The target was spotted and Steak made the first approach. It wasn't good news. Our quarry had suffered a reversal of fortunes and was now so skint that he had asked to borrow fifty quid off Steak. Fate was conspiring against us and we should have recognized the signs and gone home. Greed drove us on. We were out to plunder and complacency ruled.

Nobby had the next idea. He insisted that a leading bookmaker at White City owed him money and wanted us to help collect. Under the circumstances it seemed an easy touch and we would share in whatever Nobby could get.

We confronted the bookie outside his home in Park Lane and it all went drastically wrong. An argument developed and quickly turned into a fight on the pavement. In the débâcle that followed, two policemen arrived and Harry and I weighed in. Nobby took off, putting the accelerator down pronto.

I disposed of my cozzer who was reeling around dazed, but Harry was in trouble. His had smashed him to the ground and was lying on top of him. I went to help, but Harry was semi-conscious and the policeman wasn't going to let him go. Even in the heat of the moment I had to admire his courage.

I had no real alternative but to run. A crowd of bystanders had gathered and a few Dick Bartons were trying to stop me pushing clear. Breaking free, I made a blind dash across the heavy traffic of Park Lane. Soon I was belting through Hyde Park, my heart thumping and blood leaking from my nose across my lips.

I was free, or so I thought, but Fate was firmly against us that night. I ran smack bang into the middle of a special Metropolitan Police dog-training exercise and was brought down by a rugby tackle. The rest of the team than piled in and I knew how it felt to be the ball at the bottom of a maul.

As I came to, they were dragging me along the ground heels first, my head bouncing on the ground. I threw up before they got me into the back seat, which probably saved me getting a kicking because no-one wanted to have vomit all over them. Or maybe they held back knowing the punishment that awaited me at West End Central.

I was under no illusion as to what to expect. I had committed the cardinal sin where they were concerned – short of killing one of them. It was the one thing that you didn't do and I *would* be taught a lesson. I was screaming before we got into the station, dragged out of the car heels first with my head banging on every concrete step to the cells. There they were waiting for me.

They took it in turns, replacing each other when their fists or feet became tired. I can't remember how many there were. I was drifting in and out of consciousness; coming to and seeing fresh faces, feeling new blows and collapsing again. Vaguely I remember hearing Harry's screams. He was getting the same treatment and it sounded like they were trying to kill him. His screams were as convincing as mine; what else could he do?

Some time during the night, I tried to get up off the floor, but they were watching me, waiting for me to regain consciousness before they tried a different diversion. Two of them entered the cell, dragging me to my feet and supporting me upright to face the third cozzer, who was drawing on a pair of heavy leather motor cycle gloves. He stared at me malevolently before intoning: 'So you're the guy who bashes up policemen . . . How do you like this?'

Bosh! I got it right on the cheek-bone. Left and then a right, my head going from side to side with the impact of the blows. Again I was slipping in and out of consciousness, too far gone to feel any pain. They could have continued until I was dead, I was beyond caring.

It was daylight when I realized I was still alive. My first vision was of a highly polished elegant black brogue judiciously placed in my ribs in an effort to turn me over on to my back. It wasn't a malign gesture. As I turned, I stared up at the owner of the shoes and saw an immaculately cut Savile Row suit and inside it a West End Central policeman, senior grade.

He looked at me and asked, 'What happened to you then?'

Through battered lips I croaked, 'I tripped coming through the door.'

'Hmm,' he said, sounding satisfied, and turned to his back-up team of two. 'Clean him up, I'll talk to him later.'

When he left, they dragged me to another cell with toilet facilities. I still couldn't stand unsupported so they put their hands around my shoulders, tipped me up and held me by the waist and thighs. My head was lowered into the toilet bowl while one of them pulled the chain, chuckling to himself. 'That'll clean the fucker up.'

I was coughing and spluttering. My head was miraculously clear but I feared that the beatings were going to continue all day. I'd heard about this kind of treatment before but it was usually reserved for murder suspects, armed robbers and police killers. Why me?

They supported me back to the cell where a mattress and a blanket were thrown down and I curled up. The sympathy didn't extend to tea or food; I guessed they were saving that for later. I couldn't have eaten anything solid anyway, and where I was going there would be plenty of porridge.

A few hours later, 'Black Brogues' appeared again, accompanied by an aide with the sweetener – the cup of tea designed to loosen the mouth. Some things never changed. It was welcome when it passed through my battered lips and I sat on the mattress nursing the cup as he started asking questions.

'We know who was with you, Bruce. You don't need me to tell you that any co-operation will lead to a lesser sentence.'

I remained impassive.

'You see, what I'm more concerned about is the jeweller's on Piccadilly – you know, the Four Thin Men . . .'

My heart sank. This was a heavy bit of work and I'd assumed it hadn't been put down to us. I certainly didn't need a further charge hung on me. Had they got any evidence? I wondered, waiting for his next question.

'We have witnesses who have identified you leaving the premises. You've got no chance.'

'No comment,' I replied.

He shrugged his shoulders as if it was all relatively unimportant to him, turned and walked to the cell door. Pausing and turning back, he said: 'If you're going to take that attitude there's nothing that I can do for you . . . in any case the jeweller's doesn't really matter, you're going to get a ten for this.'

I was left alone, nursing bruises and my own thoughts. Why, why, why had I allowed myself to get involved? All the lessons I thought that I'd learned had been undone. The good times were over and it was the end of an era. Whatever happened, I was going back inside and would have a long time to contemplate my future.

That evening I was charged with robbery with violence, grievous bodily harm upon the bookmaker, and two charges of actual bodily harm on the two policemen. I didn't have a chance of probation and all I could think about was Rita, at home in the flat in Streatham. What would happen to her?

When I saw Harry's battered face, his black eyes, swollen out of all proportion, made him look like some sort of lemur. We were led into court and gave each other a wink and wry grin, assuring each other that we were still in the game, even if now we were playing to their rules.

We were remanded for a week to Brixton and exactly seven days later there was a tap on my cell door. It was Steak. He and Nobby had been nicked over the weekend after blowing the vaults of a country-town bank and taking the cash. They were incredibly unlucky, having got clean away with the money and then being nicked by chance.

We managed a few fancy legal moves to have the robbery charge dropped but we still had grievous bodily harm upon the bookmaker and actual bodily harm on the policemen. We pleaded guilty. Harry got two and a half years in total and I got a year longer, which was reasonable under the circumstances.

I returned to the Hate Factory, welcomed with open arms by the old-boy network – among then, Ronnie Biggs. He was quick to inform me that I'd had a result: he'd had me down for at least ten years. A month later Steak and Nobby joined me – it was they who'd scored the decade inside. If Harry and I hadn't been caught that night in Park Lane, in all likelihood we would have been nicked with Steak and Nobby on the bank job and received ten years. Maybe Fate was with me after all.

I knew the prison drill. The daily routine was one of hunger, cold and isolation. Everything from the clothes to the bleak cells is designed to depersonalize and crush the spirit. But what none of the psychologists and prison reformers understands is that when you feel bad, you *are* bad.

The first priority was to make friends with my cell. I scrubbed it clean to establish possession – now it was mine, the only thing I had, and it was like beginning a new relationship. It was a standard set-up: a bed, washstand, table, chair, with a small barred window overlooking the exercise yard.

There was a mirror on the wall, which was important. Some mornings you needed to stare at the reflection just to make sure you still know who you are. You need a fingerhold on reality after staring at four walls through the night.

With a little ingenuity I turned the cell into a make-shift gymnasium. I could shadow-box against the walls, dance with dusters tied to my feet to shine the floor and use the bedframe as my weights machine. I wanted to put some bulk on to my six-foot-two, twelve-stone frame.

I was working in the tool room as well as being tea-trolley boy to the screws, who trusted me not to spit in their brew. Apart from that there was bugger-all to do. For sport, I chased and killed flies in the summer; and when the 'floaters' (*books*) had been round more than once, I tried to read a few backwards to break the monotony.

It's amazing how your memory sharpens when you lie on a bunk through the night. Every poem and verse, every excerpt from a play and song that you learnt at school will come back to you. You perform concerts to yourself, singing all the words you know and humming the gaps. I relived many times my acting triumph as Bob Cratchit in my Warwickshire school's rendering of *The Christmas Carol*.

Prison was like any other closed shop with its own pecking order and a distinct language. It was easy to recognize the *cognoscenti* by the way people talked. When you asked someone what they were nicked for and they said 'Blag', you knew it was armed robbery, usually with violence. Crim argot incorporated back slang, Cockney rhyming slang, Yiddish, pikey (*travellers*), ethnic phrases and invention. If you spoke it and understood it then you were on the way to being accepted as 'one of your own' – belonging to the clan.

'Dawdy the Jook' was a pikey's term of warning – 'look out for the dog'. 'Dawdy on the hay' would indicate 'look out on the back', or 'Dawdy the jills on the hay' would mean 'look out for the man behind you' – jills being a stranger and hay being an abbreviation of haystack – back. The same phrase could also have been put as 'On your daily', from the rhyming slang 'Daily Mail – tail'.

The crim lexicon was infinitely changeable and capable of every form of permutation. For example, 'Connaught on the hay' – 'Connaught Ranger' being rhyming slang for stranger – had the same meaning as 'jills on the hay'. Familiarity with the language was of the essence or you could have problems. Nicked for 'suss' early one morning with Cobby and Paddy whilst trying to nick a car, surrounded by cozzers, we gave 'wrong-uns' (*false names*). We said we were Tom, Dick and Harry but I realized that they were not acceptable and that we were nicked, so I warned everyone to 'Guy'. This was met with incomprehension by all. Cobby and Paddy looked at me blankly and the cozzers demanded, 'Who is Guy?' I decided on a practical demonstration. With no further ado I broke free and legged it: 'Guy' meant to get away rapidly.

A pal sent me a letter and at the bottom he wrote, 'PS: Sent a stripe for the linens.' I didn't have a clue what it meant. Later he explained that a 'stripe' was a pound – pound notes then had a central stripe – for the linen drapers: the papers.

* * *

The person I missed most was Rita. It wasn't as if our relationship had been heading anywhere – you never knew with Rita. Our passionate romance had cooled a little, perhaps because of the nights I spent away from home, although each morning when I arrived home from 'work' we would be at it for hours and then spend half the day in bed.

After one trip to the South of France she thought she was pregnant and everyone was happy for a while. Of course, it was only because of the coming baby and when the pregnancy proved a false alarm things slipped back to the way they were.

When I went back to the Hate Factory, she moved to Buckmaster Road, Gran's old address, and I arranged for the rent to be paid for the entirety of my sentence. She got a job at the American Embassy in Grosvenor Square, doing short-hand and typing, and would write me letters twice a week. In my heart I knew that our relationship was floundering, but I was reluctant to admit as much. It was as if I desperately needed to hang on to something in my life.

The green-eyed monster tormented me in prison. I would read Rita's letters, looking for some hint that she had found someone else. I didn't like the idea of her surrounded by all those Yanks. I'd seen it all during the war years. Rita was too attractive not to have men swarming over her but I was in no position to keep them at bay. What I least expected was that the Lothario would come from among my friends.

I don't know when her affair started with Ernie but I could sense from her letters and dwindling visits that I'd lost Rita.

I was angry. Wall-punching, can-thumping, door-rattling angry.

Ernie was a very intelligent guy with a lot of good ideas but he was very much a percentage man, without any criminal flair or ambition. He was in it for the returns, not for the buzz. On the other hand, he was a lunatic gambler, well known at the dogs and for his attitude towards losing.

Everyone used to say what a marvellous gambler Ernie was, but they didn't know that on the bad days he would go home and smash fuck out of his wife, the television set and anything else he could reach. When he fell hopelessly in love with Rita, he split with his wife and daughter – probably imagining he was gambling on a certainty.

This was more than I could stand. I saw Ernie as taking advantage of my absence. It was a direct challenge to me and I was going to do something about it. Obsessed with revenge, I wrote to my dad explaining my feelings and hoping he could ease my torment. His reply was sympathetic but didn't help. He questioned my sanity – something I was beginning to doubt myself.

One thing was certain – I had to get out.

I made a few tentative enquiries amongst the 'escapers', the handful of players in every prison who either want to get out or want to cure their boredom by making escape plans. The latter group often take it to the farthest limits, just short of actual escape, and are relieved when there is some setback so they can start all over again.

I made the rounds, talking to the serious and the mock-serious, but none of the plans appealed to me. However, a group of the players had a scheme which was a trifle too advanced for them; they had all the equipment, keys, ropes, grappling irons, and were in danger of actually having to escape. What they really wanted was a setback so they could start again.

This gave me an idea. The prison authorities always looked favourably on any co-operation that prevented an escape. If I exposed a plot I could get my sentence reduced, but I also had to be careful of my reputation. I didn't want to be labelled a 'wrong-un' amongst my peers.

There was a blue-chip precedent, however. Some years earlier Billy Hill hatched a plot wherein a pal of his would attack a screw only to be dragged off by Billy, who then received a six-month reduction in his sentence as a reward for having rescued a prison officer. Jack, his pal, went down chokey (*the punishment cells*) for a few months but was well rewarded by Billy on his release.

I reasoned that if Billy could finesse such a deal, then so could I. To maximize my prospects of reducing my sentence, I had to make the escape plot seem infinitely dangerous. Maybe I could add a gun to the escape kit? I spoke to a mate who had connections and within a fortnight he arranged the delivery of a loaded gun.

In the interim, I spoke to the principal player regarding the escape kit. It transpired that he was badly in debt to Biggsy, who'd been running a book, and owed him five ounces of tobacco. I offered seven ounces for all his equipment – a deal gratefully accepted because it meant that the debt with Biggsy was settled and he could start the whole exercise all over again.

The gun was duly delivered, an old Browning with a full clip of ammo. It was now a very substantial parcel which could possibly earn me six months' remission. Quietly, I sounded out my friendly screws regarding possible rewards if I revealed an escape plot, although I stressed that all I had were rumours. The guards were attentive and I kept them dangling until the time was right.

On a Saturday morning while I was suitably clear of the scene, the escape kit was discovered thanks to my tip-off. The deputy governor expressed his gratitude and confirmed that I was in line for a substantial reduction in sentence. That same afternoon I was transferred to the chokey block for my own protection.

On the Monday I was interviewed by the governor, who immediately voiced his suspicion on the grounds that I couldn't give him any names of the prisoners involved. I stonewalled him, pleading ignorance, and said that even if I did have names, I wouldn't risk raising the ire of some of the most dangerous men in prison.

This sticking point turned into a private war between me and the governor, who ordered that I be returned to my normal cell.

'That's madness,' I protested. 'You're gonna get me killed.'

'Give me the names and I'll give you protection.'

'I don't have the fucking names.'

'Not good enough,' he said scornfully.

'OK. If I go back, I go under written protest. Be it on your head.'

'Fine.'

Back in my cell, I was caught in a dilemma. My colleagues all knew it was a get-up, so I was in no physical danger from them. I could swallow the governor's arrogance and give him a victory or arrange to get myself nearly killed, which would give me the victory.

Rita's affair with Ernie was tearing me up inside and it steeled my resolve. I would have to organize an attack on myself, and eventually I found an old friend who agreed to help.

On 6 July 1959, I was stabbed three times in the prison bathhouse. Two of the wounds were flesh deep but the third penetrated a lung. The knife, taken from the prison workshop, was found lying next to me when the screws stormed into the bathhouse, clearing the forty prisoners who had gathered to collect new clothing.

The jail authorities were extremely embarrassed. Newspaper reports eventually revealed that I had warned the governor that I was in danger but he had refused my request for a transfer. The Home Office was accused of trying to cover up the fact that I had foiled an armed breakout and suffered a revenge attack.

Of course, I didn't name my attacker. I was taken to St James's hospital for two weeks, during which time I had no visitors. Everyone was terrified to get involved. I was bitter but determined to fight on alone.

While Scotland Yard interviewed all the prisoners, I was quietly transferred back to the prison hospital, still in solitary confinement. With just under a year of my sentence left, I was sure that they would give me early release, or at the very least leave me in hospital. The governor studiously avoided me, knowing that he had lost our battle and was under fire from the Home Office.

My only avenue to the administration was via the deputy governor, who was decidedly embarrassed by the whole affair. It was he who broke the sorry news that I was being transferred to Durham Prison – the worst nick in the country for Londoners. The very distance from home was punishment enough. What hope did I have now of winning back Rita?

Even so, I let it be known through friends that Ernie was in serious trouble if he continued seeing her. Mutual friends tried to warn him, reminding him of my temper, but Ernie was truly smitten and love conquered his fear.

Poor guy. It wasn't long before he believed Rita might be playing around with a few Yanks. All at once, I guess Ernie realized that he had screwed up his marriage and his family. I think it became too much for him because a few months before my release I got a card from Harry's wife, saying she had 'terrible, terrible news'. Ernie had taken an overdose of insulin and had been found dead in bed.

Of course there was some talk about whether he died or whether he was killed – did the hand stretch out from prison and put him down? It was empty talk. Ernie's sister Mary believed that the affair with Rita triggered his death. No-one would ever know if the overdose was accidental or deliberate. It was sad in a way, but at the time my anger didn't allow for any sympathy.

Rita, who had alienated just about everyone, disappeared to Canada, possibly pursuing one of her many liaisons at the US Embassy. I never heard from her again.

Yet on the horizon, something brighter began to shine. Rita had two younger sisters, Barbara and Frances, and a younger brother, James. Franny was a pretty young thing, barely twelve when I first started dating Rita. There was a degree of sibling rivalry between the sisters. The younger girl would run errands for me because I was Rita's boyfriend. She was only a kid but I liked her a lot.

Soon after Rita disappeared, I started to get occasional cards from Franny. They were simple letters telling me mundane things about school and work and dances on Saturday nights.

I had nine months at Durham sewing holes in mailbags for thruppence a bag. At the end of each week, the sacks we'd repaired were taken out and burned. What was the point?

For the most part I kept my nose clean and did my bird with no complaints. Harry visited me once. He drove the five hours from London and was granted twenty minutes with me. There was no extension of dispensation for the journey – twenty minutes was the unbreakable rule.

My last night in Durham Prison was the second longest of my life. Every quarter of an hour was chimed, never letting me forget the wasted hours I had spent in that piss-hole. Franny, then only seventeen years old, was waiting for me in London. We had already planned to fly to Jersey for a week. Perhaps that's why time passed so slowly – I was too excited about the future, particularly the hours I would spend with my head cradled between her breasts instead of on some sandbag prison pillow.

We'd been writing to each other for almost a year and Franny had grown up a lot. She was no longer just a young girl seeking a father figure; now there was a bond, a mutual need. She had also filled out in the most delightful way, which was particularly evident from a photograph she sent me when she was sixteen.

There were six of us being discharged that morning. (I was serving three and a half years with maximum remission of one third – ie, I served two years four months.) We all lined up after retrieving our civilian clothes and personal effects. I had quite an expensive suit and shoes and a sheepskin coat. As we waited, one of the Geordie prisoners being released said to me, 'Can I carry your bags to the station, guv'nor?'

This was astonishing. Minutes earlier we had been cons dressed in identical uniforms and would barely have given each other the time of day. Now that I had donned my civilian 'uniform', the roles had been established and he carried my bags to the station for a ten-bob tip.

I stepped on the train to Euston with a Government-issued travel warrant and twenty quid in my pocket. In the dining-car, I sat down ready for my first proper breakfast in three years. The steward came to take my order and I was so steeped in the prison system that I said, 'I'll have bacon and two eggs – please, sir.'

Harry met me at Euston. He had made all the arrangements for my trip to Jersey. He wasn't short of advice, either. 'Bruce, just give her a good fuck, but don't get yourself involved.'

This was very much the attitude of my circle. Most of them were married and none of their wives was impressed that I was dating a seventeen-year-old girl. Women who reach a certain age begin to get very wary of younger competition. They didn't want their husbands getting any ideas from me about investing in a newer and younger model.

I told Harry, 'I don't know what's gonna happen, she's just a nice girl and I want a bit of company.'

Franny looked a knockout when I saw her at Barbara's flat. She was wearing a blue silk dress, obviously bought especially for the occasion, and she blushed when I kissed her on the lips.

She'd been to Jersey before on a camping holiday, but had never done it with style. I still had plenty of cash in my bank account and I hired a little Healey Sprite and gave her money to buy clothes. We flew from Gatwick and booked into a four-star hotel near St Helier. It was a double room. There was never any discussion about it being otherwise. It was the sixties and Franny was innocent in many things but definitely no shrinking virgin.

The hotel was an old-fashioned place, with a string quartet of old spinsters playing Beethoven and Schubert each evening. It was all new to Franny and when we sat down to dinner she saw the array of cutlery and looked nervous about which knives to use with which course. We had champagne all the way and by late evening, when the music played, she couldn't help dancing.

We had a marvellous week, although it wasn't all roses. I was still quite bitter and cynical about what had happened with Rita and let it reflect on women in general. After a few drinks I could get quite cruel verbally but Franny seemed to understand.

When we came home, we stayed with Barbara in Earls Court for a while and then moved to Paddy's place, which he graciously vacated when he got nicked for jumping bail.

My future was still a mystery. There had been no light on my road to Damascus; no magical vision of a crooked road or a straight one. I had twenty grand in the bank – enough to get me started in a legitimate business, but was that what I really wanted? I honestly didn't know.

After a few weeks I went round to see Little Fred, basically to renew the friendship and find out what was happening. Harry was quite involved in trying to buy a legitimate Renault dealership. He had met Ian Metcalf of Metcalf & Mundy, the car dealers, and he had convinced Harry that there was money to be made in selling the newly imported Renaults. You could buy a concession for about twenty grand.

Harry and I talked it over. It was certainly a safe prospect, but did I want a safe life?

Fred was still living at Strawberry Hill, Twickenham. He had a great set up, the beautiful house, gardens, an XK140 for him, a Karman Ghia for the missis. He was doing fine.

'What you gonna do?' he asked.

'Well, see if there's anything interesting.'

'This'll keep you going,' he said, handing me an envelope. This was the order of things when anyone came home from the nick. Their mates chipped together and raised a float – call it start-up money.

'No, I don't want that,' I said. 'I've come round to see what's happening.'

Viewing Fred's house and the cars helped me make a decision. This was what I wanted. It was a dangerous life, but so what? At least I'd be living well and not tied down to some crummy car dealership.

Fred told me about a businessman with stores up in the North of England whose son-in-law had asked for a raise and been told that he was already overpaid and should keep his mouth shut.

The son-in-law wasn't best pleased. He knew the old man was creaming off the take every week and was keeping the money in a safe upstairs. I was immediately hooked, and within minutes my thoughts of a Renault agency and treading the straight and narrow had been forgotten.

'We'll go up there and rope them up,' I said.

'No,' said Fred. 'You don't know what's in the safe, it's a heavy bit of work. First let's see if the safe's there.'

To me this seemed to over-complicate things, but before we could decide on a plan, our target put his house up for sale and went away on holiday for a week. He left behind the au pair minding the house and she had some sort of authority to co-operate with the real estate agents and show people around.

Fred went up with his wife and pretended to be potential buyers. While they were viewing the place, she made her excuses to go to the bathroom and found the safe in a bedroom.

The following morning, I rang up the au pair. 'I'm a friend of Nigel's,' I said. 'He mentioned that he was selling the house and I might be interested. Can I come round?'

'Oh yes, of course.'

Harry, Fred and I drove up. We parked the car and Fred waited while we knocked on the door. A nice-looking young girl answered and smiled at having two such personable young men to show around. We had no particular plan once we were inside but, at the appropriate moment, Harry asked her, 'What's in there?'

'Oh, that's the linen cupboard.'

As she opened the door, we bundled her inside.

'Stay there for ten minutes and then we'll let you out.'

We slung the safe down the stairs and loaded it into the back of the estate. Fred was brilliant at little touches and he covered the safe with a sheet and put a bunch of flowers on top. Somehow it conveyed that little smidgen of respectability because nobody would expect you to put flowers on top of a stolen safe.

As an added precaution, we didn't travel back together, it was inviting a pull. Within ten minutes we'd phoned the police and told them where the girl was imprisoned. Then Fred dropped us at a station and we came home by train.

The next day we opened up the safe at Fred's place. The information was perfect: we got fifteen grand. I was six weeks out of Durham and already had another five grand in my pocket.

20

The old team were back in business. We were confident, careful and unlikely to make the mistakes of old. Harry and I both knew why we'd been nicked. We got greedy and complacent; we thought we had an absolute licence and could do what we wanted with impunity.

We were back doing the occasional climb and nicking safes, relying on good information and gut instinct.

With money in my pocket, I bought a Triumph TR and took Franny to Paris, to live it up in style and then cruise down to the South of France. We drove south and pulled over to catch a few minutes of shut-eye in a layby. Walking to a shady copse of trees, I noticed the only people around were three farm workers in a nearby field. We didn't doze for long – just enough to take the edge off my tiredness.

'I can't find my mac,' said Franny, when we got back to the car. Stupid woman, I thought, always losing something. 'And where's the briefcase?'

Now the anchors went on. It was gone, stolen, along with our passports and our travelling money of about two grand.

How dare they rob me? I thought. What a bloody disgrace.

Obviously we had to report the theft at the nearest gendarmerie and hang about for hours to file reports and statements. We stayed the night and, finally, after a nice dinner and a few bottles of wine, my rage evaporated. I even managed to look at it philosophically and drink a toast to the farm workers. They were probably sitting back, sharing a bottle of something special and joking about the silly Englishman who left his car and what must have been his annual profits in a briefcase. I would have done the same thing.

Worse was to come though. A few hours later, further south, I took the wrong road through a town and ended up going across a level crossing at high speed. I hit something which blew the front tyre. By now I was falling out of love with the brand-new TR.

I didn't have the faintest idea where the tools were kept or that the TR had knock-on wheels. I was standing there, cursing and blaspheming, when a little crowd gathered to watch the circus.

My mood improved by the time we reached Cannes. A lot of old boys were there. Harry and Chad among them. We had a great time until the night I left the car uncovered and we had so much rain that water poured out when I opened the door. Someone had also broken into the glove compartment, ripping it out and leaving a gaping hole in the dashboard. So I thought, Na, this car is bad luck. It's not worth it.

Fortune didn't favour me on the work front, either. After several lean weeks, Harry and I met Reg in the back seat of his Roller parked up on Exhibition Road. The plan was to kick around a few ideas.

'I wish we knew someone we could kill for twenty grand,' I said, not meaning it literally, but wanting to show my keenness.

Reg wasn't in the best of moods. 'You're talking bollocks. I'd give you information about people with dough but you wouldn't steal it.'

'I'd take your money, Reg, if I could.'

In reality, you had more chance with the Bank of England than with Reg, who was so mean he had his phone and television taken away because they were costing too much money.

'What bollocks,' said Reg. 'I know someone with money and if I was to tell you who it was, there's no way you'd nick it.'

'Try me.' Reg didn't give us any more clues, but Harry and I were mystified.

Obviously, it had to be someone close to me whom Reg assumed I wouldn't touch. But the only likely contender, Paddy, was doing time for jumping bail and he was so short of cash he had me running round like a lunatic trying to sell his Porsche. Who could it be?

My mind started flicking through index cards, trying to find the answer. Who did I know with money? Click, click, click.

Suddenly, I remembered a woman I'd known when I was seventeen or eighteen. I did a bit of work with her son who was about my age, but he let the side down and went straight. Maybe Reg was referring to her. It was a vague possibility, but she was overdue a visit from me, so I took a run down to Sussex.

Ivy was about forty-five and had a ten-year-old son with her. She was quite a strange bird, who existed on the periphery for a while, putting a few jobs our way. I had a brief fling with her, and while I was in Wandsworth nick some of her letters were pretty steamy. I didn't mind a bit of titillation, but I wasn't ready for a relationship, so in effect I passed her over to Ronnie Biggs, who kept up the good work and moved in with her.

Ivy worked as a barmaid at a country club ten miles outside of Brighton. What a set-up. It looked like something out of a Peter Cheyney novel, with a grand country house and movie types in their tweeds propping up the bar, while their flash cars decorated the gravel drive. There was an enormous lake on one side and all manner of outhouses and cottages on the fringes of the main house.

'I'm looking for Ivy,' I said to a porter.

'She's in a cottage, I'll give her a ring. Who shall I say it is?'

'Tell her it's Bruce.'

He pointed me to the cottage and as I drove into the forecourt Ivy appeared at the door. She must have weighed eighteen stone and when she threw her arms around me I thought I was a goner. Through the tears, she sighed, 'Bruce, Bruce, you've come down! You have to help me. I'm in trouble.'

I extricated myself from her ample bosom and tried to comprehend how much more of a woman she was since our last meeting. 'I've been looking after some money for Paddy and it's been stolen,' she cried. 'What am I going to do?'

My first reaction was to get angry. Ivy should never have been asked to safeguard loot. I was also hurt by the fact that Paddy had me running around like a madman trying to make another fifty pound on his Porsche, but he didn't trust me enough to leave his money with me.

Ivy was crying, so I calmed her down and asked what had happened.

Apparently, Paddy had scored an enormous touch and had taken the bulk of the money down to her place. He put it in a hidey-hole under a stair, nailing it up and covering it with carpet. 'There's no need for you to go near it,' he told Ivy.

Everything should have been all right. But Paddy got caught jumping bail and was away for eight months. In the interim, Ivy had financial problems and got herself a job. She had to leave the house, so she called her son and asked him to help her retrieve Paddy's stash from the stairs.

'I know he took something out of it,' she said. 'I don't know how much and when I asked him he denied it. What could I do?'

'What happened to the rest of the money?' I asked.

'Well, I moved down here and I hid it in a safe place.'

'Under the bed?'

'No, no,' she said, 'in a wardrobe. Not all the time, though – sometimes I put it in a hole under the sofa.'

'So the rest is safe?'

'No, no, no,' she sobbed. 'It's gone.'

Ivy had been having an affair with a twenty-year-old from up north somewhere who worked as a barman at the country club.

'He was really short and I gave him some money out of it,' she said.

'What sort of money?'

'About thirty pounds – just the once.'

'No more?'

'Well maybe the odd sort of ten pounds and things like that – naturally I was going to make it up. But then, one afternoon at the club, three guys come in, hale and hearty fellows, who had a flash car and were racing faces. It was champagne all round and they were drinking it like it was being bottled in the back garden.

'You don't get too many people drinking champagne in the afternoon, and the governor of the club gets real friendly with them. He asks them what they do and they explain that they were racing people. I don't know if it was Goodwood, but there was a race meeting on the next day and they'd come down from London to have a sizeable bet. I could see the governor thinking to himself.

' "Can I have something on, could you put something on for me?" he asked.

' "Yeah sure, what do you want?"

' "Could I have a grand on it?"

' "It's your money, we're only putting it on for you." '

I could almost have heard Ivy's mind going click, click, click. She would have been thinking that she could have a bet and make up for the missing money.

'Can I have a bet as well?' she had asked.

'Sure, how much you want? Put you down for a score, shall we?' They were laughing.

'No, no, put me down for five hundred quid,' said Ivy, wiping away their smiles. It was a lot of dough for a barmaid to be holding.

Then Ivy committed the cardinal sin. 'I'll go and get it now,' she said, popping over to the cottage and coming back with five hundred pounds.

'That was it?' I said, pre-empting her.

'Oh, no, they came back the next day and gave us our money back. They said the horse wasn't right on the day. The governor asked them, "When is it going to be any good?" and they said, "Well, definitely next week." And then the governor tells them, "Keep the money and have it on for me next week." And, of course, I said the same thing.'

The guys were obviously pros. They even pressed the governor to take his money back, so that it looked genuine. The trio then spent two or three days at the club, drinking them dry of champagne. On their last morning a friend arrived in a red XK140 drop-head coupé and brought a guitar down.

He entertained Ivy's son, drawing him away from the cottage while she was working. 'That night when I got home, the sofa had been ripped up and the money had gone. The gamblers had also gone and I was left with nothing. I didn't know what to do.'

Ivy was in a fair old state, so I had a few words with the governor. He didn't know Ivy's money had been stolen but he realized that I was determined to get her five hundred pounds back. 'Well, I think they're all right,' he said, 'because they said they're coming back here tonight.'

I rang up Harry. 'Go and see a few of the lads and get a little firm together. I might need some help.'

Six of them joined me, predominant among them Big Bill Smith. He took charge, looking and sounding like George Sanders as he asked me for the details. Big Bill recognized the sting immediately.

While we were talking, the governor got a phone call from one of the gamblers. Big Bill grabbed the phone. 'We want to see you,' he said menacingly.

The guy at the other end didn't frighten easily. 'And we want to see you! Get your army on parade, we're coming down to attend to you.'

Everyone got tooled up. I armed myself with a pair of garden shears, undoing the wingnut so I had a single blade. I could slash, cut, stab, or beat them over the head. We didn't know what to expect.

Then we sat in the bar waiting and geeing each other up on champagne. After three bottles each we realized that we were in no fit state to stand upright, let alone to give someone a kicking. Luckily no-one turned up to the rumble, although Big Bill stayed the night with me, just in case.

The matter wasn't over. Two days later we heard that one of them was coming down to the club and this time we were waiting. Problem was, he brought his old mum and dad with him. They were carrying a suitcase and we figured there could be cash inside. We decided to follow them but to do that properly you really need to be organized with half a dozen cars, a couple of motor bikes and radio communication. The stuff you see in the movies with cops following a single unmarked car is bollocks.

We had three cars and as we drove we kept in touch, changing over at intervals, overtaking and then falling back, so that when this guy looked in the mirror he was never seeing the same car all the time. We managed to follow them from Sussex along a roundabout route to Northwood.

Finally he dropped his mother and father, but they took the suitcase, which seemed to rule out the possibility of cash. Then we had to make a decision whether to cop for him. We continued to follow, and finally I decided to grab him and see what he was carrying. I was two cars behind, but our routine swapping soon put us right in his mirrors. I saw him look up, see the reflection, and suddenly his door was open and he was off and running. He abandoned the car and vanished into the entrance of a shopping precinct.

A few days later, we gathered in the Star for a post-mortem. None of us held out much hope of recovering Ivy's money, but it was a good exercise to talk it over. We were joined by Little Caesar. 'A funny thing's happened,' he said, as he sat down, drink in his hand. 'I've been talking to a young pal of mine who's just had a right touch down at Brighton.'

'People are having touches all the time down in Brighton,' I said.

'Well, this one was a beauty. Ready money. The kid's a good burglar and he knows a few racing faces.'

Click, click, click. 'Can you get this pal? I'd like to meet him.'

'He's going to have a drink at Dorothy's.' Dorothy Foxon was a well-known club owner who had a place in Knightsbridge. 'They're gonna be there tomorrow morning.'

When money is involved, everyone is interested, and by eleven the next morning there were twenty of us waiting outside the club, including 'Italian Albert' Dimes, a Godfather figure at the time.

A guy wearing sunglasses and a nice suit drew up in a red XK drop-head coupé. Beside him was another young man.

'That's your bloke?' said Little Caesar. It's gotta be him, I thought, there aren't two burglars with an XK140 drop-head, red.

They sauntered into the club and five minutes later we followed.

Albert said to Dorothy, 'Fuck off, we're taking over for a little while.'

She took off and we locked the door. We closed in around them as they sat at a table and Albert spoke first.

'You're Gerry, ain't you?'

'That's right, Albert.'

'And you're a burglar, ain't you?'

'Yes.'

'Well, I got a little choice for you to make, Gerry. See, you can be a burglar with money and no legs – or you can be a burglar with legs and no money.'

The lad tried to stand but Albert put a hand on his shoulder, forcing him down.

'What's it all about? I ain't done anything.'

'You nicked some money from a pal of ours who's in the nick.'

'I didn't know. How was I to know? Some people stuck it up to me and I did the job. I'd give it back, but I spent some of it. I got debts. But I'll put the rest back.'

We eventually got three grand back, although he admitted to stealing twelve. Even then, he could have been lying. The little coup Paddy pulled was worth about a hundred grand, so by the time they sold the gear it was worth thirty or forty.

A few weeks later I had to go up to the nick and break the news to him.

'Any joy with the Porsche?' he said.

'No joy with the Porsche, and no joy with the money you left with Ivy, neither.'

The blood ran out of his face.

'Why the fucking hell didn't she tell me? I could have moved it!'

'Don't go blaming Ivy. It's nobody's fault – it's your fault for putting it down there and for not putting your trust in people who could have kept it safe.'

Although we had the names of the country club gamblers, we didn't bother following it up. Too much time had been wasted and they would simply have pleaded that the money had already been spent. You can't prove otherwise and breaking heads wasn't my way.

Some of the heavies make a living out of extorting money from fellow crims. They hear about a big bank job and then try to muscle in on the action.

They say, 'Them fucking deed boxes you nicked, I had my fucking life savings in there, now what you gonna do about it?' Or, 'You nicked my mate's money, I want it back.'

The thieves will um and ah, making excuses about having spent the money, or having earned far less than the papers reported. Eventually, a small sum changes hands to keep everyone happy and their bones intact.

If you're a thief, that's what you do for a living; if you're a gangster that's what you do for a living. Try to cross over and you will spend the rest of your life at war with people. When push comes to shove, you pay the piper and live a much healthier life.

21

Whether it was experience or boredom, my aspirations were changing. I was losing interest in country house climbs and copping chief accountants for the keys. Sure, the money was good, but it always disappeared. Five grand would last me a month or two and then I'd start worrying about the next instalment. What I really wanted was the big score – the five- or six-figure sums that could let me spend all winter in the South of France.

No longer an eager apprentice stealing to survive from week to week, I had the track record and contacts to plot bigger jobs and surround myself with experts. Security and safety were paramount: I didn't want to go back to prison. Sometimes we would spend weeks planning, staking out the location, timing movements and discussing options but eventually sacrifice it all because it didn't smell right. If this happens just once or twice, you put it down to wise counsel, but sometimes you get a run of them and begin to wonder if the golden touch has deserted you. It happened to me in 1960, when a string of major plans were scuppered by tiny details.

One of our firm's best contacts was a traveller who lived in Staines and knew people with money. He was full of possibilities, not all of them worthwhile, but we checked them out anyway. Some were dismissed outright, but others were put in the diary for later consideration.

The traveller introduced us to a porter who worked at Redhill railway station and was friendly with his local bank manager. Over a drink, they discussed a local who had just inherited a million pounds from a dead aunt.

'A million pounds? I'd like to see what that looks like!' said the porter.

'Would you? Come back at lunch-time and I'll take you down the vaults.'

So the porter arrived and the manager took him into the vault where he'd laid out some sandwiches and a couple of bottles of beer. 'We'll have some lunch in a million-pound setting, eh?'

'Very nice.'

I was intrigued. 'Was there a million pounds there?'

'Too right,' said the porter. 'It was all stacked up.'

'But could you see the bundles? Were they marked fifty grand, fifty grand, fifty grand?'

'Oh, no,' he said, 'but I could see there was over a million there.'

Of course, he was just speculating, but I began to wonder why so much money was in a bank at Redhill. Even the feeder banks rarely had more than a couple of hundred grand at any one time, and a normal high-street bank would probably have fifty grand, top whack. Redhill was only a small branch, so it didn't make sense.

The porter had also asked the bank manager about money sent through the post. Apparently, huge sums were often transferred in mailbags that were stacked on the platform until the train came through. The manager nodded his head in agreement.

We checked out the station and sure enough the bags were all laid out on the platform at two o'clock in the afternoon. But there were mailbags piled up everywhere and no indication of which of them contained money. This was the great security precaution.

Although we didn't really intend doing the bank it was worth a look, so I teamed up with Jimmy White, a well-known key man who'd been on the trot for about ten years after police linked him with the tools used in a bullion raid.

I liked Jim. Not only was he a good key man but he had this remarkable ability to be invisible, to merge in with his surroundings and become the ultimate Mr Nobody. I once cleared out a place with him and he sidled up beside me wearing a brown smock; for a minute or two I didn't even realize he was there.

Jim came with me to check out the bank and we discussed some rough plans. But before we decided anything concrete, the traveller from Staines put another piece of business our way. He was dealing with a guy who worked for a big steel firm up north and would come into town every month with some mercury which he sold for two hundred quid. The traveller then walked round the corner and sold it for two grand – a nice little earner and regular profit.

Harry and I arranged a meeting with the Northerner, using the pretence that we wanted to get hold of more mercury. Then I started asking him about the steel firm in Chesterfield.

'How many people work there?'

'Quite a few – about ten thousand workers.'

'What's the wages?'

'Ah,' he said, catching on quickly. 'Well, if you wanted to do that, it'd be easy. The cashier's department go down to the bank each week. It's about a ten-mile drive in a tilly truck – one of those army vehicles with a canvas back. They go down there with four of them sitting in the back with a big box holding the money. Then there's a driver and the chief cashier up front. The road itself is semi-rural, but the driveway up to the factory is quite long.'

It sounded promising, but the big question was, where to go afterwards? A robbery like this would cause a hue and cry, and being as far north as Chesterfield we would have trouble getting home without being picked up in transit.

The best idea would be to stow somewhere, lying low until the heat went out of the search. But the only people we knew up north had criminal records and would probably get picked up in a general sweep of the likely suspects. We knew nobody straight, and renting a house was out of the question because it could be traced back to us. It would be a hard nut to crack, but seemed such an easy score that we persevered and went up to Chesterfield to get the lie of the land.

On the first morning, the truck arrived at half-past nine. The following week it was half twelve. A week later, it was back to half nine. We went to see our man again.

'Oh it's definitely a security thing,' he said. 'There's no set pattern.'

That threw us for a while, and our regular trips to Chesterfield were costing time and money. We put it on the back burner for a few weeks and then heard that the system had changed again.

'They've got rid of the truck. Now it's a dormobile that's been strengthened.'

My first reaction was that this would make it easier, because they wouldn't be expecting anything. Unfortunately, they were still varying the collection hours which made it difficult to organize a time and location for the hit. I talked to Jimmy and we discussed how we could hide ourselves and the equipment for several hours if the dormobile was on a late run. Did we do it outside the bank, or on the country road?

Another problem was number plates. At that time these indicated the origin of the car, so if you were grafting anywhere up north you didn't want to be seen with London plates because it drew suspicion. Obviously, we could nick local plates, but this was one more moving part in the machine to go wrong.

There is an old truism among thieves that if something doesn't look right the first time, it's often best to leave it well alone. It's wise advice and, after dozens of follow-ups to Chesterfield, I put the idea on the back burner indefinitely.

By now I was starting to wonder about my touch. I even resurrected a job that a bank messenger had put up a few years earlier.

'I want to do something about your bank,' I told him.

'OK, but it's not like it used to be,' he said. 'It's tougher now and you're going to need inside help.'

Harry was interested and immediately asked about the keys. There were two: the chief cashier had one and the relief cashier the other. Both were needed to open the vault.

Each afternoon the chief cashier would leave the bank at six o'clock, walk past Selfridge's and continue for twenty minutes to Regent's Park, where his Triumph Herald was parked. We watched him bend down and undo a security lock beneath the car – an ignition cut-out.

No problem here, I thought. It's dark at six in Regent's Park. We can back a van up to his car, cop for him when he bends down and throw him in the back. Someone will then drive his car away to make the routine complete.

The relief cashier was a woman in her late twenties, whose husband also worked for the bank but for a different branch. She would finish before him and walk to Hanover Square, where they met and strolled to Victoria Station for the journey home to Thornton Heath.

This was a problem. Obviously we wanted to cop for her on her own, but she rarely left work at the same time each evening – and then she tore along the pavement at a jogging pace. She and her husband didn't always go straight home either; some nights they went to the cinema, or the theatre. Definitely wild cards.

What do they do on weekends? I wanted to know. Surely she can't walk around with the vault key in her pocket? The next Saturday morning we waited outside their house and watched them leave and catch a train to Brighton. They were out for the day so Harry and I slipped in, rifling drawers and looking for hidey-holes. Anything that Harry couldn't open had to stay shut – we didn't want to break anything and alert the couple.

We had no joy and by now a lot of the firm were getting restless. Some wanted to jack it in; others wanted to have a go. It was difficult to keep everyone together and motivated.

The next suggestion was to snatch the cashier's handbag, making it look genuine; in the commotion, someone would take a dab of the key. One of us would then step out of the crowd, collar the thief and return the purse, telling her we were taking the villain to the nearest police station.

Meanwhile, I was talking to Jimmy and he mentioned he had some work with another firm. 'Is it any good?' I asked.

'Yeah, big.'

'Can I be in?'

'I don't think so, they're all fully organized.'

He started telling me bits and pieces about the plan until I stopped him. The details all sounded alarmingly familiar.

'Jim, by any chance is your informant of Scottish origin?'

He looked up. 'Why?'

'Is his name fucking Jock?'

'Yeah.'

'Well, we're both looking at the same fucking bank.'

'No, you can't be! Christ, what are we going to do? They're gonna go mad, they're gonna think I've told you all about it.'

'Who are they?' I asked.

'It's Fitzy and Bobby Cook.'

Christ, I thought. It was a good firm, but not as good as my mob.

'The only thing to do is have a meeting,' I said. 'We'll talk it over.'

Bobby Cook was an old friend of mine but he was pretty pissed off when he heard the news. He was a good grafter, and the only guy I knew who ever got convicted for being an 'incorrigible rogue' – a fate which befell him twice. Fitzy, on the other hand, was the heavy in the firm and had been involved with the Richardsons. Not one of nature's born negotiators, he was planning to take a shooter on the job.

'Well, the obvious thing to do is pool our resources and do it together,' I said.

'Na, na, we're having none of that,' said Bobby. 'No, you get on and do it.'

I heard later that after I left, Fitzy piped up, 'If I'd had the gun there, I'd of done him. I'd of done that skinny cunt.'

It was only bravado. He loved me really.

Although we got the all clear, I didn't fancy the bank any more. Too many people now knew about the job: none of them was likely to shop us to the Old Bill but I didn't want them getting peeved afterwards and saying to their pals, 'Yeah, that was our bit of work, that one. They fucking done it instead of us.'

Security was too easily compromised so I abandoned the plan. It was disappointing but no exercise is completely wasted. Some were prospects for the future and others were learning experiences. They allowed me to gauge the strengths of the people I was working with and decide who to trust. I didn't want hotheads or heroes, or anyone likely to run scared at the slightest sign of trouble. Clever criminals don't get caught – even when times are lean.

22

Franny and I had moved into a luxury maisonette in Lytton Grove in Putney after our jaunt to Cannes. She loved the place and I felt that I'd returned to my roots.

Not much constructive was happening in the world of crime. I spent a lot of time browsing: breakfast included reading the morning papers, the Court Circular, movements of possible targets. I took *Apollo* and *The Collector*; I read the *Tatler* and all the society mags. Then I'd meet Harry for lunch at the Star or the Marlborough and kick things around, perhaps going to view a prospective target's situation to try to generate some business.

Things had changed while I'd been in Durham. The cash targets who had made their lot during and after the war were changing with the times, becoming more accustomed to using banks and safety deposits. And our circle of informants had seemingly moved on, probably retired on the money that they had earned from us. Whatever the reason, this type of information wasn't as readily available as it had once been. We had to think up new moves if we were to stay in the game. Everything appeared to be getting more organized; the days of two-man teams were being superseded by large gangs, and they were proving highly successful.

'Sooner or later we will have to move in that direction,' I said to Harry.

In the past it had been different; there had always been other pairs that we could team up with for a bit of work, but most of those were now either semi-retired or in the nick. Harry had an enormous circle of acquaintances that went back years, but they largely figured as the old breed who still thought in the old ways; they'd be good for information but not likely to be involved in the ways that were evolving.

I knew quite a few of the new breed via the Hate Factory and other similar Halls of Learning, and would on occasion bump into them at some watering hole. I went to all sorts of places, looking and listening. Information is the life blood of the business.

That was how I met Buster Edwards — at Charlie Richardson's club, the Mary Ann, in Peckham. It was a regular call-in for a quickie, as there were always a few faces there and maybe you'd get a clue. Another added attraction was the presence of the pretty girls who congregated there, strutting their stuff. The sixties were just beginning.

It seemed that everyone knew we were on the verge of bigger and more exciting things and were impatient to get started. Buster took Harry and me to meet Gordon Goody at the Castle pub in Putney, one of Gordon's major watering holes. A Putney boy, born and bred, he was the unofficial governor on the manor. He had a good reputation as a thief and in the vernacular was as 'sound as a bell'. Harry hit it off immediately with him, perhaps because of their shared Irish ancestry. In fact we all felt at home with each other and at the end of the night we felt that, should anything crop up that called for extra hands, then we had our men.

Roy James was another good contact. I knew him both by sight and by reputation. Starting out in motor cycles, he was influenced by his mechanic to switch to go-karts and soon became a member of the British team. In 1962 he transferred his enthusiasm to cars. He bought the latest Brabham Formula Junior car and entered his first official race – unofficially, of course, he had been racing most of his adult life, as a wheel man. He led the field for most of the race, before overcooking it and writing off his brand-new machine. He acquired another for the next meeting at Goodwood, and again he crashed while in the lead. The race stewards delivered a warning, saying that his driving verged on the dangerous, but Roy took as much notice of them as he did of any other authority figure. Intensely competitive, he had faith in his ability.

With his car repaired, Roy won the next race in the series, at Aintree. In fact he won so convincingly that the motoring press spoke of a new star on the horizon. They were right. Roy James won seventeen of the next twenty races, thrashing Jackie Stewart, Denny Hulme, Mike Hailwood and Jack Brabham. The only three he lost were due to mechanical failures. Esso, Shell and all the other major sponsors besieged him with offers of a contract. He broke lap record after lap record, and the World Championship beckoned. The consensus was that he'd make it – or be dead. I loved him, he was right up my street.

Roy was doing a bit of graft with Mickey Ball, and very successful they were too. They looked so young that I used to say that they should go out grafting in shorts. But they were the new breed, no doubt about it: non-smokers, non-drinkers, and fitness fanatics.

The times cast their spell. Everyone's clothes appeared to have originated in Savile Row, cashmeres and vicuna topcoats *de rigueur*, shirts from one of the names – Washington, Tremlett, Dare and Dolphin, Harvey and Hudson, Sulka, Turnbull and Asser. Personal jewellery had to have a name: Cartier was OK but blatant to the *cognoscenti*. Instead, one looked for the truly obscure that only the really knowledgeable knew about – Vacheron and Constantin, Omar Picquet, Ulysses Nardin.

My whole ideal was to present an image of understated elegance that intimated wealth and thus power. It was swanking all the way, but with the appropriate money distributed by way of largesse it opened practically every door. Restaurants were prompt in their attention, a twenty-pound note to the *maître d'* ensuring that there was never any problem with getting a table. Pruniers in St James's, Bentleys and Sheekeys were our fish places. Franny and I had our favourite, Wheeler's in Duke of York Street off Jermyn Street: you could have a small dining-room to yourself there, very private and intimate. The Rib Room at the Carlton Towers was an innovative fashion for a while, serving great beef at a time when beef was synonymous with strength: we all ate plenty of that, thinking that we needed it for our work.

At the clubs, the skirts were getting shorter. The advent of the new dances lured most of the non-dancers on to the floor, myself included. We Twisted the nights away at the Scotch, the Revolution and the Establishment, and at many other places that seemed to spring up overnight and close just as quickly. There were the clubs where you didn't eat, just drank and danced – the Astor, the Embassy – and if you were a spieler there was Les Ambassadeurs, where Chad was a member and I could always effect an entrance.

If Franny and I were looking for a quiet night on our own we'd often go to one of the smaller clubs that had a good pianist whose style we liked. People like George Shearing worked all the old standards, 'I Remember April', 'Summertime', 'Tenderly', old show tunes.

We listened to music like this at home, mostly jazz standards with Ahmed Jamal, Nina Simone, the Modern Jazz Quartet, the Jazz Messengers, Bud Powell, Charlie Parker and Dizzy Gillespie. We liked the big bands of Basie and Ellington, some of the early Kenton with Anita O'. But Frank was *the* man. Our favourite album was *Songs for Swinging Lovers* with the Nelson Riddle orchestra.

Even though she had died, my gran's place in Battersea was still the address I gave to the police when I got pulled. It meant that no-one knew where I lived. One day, however, my Uncle Jack who still resided at Buckmaster Road, rang me up to say that the police had been around and that their message was for me to get in touch with them urgently – no bollocks!

They had left a name I knew, one that conveyed respect. I was mystified, whatever could they want? As far as I knew I was clean. I played it straight, ringing up the nick and getting through to an aide.

'Come on in,' he said, 'the guv'nor wants to talk to you.'

I was sure that he did – so did a few others in his position. Whatever they wanted it was doubtful that it would be anything in my favour.

I arrived at Wandsworth police station about eight.

'Hello, Bruce,' the chief inspector said, standing up from behind his desk and extending his hand. 'Nice of you to come in.' He was one of the old school: been there, seen it, done everything. He knew that being nice gets the best results.

'Nasty one, Bruce,' he went on. 'Someone had a bit of work over at Colliers Wood, it all went boss-eyed and they killed a guy. Now I know that ain't your game but you're on the books, they've sent your file down.' He gestured to the one on his desk. 'All I want is a statement detailing your movements on that day. It's the usual process of elimination, you know.'

Sure I knew. The first rule in the game is never make a statement. However, there are always exceptions to the rules and I had no hesitation with my reply. 'No problem, Guv'nor, you going to take it now?'

'Might as well get it over with, then you can get off and have your drink at the . . . let's see . . .' He flicked through the file. 'Ah yes, the Marlborough.' He looked at me with a twist to his lips that might be a smile.

It took less than ten minutes to give him my statement. As he showed me to the door, his parting words were: 'Have one for me – and give my best to Bob and the lads.'

Just to let me know that they knew all about me, that the tabs were always on you. I never heard any more of the murder enquiry and as far as I know no-one was ever caught for it.

Every firm needs a leader, not in a military sense but somebody who will make a decision about a plan and not let petty arguments and uncertainty slow things down. It's a particular problem when you have members of equal status and there's no logical pecking order. They fight amongst themselves and turn the simplest job into a biblical epic.

One firm included several names that would soon be inextricably linked with mine in the biggest robbery in history.

Buster Edwards was working with Gordon Goody, whom we came to call 'Footpad' because he often wore a long coat that gave him, with his height, the appearance of a street mugger. The third member of their rather loose firm was Charlie Wilson, whom I had known since the war years, and worked with since the mid-fifties when we saw ourselves as high-class jewel thieves. But Charlie wasn't making any money out of it. He had got nicked for possession of explosives and spent time in Maidstone with Harry while I was in Durham.

Buster, Charlie and Gordon were doing much the same as our firm, quite successfully, but they had no natural leader. We eventually crossed paths due to the introduction of some very helpful new gadgetry: argon arc guns. Robberies on banks and armoured cars were booming and new technology meant that security was getting tighter, but at the same time, some of it could actually benefit the criminal.

The argon gun was a high-powered electric torch that could carve through metal. They weren't available wholesale and could only be ordered, which created security problems because the police could obviously trace them back. Eventually, an old geezer who worked for an engineering firm which once sold arms to Abdel Krim during the Riff revolution slipped us a company receipt for a gun.

With a transformer, we would be in business. We found a factory in Staines which manufactured them, and decided to pool our resources with Charlie, Buster and Gordon to steal the necessary equipment. We took six – one for each firm, two for trading purposes and two in reserve.

Gordon and Buster had designs on a bank in Ireland but I didn't fancy it. They took my engineering friend to operate the torch and promised me a share for having made the introduction.

It turned out to be the worst débâcle imaginable. They figured that Ireland was full of dopey policemen and drunken bank managers and played fast and loose. After renting a car, getting oxygen bottles and sussing out the bank, they discovered that one of the two guys with them had failed to do the leg-work. This same guy and his mate spent each night at local dance halls and had a good old knees up, drawing attention to themselves, when they should have been lying low. Eventually, Buster got pulled by the police and taken to the station.

'We know exactly what you're up to,' said the inspector, who rattled off the entire plot almost by heart.

'Can anything be done?' asked Buster.

'Yeah,' said the inspector. 'Give us fifty quid and fuck off back to England.'

They dumped everything and came home.

Back in England, they started working on a bank in the City where they knew the guy who'd installed the alarms. What they didn't know was that a second set had been put in afterwards. Inside they went, disconnected the first set and started torching the vault. Meanwhile, the other alarm had triggered and the police walked straight in on them. It was a single patrol rather than the whole cavalry so they decided to run. There was a battle, nothing really bloodthirsty, and all of them managed to get away.

I got to thinking afterwards that none of this was doing any of us any good. I talked it over with Harry and asked him whether he'd be interested in teaming up with Buster, Gordon and Charlie. It turned out that they'd already been talking to him: they had information on a Securicor van that regularly delivered thirty grand to a railway depot at Old Oak.

I had a prior engagement with Chad, which came to nothing, but Harry joined the others in a run for the railwaymen's money. They went in the night before and took the bolts out of the door hinges and replaced them with shorter screws.

Even so, they were still arguing about tactics, asking each other, 'Well, what do you think?' 'Yeah, OK, but I think we should . . .' No-one was making a decision and one of them even suggested machine-gunning the doors.

'Fucking machine-gun,' said Harry in disgust. 'I'll shoulder the bloody things.'

He was a big boy, about fifteen stone, and he couldn't understand all the debate. He took charge and became the physical, if not the cerebral, leader, although he had never had to keep a gang of six in line. As far as Harry was concerned it was simply a case of smashing the door, grabbing the bags and getting the hell out. You're not going to spend five minutes making polite conversation or holding a gun to someone's head.

Harry gee'd himself up beforehand as they backed the van into the workshop area. At the signal, he shouldered the door and it flew open. Inside, about ten people, the wages staff, were so shocked they didn't react until it was too late. They were in and out within three minutes, grabbing thirty grand and making good their escape.

The job which really cemented our new partnership was an audacious hijacking of an armoured van, with less than a week between the idea being raised and the plan executed. It began on a Wednesday night when a friend of mine in the motor trade mentioned that he knew someone working for an armoured car company in Middlesex.

'Does he want to play?' I asked.

'Yes he wants to play. He's very sensible, no nonsense, you'll like him.'

The following evening we met and the guard explained how he followed a particular route each day and then drove the van home at night. More importantly, the company was under-staffed and quite lax on security. Normally, there are two guards up front and another in the back who never leaves the van. The only person who can open the rear doors is the man inside. This time the crews were operating two-handed and, once outside the depot, both guards sat in the front seat.

'What sort of money are you carrying?' I asked.

'Round about seventy grand.'

'How much opposition are we likely to get?'

'Well, as far as my mate's concerned, he doesn't want to play. There isn't any way that he's gonna defend the company's honour but he doesn't want a part of it.'

It all sounded too good to be true. With both guards relaxing in the front seat, with windows down and sleeves rolled up, they became ordinary van drivers rather than security staff.

The next morning, I watched the van leave the depot in Great West Road. The driver didn't see me standing on the far side of the street reading a newspaper. Around the corner, the van stopped while the second guard climbed out and joined the driver. Everything panned out.

I went back to the guard after his shift and laid down the law to him.

'Do you know what's gonna happen when this goes off? You're gonna have the heavy mob come down on you like a ton of bricks. They'll do everything short of hanging you. It's worth twenty years, believe me, and you can forget about your wife and kids, you won't be seeing them again. All it's gonna take is your mate to start singing and it's over.'

He listened and nodded. 'That's OK, I know the risks. The only person that's gonna get me nicked is me.'

'OK, that's basically it,' I said. 'When the job's done you won't hear from me for a month. Then you'll get your money.'

'How much?'

'You'll get a full whack.'

'How many of you will be on it?'

'I don't know, four maybe five.'

He did some quick calculations in his head. 'Fine.'

I looked closely at his route and worked out several locations where we could hit before the van had dropped any money. Then I pulled in Charlie and Gordon to form the nucleus of the team. Gordon was worth three men because of his 'Footpad' looks. Charlie's bantering shout of 'Put it back on, you ugly bastard!', accompanied by a grin, was a regular occurrence when Gordon took off his stocking mask.

Harry came with me when I checked and re-checked the route, working out exactly how and where we were going to stop the van. Eventually we decided on a road which wasn't particularly busy and featured a cut-through street.

I was to tail the van from the depot at six in the morning and overtake it before it reached the road. I could get there five minutes ahead and alert the others who would erect diversion signs for road repairs. As luck would have it, there were genuine roadworks further down the cut-off road.

I didn't tell the guard where we were going to hit them. 'It's best if you don't know anything whatsoever,' I said.

'But it'll be some time next week?'

'Yeah, some time next week.'

The diversion signs were stolen from building sites and kept in the back of a parked van. The getaway car was also in position and we were set to go.

I watched the van leave the depot, catching a glimpse of the nervous-looking driver. Down the road he was joined by his mate, as per normal, and I overtook them and headed to where the ambush was planned. Harry and Gordon saw me arrive and quickly set up the diversion signs. They were dressed like road workers in overalls and heavy boots.

Meanwhile, I turned the car around and waited. It was my job to pull up in front of the van, forcing it to stop, while the others piled in on the security guards.

We were waiting, my hands clammy on the wheel and eyes sweeping the street. What I couldn't see was that a night-watchman from the genuine works site had wandered up the road and seen the diversion signs. He scratched his head, wondering what was going on, and began taking them down. He dumped them on the grassy verge and wandered away.

Gordon and Harry sprinted out of hiding and re-erected them just before the van came into view.

This is where I deviated from the plan. Instead of simply pulling out in front of the van, I rammed it head-on, so that my chest hit the steering wheel and I heard the metal crunch and twist. The guards were totally shocked as the doors were flung open and rough hands pulled them out. They were coshed over the head, only glancing blows, designed to mark but not injure them.

Meanwhile Charlie crawled into the back and opened the door. We formed a chain and slung boxes from hand to hand into the boot of the car. Three minutes was all it took. We drove off, leaving the guards dazed but unhurt. A few streets away we parked the car and transferred the loot to another.

We scored more than sixty grand. It was a brilliant coup and my star was rising, certainly with Gordon and Charlie, who suddenly were looking at me as if I was 'the man'. Not as the leader – no titles were ever conferred – but as 'the man' whose opinions and strategies were given weight.

In the underworld, word spread quickly. If I had the respect of people like Gordon and Charlie, then I was worth following. To a certain extent it gave me power, which could be used in various ways.

A month later, I saw the driver and gave him his eight grand. He deserved every penny for, just as I'd predicted, the police gave him a terrible time. I met a doctor from Chelsea who told me how he'd been asked to help investigate an armoured car robbery. He had to examine two security guards to see if their injuries had been self-inflicted.

'The driver and his mate were suspects,' the doctor said. 'It was diabolical. They said they were attacked and rammed, but the police didn't believe them. Apparently they'd been seen unloading the boxes at the side of the road.'

My initial reaction was amazement. Obviously, the police thought they had the right men. They interrogated them for days, claiming they had eye-witnesses and admissions from accomplices, the works. But the driver and his mate kept stum and there was nothing the police could do about it.

Throughout all this, I was overseas. Chad had instilled in me the policy of never being available for questioning regardless of whether you were likely to get pulled in by the police or not. The best defence is not to be there.

The firm made a loose arrangement to meet in Paris a week afterwards. Meanwhile, Franny and I spent three days in Amsterdam, staying at the Amstel and cruising the canals in floating restaurants and bars. When we got to Paris we booked into the George V, but after four days nobody had turned up. I made one or two calls to London and there seemed to be nothing connecting us to the armoured van job. Nobody had been pulled in for questioning. So where were they?

I had someone visit my flat and ask the porter and gardener if police had been around asking questions. The answer was no.

Ten days later, I came home from Paris not knowing what to expect. It turned out that Gordon and Charlie had disappeared to the country. Meanwhile, Harry had told his wife that he was going away, then taken the key to my place and spent ten days locked away with another young lady having a torrid romantic tryst.

'Fuck going to Paris,' he said. 'I've got her here and that's it.'

Eventually he divorced his wife and he married the girl. They were together for the next 26 years.

There were bits and pieces of work over the next few months, none of which made the headlines. I had spare time and plenty of money – I could afford to pick and choose.

Paddy had finally come home from the Hate Factory, a little poorer than he anticipated because of the money Ivy lost, but he was never one to run short. Having been away for nine months, he ordered a coming-home present for himself – a customized racing Healey. Having owned an Aston and a Porsche, he couldn't resist this machine, which growled like a rabid dog and seemed to be rocket propelled.

I drove it home from Worthing for him and gave it some stick. After pottering around in the Gordini and TR, the modified Healey was a seriously fast car that created a whiplash effect among pedestrians turning their heads to catch a glimpse. Of course, I couldn't resist getting my own. It cost £850 second-hand and was part of an experimental series that had disc brakes all round.

In July I was back in France, where Franny and I rented a flat for the summer. Paddy had bought a thirty-foot boat and decided to tow it down to Cannes behind the Healey. It was incongruous seeing a bloody great thing being towed by such a small car.

Mickey Ball, another celebrated wheel man, had also bought a Healey, a red and black one. He and Roy followed us down. It was bizarre really; there were three of us buzzing around Cannes in almost identical cars, driving like maniacs.

Peter Scott was also there in his 3.8 Jaguar XK140 fixed-head coupé, which had once belonged to Little Freddy. It was like an overseas conference for London's criminal fraternity.

Franny and I spent a few days at the Château Madrid, which had once been one of the Grimaldis' palaces. We would sit and take lunch on the terrace, looking down over the coast. Later we would meet the others for a drink, before wandering along the promenade to dine, fashionably late.

With everyone driving sports cars, it was a race every time we got behind the wheel. The women were terrified. They knew that at the end of the night, wherever we were, it was going to be a hairy ride home as the three Healeys raced along the narrow, winding roads, sliding into corners and accelerating away. Fortunately, I had better braking, but not the same power as the others.

During the day I slept, lounged around the pool and even tried my hand at water-skiing with Roy and Mickey, who were mad keen. They were both little guys and used to make me sick the way they carved up the water, while I was so uncoordinated I spent most of the time getting water up my ring. Of course it didn't help when they'd yell out, 'Are you all right now?'

'Yeah, I'm fine,' I shouted back, clinging on to the tow rope for grim death.

'Are you sure you're all right?'

'I'm OK, really.'

Then the knife would come out and they'd cut the rope and I'd swallow six gallons of water while they were laughing and rolling around in the boat.

Down at the Chunga one night, a madhouse café-cum-restaurant next to the Martinez, we suddenly got to talking about running with the bulls in Pamplona. About twenty of us decided to go, but for one reason or another – ie, they sobered up – this was whittled down to just three: Chad, Paddy and myself. Franny was quite happy to stay with her sister Barbara while we embarked on a men-only expedition.

We pumped up the tyres, changed the oil and set off one morning, bombing along the coast on a six-hundred-mile journey to Pamplona. Chad was with Paddy and I had the luggage. It was almost like a race.

When we got to Biarritz we'd been driving all day. Paddy pulled into the Hotel Palais and immediately smashed into the front wall. After spending so many hours staring far ahead, he couldn't adjust to the shorter distance and didn't stop in time. There was no great damage apart from his pride.

That night, we tore up the town. Chad had some dodgy traveller's cheques and even dodgier dollar bills which he'd nicked from somewhere, so we were loaded. We ended up having a party with some girls who all got paid in crooked dollars and thought we were millionaires the way we lavished money on them.

Come the next morning, all a bit bleary-eyed, we were packing up when I realized that I didn't have my passport. I was straight on the phone to Franny, obviously blaming her because I was so angry at myself.

The nearest airport was miles away and flights were irregular. The quickest way for me to get the passport was to drive back to Cannes, pick it up and then drive back again –

a journey of five or six hundred miles. Not surprisingly, I was rapidly losing interest in Pamplona.

Chad and Paddy were undeterred. They decided to drive on, book in and wait for me.

So I set off, still relatively early, before the heat took hold of the day. I was driving with no shirt on, carrying a bit of excess weight because I no longer needed the ability to run or climb like in the past. As the miles disappeared, my mood grew brighter. The scenery was beautiful and it was a lovely day to be driving.

On a straight stretch of road not far from Arles, something happened ahead. I slowed down a little and saw two cars, Citroëns, racing each other along the tree-lined road. One of them lost control and they bumped together, bouncing off and sending a car spending into the path of a lorry coming in the other direction. The collision sent the lorry directly towards me and it literally sheared the Healey in half and then careered into a tree.

I remembered thinking, This is it! and then I passed out.

Coming to, I had the awful realization that something was wrong. I leaned over to get out of the car and put my arm down. It was simply hanging there on a flap of flesh and fibre. There was smoke coming from the engine and any second it was going to explode. I managed to crawl out before collapsing again.

This time I came to and was staring up someone's bare legs. It was a monk, and I could vaguely see a big pair of hairy bollocks under his habit. He was intoning some Latin litany over me and all I could think was, This is France, they mustn't cut off my arm, what's the French for 'Do not cut off my arm'?

'*Ne coupe me bras. No coupe me bras*,' I mumbled.

When the ambulance arrived, there were crowds of people around me. I heard them talking, '*Il est mort*.' Who's dead? I'm not fucking dead, I thought. Later I discovered they were talking about the lorry driver, whose head had made no impression on the tree.

As I was lifted into the ambulance, I was telling them, 'Don't cut off me arm, *ne coupe me bras*, don't cut off my arm.' Finally one of the paramedics said, in quite good English, 'You don't have to worry, we're not going to cut it off. You'll be all right.'

When I regained consciousness I was lying in bed with plaster where my arm used to be. In a panic, I tried to move my fingers, just to make sure they were still there. It was a small private hospital which had been the asylum where Van Gogh had been at Arles. Now owned by a surgeon, it was stinking hot and full of flies and I lay there sweating, with only a towel over the family jewels for decency's sake.

Franny arrived with her sister. The accident had been headlined in the press as 'Two dead, two injured' – the tourist, me, was one of the dead. They booked into the Caesar Hotel in Arles so they could visit every day. Harry also arrived, and Roller Reg. They had nearly got killed on the way when Reg fell asleep at the wheel of his new Sunbeam Alpine.

I was lying in bed reading one morning, tired of staring at the same whitewashed walls and counting flies on the windowsill, when Franny arrived on her own. She sat on the side of the bed, stroking my face with a cold flannel. I thought she looked nervous, but more beautiful than I could ever remember.

'Bruce, I've got something to tell you,' she said. 'I know this probably isn't the best time, but at least you can't run away.'

My God, what's she done? I thought.

Franny took a deep breath, looked straight at me, and said: 'I'm pregnant.'

If Franny had told me she was pregnant before the accident my first reaction would probably have been to suggest an abortion. I would have told her that I didn't want the responsibility. Maybe my brush with mortality made me realize that you can't plan everything in your life. I could so easily have been killed in the accident.

I realized that really we have very little control over our destinies. There was no point in worrying about what might happen if I got nicked. What would happen to my wife and child? Who would look after them? No-one knows what the future holds and you can't spend a lifetime second-guessing Fate.

Deep down, within all of us, there is a desire to establish a mark and leave some trace of having existed. What better legacy than to create another life, a child? I was about to be a father. Naturally, I wanted to give my kid a better start in life than the one I'd had – probably the very same thought my dad had had when I was born.

There was nothing very romantic about my marriage proposal. Looking like a leftover from a Hammer horror set, naked except for the strategic towel, encased in plaster from the waist upwards to the neck, my left arm pinned and plastered, elbow at right angle to my torso, I said, 'We'd better get married then.'

Franny, face flushed with emotion and hot from the sun, looked up from her administration of the cold flannel over my battered body and said, 'I'd like that, I would.'

A fortnight later I got an ambulance to Nice airport and was flown home. The French doctors said I would probably have to spend another two months in hospital, but when I got to St Thomas's a doctor looked at my arm and asked me who had performed the surgery.

'You're a very lucky man, Mr Reynolds,' he said when I told him. 'Your arm was saved by one of the best surgeons in Europe. You couldn't have been in better hands.' He told me to go home and a few weeks later he cut off the plaster and put my arm in a sling.

Having moved out of Lytton Grove before going to France, Franny and I were homeless. Initially we stayed at Mickey's place at Earls Court because he was still in the South of France, and from there we rented a flat in Putney Hill. For the first time it was an unfurnished place and Franny set about nesting with a rare passion.

I, too, had changed. Before the accident, I was just taking things as they came. I didn't really think in terms of the future; I didn't want to get married or be tied down. Deep down I knew that the life I was leading didn't promise marital bliss and a happy family. Inevitably, I would be caught, and you can't leave a wife alone for years without something happening. You're not the same person when you come home.

We planned to keep the whole affair secret and marry quietly at St Mary Abbot's Kensington Register Office, but a wedding photographer gave the game away when he was sent to Paddy's address instead of my own.

'What's all this about a wedding, Bruce?' asked Paddy.

I had to come clean.

Any thoughts of a quiet ceremony were noisily shouted down.

On 7 September 1961, I said, 'I do' to Frances Margaret Allen. The bride looked radiant, dressed in a brown silk outfit by Mary Quant. I wore a suit from Kilgour, French & Stanley. Among the spectators were Rick, Roy, Mickey, Paddy, Roller Reg and Harry, and a jolly good time was had by all.

23

We went to the south of France for the honeymoon, spending a week in Nice and another on the Riviera. The second half was spent scrabbling in the dirt on our hands and knees trying to find buried treasure.

It was the hoard from a jewel robbery that had had its beginnings years earlier when Chad and I had looked through the windows of Van Cleef and Cartier, wondering how we could get our hands on the baubles inside.

Before the accident, when we were living it up on the Riviera, we had reviewed our prospects, tailing a few people home from the casinos and making tentative plans. Roy found a particularly interesting target. There was a jeweller's in the foyer of a luxury hotel whose prize possession was a 30-carat emerald. The stone was valued at almost thirty grand.

All the big jewellers had been hit, at one time or another, by the heavy French mobs armed with machine-guns. Security was tightened but at this store the woman had an assistant who at the end of each day removed all the valuable pieces, leaving what you might term the bread-and-butter stuff. She used to take the prime pieces home with her every night and it was a simple plot to follow her down the main road, force her over and take the suitcase out of the car.

While I was recuperating from the accident, Roy asked me if I wanted in.

'Do it if you can, it's entirely up to you,' I said. 'Just save me a whack.'

There were no problems. The guys even found time to do another bit of work and together the two coups were worth about a hundred grand. Of course, this was the insurance 'scream' – the actual returns were far less.

They brought some of the gear back with them, but decided it was safer to bury the rest rather than risk getting pulled by Customs.

When Franny and I left for our nuptials, Roy gave me a map and asked me to do some digging. For the first five days it was like something out of *Treasure Island*. Armed with shovels and tattered instructions, it was a matter of eight paces to the east, turn west at the old tree stump, twelve paces to the north, all that sort of thing.

But try as we might we couldn't find the jewels. Eventually I rang up Roy and he flew over for one night. Of course we'd been digging only a few inches from the prize, which was wrapped in a cloth about nine inches underground.

I had a hidey-hole built into the sub-section of the Mini that we had taken over. It was just large enough to wedge the parcel inside and re-fix the panel. Coming back through Dover, we were stopped by Customs in a random search. I opened Franny's bag, having forgotten that inside were several pages of pornography torn from a book by the Olympia Press. It was indescribable filth; the Customs officer took one look and announced that it was confiscated.

On the night of 22 March 1962, I was on a coup at the Chelsea residence of the Rothschilds, a high-profile family who were always on the books. Lady Rothschild had the sort of jewellery that went with the rank – almost Royalty, and perhaps even richer. We were after the jewellery and anything else we could find.

It seemed simple enough. Knock at the door, tie up the occupants and clean out the place. What we didn't realize was that the gate which led to the front door, and which was open during the daytime, was locked in the early evening. There was no way we could climb over it, press the doorbell and expect anyone inside to answer. The element of surprise would be entirely lost.

I called the job off and went home. The telephone rang, as I tried to sleep.

'Your wife has had a son,' a nurse said.

Nicholas Rufus Reynolds had been born at six o'clock in the morning at St Mary Abbot's, weight: six and a half pounds. As I held him in my arms, I was consumed with love for him and Franny; tired as she was, she had never looked lovelier – glowing with satisfaction, her world now complete. She gave me a painful smile and looked proudly at our baby boy, who was swaddled in a hospital blanket with only his face visible – a round, full face, almost cherubic, with a presence that commanded attention. My dad christened him 'The Bishop' the moment he saw him later that day.

After Nick was born Franny went to recuperate with Dad and my stepmother Amy in Dagenham. My family ties had grown stronger since leaving prison and Amy had badgered me for two years to marry Franny. 'If she's good enough to live with then she's good enough to marry,' she had chided.

I discovered that Amy was not as I'd imagined over the years. She had a sense of humour and a very warm character, and as time moved on we became very fond of each other. She'd been intimately involved with Franny and me from the outset, creating the family atmosphere that we'd never had.

You have to live with someone before you really know them. I got to know Amy and respected her views; she came to recognize mine, and, without being in full agreement, she accepted me honestly for what I was. We laughed together at stories from the past.

'You were', she said with a wry grin, 'a bit of a handful!'

After a week at Dad's, Franny came home. It was a big thing for us both; now we had our first real home, and a baby.

To an outsider we must have looked like any other family – taking Sunday walks to the Green Man, pushing the pram, a pint of Young's Best Bitter and then home for roast beef. But domestic stability and an extra mouth to feed didn't change my life. I still had the hunger.

Gordon came up with an interesting piece of information from one of his many ladies. He was a mad cocksman, who managed to pull a succession of good-looking birds – many of them happily married, or in long-term relationships. One of his amours was also having an affair with a guy who owned half a dozen good restaurants and was always boasting to her about how he didn't believe in banks.

Originally he came from Italy and had inherited a love for keeping his cash close at hand. He lived in a big house in Clapham, not far from the Common. Although he was rarely at home, he had a girlfriend who spent so much time in the house I could have sworn she was more guard dog than live-in lover.

Somehow we had to lure her away for long enough to get inside.

Again the plot was simple. One of the firm went round there at about half-past seven, dressed in a dark-blue mac and peaked cap. He knocked on the door and waited for her to answer.

'Madam, could you get dressed and come with me please, your husband's in hospital.'

'What is it?'

'Nothing seriously wrong, he's had a fall. He's asked for you and the doctors want you to be there. There's nothing to worry about. There's a car waiting to take you to him.'

She collected her coat and was driven to St George's Hospital by Hyde Park. Parking out front, the driver said, 'Go into reception, give your name and they'll direct you to the right place.'

Off she went. We reckoned we had a minimum of about forty minutes from the time she left the house to when she discovered it was a ruse and returned home.

It went without a hitch and we cleared three grand.

Old-fashioned pillow talk was a Godsend, particularly because a rich man can make no greater enemy than a spurned lover or a jealous wife.

A pal of mine had a girlfriend of twelve years' standing who worked for a married businessman with an office in Park Lane. As far as I knew she wasn't having an affair with her boss, but he was certainly doing his best to get into her drawers. Having her work late one night, he tried to impress her by pulling out trays of uncut stones: diamonds, emeralds, rubies, the works.

Well, just before his business went to the wall (he'd been milking the company for years along with his partner – they eventually got nicked and got five years apiece), he moved the contents of the office to his manor in Bognor.

'The safe went too,' my pal said, 'but she doesn't know what was inside.'

'That's good enough for me,' I said. 'We'll go down and have a look.'

The house was on a sought-after estate called Pagham, full of mansions with swimming-pools and two-car garages. At the local library, I checked the electoral roll and discovered there were two people living there, both surnamed Paxos, and prefixed with Leonard and Joan. Unfortunately, we also discovered that the house was rarely empty. We would have to do it at night and tie them up.

At three o'clock, Harry, Roy, Chas, Gordon and I moved in, taking out a pane of glass by the door and reaching inside to unlock the bolts. Our ringer, a Jaguar, was parked on the street with the keys in the ignition to make a quicker getaway.

All of a sudden I heard a warning whistle. PC Plod on his bicycle was riding down the road, shining his torch into the front yards. He saw the Jaguar, didn't recognize it, and peered inside. Next minute, the door was open and he plucked out the ignition keys and slid them in his pocket before riding off into the night.

What's his thing? I thought. He must have assumed he was protecting one of the owners by safeguarding his car keys. Back at the station he would write up the occurrence book and return the keys in the morning.

Of course, he could also check if the car was stolen – a risk we couldn't afford to take. Regretfully, I called off the job. Roy made a makeshift key from silver foil and managed to get the car started. We retreated to a caravan owned by an obliging publican who'd said we could flop there for a few days, saving the journey back and forth to London.

We tried again the next night, but just as we pulled out of the caravan site I spotted a police car. Obviously Old Bill didn't like the look of us because they gave chase. Soon we were tearing through Worthing, screeching around corners and steaming over intersections at high speed, trying to shake them off. No sooner had we lost one patrol car than we drove down a road and found another two waiting for us. They chased us almost all the way back to London. At one point we thought we'd lost them until we reached a small one-lane bridge coming down the coast. As we slowed to cross, a patrol car almost drew level and we took off again. But Roy was at the wheel and our pursuers didn't stand a chance.

It has always been one of my failings that I can't let go of something. I wanted this job badly, in spite of the false alarms. It promised to be a right touch and so I did my best to keep the others jollied up. We went down once again and this time managed to get into the house. The guy and his wife were sound asleep when we pounced and trussed them up against chairs.

Straightaway, the woman said: 'You're too late, it's all gone.' She was a right old battle-axe, cursing at everyone and stamping her feet. Five of us cowered as she ranted. 'Get me another cushion. I insist on having another cushion here. Don't you dare tie me. Why don't you take those masks off? What's the matter with you? You're all cowards, aren't you?'

Anyway, we cut the safe open and lo and behold there was nothing inside, apart from bits and pieces – barely enough to pay expenses. We trawled through the rest of the house without success, apart from discovering that the businessman had a villa in the South of France.

That's it, I thought: that's where he's got the stuff. Now who can we get to finance the trip to the South of France?

I costed the trip. It would mean spending three weeks, hiring cars and – naturally – staying somewhere like the Carlton in Cannes. The whole exercise would cost several grand, which was OK if you were guaranteed a big score from the villa. In the end, I couldn't get anyone interested in financing the job, so it died a natural death.

As one door closed, another opened. Through a guy in the Midlands who ran a chain of betting shops, we learned that each week the football pools coupons and money were collected from him, taken to the nearest railway station and put on a train to William Hill in central London. His own shops contributed a grand, but with other betting shops likely to have the same routine there was potentially a big score.

A lorry delivered the mail bag to Redditch station. We knew the route and timings, so when the truck parked Harry manoeuvred a car behind it, boxing the driver in. I strolled over and took the mailbag off the seat next to him.

'What are you doing?' he shouted.

'What do you think I'm doing? I'm robbing you, you stupid bastard!'

We sped off with three grand – a nice morning's work. But if three grand came from this small area what about the rest of the country? The train could have been packed with pools takings, all being transferred to William Hill. And because of the timings of entries, most would be transported on the same day.

The following week we were waiting at King's Cross Station as the train arrived. Bang on schedule, an estate car pulled up and about thirty bags were loaded into the back. Following at a discreet distance, we tailed the van all the way to a head office of William Hill's near the Barbican.

Thirty bags! We had got three grand from just one of them. This promised to be a nice bit of money and, more importantly, there were only two people driving the vehicle – hardly what you'd call tight security.

I had already co-opted Charlie and Gordon for the job when our contact in the Midlands put a dampener on things. He had found out that, although he had a particular arrangement to send money, most betting shops sent cheques.

For a week we had lived in hope, but not all was lost. A thought had lodged – a very interesting one – about how much money was being transferred around the country on trains. It wasn't an original idea. Harry told me how Billy Hill would always tell his boys that 'trains are the thing'. He would send his gang out to railway stations to see what they could find, although I couldn't understand the logic. You can see all the mailbags you want, but it won't tell you what's in them. For that you need inside information.

In late 1962 Buster Edwards stumbled upon just that. He was told about heavy boxes, which he believed to be the wages for railway workers at Swindon, that were loaded under tight security on to the Irish Mail train each week at Paddington.

Buster and Gordon went to Paddington for a recce and followed the boxes on to the Irish Mail. They got off at

Swindon and saw them being unloaded. Again, security was tight; the only way of taking the money would be to stop the train between stations by pulling the communication cord.

We decided to have a trial run. Buster and Flossy (Bill Jennings) went on the train; Gordon and one of his associates drove to a disused factory, which bordered the line at West Drayton, where they would do the pick-up.

Flossy shut himself in a toilet on the train and Buster waited outside. When they reached the signal box at Hayes, Buster banged on the door and Flossy pulled the communication cord. There was a screech of steel and the train braked to a halt. Buster and Flossy jumped down on to the track and found themselves directly alongside the factory. They cleared the fence and were picked up by Gordon in a lane.

A date was fixed for the robbery and we assembled at Paddington. This time, a fellow called Bonko (Denis Marlowe) was going to drive the van. Gordon, with a crowbar under his coat, joined the rest of us on the train. As before, Flossy hid in the toilet and Buster stood outside. The rest of us stayed in our seats until the train reached Ealing. Then, one by one, we got up and walked down the corridor towards the guard's van at the rear.

Gordon smashed through the lock and leapt into the van, keeping his crowbar raised to give the guard the message. Charlie and I set to work on the boxes, both of us armed with bolt cutters. We'd known they would be secured to the wall of the carriage, of course, but this was ridiculous. The boxes were fucking festooned with chains. We set to, totally engrossed in what we were doing.

Back along the corridor, meanwhile, Buster had seen the signal box at Hayes and banged on the door of the toilet. Flossy had pulled the communication cord, but nothing had happened. He pulled it again. Nothing. He came out into the corridor and ran with Buster along to us in the guard's van. They burst in as Charlie and I were still going at the chains like lunatics and just as the others were opening the outside doors, ready to offload. To their horror, they saw the first buildings of the factory premises shoot past.

Buster grabbed a likely looking control wheel and started turning it like mad. The brakes engaged and the train slowed to a halt – the best part of a mile from where Bonko was waiting for us with the van.

'We're fucked,' Gordon said succinctly.

There was nothing for it but to run. Some of us grabbed boxes and jumped down on to the tracks. But though they were made of wood they were lead-lined and extremely heavy. Buster dropped his first, then I mine. Charlie managed to carry his as far as a pig farm which was next to the factory, but when the farmer came out of his house with a large dog, he dumped it in a hedge.

'The train's stopped,' Buster beamed at the man. 'We're going to get help.'

We all jumped the hedge and ran through the farm towards the factory. Bonko was waiting patiently in the van, and as we jumped in the back he gunned the engine. Only Gordon had managed to come away with a box. As the van sped towards London we jemmied it open. It contained precisely seven hundred quid.

24

Rather than be disheartened, I vowed to strike back. The next target was also ambitious but the size of the prize was worth it.

Charlie had been introduced to a man who worked in Comet House, BOAC's admin offices at London Airport (as it was known then). The guy had inside info on what happened to the wages of the entire staff of BOAC.

Comet House was the largest building in a complex of offices and warehouses on the south side of the airport, separated from the passenger terminals by runways. The A4 from London to the South West ran along one side, and on the other side of a tall wire fence was a small road used by airport vehicles.

However, the most interesting building as far as we were concerned was not Comet House but one a few hundred yards away: a branch of Barclays Bank.

'A security van arrives outside it each Tuesday morning,' the informant had told Charlie. 'Two guards load a box on board that contains between three and four hundred thousand quid in wages. Then the van is driven over to Comet House.'

The van was always followed by three cashiers, and sometimes, even though it was only a very short distance, by a police car as well. Charlie's informant envisaged lifting the money from the vault in the bank – which only goes to show what ordinary, law-abiding citizens know about the science of robbery.

I spent some time walking round the buildings, an easy thing to do in pre-terrorist days. I could see only one major obstacle. After the five-minute journey from the bank to Comet House the police car waited while the money was carried inside. Any snatch while the patrol car was near by was likely to end up in a bloodbath, and I didn't fancy going in that strong. Then again, this was a very tasty bit of money.

Back in London, we pulled together the best firm available. Gordon was already on board and Buster, who was living with his wife as Mr and Mrs Derek Glass at 214 St Margaret's Road, Twickenham, didn't take much convincing.

Dressed as smart executives, Gordon and Buster took a drive out to the airport one Tuesday morning. They wandered around Comet House as if they belonged to the place. Gordon hung around in the foyer, apparently engrossed in a copy of the FT, while Buster took the lift to the top floor and went into the Gents. As he stood at the urinal he realized he could see the entrance to the bank, and proceeded to take the longest piss in history. At last the security van arrived, and once the box was loaded he timed its journey from the bank to Comet House.

Gordon watched from behind his newspaper as the two guards offloaded the heavy box on to a trolley and wheeled it through the main doors and past him to the lift. The lift doors closed and he watched the floor indicator lights. As we expected, it stopped at the first floor, the cashier's office.

Buster travelled down in the lift and the two of them sauntered back to their car. On the way, they passed two young chauffeurs who were chatting in the front seat of a spanking new Jag. Roy James and Mickey Ball, the best wheels men in London, were ready, willing and able.

The first full meeting of the firm was held in Buster's flat. There were eight of us – Roy, Mickey, Gordon, Charlie, Buster, Flossy, Harry and the thief of the moment – me. We'd all been to Comet House by this time, and the general consensus was that the job was a goer. I agreed with Gordon and Buster that the only way to do it was a snatch, and made a few suggestions.

The final plan was that some of the firm would enter the building disguised in bowler hats and suits, then hide in the Gents on the top floor until they saw the van pull away from the bank. They'd go down in the lift and overpower the guards as they waited in the foyer. Roy and Mickey, dressed again as chauffeurs, would be in two Jags in the car park. The money would go in the first vehicle with three members of the gang, and everybody else would pile into the second. The getaway would not be back out of the main entrance but along the perimeter road and out through a gate. In theory we'd be in Hounslow before the police reached Comet House.

I still wasn't entirely satisfied and kept raising questions, trying to point out the flaws. 'Well, what if this happens? Or if the police decide to do this . . .'

Of course, the others howled me down. 'Christ, Bruce, how often is something like that going to happen?'

'It's not how often I'm worried about, you only need to get it once.'

Although it seemed a little hit and miss, finally I relented and went along with the plan. The agreement, however, was that if the police were escorting the van, we would abandon the job.

Gordon began looking for a way through the wire fence for our escape route. On a recce one night, he discovered a gate secured with a padlock and chain. He drove with a friend in his own Jaguar to ironmongers all over London in search of bolt cutters. He ended up buying two pairs, and the night before the robbery he drove out to the airport with Buster and cut the chain.

By 9 a.m. on Tuesday 20 November we had taken up our positions around Comet House. Roy and Mickey were in the driving seats of their Jags; I sat behind Roy, studying my copy of the *FT*; behind Mickey was Bonko. Both of us carried furled-up umbrellas in which the stems had been replaced by iron bars.

Gordon, Charlie and Harry took up station on the fifth floor, where they were joined by Flossy and Buster, all dressed in suits and a variety of hats to conceal their rolled-up stocking masks. Gordon, who had dyed his hair black, wore a checked cap and a false moustache. Flossy stood by the lift, waiting for a signal from Buster who was watching the bank entrance from the urinal.

The van arrived and the money was loaded. Buster was just about to give the signal when a police car drew up; he know at once that we'd have to abort. Down in the car park, we saw the same thing and knew that the job was off. There had been a chance of it happening, so everybody was rather philosophical. There would be other Tuesdays.

The following Friday night, Gordon checked the gate and discovered that the broken chain had been replaced. This was a problem, because if we cut the chain again an alert security man might work out that something naughty was afoot. Gordon therefore visited the old metalsmith in Chiswick who had fitted the iron bars to our umbrellas and got him to provide a false link for the chain. It looked just like the others, but was cleverly made to pull apart. Gordon went out to the airport again, cut the chain, and introduced the false link.

The following Tuesday we repeated the plan. As before, each of us had his favourite cosh concealed in a special pocket in his trousers or in the umbrellas. Gordon favoured a Guardia Civil truncheon he'd acquired in Madrid; Buster's was a foot of inch-and-a-quarter piping, filled with lead and bound with tape. Charlie carried a length of cable, also bound with tape.

Gordon, Charlie and Harry followed Buster into the Gents and found to their dismay that this week the room was supervised by an elderly cloakroom attendant. He hadn't been there the week before, or on any of the recces. They spent many minutes washing their hands, straightening their ties and generally preening themselves, trying to distract his attention away from Buster. The old boy was clearly interested in why this executive in a pinstripe suit should be spending so long at the urinal without anything seeming to happen. At long last, the security van drew away from the bank and Buster zipped himself up. It was the signal for Bill that the job was on. The van was unescorted.

The two Jags were in the car park adjacent. Bonko and I were in the back seat, wearing bowlers and looking every inch the city gents. We saw the wages van go round with the three security guys and stop in front of Comet House. As they went inside, we followed.

Upstairs, the lift arrived and Flossy threw the switch to keep it in position. The others filed out past the puzzled attendant and Buster went to the window in the corridor overlooking the entrance of Comet House. After several seconds he checked his watch: the van should have arrived, but it hadn't. The lift bell kept pinging as people on other floors impatiently pushed the call buttons.

Then, just as Flossy came out of the lift to ask Buster what was going on, they spotted the roof of the security van below. The two of them jumped into the lift to join the others and pressed the button for the ground floor. The lift started going down, then stopped. They were on the third floor. The five men swiftly turned to face the back wall, fearful of showing their faces to whoever was waiting. But nobody was there; whoever it was must have got tired of waiting and used the stairs. The doors closed and the lift descended. It stopped again, this time at the first floor. Again, nobody there. This time, as the doors closed and the lift started to move, the blokes pulled down their masks and produced their coshes.

There was an explosion of bodies as the five burst into the foyer. Everybody had a job: Gordon's and Charlie's was to attack the guards, Harry's and Flossy's to grab the box. One of the guards caught a blow behind the ear and went down. The other one dodged the coshes and made a run for the door. He ran straight into Denis and me. Denis gave him one across the head with his umbrella and he hit the floor. Just the three cashiers now. Two of them hit the deck without being asked, but the third one stood rooted to the spot, grinning at Buster as if he'd gone mad. Buster whacked him one and he fell to the floor.

Harry and Flossy made it to the door with the strongbox and the two Jags reversed at high speed to meet them. Hurling the box into the boot of Mickey's vehicle, they leapt in the back, closely followed by Denis. Behind them, running backwards, coshes at the ready and eyes on the door of Comet House, came the rest of us. We piled into Roy's car and he hit the accelerator.

We screamed out of the car park and on to the narrow perimeter road. Roy followed the fence until we came to the gate. There Buster and Charlie jumped out, both armed with bolt cutters. With Charlie guarding him, Buster ran to the gate. We saw him hesitate. He couldn't find the false link. Finally giving up, he used the bolt cutters on the chain and pulled the pieces out of the way. He swung the gate open.

As we drove out a member of the public in an Austin A40 saw what was happening and reversed, attempted to close the gap, blocking off the exit. Mickey's Jag surged on to the main road and braked almost immediately. Looking in his rear-view mirror, Mickey saw what was happening. Roy swerved to avoid the do-gooder, grazing his wing, and accelerated hard to the traffic lights, overtaking Mickey on the way. Just as we got there, however, the lights changed to red. With Mickey behind us, there was every chance that if he ran the lights, he would be hit by the cross traffic. With incredible instinct Roy swung across its path and stopped. A petrol tanker coming away from the lights screeched to a halt yards from us. All the westbound traffic was halted. A second later, Mickey was past us and Roy's foot hit the floor.

We drove fast to the garage where we were going to work the changeover. The strongbox was transferred into a van and Mickey set off in it for the place where we were going to cut the money up: Jimmy White's flat in Norbury. The Jags were abandoned with the bolt cutters still on the back seats.

Roy and Gordon were planning to travel on a motor bike but it wouldn't start, so Gordon left on foot for the underground station and went home to change out of his disguise. Buster took a bus to Vauxhall, picked up his car and drove to Jimmy's. Some of us were already there and one or two wanted to open the box immediately.

I said, 'We ain't going to open it yet. Everyone's got to be here – that's half the buzz.'

Course there was one or two people, Harry in particular, who insisted on lifting the box and shaking it around like an unopened Christmas present. 'How heavy is it? There's something shaking round inside.'

Gordon was the last to arrive, just as the first news of the robbery was going out on the radio. Denis broke the lock and forced the metal container open. Eight heads peered in and saw a single parcel.

'There's no way that's four hundred grand!' said Buster.

The parcel contained bundles of bank notes. We started undoing them. 'Oh, it's not too bad,' someone said, 'there could be three hundred grand.'

'No, you're talking nonsense,' I said. 'They're tenners and fivers. We only got sixty grand.'

When the count-up was finished, I was right. We had scored sixty-two thousand – disappointing considering we were expecting four hundred. By the time we had paid the guy who stuck up the business and looked after Jimmy for lending us his flat, we came out with six grand apiece.

Harry took it harder than most. He'd had enough of going out, risking all and things not always going to plan. The stress was enormous; he'd reached the end of his tether. He took me aside afterwards. 'I've had enough, Bruce. I had this down for retirement money. I was gonna put it into a business with Max.'

'What do you mean?'

'I expected more but six grand will have to do. We had some great times, but I'm giving it up.'

OK it was a disappointment, but to me and the rest of the guys it just meant we kept on going. Retirement money is one of those things. Everyone thinks that when the motherlode is struck, they will settle down and give the game up. It rarely happens, of course. Maybe it's in the blood.

As usual I had already made plans to disappear overseas until the heat went out of the police investigation. I flew straight to Paris and from there to Tangier, where Gordon joined me. After two weeks he sailed to Gibraltar, hoping to line up some watch smuggling. Meanwhile I flew back to Paris and Franny joined me. She left Nick with Mary Manson and another friend, Rene, who had looked after him before. Mary always had children around her – her own daughter's children or someone else's.

We spent Christmas in Paris, almost a ghost city in late December. There were only six people in the dining-room at the George V on Christmas Day. Afterwards we rented a car and spent New Year in Tours at the invitation of a nice chap who worked for Unesco and wanted us to meet his family. Then we drove south, booking into the Metropole at Monte Carlo.

We were there for a month, alternating between nights out on the piss drinking champagne or lying in bed reading Ed McBains and eating chocolate. During the day, we went on long walks and had egg on toast and English tea at the Scotch Teahouse. Although it seemed very refined and romantic, beneath the surface Franny and I were having problems. Perhaps it was being away from Nick, or the pressures of spending so much time in each other's company. Whatever the case, we were drinking too much and the fights began.

One night we came home pissed and as I was following her up the stairs I gave her a playful smack on the bum. Obviously, I hit her too hard, because instead of treating it as an affectionate gesture she got the hump and gave me an earful. The old alcohol reacted and I chased her up the stairs into our room, where she had locked herself in the bathroom.

I got undressed, but wasn't about to sleep the drink off. Instead I climbed out the window stark naked – we were on the fourth floor – over the balcony railing, and got in through the bathroom window. The last thing I remembered was chasing Franny, trying to whack her bum with the toilet brush. I collapsed on the bed laughing.

Next morning, I woke and she was gone.

'She came down and booked another room last night,' the desk clerk said.

When I found her room I tried to apologize, using my best hangdog expression.

'This can't go on,' said Franny. 'This is madness. We can't be drinking if this sort of thing happens.'

'I think that the best thing really is for you to go home,' I said.

'Yes, I thought the same thing. We can't live like this.'

At midday, we drove to Nice airport and booked her a ticket. With a couple of hours to wait, we went to the Negresco. It was absolutely beautiful. Sitting there, drinking our fourth champagne cocktail, the world started to look different. I looked at Franny and thought, What does she want to go home for? And I could see she was looking at me thinking, This is madness, why am I going home?

Unfortunately, neither one of us wanted to put it into words.

Almost in tears, I saw her on to the plane and waved goodbye before returning to the hotel. It was totally crazy and I had no idea what I was going to do. The next morning, I received a telegram. Opening it, I feared the worst, but instead of saying she wanted a divorce, it simply read: 'Arriving back at five o'clock.'

Franny brought Nick with her, and we started looking for a house to rent. There was a real estate agency in Antibes called Scott-Douglas which was run by a typical Englishman abroad with strangled vowels and no taste in summer clothes.

'Are you any relation to Jimmy Scott-Douglas?' I asked him.

'No. Is he a friend of yours?'

'Yeah.'

Sir James Scott-Douglas was a larger-than-life real character, best known for his involvement in motor racing. He was also a regular at the Star and the Marlborough, which was how I'd met him. He spent his life living it up on a variety of bequests that had been left to him by rich relatives. Whenever one of these arrived, he would take off on wild jaunts with his cronies, trying to spend the money in record time. On one expedition, he bought a boat, freighted it up with booze, and set sail with half a dozen pals to nowhere in particular. They ended up a year later stranded down in Mara, where he sold the boat, had one last binge and came home.

Once it was established that I knew Jimmy, the agent thought I had a pukka background. He looked through his books and said, 'We've got this very nice villa at Haut de Cagnes.'

Haut de Cagnes was very much an arty spot, more exclusive than St Paul de Vence because it was full of people who were either famous or on their way to being famous. The villa we rented belonged to a Swedish chap who'd married a Scots lady. When he died she wanted to sell the property for £40,000 – peanuts compared to what it would cost today. It was a beautiful place – an old farmhouse built in layers up a hillside so that from any room you could look out across the rolling countryside. I loved the spring sunshine, the views of the Alpes Maritimes, the mimosa, the bougainvillea, the lemon trees in the terraced gardens. Most of all, I loved spending time with Nick, watching him grow and utter new words. Franny, too, was happier than I could ever remember. She had my undivided attention, free from the stresses and traumas of 'business'. Although she had never really understood me or what motivated my career, she accepted it because love is like that.

The house had a huge wine cellar which we were welcome to use. 'Just tick off what you've had, we'll sort it out later,' the agent said. We took him at his word.

It was wonderful. There was a little market in Cagnes where we got our supplies and once a week we would run into Monte Carlo to see an English film. Harry came out and spent a week; and later my stepmother Amy, who had become a doting grandmother to Nick.

Our four months in the villa was the realization of everything I had ever worked towards. Maybe I was role-playing to a degree, but I became that person. I was rich, successful, with a wonderful wife and son, living in one of the most beautiful locations on earth. I wore polka-dot bow-ties from Sulka, shirts from Washington Tremlett, suits from Kilgour French & Stanley, shoes by Lobb. I was the image that I created.

When I returned to London, I came back a different person, stronger, more certain of my power. If I told people to do something, they did it. My confidence was absolute.

The police had moved swiftly against what Fleet Street called the 'City Gents' gang, guessing almost immediately who was involved. The detailed planning pointed the finger at Buster and me, and Roy and Mickey were the only drivers in London capable of doing what they'd done. What was more, officers remembered seeing theatrical make-up when they'd last raided Gordon's flat.

By the day after the coup they'd pulled Charlie, Gordon, Roy and Mickey. There was a line-up at Cannon Row which by all accounts was more pantomime than identity parade. Roy wasn't much bigger than five feet four and Gordon was at least a foot taller. In the identity parade, they gave everyone a bowler hat and false moustache and said, 'Put these on.' Roy's hat came down over his ears, while Gordon's sat on top of his head and made him look eight foot tall. Was it any wonder that no-one was picked out?

Since no evidence had been found in the men's homes, the police had no alternative but to let them go. That was when Gordon had left the country, flying to join me in Tangier.

However, the Flying Squad were not about to give up. By the second week of December they were ready for another identity parade. Gordon had returned to England and together with the other three was taken to Twickenham police station. Again they were dressed in bowler hats and false moustaches. One by one the witnesses filed past. Then the suspects were told to change into workmen's overalls. Still no joy for Old Bill.

They did, however, find one piece of evidence. The ironmonger who had sold Gordon the bolt cutters had been suspicious and had followed him outside and jotted down the registration number of the car. Brought in front of the identity parade, he wrongly identified Mickey as being Flossy, who had been with Gordon. Mickey cracked. He realized that he looked a lot like Flossy, and knew that if he got blamed for the violence in the foyer he could be sent down for a very long time. He confessed to the officers present that he was guilty, but only as the driver of a getaway car.

There were two more identity parades that week. Roy was released, but both Charlie and Gordon were identified by witnesses and charged. They refused to make statements: they knew that a charge was not the end of the war, just the start of another battle.

Mickey immediately went to work trying to cop a plea. He eventually got five years for being the driver. The others were charged, pleaded not guilty and were remanded in custody.

All the while, I was relaxing in France, wining and dining and being kept abreast of developments by Harry.

'It seems to be all right,' he told me. 'I've spoken to someone at the Yard. Fifteen hundred quid and your name gets taken off the list.'

The last thing a professional crim needs is a squeaky-clean solicitor. The best sort of brief is one who can dream up good alibis and dispense 'drinks' to whoever requires them – usually policemen and witnesses.

Gordon's brief was called Brian Field, a solicitor's clerk for John Wheater & Co. He was only in his twenties, but he had his head screwed on and had acted in the past for Buster and Gordon. Their relationship was not the normal one between solicitor and client; it had hidden depths, which involved supplying Gordon with good information about the contents of his clients' country houses. A measure of the success of the relationship was that Field's employer, John Wheater, owned a battered old Ford and lived in a rundown neighbourhood, but Brian drove a gleaming new Jag and had a beautiful house in Pangbourne.

Brian moved to get Gordon bail. Normally, given the seriousness of the crime, this would have been out of the question, but Charlie's pals had been handing out thick envelopes and bail was granted without opposition. Concocting a watertight alibi was a little more difficult, but again Brian came up with the goods. On the morning of the robbery, so the story went, Gordon was in Jermyn Street visiting his shirtmaker. He'd gone into a coffee shop, and had knocked into a customer, causing him to spill coffee on his trousers.

Brian also made arrangements to discredit a witness who said he'd seen Gordon from the top deck of a double-decker bus, getting out of a Jaguar. Hiring a similar bus, he went with an 'independent' photographer and took pictures of the Comet House car park that proved that the man could not possibly have seen what he claimed to have seen.

At the trial, Charlie was acquitted at the end of the prosecution case upon the direction of the judge. Two witnesses swore that they had seen him, but in different places and at exactly the same time. The defence that Brian had prepared for Gordon did not fare so well. The alibi was challenged, and in any case several witnesses swore that Gordon had been at the scene.

Gordon decided that he'd have to nobble the jury. From where he sat in the dock he studied the faces of each of the twelve people in front of him. He picked one man who looked weak and – still being free on bail – followed him after the day's proceedings to a house off the Finchley Road. He returned later that night with Buster and knocked at the door. There was no reply.

The next day was the last day of the trial. Gordon got up early and drove back to Finchley. Just after nine o'clock, he saw the juror come out of his house. Gordon drew up alongside.

'Fancy seeing you here,' Gordon grinned. 'Can I give you a lift?'

The man did not seem too put out, and as they drove towards the Old Bailey they chatted about the way the trial was going.

'What do you think the verdict will be?' Gordon asked.

The man did not answer immediately. He stared straight ahead at the road, then turned his head and said, 'I've done a bit of bird myself, you know.'

'Well then, you'll realize there's a little present in it for you if the verdict is not guilty?' Gordon said.

Opening the glove compartment he handed the man a bundle containing five hundred pounds in used fivers.

'No need for that,' the man said.

They shook hands on it and Gordon parked the car. They went their separate ways into the courtroom.

Summing up, the judge reminded the jury that by law their decision must be unanimous. The foreman returned after several hours and announced that they were unable to agree. The judge sent them out again, but again they returned with the same result. The judge had no alternative but to order a retrial.

Gordon had paid handsomely for Brian Field's skills but decided that next time round he could not rely on the goodwill of jurors. He decided to tamper with the evidence.

The witness on the bus had been discredited by the photographer's evidence, but the ironmonger still swore that it was Gordon's car that he had seen Mickey Ball climbing into. The theatrical make-up found in his flat could not readily be explained away either, and another witness was adamant that it was Gordon who had hit him.

Gordon visited the owner of his flat, an actor, and got him to claim that the make-up was his, left in Gordon's flat when he was collecting the rent. The ironmonger was more difficult to deal with. The bolt cutters had been left in the abandoned Jaguars, and forensic evidence clearly linked them with the severed chain. The ironmonger stood by his claim that he had seen Mickey Ball get into Gordon's car. Since Mickey had pleaded guilty, Gordon was heavily implicated by this evidence if it was proved. However, Gordon knew that it had not been Mickey that had bought the bolt cutters. Gordon therefore got the friend who had actually done the buying – and who did in fact look quite a lot like Mickey Ball – to come to court dressed in workman's overalls.

The toughest evidence to deal with was going to be that of the witness who claimed that Gordon had assaulted him. He was quite emphatic that the man in the checked cap had hit him, and that the man in the checked cap was Gordon.

Gordon's solution was ingenious. The cap had come off during the struggle in the foyer, was in the possession of the police, and formed part of their evidence. For a mere two hundred pounds, however, a police officer was willing to replace this cap with a similar one three sizes larger. All that remained now was for the witness concerned to be persuaded to embellish his evidence a little.

Early one Sunday morning, Charlie, Gordon and Buster drove to Harrow where the man lived. Gordon could not be seen to be interfering with a witness, and when it came to the gentle art of negotiating Charlie was hardly one of the kid-gloves school, so Buster offered to do the dirty work. The outcome required was that the witness was only prepared to swear that Gordon was the man who had hit him if Gordon was wearing the cap.

The other two waited in the car at the bottom of the street while Buster went and knocked on the door. A young woman answered.

'Can I have a word with your husband?' he asked.

'Come in,' she said, leading Buster into the lounge.

The husband put down his newspaper and they shook hands.

'I'm a friend of Gordon Goody's,' Buster started. 'He saw you smile at him in court and wondered if, er, you might be prepared to help him?'

The man reached for the telephone on a small table beside him.

'I'm going to call my brother,' he said. 'Don't worry, we were expecting something like this.'

The man spoke into the phone for a few seconds and then rang off. 'He'll meet you in five minutes in the pub around the corner,' he said.

Buster left the house and walked back up the street.

'What do you reckon?' he said to Gordon and Charlie. 'Shall we clear off before this gets serious?'

'It's up to you,' said Gordon. 'But you know we'll cover you.'

Buster shrugged and walked to the pub while the others followed him in the car. He installed himself at a quiet table in the corner and watched the door. A few minutes later, a large man entered and came straight over to Buster's table.

'Let's speak in my car outside,' he said.

As they got into the vehicle, the man turned to Buster and said, 'You know, we don't want any trouble from you people.'

Buster grinned, reaching inside his coat and pulling out a wad of notes. 'Nobody's going to get hurt,' he said. 'We just thought that for a little drink your brother might add something to his evidence.'

'No need for money.' The man waved it away. 'We just don't want any violence.'

Buster explained about the cap and the man agreed that his brother would meet with Gordon sometime to rehearse his lines. He dropped Buster at a street corner; moments later he was picked up by Gordon's Jag.

At the second trial, all of Gordon's brilliant planning came to fruition. The actor gave evidence that the make-up was his. The forensic expert from the Home Office laboratory said that

there was no doubt whatsoever that the chain had been cut
by the bolt cutters found in the abandoned vehicle. The
ironmonger swore that it was Mickey Ball who had bought
just such a pair of bolt cutters from his shop on Euston Road
– but when it came to cross examination by the defence, he
spotted Flossy, who was sitting in the front row of the court
wearing workman's overalls. The ironmonger stopped in
mid-sentence. He was no longer sure about Mickey Ball. His
evidence collapsed.

The nobbled witness gave the same evidence as before, but
with a little more emphasis. Yes, Gordon Goody, wearing the
checked cap, was definitely the man who had rushed at him
in the foyer and hit him behind the ear.

'And if Gordon Goody was not wearing that cap?' asked
counsel for the defence.

'Then it could not have been Gordon Goody.'

The cap was produced and Gordon was asked by his brief
to put it on. It was handed up to the dock and Gordon stuck
it on his head. It fell over his ears and eyes.

When the jury returned its verdict of not guilty Gordon was
jubilant. Coming down into the well of the court, he passed
the prosecution benches. The chain which had fastened the
gate in the perimeter fence was lying on the table in front of
the prosecuting counsel, who was gathering up his papers.

'Well done,' the lawyer said with a knowing smile.

Gordon picked up the chain and smiled back.

'Your expert ain't much good, is he?' he said. 'I mean, he
never even noticed this.'

And holding up the chain in front of the astonished
barrister, he pulled apart the doctored link. Laughing loudly,
Gordon Goody left the Old Bailey a free man.

25

I had a couple of ideas about trains. Our less than successful
attempt to rob the Irish Mail at Swindon had whetted my
appetite and illustrated the immense potential. Similarly, the

firm's collective knowledge, which consisted of half truths, rumours and exaggerations, all pointed to the railways as being especially vulnerable.

Scouting about for an opening, I remembered that a few years earlier a contact told me how the payroll for Vauxhall's car plant at Luton was made up at the London offices and delivered under heavy escort to Euston Station. There it was entrusted to a single guard for the journey north to Luton, where it was met by another heavy escort. Well worth a look, I thought. Alas, times had changed. In the interim, Vauxhall had rearranged their payroll system, having the wages made up in Luton instead of London. Back to the drawing board.

I remembered Geordie, an old friend who had been part of the Chelsea scene, a one-time street photographer who worked Trafalgar Square, the Palace, the Tower, all the tourist haunts, before abandoning his artistic career for the more plebeian role of porter for British Railways at Waterloo. Geordie loved a drink and I found him propping up the bar in the Angelsea in Chelsea, one of Reg's haunts. It had good beer and a dartboard – all Geordie needed to feel he was in heaven.

Suitably lubricated, he was very gregarious and forthcoming.

'What goes on there?' I asked, handing him another pint. 'Are you loading anything valuable?'

'Well, there's the money train that comes in, but you can't do nothing with that, there's a hundred policemen waiting for it. And there's the gold train, but you can't do nothing with that either.'

The gold train was a weekly delivery of approximately a ton of gold, shipped from South Africa by the Union Castle Line to Southampton. It was transported by rail to Waterloo and met by an assortment of police, Bank of England officials and security, and taken off under heavy escort to the Bank of England. Geordie's verdict – impossible.

That left the train described by Geordie as the 'Money Train'. This originated in Bournemouth, picking up the goodies on the route to Waterloo, where it was also met by heavy security.

'What's the last stop?' I asked Geordie.

'I think it's Weybridge.'

This is what I loved about the 'game', fitting all the bits together, starting with an idea and kicking it around within the firm until there was a general consensus and a rough plan of action. Generally these 'board meetings' took place at Buster's flat in Twickenham. The usual complement was Buster, Gordon, Charlie, Paddy, Flossy and me. Harry had retired and gone into the textile business.

The first priority was observation, usually done in pairs. Four eyes see more than two and it was sod's law that if you worked single-handed the five minutes you disappeared for a piss would see something vital happen. Two people also countered the problem of interpretation – no two people saw a scene exactly alike.

We began with the gold shipment. Paddy and I took a commuter train down to Southampton, noting areas of interest and possible ambush sites. Going into the docks, we found the *Union Castle* ship and watched passengers streaming off the gangways *en route* for taxis and trains. On the dockside, we watched a security coach shunted into position and a container winched out from the hold. Locked and bolted in the presence of uniformed guards and plain-clothed security, the coach was joined up to the tail of the train and a security man took up position in the adjoining carriage.

This was interesting. The guard was effectively isolated from the gold with no means of entry into the bullion coach once the train was moving. It was vulnerable in transit.

Meeting with Gordon and Buster that night, we swapped reports. They had been to Waterloo and watched the bullion arrive. As Geordie had indicated, security was enormous and there was little chance of a snatch at the station. It was decided to swap positions next week and review it again. Gordon and Buster went to Southampton and I staked out Waterloo. We reached a consensus – the only possibility was to hit the train in transit, probably at Micheldever.

Our major problem was logistical. What equipment would we need to remove, load and transport a ton of gold? And how much time would we have before the opposition reacted? It was all very tempting, but the problems were enormous. We came up with some imaginative solutions but none was foolproof. We decided instead to look at the money train.

On a Tuesday night, Paddy and I drove to Weybridge in a 'clean' old Austin A55, parking well away from the station. The train was due in Weybridge at three o'clock in the morning so we arrived at two and walked through a very tasty area, wary about being seen. To be pulled would automatically rule out the whole business, because our names would be taken and possibly traced back to the job.

Crossing a railway bridge, we found ourselves on the run-down Brooklands racetrack, a ghostly relic which before the war was Britain's premier motor-racing circuit. It was scarcely comprehensible that cars had once lapped around it at over a hundred miles an hour.

Creeping through the woods we came down on to a plateau railed off from the track and overlooking the station. It was the perfect observation post. We could see the entrance to the station, the steps leading down to the platform and beyond to where the pick-up would probably occur.

My thoughts were broken by the sound of a police car, travelling at high speed with headlights blazing as it spun into the station yard. For a split second, I froze, fearing that we'd been seen. Pressing closer to the damp ground, we watched the police car stop twenty yards beneath us. Static from the police radio muffled their conversation as one of three occupants got out and checked the station doors. He got back in the squad car and they roared off into the night.

What was all that about? I thought.

Moments later the police car reappeared, this time on the opposite side of the railway cutting and the headlights seemed to focus directly on our prostrate figures. What the fuck was going on? Have they seen us? Should we run?

The police radio buzzed and crackled. Nobody got out of the car. It remained there, waiting. Pressed to the ground, I looked at Paddy. I could almost hear his heartbeat keeping time with my own. Suddenly, another police car hurtled from the darkness, stopping directly beneath us. Two policemen got out and nonchalantly lit cigarettes.

I heaved a sigh of relief and so did Paddy. They weren't chasing us. The boys in blue, like us, were simply waiting for the train.

The impasse was broken by the sound of a heavy motor vehicle. A large Royal Mail box lorry descended to the station, turned around and stopped parallel with the police car. The three occupants, two uniformed postmen and a railway official, greeted the police with cheerful *bonhomie*. The scenario was now clear. The police had secured the area before the train's arrival. The truck was obviously carrying High Value Packages to be loaded on board. The train had picked up similar consignments along the length of its journey.

One thing bothered me. If the lorry was holding such a valuable prize, why were the police and postmen so relaxed and jovial? They congregated together, laughing and smoking, unconcerned about their treasure.

Paddy heard the train first. The English Electric Diesel locomotive slowed down under power drawing into the station. Beneath us, the group broke up and took up positions with a spate of radio activity. The railway official opened the station doors and disappeared from view with the two postmen. Where were the bags to go on the train? I was mystified.

The platform itself was obscured by the carriages. We couldn't see what was happening until the diesel engine started thumping louder and then rumbled off towards Waterloo. Suddenly we saw the postmen pulling a four-wheel trolley weighed down by plump mailbags. Beside them was the railway official.

So that was it! The money train wasn't collecting: it was delivering. Our assumptions were all wrong.

They wheeled the trolley adjacent to the Royal Mail truck, unlocked the doors and proceeded to load up. I counted seven bags. The doors were locked and they clambered aboard the truck, whistling an 'OK' to the police car. As the gears engaged and it began moving, the police car slid in behind, forming a convoy. On our side of the tracks, the other police car also began moving. After the headlights had swung past us, I propped myself on one elbow, turned to Paddy and enquired, 'Well, what do you make of that?'

We lay still for ten minutes before I gestured it was time to move. My head was full of questions, but the discussion would come later. For the moment, we had to cross Brooklands and get back to the car without being pulled.

The silence continued until we were clear of Weybridge and on our way back to London. What had we seen? Mailbags coming off, not going on; and the whole exercise monitored by the police. The authorities were never frivolous when it came to the costing of police manpower. There had to be money involved – a substantial amount.

But why was it coming off at Weybridge? Was the police presence at Waterloo all part of a security subterfuge? Nothing could be ruled out. The convoy from Weybridge Station had to be followed; maybe it was being secretly moved to London by road – a brilliant idea, but perhaps a trifle too elaborate.

The firm gathered to consult. We realized that we would have to step up a gear and give Weybridge saturation surveillance over a month to try and determine the pattern of events. Unless we knew the entire story, too much was left to chance.

A month later, we had ruled out security subterfuge. Nor was it likely to be top secret documents for the British Aircraft Company's works in Weybridge. We were unanimous – it had to be money. It was banking policy to monitor how much was held at each branch. Cash balances from Bournemouth and all stops to Waterloo would be forwarded to the head office in central London, together with whatever old notes had to be taken out of circulation. These were collected by the Post Office on a Monday afternoon and lodged at the Post Office till early Tuesday morning when they were delivered to the connecting train service.

Tuesday morning saw the largest number of mailbags collected. The maximum was 32, the minimum 27. On other days, there were as few as three bags. The police escort varied only occasionally, but for the large collections there were always two cars. After being picked up from Weybridge station, the mailbags were taken to the main Post Office in the high street, where they were unloaded and secured behind locked and alarmed doors.

We investigated the vulnerability of the PO but discovered that there were six night staff on duty, and it was a popular dropping-in spot for the boys in blue. No, the logical place to hit was the station yard, where we knew the opposition numbers.

The plan was a simple ambush, a three-pronged attack from different directions. The first attack would take out the police radios in both cars. Violence would be kept to a minimum. We'd use surprise rather than mindless thuggery. It wasn't my style to draw blood: apart from the humanitarian aspect, it created a bad press which made the consequences more severe in the event of capture.

Two Jaguar 3.4s were stolen – at Roy's insistence they had to be 3.4s and not 3.8s. Apparently they had less power but handled better and would guarantee a good, safe ride. Meanwhile, Jimmy had prepared two cylinders containing compressed air and fuller's earth. When released into the enclosed space of a car, the mixture rendered the occupants helpless. The cars and equipment were all stowed up in two garages that Jimmy had rented.

Now it was just a question of when?

Unfortunately, Fate was working against Weybridge. Perhaps it was the length of time spent planning, which created an inertia; or it could have been the vacuum created by not knowing the size of our prize. Whatever the case, the momentum slackened. It came to a complete halt when Jimmy's garages were broken into and the two Jaguars with all the equipment were stolen. I tried to maintain the enthusiasm and hold everyone together but the impetus was gone. That was when Gordon and Buster came to me with another proposition – not all that dissimilar, but with one vital ingredient: inside knowledge.

Brian Field was the bent solicitor who had defended Gordon during the Airport trial. He also knew Buster quite well and had done some work behind the scenes to make sure he stayed out of prison. Brian not only defended criminals, he mixed with them and provided them with information.

Early in May, Brian contacted Gordon and, along with Buster, arranged a meeting with a man they came to know as the Ulsterman. Even this name was tenuous. Gordon had secretly checked the inside of the mystery man's jacket and come up with an Ulster address. They met on a bench in Finsbury Park. He told them about a train that travelled regularly between Glasgow and London carrying a large consignment of mailbags that could contain as much as six million pounds.

'Are you interested?' he asked. 'Can you do it?'

Gordon and Buster simply nodded, stunned by the scale of the prize.

The Ulsterman then gave them a detailed breakdown of security and the timetable of events. Between fifty and eighty mailbags were transported in a High Value Package coach on the overnight train to London. These contained surplus-to-requirements cash from all the banks in Scotland, as well as other banks adjacent to the route going south. At holiday time, there were often five times as many bags. The High Value Package coach was normally the second from the diesel loco. Inside there were five postal workers. In a separate section of the train were seventy postal sorters going through the overnight mail.

The Ulsterman could supply further information when needed, and a meeting was arranged for the following week.

Gordon and Buster came around to the flat and I could see that they were bursting to impart some valuable knowledge; however, there is always an established code of decorum to be observed. Serious talk cannot be conducted without a drink in hand.

I gave Gordon his usual Jameson's Irish whiskey; Buster and I had beers.

I look at Gordon quizzically. It was his stage and he was very good at filling it. Leaning forward, pausing, dropping to a whisper, he knew all the subtle tricks to entrance an audience. Slowly he revealed details of the meeting. Finishing with his charming wolf grin, he asked, 'How do you like it?'

'Sounds great,' I said, keeping my reply cool. Inside I was screaming, This is it! Fucking hell, this is it!

I looked at Buster, his face aglow with enthusiasm.

'Six fucking million!' he said breathlessly. 'What should we do about the gold train or the Weybridge thing?'

'Fucking forget 'em,' I said.

We all grinned broadly and started laughing. It did indeed sound like a great bit of work. As much as I tried not to think about it, deep inside I was thinking about Eldorado. 'Lay it out for me again,' I said. 'Let's kick it around a bit.'

Gordon went through the information, this time with interjections from Buster and questions from me. Ideas abounded. We were all very excited and wanted to get it all settled there and then – an impossibility because we still had much to learn. With notebook in hand and the drink tasting better all the time, I listened to the story for a third time.

This prospect excited me enormously. What set it apart from the other possibilities was the inside information. Here there was an indication of the size of the prize, at least a million – anything beyond that was largely academic. But could it be done successfully? Not for the first time, I wondered if we were being set up by the boys in blue. I was always wary of renegades and didn't particularly know Brian Field. Could it be an elaborate plot to round us all up and put us away?

I refused to get carried away.

A few days later, the nucleus of the firm had been recruited and we assembled for the all-important meeting to discuss a basic plan. Given the prize at stake, it was going to be an exciting session, tossing around ideas, arguing and listing priorities. This was the part I loved – the plotting, the intricate mind games to second guess and then triple guess the police, covering all the angles.

Again we met at Buster's flat. I parked the Lotus three streets away and walked over. Flossy was already there; he and Buster were inseparable. We had a cup of tea and waited for the others to arrive. Charlie and Gordon turned up together, closely followed by Roy, who was bubbling with enthusiasm as ever. We chatted about motor racing until Jimmy White and Alf Thomas arrived.

Alf was a notable recruit. A mate of Jimmy's, he had given us some advice during the surveillance at Weybridge. He was a big old boy, very reliable, and would have been useful for the money train because he had the muscle to disable the police cars by tipping them over before we sprayed them with fuller's earth and compressed air. We were going to need some hard men and Alf fitted the bill.

All ideas were permissible at this session, from the sublime to the ridiculous, from reality to fantasy: out of them all would come the plan. I took out the maps, spreading them across the kitchen table. London to Glasgow was roughly a distance of 400 miles, a large canvas on which to project the masterwork.

We knew what time the train left Glasgow and the journey times, but still had to decide how and where we were going to lift the mailbags. Euston was out of the question. The reception committee there looked like a police college open day. I considered the possibility of striking as the train slowed before reaching the station. Unfortunately, in such a heavily populated area, the alarm could be raised by somebody looking out their window and phoning the police.

Increasingly, it looked like an out-of-town job – a far more dangerous proposition. How do we get home if the opposition is out in force? Or if the distance is too great? Once the alarm sounds there will be roadblocks and blanket police presence. The nicks are full of guys who have tried out-of-town work and failed.

The most likely option was to establish a base post near the strike point. There could be no hotels, no registering or contact with locals. Staying with friends was also out of the question because most of our associates had criminal records and would be subject to police checks, as well as police pressure. By the same token, if they didn't have criminal backgrounds, how could they be trusted? How about renting or buying a house? There would be witnesses to the transaction. Who could we get to act on our behalf? How did we ensure their trust? Money?

When the meeting finished these questions were still unanswered, but decisions were made to push ahead with surveillance and locate a possible strike point. I rang Paddy and arranged to meet him the following morning at ten.

I drove over in my new, scarcely run-in Lotus Cortina – a dynamite car; Jim Clark was trouncing everyone in the Production Car Races driving one. We drove to Euston and boarded a train going north – a slow one that stopped at every station, giving our eyes a chance to survey the terrain.

We sat alone in our first-class carriage, suitably attired, and talked openly of possible sites. I had a picture in my mind. I was looking for either a disused station or a junction point where we could take the train off the main track and out of circulation, and somewhere which had the facilities for unloading the mailbags and transferring them to vans. Periodically I paced the corridor to see if it was greener on the other side. People brushed past me, oblivious to our intent, although I wouldn't have been surprised to see Buster, Gordon, Charlie and Roy, done up in some guise. They would be out as well, ducking and diving, discreetly digging for inspiration and information.

We passed through Brent, Wealdstone, South Oxhey, Bushey, Kings Langley, Hemel Hempstead, all more or less built-up areas not suitable for our purposes. After Hemel Hempstead we began to see some open spaces before we hit Berkhamsted, and even more before Tring. After Tring, crossing the Chiltern Hills and the Ridgeway, this began to look like our sort of territory. The run up to Cheddington and Leighton Buzzard was open on both sides, with connecting roads that crossed over the tracks. My senses began to twitch. There was a road, the B488, running parallel to the track – quite a good road which curved and disappeared under a railway bridge beneath us. There were no houses immediately in view. I could picture the train being stopped on top of the bridge and it would be a simple task to throw the bags down.

In my heart I knew this was the place, this was it. Nonchalantly, I gestured to Paddy. 'What do you think?'

He nodded his consent, happy to rely on my judgement. It was my vision; he couldn't see what I could see. Although tremendously experienced and successful, the heavy graft was new to Paddy, but I was happy to have him aboard. He was tried and trusted, the real McCoy.

We got off at Stony Stratford and had lunch before catching the train home. As we passed the railway bridge, I silently murmured, 'I'll be back.'

The following night, we assembled at Buster's – all the old crowd from the Gold and Money Trains.

I put forward the target point at Cheddington, pointing out the pluses. Roy said he'd take a drive up there and work out a time for the route home from the target. I could see he was relishing his involvement; this was right up his street. I liked the idea myself of a hit and straight drive, but it didn't appear feasible.

Now the biggest question dominating our discussions was how we were going to stop the train. There were no passengers on the TPO (*Travelling Post Office*), ruling out inside action via the communication cord – highly fallible, as shown by the Irish Mail fiasco. Anybody with half a bit of sense knows you can lay a sleeper across the line but the aim was not to alert the driver and crew that anything unusual was happening. No, we had to be certain and we'd get only one chance. We asked ourselves, how does the train stop normally? Answer: the signals.

'Does anyone know how to do it?' I asked.

There was silence.

'Does anyone know a signalman?'

Buster raised his hand. He had a friend, Roger Cordrey, who had been working with a successful South Coast firm doing train robberies.

'Can we poach their expert?' I asked.

'I don't think so, they're a very close little firm, they'll all want to be in.'

Jimmy spoke up and everyone listened with respect. A wartime paratrooper, a survivor of Arnhem, and on the run for years, wanted for a bullion robbery, he knew more than most. 'With seventy to eighty staff on the train, the extra firm could be an asset if things go boss-eyed,' he said.

There were general murmurs of agreement.

'There's enough dough there anyway, no-one's greedy; fucking hell, we're nicking a train.'

Gordon raised the point about security. The more people who knew about the job, the less our security. True, but could we do it properly without them? Buster said he would approach the South Coast gang, suppressing the details but giving them a basic outline. With mutual respect, he thought they would agree.

By common agreement everyone was allotted tasks. The octopus began stretching its tentacles. We needed information. We needed to submerge ourselves and think of nothing else.

The next morning, Paddy and I set off in his 3.8, driving up and around the target area. The more I saw, the more I liked it. I plotted a route which took us south in a dogleg on to the Thame road. It was a great route, B-roads all the way, crossing two main roads in all. Shades of Chad – he'd be proud of me, I thought. I'd learnt backroads from him – if the alarm went up prematurely they couldn't erect roadblocks in time. More importantly, I wanted to consider a stow (*hiding place*) in the area, somewhere to lay low for a few days until the heat disappeared from the search. Thame was about seventeen and a half miles from the railway bridge, as the crow flies. By road it was closer to thirty.

On 24 June I called at Midland Mart's estate agents in Thame and asked about properties for sale. It wasn't a long list so we planned to view them all, but the first, near the village of Brill, some 27 miles west of Bridego Bridge on the other side of Aylesbury, was immediately attractive. Quite apart from anything else, Leatherslade Farm didn't appear on Ordnance Survey maps. Shortly after leaving Oakley there was a dirt road which led up the hill to the farm, with just two outbuildings at the foot of the dirt road. Isolated and remote, hidden by the trees, it held a commanding position over the countryside. It was not visible from the road and there was only one narrow access lane.

Midland Mart's details explained that it offered a sitting-room, dining-room, kitchen, bathroom and four bedrooms. In the grounds there was a hangar-cum-garage and a cobbled-together shed politely described as a workshop. Water was from the mains, the electricity from a diesel generator. All in all it wasn't much to look at, but it was perfect for our purposes.

It was then that I made a major blunder – we stopped and knocked on the door. By talking to the owner, I was creating a potential link between myself and the crime, but I assumed that this robbery would be no different to any other: it would make headlines for three or four days and then die a natural death.

Mr Rixon was an affable type of guy and willingly showed me around. Perhaps the sight of Paddy's 3.8 Jaguar keened his appetite for a quick sale: he was enthusiastic to sell and willing to deal. I said that my interest was genuine and that I would be in touch. When I informed the group, after an inspection from afar by Buster and Gordon, it was decided

Early passport photo

Above Hunting with Harry, Cannes

Right Reynolds in Cannes

Above 'Sprite'ly with Franny

Right With Franny in Cannes

Above
Entertaining
at the
Embassy Cl
with Frann
Barbara, Ma
Lulu and Pa
Opposite an
Bruce, Pade
Harry, Mich
and Charlie

Above At the
Astor. Seated at
the table are
Franny, Paddy,
Barbara, Bruce
and Mary
Manson.

Right Bridego
Bridge with
plundered
train. (Camera
Press)

Right Stretch of line between Sears Crossing and Bridego Bridge. (Camera Press)

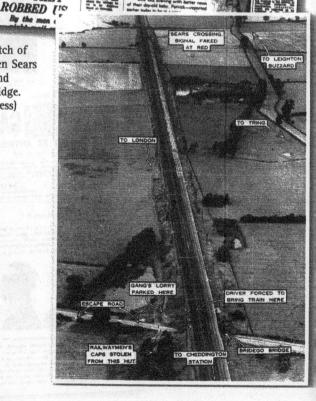

METROPOLITAN POLICE

On the 8th August, 1963, the Glasgow to Euston mail train was robbed of about two and a half million pounds.

Substantial rewards will be paid to persons giving such information as will lead to the apprehension and conviction of the persons responsible.

The assistance of the public is sought to trace the whereabouts of the after described persons:

RONALD EDWARDS, alias RONALD CHRISTOPHER EDWARDS, also known as "BUSTER," aged 32, 5ft 9in., stocky build, complexion fresh, hair dark brown, eyes brown. London accent, scar left of nose and right forearm.

JUNE ROSE EDWARDS, née ROTHERY, aged 30, 5ft. 2in., hair fair. May be accompanied by daughter NICOLETTE, aged about 3 years.

BARBARA MARIA DALY, née ALLAN, aged 22, 5ft. 1in. hair brown. May be pregnant and accompanied by daughter LORRAINE PATRICIA, aged 1 year.

JOHN THOMAS DALY, aged 31, born New Eam. Eam, antique dealer, 5ft. 11in., complexion fresh, hair dark brown (wavy), eyes blue, scar right of forehead.

BRUCE RICHARD REYNOLDS, alias RAYMOND ETTRIDGE and GEORGE RACHEL, aged 31, born London, motor and antique dealer, 6ft. 1in., complexion fresh, hair light brown, eyes grey (may be wearing horn-rimmed or rimless spectacles), slight cleft in chin, scar left eyelid, cheek and right forearm.

FRANCES REYNOLDS, aged 20, 5ft. 3in., slim build, hair brown.

ROY JOHN JAMES, aged 27, born London. 5ft. 8in., medium to slim build, complexion fresh, hair brown (wavy), eyes blue, scar right of forehead.

JAMES EDWARD WHITE, alias BRYAN and JAMES EDWARD WHITE (uses many aliases), aged 43, born Paddington, London, cafe proprietor, 5ft. 10in., slim, complexion sallow, hair and eyes brown, wears moustache, Royal Artillery crest tattooed right forearm.

Persons having information are asked to

Above Police 'Wanted' poster.

Right The *Police Gazette*.

POLICE GAZETTE

PUBLISHED BY AUTHORITY.

NEW SERIES   FRIDAY, AUGUST 23, 1963   No. 168. Vol. 1.

Matter for circulation under the headings, "Commonwealth Citizens" or "Aliens" should be addressed "THE ALIENS REGISTRATION OFFICE, 10, PICCADILLY PLACE, W.1."

With all other manuscript for publication the envelope should be addressed "THE COMMISSIONER OF POLICE, NEW SCOTLAND YARD, S.W.1." with "T.P.O.(P.G.)" in top left corner.

JOSEPH SIMPSON,
The Commissioner of Police of the Metropolis.

Wanted

1. **Bucks, Aylesbury Co.**—ROBBERY, 3 a.m. 8th inst., at Cheddington, vide Case 42, 22-8-63. Stopped express train, attacked driver, entered travelling post office attached to train and stole 120 post bags containing about 2½ million pounds in currency (about £20,000 in Scottish and Irish notes). BRUCE RICHARD REYNOLDS, alias RAYMOND ETTRIDGE and GEORGE RACHEL, C.R.O. No. 41212-48, b. London 7-9-31, motor

dealer/antique dealer, 6ft. 1in., c. fresh (slightly suntanned), h. R. brown, e. grey (wears horn rimmed or rimless spectacles), fairly well spoken, slight cleft in chin, scar l. eyelid and cheek and rt. forearm. Conv. for larceny, assault on police, receiving, causing g.b.h. with intent, shop, house, workshopbreaking, etc. at Omar and M.P. (C.O., C.O.4, G, F, L, P and W). Last 30-5-63—fined. Is the holder of Passport No. C.306103, issued at Marseilles, France and during the past year has visited Gibraltar, Spain, Monte Carlo, Paris, North Africa. Represents he is in business as an antique

Passport photos of Britain's most wanted man. (Captain East/Peter G. Wickman)

Reynolds jailed with £150,000 secret

CM15JAN69

By RICHARD HERD and ARTHUR TIETJEN

BRUCE Reynolds, one of the leading members of the Great Train Robbery gang, was jailed for 25 years

BRUCE REYNOLDS

said: 'Well, this is it, I suppose. I'm glad it's all over.

'It is no life for anyone, always shifting about. I had been thinking for some time of giving myself up, but I was frightened to because of the long sentences the others got.'

Above Det. Ch. Supt. Tommy Butler: the cop who just wouldn't give up. He made a vow not to retire until Reynolds was behind bars. (Syndication International)

Left Bruce's first passport photo on release from prison

FREE! GREAT TRAIN ROBBERY'S MASTERMIND

Bruce Reynolds, who masterminded Britain's Great Train Robbery, strode out of Wormwood Scrubs Prison this week after nearly 10 years behind bars.

The once elegant Reynolds, now grey-haired and 47, emerged a new man in more ways than one.

Reynolds, who wants to be a male model, has shed much of his 15 stone. He looks long and lean.

But his bankroll has grown fat.

He has about $16,000 for helping author Piers Paul Read compile the official version of the robbery which netted the gang about $4 million in 1963.

He is enjoying a renewed notoriety with the

Above Promo shot for the film *Buster. (Left to right)* Ralph Brown as Ronnie Biggs, Michael Attwell as Gordon Goody, Norma Heyman (the producer), Larry Lamb as Bruce and Phil Collins as Buster Edwards.

Above Bruce with Ronnie Biggs. The first time they had met in thirty years since the robbery.

Right Publicity shot for BBC documentary *Everyman*. (Penny Tweedy)

Below Bruce and Ronnie at Ronnie's seventieth birthday party in Rio. (Tony Hoare)

Left Bruce with Howard Marks and Robert Sabbag at Filthy McNasty's. (Greg Smith)

Below Refuelling Capo Verde. Bruce with pilot, Ronnie Biggs and son Mike.

Left Bruce giving a talk at Karl Marx Library (Greg Smith)

Below The Reynolds boys: Ziggy and Otto (Bruce's grandchildren), Bruce and Nick. (G. Feltham-Pari that we place the matter in the hands of Brian Field. The farm would be purchased through the firm of John Wheater.

The farm was brought for £5,500, nominally in the name of Leonard Field (no relation to Brian) after some finessing by the solicitors concerned, and upon payment of £550 (10 per cent) the contracts were signed and vacant possession granted.

At our next meeting in Buster's flat, the South Coast boys arrived. Roger came on his own and then all the big boys, Tommy Wisbey, Bob Welch, Jimmy Hussey and Frank Munroe. They seemed a strong, safe bunch. Big Jim had worked with 'Old Wal', a powerful old boy who was rumoured to have tied a few people up in his time to settle arguments, as well as for straightforward business reasons. On one particular job he emerged from a building with two night-watchmen he'd captured, one under each arm!

Big Bad Bob Welch (bad being an affectionate term) was a very bright guy, intelligent and strong. Tommy, an ex-Army ex-boxer, was a gentle giant and a gambler with a betting shop who knew how to calculate the odds. He was the strength behind the South Coast raiders. Frank Munroe was the motivator and Roger the schemer. All of them fitted together perfectly.

Buster did the introductions and the banter dropped. I took the floor with the blackboard at my side and ran through the basics again. 'It's simple enough,' I said. 'The train leaves Glasgow loaded – could be as much as five or six mil.'

Gasps, phews, fucking hells.

'We stop it at Sears Crossing, disconnect the loco and the two coaches and drive it to here – Bridego Bridge. There we unload it and drive away to our stow, the farm. No problems.'

'How do we drive it away?'

'We get the driver to drive it. If he won't co-operate, then we have our own driver.'

'How good is the information?'

'We don't know. But all he's said so far makes sense. Right, Roger?'

'Right, Bruce. He knows what he's talking about.'

'In any event, he's Brian Field's man,' I said. 'I don't think that Brian's going to risk his career unless he has total confidence in him.'

There were mutterings of agreement, a general consensus that we shouldn't be nit-picking; you don't get invitations to a six-million-pound party every day.

'What about the farm – are the arrangements sound?'

'Yes, that's in Field's corner. All settled, his firm is getting well paid. But they don't know who is involved.'

'Field does.'

'I know, but without Field there's no business. Either we've got confidence in him or we haven't. I'd say that we have.'

'That's OK then, I just wanted to know.'

'Of course you wanted to know. We all want to know. We've got to feel right about it. This is the time to build it up and then try to destroy it, OK?'

'How does our man know all this?'

'We don't know. It's all on trust.'

'He says that the security coaches will be out of action. Can we believe him?'

'The same answer – it's all on trust. If you believe the first part then you must believe what follows. Remember, if his information is incorrect there's no pay day for him.'

'And none for us,' someone piped up.

'True, but if we are going to do it we have to believe in it. It's up to you, we know where we stand. We won't know till afterwards if the yolk is on us, but this is like any other bit of work – maybe a trifle ambitious with a larger prize, but basically it's just a bit of work like any other that you've done.'

There was a hum of conversation and a bit of ribaldry before Charlie called out, 'Now, now, lads – listen to teacher.'

Turning from the blackboard I smiled and said, 'Teacher knows best.'

I did a rough sketch outlining the salient details, from where we would stop to how we would separate the loco and the two coaches and who would do that. Then the capture of the driver and his fireman mate, the driving away of the loco and coaches, the final stop at Bridego Bridge. The heaviest and strongest would be in the assault group, I said, and they'd be unloading as soon as they'd secured their objective. Everyone would then join the gang passing the bags down the embankment and on to the truck. 'It's a piece of cake,' I said.

'It's easier than hijacking a lorry on the M1,' Buster said. 'We haven't got any other traffic to worry about.'

The simple analogy cut across any lingering doubts, though one query was raised. 'Won't there be any other trains on the track?'

'There's none scheduled,' I said. 'We have an all clear.'

'That's handy, very handy,' Bob said. 'We can do as we like.'

'As I see it, the key scene is the taking of the loco and the two coaches. If this isn't done quietly and efficiently, then we could have problems and the business'll be fucked. There's seventy sorters in the rest of the carriages and we don't want a row with them, do we? We've got to do it without them being aware. Roy and Jimmy have been working nights.'

'I hope they're getting overtime,' Tom said.

'They hope so too! They're confident they can do it without problems and with the minimum noise. They're right for the job – both technically aware, both fit, and both the right height to get under the coaches for the uncoupling. I'm not relying on their word that they can do it – we've seen that they can do it.'

Gordon nodded. 'That's right, sweet as a nut, no problems there.'

'Once we've got the loco and coaches to Bridego Bridge then it's ours. I can't see any real problems – there's five postal workers in the High Value Coach, you lot should cop for them in no time.'

I eyeballed Gordon, Charlie and Buster, then Big Jim, Big Bob, Big Tom and Big Frank. There were rumblings, flexing of muscles in their confidence, as Big Jim replied drily, 'I should think so.'

'That's it then. Big Alf will drive the lorry. He's had plenty of experience, it's his game. And before anybody asks, yes, he does have an HGV licence.'

'That's good,' Charlie quipped. 'We don't want Alf nicked for driving without a licence, do we?'

Alf smiled. He was a big old boy, didn't say much, but he knew what he could do, he didn't have to advertise himself.

'Nobody's going to get nicked on this one if we all stick together. Just remember that. Any other questions?'

Almost hesitantly, Flossy asked, 'Will the train stop at the signals?'

'The train has to stop. The driver is bound by the book, and we know what the book says: the amber is the warning preparatory to stopping and the red is the stop. He has to stop. He'd be going against all the rules if he didn't. He's an experienced driver, years of service. They're all hand picked, the élite, these mail train drivers. Is that right, Roger?'

'Right. These drivers are conscientious, depend on that.'

'But suppose he doesn't,' Flossy laboured the point. 'You hear of them having a drink and all that – suppose he's one of those, what'll we do then?'

It was not a question I was enthusiastic about; I recognized myself that it was the one imponderable.

'Then we all go home and wait until Christmas, then have another go.'

'He'd better stop,' Charlie said, 'otherwise I'll report him.'

'He'll stop,' said Roger, speaking with the authority of the railway expert that he was.

But would he? I wondered. There were no guarantees. This one had to be left to fate.

'OK then,' I rounded off, 'till the next time. In the interim Buster will keep in touch. We'll try to minimize these major meetings – we don't want curiosity to kill the cat. People will wonder what we're all doing together, and it could look a bit dodgy.'

I arranged the next major meet to be at Wimbledon Common. We could take a ball and have a kick around, so we wouldn't look out of place. 'From now on, more than ever, security has to be the name of the game. You don't need me to tell you that, but I'm going to: just remember the old wartime slogan – be like Dad, keep Mum! See you next time, and be lucky.'

By the time of our next meeting, Gordon and Buster had seen the Ulsterman; everything was fine. Roy and Jimmy had been to Euston viewing the target as it pulled in, noting there were two types of HVP coach – one manifestly a newer design and more secure. It was no great problem; we could still effect an entry but it would take a little longer.

Surveillance now went into full swing. Cruising the environs of the target point, I discovered an army base at Bicester. Regular convoys of army vehicles trundled through the B-roads. This sowed the seeds for an idea. For the robbery we would adopt local camouflage and pretend to be an army convoy. We could duplicate Divisional insignia on our vehicles for added authenticity. We could be an élite unit on night-time manoeuvres and this gave us the self-designated authority to assert ourselves over lesser authorities such as the police, if some local bobby stumbled in on the job in progress. I liked it; I could live out my fantasy and indeed be 'the Major'.

Further reports from the Ulsterman indicated our concerns regarding the more secure type of HVP coaches were groundless. He was emphatic that on the night in question the older, less secure type woud be in use. Great news, but who was this guy who could effect such a guarantee? We grew suspicious and kicked around the possibility of a massive set-up. All of us in the bag in one fell swoop, jailed, out of circulation for a very long time. We knew we were on 'their' hit list – the publicity over the Airport had seen to that.

'Don't look too deeply,' someone had told me years ago. I knew what he meant: you could flounder in your own paranoia. No-one seriously believed it could be a set-up; it was too ambitious for Old Bill – they had far more restrictions on their activities than we did. Nevertheless, the possibility was always there.

Roy and Jimmy had been to Royal Oak, the main rail depot for Paddington, gleaning general info, acquiring locks, studying coach construction, uncoupling, loco controls, anything that might be of use to us. You can never have too much information – it is the life-blood of a good criminal.

Most of the equipment we needed was already at hand. Having spent much of the summer messing about with Weybridge, we had collected the necessary bits and pieces, such as radios, uniforms, and railwaymen's boiler suits. We needed very little hardware and less than eight weeks of preparation. That's the beauty of trains; they run to a set timetable. Instead of waiting all day for something, you can arrive at three in the morning, knowing that within minutes the locomotive will come thundering past.

I was co-ordinating all the material collected, as the project acquired its own momentum. Roger and I were spending long nights doing recces together at Cheddington, bivouacked on the side of the embankment, sipping Bovril from mugs and discussing coups of the past. He impressed me with his grasp of the situation, his quiet confidence and technical know-how.

Together we had worked out the detail of the plan to stop the train at Sears Crossing, uncouple the diesel loco with its two coaches and take it to Bridego Bridge. But we still had to overcome the problem of who would drive the train. What if the official driver refused to co-operate. I could imagine the scenario.

'Drive it or I kill you!' he's told.

'OK, kill me then.'

A perfect stalemate.

'Could we drive it?' asked Roy confidently.

Gordon grinned. 'How hard can it be?' he said. 'I'll look for a manual.'

What he found was a children's picture book for eight-year-olds about 'Tommy' driving the Royal Mail train. It had coloured diagrams and a story of how little Tommy rode in the cabin and watched the driver at work.

Armed with this high-tech information and fortified by wine, Gordon and I ventured to Euston Station late one night and found a train parked up on a siding. It was two o'clock in the morning when we clambered into the cabin.

'OK, what do you think?' I asked, staring at the buttons and levers.

'Well, that looks like the brake,' said Gordon, gingerly releasig it. 'And this is probably the dead handle.'

As we experimented with different levers, the engine rumbled, coughed and spluttered into life. 'Hey, we're in business!' I cried with a grin. 'OK, let's take it steady. Ease forward.'

The locomotive cranked into motion. Gordon was craning his head, watching the track for obstructions or on-coming trains.

'Brilliant. OK, let's stop now,' I said, growing nervous. Gordon pulled on the brake and the train picked up speed.

'You can stop now,' I said, more urgently.

'I'm trying.'

'Come on, don't piss around. Stop the fucking thing.'

'I can't stop the fucking thing.'

We were cursing and blinding, pulling on every handle within reach. Meanwhile, the locomotive continued to rumble forwards at three miles an hour.

'I'm outa here,' said Gordon, bailing out of the doorway. I followed, leaping on to the gravel and sprinting along the tracks. We didn't wait to see where the train finished up.

There was no mention of the incident in the next morning's paper. I figured it had probably crashed into a shed or been sidelined at a junction box. Maybe it had happened before with kids mucking around in the locos.

Obviously there was far more to driving a train than met the eye.

The search for a driver had become a sticking point, with everyone in the firm racking their brains to find a solution. It arrived purely by coincidence when I took a day off to recharge the batteries and drove down to Redhill with Franny and Nick to visit my old sparring partner from Borstal days, Ronnie Biggs. I had occasionally seen Biggsy in the intervening years. We talked then of a few plots but nothing emerged; we were both trying to make up for the years that we had lost inside, and other commitments prevented a closer involvement.

Ronnie was much more of an entrepreneur than I and had done well for himself since getting released. He had a small carpentry business, a wife and kids, and seemed happy. But then, he always did. I remembered seeing him after his last arrest when he hobbled into the Hate Factory, his eyes blackened and his testicles swollen from a beating. He was a straight-up guy, obdurate in the face of police 'questioning'. Our years in prison together reinforced the camaraderie. How could I forget the hot cocoa in the treacle tin, swung line to line, cell to cell and lowered to me – the first hot drink I'd had for three days? You had to feel affection for a guy who did that for you.

He was sitting in the living-room, his feet on a coffee table and eyes half shut, when I asked him about business. Biggsy was never a big-time operator – he seemed to drift from one job to the next, some of them legitimate.

'Things are pretty quiet,' he said. 'I'm painting some old boy's bungalow at the moment. He's a nice guy – he's promised to take my lad out soon on his train.'

'On his train?'

'Oh yeah,' said Biggsy, 'he's an engine driver. Mainly shunting now because he's getting on a bit. Hey, why are you looking at me like that?'

'Can you talk to him?'

'About what?'

'A job. A good earner. I need a driver.'

Biggsy's eyes lit up and I could hear the wheels crank into motion. 'Yeah, well, he knows I done time. When I told him about doing bird in Dartmoor he got quite excited. I guess he figures I've led an exciting kind of life. He even said to me, "I wish I'd known about that, Ron, when I was younger."'

This sounded very promising. 'I'd like to meet him. Tell him there's a nice bit of money involved, but he must be able to drive an English Electric Type 3000.'

Three days later I went back to see Biggsy.

'Yeah, he's only too pleased, what we gotta do?'

'Hold on,' I said. 'It's what he's gotta do – there's no need for you to be in it.'

'Well, I'd like to be in it.'

'It's not in your best interests,' I said. 'Look at it this way. You get fifty grand for having introduced us to the driver. Easy money, no questions asked. Why risk taking it further?'

'Fifty grand?' Biggsy whistled through his front teeth. 'Christ, what sort of money's involved?'

'It's big, big money.'

'I want to be in it. I want to be in it!'

Biggsy couldn't be dissuaded. He had ambitions, and this was the biggest operation he'd ever heard of. He couldn't turn his back and walk away.

Later that night, I put it to the firm.

'I can't see why we need him,' said Gordon.

'None of us have worked with him. What do we really know about him?' asked Buster.

'I've known him for years,' I reassured them. 'He's sound as a bell.'

Roy rejected the idea on the basis that we didn't need a train driver, and without a driver we didn't need Biggsy. 'I'm pretty sure I can handle the train,' he said.

'Not pretty sure, we gotta be one hundred per cent sure,' I said.

'You're just complicating things,' said Roy. 'Keep it simple.'

Finally it was put to a vote and it was passed overwhelmingly – we use our own driver. By the back door Biggsy had joined the firm.

26

We now had to make a final decision on the plan.

Roy was against a lay-up at the farm. Instead he favoured a fast drive home in a fleet of 3.8 Jaguars with the back seats discarded and loaded with the mailbags. It sounded reasonable, but eight or ten Jaguars parked up in a lonely place at night would arouse suspicion. Similarly, there was a certain reluctance about the load being divided. No-one would know how much each car was carrying, which could lead to dissatisfaction and distrust. Then we had to rendezvous to divide the dough. Even in central London you can't afford to have eight Jags parked up in proximity. Roy gracefully accepted the majority view. We were now unanimous. With the location, the route, the farm and the train driver fixed, all we needed was the date and confirmation from the Ulsterman.

Biggsy's retired train driver, Peter, was a small man in his fifties, with a nicely timed sense of humour and a detached air about him. It was almost as if he didn't realize that what we were planning was for real. He confessed that he had no experience of the big English Electric diesel loco but explained that the principles were all the same. To make sure, he arranged to cadge a ride from Euston in the name of railway freemasonry and familiarize himself with the controls.

'Don't plan any holidays in August,' I told Biggsy. 'And let me know if Peter's exercise is a success.'

The equipment was ready – handcuffs, army uniforms and blue railway overalls, bedding, camp stoves, torches, four walkie-talkies and a VHF receiver to monitor the police and emergency services. Transport-wise, we needed an army-type lorry and two Land-Rovers for the hit, gambling that the load would not exceed the vehicles' capacity: any more than that and we would have to leave it behind, but no-one was going to be disappointed with three tons of dosh to share out.

Jimmy and Alf volunteered to get the lorry and one of the Land-Rovers, buying these at auction. I forwarded the money, making sure it went into my accounts book. For some reason, I appeared to be financing the project. Jimmy and I decided to steal the second Land-Rover, taking a light blue version from Oxendon Street, near Leicester Square in the West End and passing it on to Gordon for him to paint khaki. He changed the registration from 296 P00 to BMG 757 A.

Roger almost second-guessed my thoughts when we worked together. We had the same eye for detail. Perhaps the only difference between us was that he loved the horses and was a mad-keen punter. He could rattle off the results of past classics as if reciting multiplication tables. It was Roger who pointedly remarked that Reynoldstown had won the Grand National in 1936.

'Is there an omen in that for the year 1963?' I wondered.

'Better than that,' said Roger. 'Reynoldstown had won it before, in 1935 – only a few horses have done it twice.'

'Remarkable,' I said. Then, feeding his ego, I asked, 'What won it in 1937?'

He'd been waiting for this. Pausing to let his smile begin, he calmly announced: 'Royal Mail!'

'Fucking hell!' I exploded.

'I thought you'd like that,' said Roger, a twinkle in his eye.

A low-key rehearsal was organized, with everyone taking up positions at Stewarts Lane depot near Nine Elms in Battersea. We had been over it time and time again at Buster's place, using blackboards and maps, but nothing could replace a proper outdoor rehearsal. I had taken endless stick over my blackboard manner, all in good humour. It was time to find out if teacher really did know best.

The positions were decided. I would signal by walkie-talkie the approach of the train to Paddy at the dwarf signal; my signal would simultaneously be picked up by Roger and Roy on the signal gantry and alert the attack group on the track. Roy and I would sever all phone lines in the area shortly before the train was due to arrive. When it stopped Roy and Jimmy would uncouple the loco and the front two coaches whilst the attack group would capture the driver and fireman, replacing them with our driver, Peter, with Biggsy to hold his hand.

Upon capture and uncoupling Peter would drive the loco and coaches to Bridego Bridge. The firm would dismount from the loco and break into the HVP coach, capturing the five workers inside before forming a human chain to pass the bags down to Alf and the lorry. It was as simple as that.

Although everyone knew his own task, all roles were interchangeable, in case for some reason someone was missing or was incapacitated on the night. We had an abundance of manpower.

Everyone had to make their own arrangements for after the robbery. I'd already made mine. On the following morning, Mary and Rene would be in Thame with a vanload of antique furniture. I would pick up the van from them, return to the farm, load it with my share, hidden behind the furniture, and return it to Mary at Thame. They would then drive it 'home'.

I felt secure in all of this. Everything was under control. Gordon and Buster had their last meeting with the Ulsterman and he recommended 7 August: it was just after the Bank Holiday, which meant that the ultimate prize would be greater. His last words were truly inspiring: 'I've got another, bigger job for you after this.'

They had a phone number where he could be contacted on the night of the sixth, to confirm that the coast was clear. Meanwhile, Brian Field had obtained the keys of the farm and we planned to arrive there on the fifth or sixth for last-minute preparations. Paddy, Jimmy and I would pick up Biggsy and Peter from Victoria, together with the provisions and equipment. The others would make their own way, alone or discreetly in small groups with the assistance of Brian Field.

All that remained was for me to go home, recheck my gear and say goodbye to Franny. She had been busily stitching crowns on my Airborne smock and the winged dagger on my SAS beret. As always, she didn't ask any questions, but she obviously knew that something big was going down. She'd seen it all before.

My last task was to hide the Lotus Cortina. I had driven it around the Cheddington area during recces and parked it up in various fields by night, leaving it covered with a camouflage net to break its silhouette. I was fairly sure no-one had seen it but arranged to leave it in Twickenham at Willments, the Ford competition specialists. The purpose was twofold. It would be out of sight from Old Bill, and the tyres would be changed – particularly important because the police were not averse to fitting people up with tyre treads 'found at the scene of the crime'!

27

The August moon was as white as a five-pound note.

Parking the Land-Rover off the road, close to the abutment of Bridego Bridge, I clambered up the embankment, slipping several times on the damp grass and loose rock. At the top, I paused to take a piss. It was more than just relief. Perhaps, subconsciously, I was establishing territorial boundaries like a tom-cat or a lion. This was my domain.

From the top pocket of my camouflage smock I took out a leather cigar case and selected a prepared Montecristo No. 2. Moistening the tapered end, I struck a match, carefully ensuring the flame burned the leaf evenly before I drew in the smoke. I exhaled into the night air; as it blended with the darkness, the thought ran through my mind: I have brought Cuba to Buckinghamshire.

I knew I wouldn't have time to finish it, but a Montecristo No. 2 is a fine companion to have whilst awaiting your destiny. I knew this would be my greatest moment, a night to remember. Whatever happened in the next few minutes, my life would never be the same again.

I looked at the glowing hands of my Omega stainless-steel watch. 2.45 a.m. Only fifteen more minutes to destiny. That's how I saw it. From my first crime to my last, through the triumphs and the sorrows, this was what I had waited for. My Eldorado.

Visions of Drake and his motley crew at Panama, of Max my old cell-mate who had continually exhorted me: 'You've got to sack a city.' I hoped Max would not be disappointed that it was just a train.

I looked down at the tracks, at the illusion of the rails coverging in the distance, where soft lights marked the outskirts of Leighton Buzzard. Ten minutes more and I should see the darkened mass of the train, picked out by side lights. I would hear it first, of course, drifting on the warm night air and rumbling through the rails at my feet. Maybe I would smell diesel.

I wondered what the others were thinking. I'd set off with fifteen minutes to go, dropping Paddy off at the nearest point to the dwarf signal before taking up my observation post some eight hundred yards from Leighton Buzzard Station. When I left they were all loosely congregated in their own groups, clustered in the lee of the embankment, with the exception of Roger Cordrey, who was on the gantry preparing the equipment that would effect the red light and eventually halt the train.

Buster would be with Gordon, Charlie, Roy, Jim and Flossy. The South Coast boys – Big Jim, Tommy Wisney, Bobby Welch, Frank Munroe – would be together. Big Alf Thomas would be floating; he was the sort of guy that could fit in anywhere and do anything.

All afternoon I had prowled the various rooms of Leatherslade Farm. I told myself I was maintaining morale, but there was no sign of weakness, only irritation. Waiting is always the most difficult time; it is when people look inwards and begin asking themselves questions.

The scene was reminiscent of all the war films I'd seen, the strung-out faces, the perpetual fag hanging from dry lips, the long silences. Buster was pushing cold chips around a plate with a fork; Paddy playing patience, flicking cards theatrically and cursing his luck; Roy cleaned and re-cleaned his hands, scraping oil and grease from beneath his fingernails; Biggsy stared out of the window as if watching the grass grow; Big Jim chewed gum like cow's cud and pressed his arms against the doorframe as if trying to topple the house; Flossy couldn't stop talking – he kept telling stories of how he used to rustle horses in the Midlands.

Only Gordon was absent. His late arrival was cause for concern. I couldn't afford to lose him; even though everyone had rehearsed everyone else's job, he exuded such confidence that he could instil success in others. Like Harry, Gordon was a man who could funk things to happen by positive thought.

I was getting worried. Gordon was cautious, an admirable trait but it could be carried to the extreme. That was the difference between us. I would gamble everything in the pursuit of the objective and Gordon would not. In truth, he was more professional than I. For one thing, he would never have shown his face when renting the farm. Nor would he have opened the door to My Wyatt, the neighbouring farmer who called in to ask if I wanted to continue the pre-existing arrangements for the rental of the adjoining fields.

After the event, I always knew Gordon was right. But to me everything was secondary to getting things done. Buster was very much the same. He was always the first volunteer for anything a bit awkward.

Finally, at eleven o'clock, Gordon staggered in with a bottle of Jameson's Irish whiskey in his hand. 'The hit is off,' he said. 'Postponed for twenty-four hours.'

Gordon had been at Brian Field's house in Pangbourne, awaiting the confirmatory phone call from the Ulsterman that tonight would be the night. When the call finally came it was to say that the hit would have to be deferred. He had been in no great hurry to get to the farm to inform us; after all, we now had an extra twenty-four hours to play with.

We were all mightily pissed off: another twenty-four hours of waiting.

At eleven o'clock on the seventh we changed into our 'uniforms' and prepared ourselves. Hardly a word was spoken. I suddenly felt a great sense of affection for my 'troops'. Charlie I'd known since I was a child returning from evacuation. Paddy and Biggsy from my late teens, Gordon from my late twenties. They were a part of my life. I trusted them implicitly.

Everyone moved with a sureness and sense of purpose which belied their nerves. The previous night's preparations had acted like a dress rehearsal. There would be no more calls saying, 'Not tonight, Josephine;' this was the real thing. The atmosphere had radically changed. We were moving, the show was on the road.

Filing out of the house into the cool air, we merged into selected groups. Not quite Guards material, I thought, but we weren't applying for jobs with the Bank of England. The uniforms had been left to individual choice and the lack of uniformity showed. We resembled an old black-and-white photograph of irregulars in Popski's Private Army or the Long Range Desert Group. It was exactly the effect I desired.

I looked exactly like 'The Major' in brown jump boots, olive drabs, a camouflaged Airborne smock, gold-rim glasses painted black, a close-cropped military haircut crowned by the sand-coloured beret of the Special Air Service with its dagger badge and motto, 'Who Dares Wins'. It stood for everything I believed in.

But the uniform wasn't self-indulgent fantasy. Locals were unlikely to be suspicious of an army convoy parked under Bridego Bridge in the early hours. PC Plod would similarly be unconcerned, and if he did ask questions I would place him 'under arrest' for the duration of the operation. Sure, he'd cough, splutter and protest, but as 'The Major' I would inform him curtly that I was in charge and carrying out my duty as part of a military exercise.

It was a marvellous summer's night, the air still warm from the day's sun as we drove down B-roads in the moonlight watching the shrubs and hedgerows appear in the headlights. The route had been defined to cross just two main A-roads. The radios were tuned to the police frequency but there was no activity. The previous night, the only major call had been to a break-in on a cigarette machine.

'Sgt Paddy' was driving one Land-Rover, and he appeared to wear his stripes with pride. Periodically, I reassured him about directions. We'd been over the route a few times together, but I knew it better than most. I hadn't wanted people bombing up and down country lanes drawing attention to themselves and maybe getting a pull from Mr Plod, leaving their names on file to be dredged up later.

Sedately we criss-crossed Buckinghamshire, seeing little traffic and only one solitary human, a guy hitching at the side of the second main road. He wasn't going our way. We passed the country estate of Mentmore, home of 'landed gentry'. Their wealth and privilege had in all probability been founded on similar acts of brigandry. Not much chance of Ks being given out for tonight's good work, however!

We ran past Rowden Farm – their phone would be cut later – and pulled up at Bridego Bridge at 1.30 a.m. We disembarked and huddled in groups with time enough to spare. Several of the firm climbed up the embankment to review the landscape and note points of interest: the signal gantry straddling the lines, the dwarf signal beyond, the telephone that connected up directly to the signalman in his box further down the line. We jemmied open the railway hut, removing tools and items of railwaymen's clothing. Then we turned the vehicles to face in the right direction.

I went off with Paddy and Roy in one Land-Rover to cut the preselected telephone wires. Roy did the climbing, showing the agility that had confirmed his status as a major talent on the Riviera jewel circuit. Then we returned to Bridego Bridge.

The walkie-talkies were taken up the line a distance and tested yet again. Then, shortly before two-thirty, we congregated *en masse* close to Sears Crossing to go over the plan a final time. There wasn't a lot left to talk about. The vacuum was filled by jokes and quips, all puerile and meaningless, but at least they released tension and kept everyone thinking positively.

At around two-forty, I said my last words with the guys, before setting off with Paddy to take up his position at the dwarf signal.

'All right, chaps?'

'You sure it's always on time, Bruce?' someone asked.

Roger answered, 'Never more than five minutes late, never more than a minute early.'

'Let's hope it stays that way.'

'Yeah, we don't want any delays tonight.'

'Or strikes.'

'No worries about strikes,' I said, 'our man has guaranteed that.'

'Who the fuck is he, Dr Beeching?'

'Could be. Could be anyone. Who the fuck knows? Who the fuck cares?'

'Well, it's a good night for it, anyway.'

'Listen,' I said, 'any night you nick a few million is a good night.'

I sauntered over to Alf and Jim. 'Right, Alf? Right, Jim?'

'We're right.'

I looked at Roy. His face was as composed and focused as in the picture I'd seen of him in the motoring press the week before, sitting in the cockpit of his Formula Junior Brabham at Goodwood. He'd beaten Jackie Stewart that day; surely he'd be the next World Champion? I rubbed shoulders with him in a gesture of intimacy.

'It's a great night for the climb, Bruce,' he said, nodding his head at the bright moon.

'My favourite,' I replied. 'A hunter's moon, the poacher's friend.'

'Think we'll poach this one, Bruce?'

'I feel it in my water.'

'I hope so, I've got a new engine ordered.'

'You can go to Ferrari's after this lot, Roy; you can get any car you like.'

'You fancy a Ferrari yourself, don't you, Bruce?'

'I'd love one. Especially the GTO. That's some machine.'

Big Jim Hussey cut in. He'd had experience in the car trade. 'They're useless as an everyday car,' he said. 'Always need a tune-up, and the fucking spares'll cost you the earth.'

'I should fucking worry,' I said. 'I'll have it tuned up every other day – with what I've got coming I can afford it.'

Charlie was listening. 'Gordon will buy a new car, won't you, Gordon?' he said.

'If I can afford it,' Gordon said.

'You can afford a Bentley Continental now,' Chas grinned.

'I wish I could. I'm fucking skint at the moment.'

Everyone laughed. Gordon's caution with money was legendary.

'You were skint after the Airport when we'd just cut up sixty fucking grand,' Buster piped.

'Well, I was. I had a lot of debts to pay,' said Gordon defensively.

'You gotta lot of debts to pay after this one,' Chas said. 'You'll be skint again.'

'Bollocks, I'll be all right after this one.'

Chas looked at Gordon for a moment of two, and then, using our nickname, said, 'For fuck's sake, Blue, put your mask on. You're so ugly.'

Laughing, Gordon pulled his stocking mask down over his face.

It was time to move and I had the last word.

'See you at the bridge. Be lucky.'

With Paddy at my side we set up the marker that indicated where the train should stop. Then we drove back to Sears Crossing bridge, where Paddy got out to go to the dwarf signal. I continued northwards on the B488 running parallel to the tracks, to the bridge beyond where I would establish the radio link-up.

Standing on the embankment I saw the locomotive, lighting up the sky as it hurtled towards me. I stood up confidently, 'the youngest major in the British army', and felt my stomach turn. For an instant, the consequences of my actions hit me. For a split second I had a vision of the bad old days in prison being kicked to death by a handful of sadistic screws in a cell with a bloodstained floor. It passed just as quickly as it came and I sent the signal for the final act.

'This is it! This is it! This is it!' The walkie-talkie crackled in my hand.

'Check.'

'Check.'

'Check.'

The replies echoed slightly before being engulfed in the roar of the diesel already braking hard as it responded to the cautionary amber of the dwarf signal. Slowly the metal monster decelerated, amid grinding metal and fumes, until it barely edged forward and stopped at the glowing red signal at Sears Crossing.

Feeling remarkably calm, I stretched and wandered down the embankment. So far so good. As per railway regulations, I paced out the required distances to place detonators on the line behind the stationary train. Returning to the Land-Rover I drove off to pick up Paddy at the Sears Crossing bridge, throwing away the stub of my cigar.

Paddy was waiting for me, a cool grin on his face. 'OK, we've stopped it.'

Driving back towards Bridego Bridge, we saw the stationary English Electric Locomotive a few hundred yards away with its full complement of coaches. I stopped and turned off the ignition. Each sound told the story. Clanking metal – that would be Jimmy and Roy uncoupling the 'loco' and the two coaches from the rest of the train; distant muffled voices, and then an ominous silence, quieter than quiet, as if everything had shut down for a second before the night noises of the country recommenced. It was like watching a well-rehearsed performance unfold on the stage. In my excitement I wanted to shout, 'Bravo!'

Paddy and I leant forward in our seats when we heard the loco's diesel throb into life. We waited. There was no movement. Looking at each other, our eyes asked the obvious question. Paddy shrugged.

It was only later that we learnt that, inside the cabin, a problem had emerged. The train driver, Jack Mills, had been coshed in the initial assault on the locomotive. Our ex-driver Peter was then unable to 'get a vacuum' to set the loco in motion. Mills, although bleeding, was told to take over the controls.

The diesel revved again and this time, almost impercep- tibly, a gap opened between the moving and the stationary carriages.

'They've got it,' I said, shaking Paddy's hand. I tried to start the Land-Rover but in my excitement forgot to turn on the ignition. Paddy leant over and switched it on for me with a grin. Thank God for sergeants, thought the 'major'!

Keeping to the road, we followed the loco, speeding up as we neared Bridego Bridge to give ourselves enough time to park up, climb the embankment and direct the train to its final stop at the marker post.

I saw it coming slowly, with the cab seemingly supporting the whole firm, their arms waving, shouting commands and offering encouragement. Marvellous, just marvellous.

Stopping at the marker, the firm clambered down and we immediately began the assault on the High Value Coaches. Leading the way, Charlie smashed the window with a large axe and then hurled himself through, closely followed by the rest of the assault team – Jimmy Hussey, Gordon, Bob Welch, Buster, Tommy Wisbey, 'Big Alf' and Frank Munroe. In less than a minute the doors slid open and bags began to spew out on to the embankment. A chain was formed and the bags passed hand to hand down to the lorry.

I caught sight of Peter, our reserve driver, who didn't look at all well. Reality doesn't sit too well on some people's shoulders, and he'd seen blood and didn't like it. He was taken to one of the Land-Rovers to sit it out with Biggsy. Bobby, meanwhile, was attending to Jack Mills and the fireman. He'd given them cigarettes and was calming their fears. After checking they were all right, I returned to help in the mailbag chain, realizing that time was running out if we were to keep to our schedule.

'That's it, chaps,' I eventually cried, checking my watch.

'But there's only a few left,' said Charlie.

'Fuck 'em, time's up, let's get on the road.'

I had a last look inside the coaches; nobody was going to be left behind on this one. A further check of the vehicles established everyone was present and I took my place in the lead Land-Rover as we headed off into the night to the temporary sanctuary of Leatherslade Farm.

The mood was quiet and subdued in my Land-Rover. Paddy and I gave each other grins of satisfaction. Looking across the darkened fields, I didn't know whether to yell or to cry. We'd done it!

The twisting country lanes threw back the echoes of laughter from the lorry behind. There were no reservations there; they were enjoying themselves, joining in with Tony Bennett on the radio singing 'The Good Life'.

As we pulled up in front of the farmhouse at 4.30 a.m., smack on schedule, the VHF scanner crackled to life.

'You won't believe this,' said one officer over the airwaves, 'but they've just stolen a train.'

The bags were eagerly unloaded and stacked along the living room walls and in the hallway. Soon there was precious little room for us to gather amidst them to view the spoils. As if on cue, men began ripping open the bags and stacking the parcelled contents. As each bag was emptied, Gordon checked it for homing devices. We didn't want any gatecrashers at our party.

I surveyed the scene with pride, the healthy stack of bundled banknotes a tribute to our endeavour. I thought, I'll never see that amount of money again, certainly not in cash. Around me a party was starting, each man getting off on the greatest, most cynical drug in the world – money. Yet deep inside, I could already feel an emptiness, a sense of anticlimax. So we've got it; what do I do now?

Suddenly I remembered it was Biggsy's birthday and I wished him the best. Then I went to each of the firm and thanked them for their efforts. I was tired, I'd had enough. 'I'm going to hit the sack for a couple of hours,' I told Buster. 'I'll leave you to supervise the final counting and divvying up.'

I slept deeply for two hours and was awakened by Buster, who told me the score: 'Two and a half million, mate!'

'How do you feel about that?' I asked.

His reply was succinct. 'That'll do nicely,' he beamed.

I guessed it would.

28

Two million, six hundred and thirty-one thousand, six hundred and eighty-four pounds! (*At 2003 prices, the equivalent of over £35 million pounds.*)

The sheer size of the prize was staggering and unprecedented – the stuff of dreams. Soon, as publicity spread, it would capture the imaginations of the general public like no other robbery before or since. Within hours the news was being wired overseas and the hold-up of the Glasgow-to-

London Post Office train would become front-page news internationally.

Celebrating at Leatherslade Farm, none of us had any idea of how famous, or infamous, we were becoming. The 'Great Train Robbery' was about to enter criminal history and become part of British folklore. By the following afternoon, it was already the major talking point across hotel bars, garden fences and office tea trolleys throughout the nation.

The reason was primarily to do with the enormous amount involved. Johnny Haynes, the Fulham and England footballer, had just become the first member of his profession to earn £100 a week. The average male wage was less than a fifth of that. Our whack of £150,000 each was equivalent to the biggest football pools win of the time.

The way many of the public saw things, it was an unimaginable sum in untraceable notes that had been stolen from large, anonymous banks and 'nobody had been hurt'. The driver, Jack Mills, had been hit twice as he struggled with the assault team, but he was never unconscious. Charlie had made him comfortable, patching him up and offering him a cigarette as they sat on the grass verge beside the tracks.

'I think you're real gentlemen,' Mills had said.

Charlie asked: 'Do you want any money? We'll leave it on the grass verge for you.'

Mills had shaken his head.

I didn't anticipate staying at the farm any longer than I had to but had made provision for emergencies by stocking up the larder. We had enough food to last us for weeks if we found ourselves under siege. Every eventuality had been considered, I thought, but I was wrong. What I couldn't have foreseen was the importance of the solitary hitchhiker we had passed on the road to Sears Crossing.

The radios were crackling all day, both the VHF and the conventional wireless. The activity was awesome, with the boys in blue buzzing everywhere. The news bulletins kept upping the ante on our take, starting originally at a million, then creeping upwards as the day wore on. At one point, when the announcer spoke of one and a quarter million, one of the blokes called out, 'Think again, clown – there's two and a half million here.'

Then the news was broadcast that an aircraftman hitching a lift had been passed in the early hours of the morning by what he took to be an army convoy. The police were very interested in this convoy, and anybody who had knowledge of it was asked to contact their local police station.

I knew that Mr Wyatt, a local farmer who had previously rented fields from Mr Rixon at Leatherslade, had seen the army lorry when he visited to ask about the fields. I had told him that I was just there to supervise the workmen and we would have to ask the new owners. I promised to put in a good word for him. What if he had heard the radio broadcast?

Discussions raged about what we should do. We eventually agreed that the police would be inundated with sightings: after all, there was army traffic in the area, plus any number of agricultural vehicles that might easily be mistaken for military ones. In any case it was early days, and I knew that it would take time for the police to mobilize. Once they'd got up a head of steam it would be a different story; then, the pressure would be inexorable.

I felt quite happy that their manpower would not extend to large-scale searches, though if they started asking about recent property transactions I didn't trust Brian Field to stand up to questioning for more than an hour or two.

For now, however, it was a safe house. We were on a high, but alert. People began clearing up, disposing of all combustible evidence in the stove and wiping down every surface and object.

The radio announced the latest figure of 'just over two million pounds' and everyone cheered. I imagined Franny sitting close to the television with Nick on her lap, attentive to any news of her beloved and funking for me all the way.

The very same thoughts were being voiced by some of the other married or romantically inclined members of the gang. Other voices spoke of what they planned to do: businesses started, clubs opened, holidays of inordinate length, yachts to be bought and sailed around the world. For Roy it was to be the latest in motor-racing technology; he'd surely make World Champion now. For me, I thought: I'll put Nick's name down for Harrow – not Eton, that was too common. Winston Churchill had been at Harrow, and that was good enough for my boy.

Everyone had made their arrangements for leaving the farm. Even so, there was a certain amount of apprehension about splitting up. There was a strength in numbers and we were prepared, if necessary, to fight for our lives.

I left early the next day after setting an example by wiping down yet again.

'Why don't you open a fucking office cleaning business, you cunt?' Charlie said. 'You'd be good at that.'

I laughed and said, 'Get on with it – you don't want to leave any dabs, do you?'

'Fucking dabs,' he said. 'There won't be any fucking surfaces left in a minute, let alone fingerprints.'

'That'll suit me fine, Chas,' I said as I looked at the line of men behind me, each with a damp cloth in his hand, wiping everything in sight.

I said my goodbyes and walked out into the warm sunshine, dressed in a Burberry sports jacket, Simpson's cavalry twills and Fortnum's chukka boots. As I walked along the lane towards the bus stop, a car stopped beside me. Two colonel types inside asked me if I wanted a lift. Dressed as I was, they obviously recognized me as one of their own.

I climbed aboard and immediately joined the conversation. It was on the obvious topic.

'They should be bloody well horse-whipped!' said the driver with outrage.

'Yes, yes,' brayed his companion.

I could not let this go without adding a little something of my own.

'That's right, sir,' I said. 'Teach those blighters a lesson.'

They dropped me off in Thame where good old Mary and Rene were waiting with the van. There was little time for pleasantries. We did the changeover and I drove back to the farm, loaded two whacks, Paddy's and mine, and together we returned to Thame. Then, after handing the van back to the good ladies, we caught the Greenline bus to London.

When the bus arrived at Victoria we took a cab to Mary's house in Mitcham. Mary and Rene had already arrived; we sorted out the money and put it in a lock-up I'd rented near by. It was hidden under stacks of furniture, so it would take anyone an hour or more to get to it.

The following day, I was reunited with Franny and Nick. I gave her a hug, burying my face in her hair and spinning her round and round in the kitchen until her feet left the ground. Home had come the conquering hero, exactly four hundred years after Drake sailed home from Panama to Plymouth Harbour with the £50,000 he'd secured from the Nombre de Dios treasure trail in Panama.

Franny only had a vague idea what we had planned. I didn't tell her everything because crime was very much a man's world. Now she was overwhelmed, excited, confident that I could handle what happened next.

From the outset it was obvious that we would be targeted: the London Airport Robbery had put us in the frame. There were only a couple of other firms capable of work like this – a view repeatedly put forward by the top jollies at the yard.

Of course, Franny and I couldn't stay in Putney. If I was linked with the robbery, I wanted to make sure I wasn't available for questioning.

Nick was farmed out to Mary and Rene and we packed a few things in suitcases and moved in with a long-time friend, the Captain, who lived in a big mansion block in Queensway with its own porter. Of course, he wasn't a captain at all. His real name was Alan and he'd started off as a freelance photographer in Trafalgar Square, taking pictures of tourists feeding the pidgeons and doing some film work as an extra, including lounging around in a toga and tunic in *Cleopatra* with Liz Taylor and Richard Burton.

The Captain lived in a fantasy land of role-playing and skullduggery. He'd call himself Captain Alan and dress accordingly. Then the next day, I'd see him walking down the King's Road in cowboy boots and a leather jacket.

I could, however, trust the Captain, which was important when there were armies of informants hungry for their whack of the £260,000 reward money that had been announced within days of the robbery.

Informants are a misguided breed. The police may find them useful, but they regard them with contempt. Why wouldn't they? What sort of person shops a person for money? They spill their tittle-tattle to policemen who promise never to divulge their sources but the guarantees are always hollow. After all, what is a promise to an informant?

It was only much later that I learned that the official version of how the police linked us to the 'Train' was that Ernie Millen, then Detective Chief Superintendent, the chief of the Flying Squad, together with George Hatherill, Commander of C Department, visited an informant in prison who had contacted them via his barrister. He gave them the names that they wanted, names that were already on their hit list.

Now they had confirmation of a kind – more than enough to go on.

Five days after returning to London, I became increasingly disturbed by the lack of confirmation that the farm had been cleaned up. The plan had been to leave absolutely no trace of having been there – no fingerprint, tyre mark or mailbag. I expected to hear that the job had been done, but, with no confirmation, I called a meeting of the few of us who were available.

We met outside a transport café on the North Circular, well off our plots. As ever, Buster was already there when I arrived and we waited for Charlie and Roy. The sight of them appearing in Charlie's Rover 3.5 coupé gave me a temporary lift; it was good to be with the guys again.

We presented an incongruous quartet in the transport café – Buster and I immaculately suited and booted, while Chas and Roy were in smart casuals. Sitting around a bare wooden table, we nursed our teas and kicked around the problem. In the absence of confirmation we decided to go back to the farm ourselves that night and clear out the mailbags, the only clue linking Leatherslade to the robbery. The original plan had been that Jimmy would take them away in the lorry for disposal elsewhere, but it had to be scrapped the moment the vehicle was reported by the hitchhiker.

Over the next cup of tea, Buster went out for the afternoon paper. I saw from his face as he returned that something terrible had happened. Without a word he placed the paper on the greasy table.

'HIDE-OUT DISCOVERED', screamed the headlines of 13 August.

'Well, that's that,' was the general reaction, and I had a deep sense of foreboding. The moment I saw the front page, I somehow knew that I would go to prison again. It was a powerful feeling, but I tried hard not to let it show.

To give myself time I took out a Montecristo, cut it, lit it, and fitted it into my Dunhill ivory-and-gold cigar holder. Oblivious of my surroundings I puffed a dollar's worth of cigar smoke into the atmosphere as a gesture of bravado before saying, 'Well, what's the next move?'

Charlie said, 'Let's go down there anyway – we can cop for whoever is there and clear out the place.'

Charlie meant it, that was obvious; with him it was never bravado. But it made no sense. There would be more Old Bill down there than the passing-out parade at Hendon Police College.

'They haven't got us yet,' was the consensus. The 'game' was still on.

So were we suspected? Probably, but there was nothing to worry about. We were all confident that we hadn't left any identifying trace behind. From the outset we had all worn gloves, the most elementary precaution on any bit of work, let alone the biggest heist in history.

My principal concern was Brian Field and his associates. They had handled the conveyancing and purchase of the farm, and it was only a matter of time before they were interviewed. How would they stand up to heavy interrogation? I know they wouldn't last long before they would be co-operating fully in the vain hope of evading jail terms. They had always been the weak link, one that we had accepted in our confidence that the farm would never be associated with the robbery.

'Look at this!' Roy said, stabbing the newspaper with his forefinger. 'Fucking Tommy Butler's in charge of the London end.'

We all knew of Butler. He was the Flying Squad's number-one 'hit man', a dedicated career policeman who knew how to get results. He went back a long way – all the way to Cyprus where he had advised police on the island how best to combat the terror group EOKA and its leader, General Grivas.

Then, he and Peter Vibart had turned their attentions to Soho and successfully pursued underworld heavies like Billy Hill and Jack Spot – successful to the point of curtailing their activities and earning respect. They had also investigated corruption involving the Chief Constable of Brighton and two of his top CID men in a case that shocked the nation because of the high rank of the senior officer concerned. The Chief Constable was acquitted but sacked and two CID men were convicted.

Later, both Butler and Vibart were accused by a bookmaker of having fabricated evidence, but neither judge nor jury believed that the members of the most respected police unit in the country were capable of such a thing.

Tommy Butler wasn't a typical squad man. His rise through the CID ranks was meteoric, from detective sergeant to chief superintendent in less than ten years. A non-smoker and moderate drinker, he was a life-long bachelor who lived with his mother in west London.

Looking around the café table, I could sense the disquiet. The dramatic news had left its mark.

'At least we know what we're up against,' I said, but there was no reply. We were reluctant to end the meeting and the reinforcing element of being together. No-one wanted to be on their own but it was the only way that we were going to survive.

Chas looked at me holding the burning Montecristo and said, 'Give us a puff of that, you greedy bastard.'

Astonished, I passed him the cigar in its holder and he took an exaggerated draw, puffing out the smoke with an involuntary cough. 'Fucking hell!' he said, laughing loudly. It was a personal show of contempt to the world and, in particular, to Tommy Butler. Chas was telling them to do their worst.

Taking back the cigar, I considered my old boyhood friend – the first friend I'd made when I returned from evacuation in 1943. The last time that I'd seen him smoking was in the 'gang' hut, the Anderson shelter in his back garden.

We shook hands and wished each other luck.

We had thrown down the challenge and the Establishment had picked it up. There were no rules to this game, no umpires to ensure fair play, it was us versus them – no holds barred! That's the way 'they' played it.

By the following day, the papers revealed what clues had been found at the farm. 'Arrests are imminent,' said the Yard in a typical press statement, designed by the hunters to flush out the hunted. They hoped that the spectre of long years in prison would create panic and force errors.

The daily newspapers also revealed that among the specialists sent to the farm was Detective Superintendent Maurice Ray, a fingerprint expert and an old drinking acquaintance from Ben Slennet's pub, the Marlborough. As fellow regulars we had enjoyed the not irregular after-hours piss-ups. Maurice and his mob were very good but in my view they were going to be disappointed. They'd find the same blank surfaces as when they printed the locomotive and the coaches. We'd left nothing behind.

Even so, the next media revelation dropped like a bombshell and destroyed my confidence. Roger Cordrey and someone I'd never heard of, a man called Bill Boal, had been arrested with £141,000 in their possession – cash that was directly linked to the 'Train'. In addition, several of their relatives had also been picked up and charged with receiving.

Roger was the last person that I'd have expected to be nicked. He was so low profile and extra careful. As it turned out, he was bloody unlucky. A policeman's widow had become suspicious when he paid three months' rent in advance for her garage and she phoned the police. Rotten luck, or maybe it was Fate: who knows why these things happen? It was certainly bad news for the South Coast Raiders, Roger's old gang. They'd be firmly in the frame; the clever among them would go underground and stay there.

At least it took the heat off us for a while. There was no obvious connection between the two firms and police enquiries would be complicated by a new list of suspects. It was already burdened by two county police authorities and Scotland Yard's Flying Squad, all seeking priority and dominance over each other.

On 22 August, I went house hunting in the Midlands with Freddy, hoping to buy a place and hide there under an assumed name until the furore died down. Franny didn't come with me; she decided to go shopping in Oxford Street and to have her hair done at Vidal Sassoon's.

Although miles apart and on different errands, we both saw the midday papers at about the same time. Franny told me later that she had just left the salon and was walking past D. H. Evans when she suddenly saw my face staring up at her from a newspaper poster.

'TRAIN SUSPECTS NAMED BY YARD.'

There, on the front page, were large photographs of myself, Charlie Wilson and Jimmy White. All of us were wanted for questioning.

Franny said her hands were shaking as she read the story at a nearby tea-shop. I think she finally realized that it was not an exciting game. It was very serious.

The issuing of photographs of suspects was almost unprecedented. From a legal point of view it was considered to prejudice the chance of a fair trial because it gave undue attention to the suspects and could lead to a direct bias against them in the eyes of a future jury.

The police were pulling out all the stops.

But why was Jimmy White a suspect? He wasn't a known associate of ours; he had been on the run for years and was very discreet in everything he did. Only the real insiders knew of his association with us. Obviously someone had talked – someone who knew what they were talking about. It didn't look good at all.

Franny realized that she couldn't go back to the Captain's flat because the porter had seen us. If he recognized the photograph, the police could already be round there. Meanwhile, I too had seen the story at a newsagent's in St Albans high street.

'Where's Franny?' I said rhetorically to Fred.

I found a call box and phoned. No reply. Had she been picked up? I couldn't go back and see and there was no way of contacting her. Suddenly the heat was on.

Concern for Franny shifted abruptly. What about the money? That had to be the priority. It tied me in directly to the robbery; I had to get it out of the garage that I'd rented in my real name. Even as I had the thought, I was conscious that the estate agents could be reading the newspapers too. Maybe they'd already called the police hotline. Fucking hell! The cozzers would go to the garage and clear it out – two whacks, mine and Paddy's, a quarter of a mil. That would be me tied nice and tight into the robbery.

'I've got to take a chance and try to get there before Old Bill,' I said to Fred. 'They could come at any time – all depends when the estate agents read the papers.'

It was one o'clock and we were in St Albans. It would take me an hour and a half to get back to Lodon, and then I had to get a van and some help.

'Hold on a minute, Bruce,' Fred said. 'Think about it. You're putting yourself bang on show. They could be there now, just waiting for you to turn up. Or they could turn up while you're loading. You're better off forgetting the money – at least you've got your freedom now.'

'I know, Fred. I've already thought of the worst scenario – getting nicked, and with the money. And half of it's Paddy's as well. He's uncontactable – he's swanning around Folkestone. No, I've got to give it a go. Maybe the agents won't see the papers until later, and Old Bill will just log it with all the other sightings.'

'But, Bruce, I've done all the arrangements, and they're for later in the month. I can't move them forward. Where would you move the money to?'

'I'm up shit creek there, Fred. Everyone I know has either had a spin or is expecting one. Any ideas?'

'Maybe Cyril? He'd sit on it for a few weeks. He's safe enough with money – he's got more than God. He'd look after it just for the buzz. In fact, he'd dine out on the story for years of how he looked after the Great Train Robbery money – and you can bet that he'll let his chief constable pal know all about it . . . after the event, of course!'

'Can you ring him and confirm that?'

'There's no way that he'll refuse me, Bruce – I know too much about him. Go and get the dough and drive straight up to his place. I'll be waiting. But be careful – they'll give any van a spin at the moment, and vans are not that common around his way.'

'I'll be moving then. Be lucky!'

'You be lucky, Bruce. See you later.'

I drove directly to see Tony, an old cycling pal who was as straight as a die but who wouldn't let me down. He didn't: he volunteered his van at once and we drove to the lock-up garages. I had a quick scan of the area, but unless Old Bill were very good at camouflage we were all clear. I lifted the door and tunnelled my way through the furniture towards the back wall. And there, just where I'd left them, were the holdalls. I passed them back to Tony, who stowed them as quickly as he could in the back of his van.

Tony's face was drenched with sweat as he drove north. He looked as if he had just realized what he was involved in, and wished that he wasn't.

I was pleased with myself. By prompt action I'd saved the day, though I knew that luck had probably played a major role too – and maybe all the prayers I'd uttered, and all the funking I'd done.

'You know I'll look after you, Tony,' I said. I felt guilty; I'd used him selfishly, placed his liberty at risk, and all in the name of friendship.

'Bruce,' he replied emphatically, 'I don't want anything. Well, I do – and that's to get rid of this lot and get home.'

'I understand. Relax, eyes on the road, we're almost there.'

At that moment we passed a police patrol car that was stationary on the hard shoulder. It had pulled in a large van that looked very similar to ours. Tony stiffened with shock and the vehicle veered.

'Easy does it,' I said. 'That could have been us, mate, but it wasn't.'

In the plush stockbroker belt of a Northern town, I directed Tony into the drive between Cyril's house and a large garage. The instant the bags were out of the van and on to the asphalt he revved the engine and wanted to be away. I waved him off. He'd been a pal, a real pal.

Cyril chuckled as he struggled up his loft ladder with the bags. To him this was all a game. He offered me a large brandy, which I accepted not because I felt like celebrating, but to steady my shattered nerves.

Now that the money was safe I could turn my thoughts to locating Franny, and then finding the two of us a stow. Fred dropped me off in London and I called Harry from a public phone box.

'I've made a few calls,' he said. 'Everything's fixed. You're booked in at Rick's. Franny is OK, she's staying with friends of friends and will join you as soon as you're settled.'

I knew that Rick's place could only be temporary. He had been at our wedding and featured in the photograph. Old Bill would be around to visit his place in Wimbledon sooner or later – and probably sooner rather than later.

By the time I got to Rick's flat, Charlie had already been arrested at his home. I was worried sick about Franny with no way of contacting her. Then, as the days went by, Rick was increasingly nervous and his wife was continually looking out of the window. Meanwhile, I was polishing off a daily bottle of vodka, just to hold myself together.

Days went by and from the seclusion of my 'safe house' I read all the papers, marvelling at the imagination of the Press and at the same time being sadly reminded of my plight as the suspects were nicked one by one. The domino effect had taken hold and it was just a matter of who would be next. I knew one thing, it wasn't going to be me!

Finally Rick said to me, 'They've got to come round soon. I think you should really go. I've spoken to someone who can help.'

I couldn't blame Rick for being scared. I was scared. But from that moment I passed out of the hands of friends into the hands of people who were subtly yet fundamentally different. My new protectors were 'gangsters' who earned their money as much by intimidation and graft as stealth and ingenuity. Thankfully, they were good friends with Charlie and I had few worries.

My first safe house was a pre-fab near Crawley owned by a man called Toby One-Leg. A couple of hundred pounds changed hands and I was transferred late at night by car.

'You'll be all right, there won't be any callers,' the one-legged man said, moving out and leaving me on my own.

That first night I got to sleep on half a bottle of vodka. At midnight there was a tapping on the door. Do I answer it, or not? I thought.

I was in the hallway, pressed against a wall, trying not to make a sound. The knocking became more insistent and then

I heard the letter flap go up. A woman's voice said, I know you're there. I've heard you moving around, darling, now open the door, there's a lovie.'

I thought, What is this?

'OK, but I'll be coming back,' she said and left.

I didn't know what to do. Who would she bring back? The police? I got dressed and went to a phone box on the corner. I phoned up Harry and he called through to my minders who came round and picked me up.

They were mystified as well. Finally, we discovered the truth. It transpired that my one-legged host had been slipping one to the bird next door and she had come round looking for a bit of rumpy-pumpy.

The heat was enormous. The daily papers were devoting page after page to the story, increasing pressure on the police. For their part, the Old Bill was throwing everything at the case – dozens of detectives, radio appeals, daily press briefings. Police were raiding as many as fifty addresses a day. You'd have thought we'd stolen the bloody Crown Jewels or massacred several busloads of senior politicians.

When I did hear from Franny, it was via the family solicitor. She had gone to him and told him the situation and he arranged for her to stay at a house in Canterbury. A week later, I finally made contact with her. She was told to take a train to Victoria, put her suitcase into a locker and take the tube to Tooting Bec Station. Then she was taken to a flat in South London where we were finally reunited. We hugged each other, trying to draw strength.

I had no idea what we were going to do next. Safe houses were at a premium and help was thin on the ground. Anybody who'd had any form of contact with us had been turned over by the Flying Squad. It was such a terrifying experience that they closed their doors; we were too hot to handle.

Tommy Butler aimed to cut us off at the roots and the policy was working.

If it was difficult for me, it was doubly so for Franny. She had never experienced life on the run, never contemplated that she would have to leave her home, her friends, her son.

She even had to change her appearance, lopping off her expensive Vidal Sassoon hairstyle and dying her hair a ghastly ginger colour.

We arranged to move into a tiny flat near Clapham Common with remote friends. We had a bedroom to ourselves but it was terrible sharing a place with people we hardly knew. And being Clapham, my old stomping ground, I couldn't venture outside.

Meanwhile, I authorized Freddy to collect the money from Cyril, ready for him to put it down gradually, filtering it into various accounts to break down the bulk.

One day, Franny went shopping with the woman of the house. It was 30 August, 22 days after the robbery. They wandered into a nearby butcher who said cheerily, 'Best fillet as usual, Mrs Reynolds?'

She nodded dumbly. It was her old butcher from Putney, now moved to a new business. Franny stumbled out, clutching the meat, and walked to a nearby pub for a vodka and lime to steady her nerves. A TV screen flickered above the bar and the news was on. Franny raised her eyes and suddenly saw her own face on the screen, alongside my own.

'Wanted in connection with the Great Train Robbery . . . Any person who can give information . . .'

Franny left immediately and ran home without raising her eyes from the footpath. We had no choice but to move again.

29

Already I was learning that being on the run cost money. It wasn't just a case of repaying favours, but a rather subtle form of extortion which would soon become far worse. Besides being gangsters, my minders were also into the dog-doping business. Despite the best-laid plans, this was a flawed occupation and I found myself being milked for readies.

The approach was fairly standard. 'We haven't got enough money to put on the dogs tonight, can you lend us?'

Of course, it wasn't a loan. They knew I had money and they wanted a slice. Up to a point, I didn't mind. They weren't overly greedy and it cost me about three grand. Unfortunately, it was a sign of things to come.

Franny and I moved into a flat above the cleaner's in Handcroft Road, Croydon. It was a small, one-bedroom place on the first floor, with the windows overlooking the road. After spending a few days cleaning off the grime and filth, I paid a couple of grand to have a bath put in, using workmen who were friends of the family. I stayed out of the way.

Paddy, too, suffered at the hands of the jackals. After the robbery, my share of the money was safeguarded by Freddy, who also looked after Paddy's whack. We made an agreement about access – knowing that the police would use blanket surveillance to recover the cash. Fred had a banker friend who was filtering it into the system; it would be available once the hue and cry was over. In the meantime, I had kept £5,000 aside as movers money and we were living on that.

Harry visited me. 'I've had a call from Paddy. He wants to see you, it's very very important.'

'How are we going to do that?' I asked, knowing the risks involved in venturing away from the house.

'The guy that's looking after him has made arrangements with me. I'll drop you at Baker Street tomorrow night at eight o'clock. He'll have a car waiting there. He wants you to lie down in the back seat so you don't see where he's going. He'll take you to Paddy. I'll be back at Baker Street at eleven to pick you up. OK?'

It was a risk, but I was sick of being indoors and wanted to see a friendly face. As arranged, I was picked up and my head covered with a blanket during the drive. It wasn't far, but when the car stopped I knew exactly where we were. It was an area that I'd worked – Bryanston Square, just behind Marble Arch. We were talking serious money for some of the flats and houses.

Paddy met me at the door and ushered me inside an enormous place, expensively decorated, with real touches of class. Someone was with him.

'This is Percy,' he said.

My mind began working overtime. Who was this Percy? In our business it paid to know everyone, by reputation if not in person, but I'd never heard of this guy and he made me nervous. It was quickly obvious that he spoke the same language, although with a more cultured accent, and deep down I sensed he was one of us. He knew what we were talking about.

'I gotta have me money,' said Paddy.

I shook my head. 'Come on. That wasn't the arrangement at all. The deal was that Fred would look after the money until the heat was off. He can't dig it out just like that.'

'I've gotta have it.'

'Why have you gotta have it?'

'This guy and his partner are gonna invest it for me.'

'Are you absolutely sure?' I asked. 'Do you know these people?'

'Yes, I know 'em. I'm sure.'

But I didn't know them and I sure as hell didn't trust them.

'They're a hundred per cent,' added Paddy.

'Well, the only thing I can do is ask Fred. I'm not promising anything because I'm not going to jeopardize my money, and that's what you're doing by asking for yours. The last thing Fred said to me was, "Don't start fucking about with it, Bruce, or you can have it all back because I don't want the aggravation." That's because he ain't getting any dough out of it. I'll ask him, OK? No promises.'

'I got to have it,' said Paddy, sounding desperate.

The whole scenario puzzled me. It didn't smell right. I excused myself and went to the bathroom. Locking the door, I had a pee and then opened the medical cabinet. There was my answer. There were two bottles of pills prescribed for a Mr Michael Black.

This was a name I knew.

When I left I said nothing to Paddy. I knew what it was all about.

Harry was waiting for me at Baker Street. As Percy opened the back door of his car to drop me off, he said, 'We'll have the same sort of meet next time.'

'All right, Mickey,' I replied.

He looked at me and gave me a half smile.

Harry didn't know of Michael Black but I filled him in as we drove back to the mews house.

Michael Black's real name was Michael Hackett, a former Leicester boy who had originally been taken under the wing of Taffy Raymond in the early 1950s. Taffy was one of the older climbers who was good at finding up-and-comers, normally at the Billiard Hall in Windmill Street or somewhere like that, and he would 'educate' them and set them to work.

Mickey Hackett had a natural talent for climbing. He was quite fearless and later did some work with Chad, who saw the potential and virtually nicked him from Taffy. Mickey was a good grafter but his world was what I termed low low-life, whereas Chad mixed with high-class low life. Together they became half legendary as 'Chad and the Kid' and scored big on visits to France for about three years running. On a job in Southport, they found a safe amongst the old shirts at a garment factory. When they pickaxed it open, money tumbled out. Some said it was seventeen grand, but I heard it was up to fifty.

'Why has he surfaced now?' I asked Harry.

'Well, Paddy is an old friend of Chad's. Maybe he introduced them. In any case, what can you do? Paddy's a big boy. It's his decision.'

Fred was indeed pissed off to start with when I asked him to fetch the money.

'It's all right, I understand,' he said eventually. 'It's lucky that it's not been filtered.'

When he contacted me the next day he was flapping. 'We've had a fucking close one, Bruce,' he said.

Fred had called at his aunt's house where the money was stowed. He had his own key, but for some unaccountable reason it wouldn't open the door. He knocked and got no response, so he called loudly through the letterbox. He heard disjointed voices and movements but no-one answered the door. He went round to the rear of the house and found the back door swinging open.

'The house was in a shambles,' he said. 'I knew straight-away that the house had been sprung. I ran upstairs to the box room, shitting myself all the way.'

The door to the box room was open, with clothes strewn all around, but the three suitcases were where he had left them – locked and intact.

'Fucking hell, Fred,' I said. 'So they were in there when you knocked?'

'Yeah, it's unbelievable. My aunt's nearly always there, and this was the first time that I'd called so early. Thank God they didn't find the money. What could I have done? What could I have said to you? Would you have believed me?'

'I'd have believed you, Fred. But do you reckon they were after the dough, or was it just a fluke – you know, opportunists at the drum up?'

'I can't see how they would have known anything about the dough. They took a few trinkets, so I suppose they were opportunists. I've moved the money again, and now that Paddy wants his whack it'll make things easier for me. I can get Paddy's to you in two hits – is that OK?'

I didn't like the idea of driving across London freighted up with forty-five grand, and I liked even less the idea of having to do it twice. I debated whether to warn Paddy about what had happened, but his confidence in his minders was absolute. Anyway, Harry was right – he was a big boy and he had made his own decision.

I delivered the final instalment to Paddy and Mickey's partner at his flat in Bryanston Square. He began talking about what they were planning to do for Paddy – how they were going to buy property and change his identity.

He eventually said to me, 'How are you fixed? Are you quite settled where you are?'

'Reasonable,' I replied.

'I could help you there. A friend of mine is a major-general who's just been posted to Germany for three years as part of the occupation of the Rhine. He's got a lovely mews place – space for three cars, six bedrooms, three jacuzzis, the whole lot.'

It sounded too good to be true. 'I could be very very interested, sure. How much is it gonna cost?'

He put his hand on my knee. 'I wouldn't charge you a penny – you can have it.'

I smelt a rat. If I'd been in his position, I'd have been looking to earn some money. This was unnatural. This guy was offering something for free.

Before I left, I took Paddy aside. 'Don't trust these people,' I whispered. 'Get the hell out.'

'You're fucking wrong. You don't know 'em. They're fucking one hundred per cent.'

At 6.30 p.m. on 3 December, we heard on the radio that Paddy and his wife Barbara had been arrested in Belgravia. Absolutely gutted, we decided there was nothing that could be done except get hopelessly drunk and try to forget the setback.

I was drinking downstairs, as was my habit, when I said to Franny, 'It's about time we checked the briefcase.' I always kept my movers money close by in case we had to leave in a double hurry.

'I haven't seen it,' said Franny. 'I'll go up and get it.'

She went upstairs and was coming down again when there was a knock on the door.

'There's a policeman looking through the window!' she whispered.

Christ! I'm nicked, I thought. And then I remembered the last thing my solicitor had said to me. 'If you get caught, don't get caught with any money. That's going to be the principal evidence against you, so don't get caught with any money.'

Where was the briefcase?

Franny opened the door, all sweetness and smiles.

'No, there's nobody here,' she said. 'No, I didn't report any intruders.'

'Well, there's a ladder up to the window,' I heard the officer tell her.

'I don't know anything about it.'

'Do you mind if we come in and have a look round?'

I quickly took my clothes off and crouched naked behind the sofa. As they came into the room I rather shamefacedly stood up, my hands shielding my privates.

It was a ploy I'd used once before when I was caught with a girl in a stolen car on Mitcham Common. Confronted by a naked man the officers immediately became self-conscious, averting their eyes, and not looking directly at my face.

'You see,' said Franny, almost in tears, 'my husband's away and this is a friend who, um . . .'

The policeman looked even more embarrassed. 'Sorry madam. We were just following up a report. No harm intended. If you could just give us your name, sir?'

'Bert Smith.'

'And your address?'

I gave a false one in Battersea, although I made sure the street and house number existed in case they knew the area.

'Well, I'm sorry to have disturbed you, sir; and you, madam. All right then. We'll be off.'

Of course, even as they disappeared, I knew that we would be moving again. The burglary report was indeed genuine. Franny had lost an eternity ring and other bits and pieces, along with a few hundred quid in loose cash. But not the briefcase. It was safe.

I barely had time to consider the losses. The police could easily get back to the station, glance up at the 'Wanted' board and recognize me from my photograph. I contemplated starting a bonfire in the garden and burning three grand, positive that they were waiting for me outside.

Although I couldn't think straight, I knew it was pointless sitting around waiting to get caught.

Over the next 48 hours everything dove-tailed together. For every setback came an opening. On the same day Paddy and Barbara had been nicked the news arrived that the contracts had been exchanged on the mews cottage we were buying in Kensington. The Captain had done the business as nominal buyer and was holding the keys.

I kissed Franny goodbye, telling her, 'I'm going to pick up the keys and move into the other place. I'll be back tomorrow and see how everything is. The Captain or Harry will know where I am.'

I walked on to the road and hailed the first cab I saw.

'I need to get to Clapham Common.'

'No, I'm going home, guv,' he said.

'I'll give you a tenner.'

He dropped me at the big cab rank opposite the Common. I killed a minute or two then took another cab to Victoria Station and walked through the crowds to another cab rank at the far side. Then I took another cab to the Captain's place.

It was awkward avoiding the doorman but I finally managed to get inside and at one o'clock in the morning I knocked on the Captain's door.

Naturally, he was not impressed about being woken.

'It's me,' I whispered.

'Fuck! What are you doing here? Here's the key. Get out as quickly as you can!'

I went through another elaborate series of cab switches before I reached the house in Albert Mews. It was a perfect spot, a tiny dog-leg of a street with a narrow entrance that you could easily miss. Even with an A-Z it was almost impossible to find. Being just renovated, the carpets and curtains were spanking new but I didn't have time to enjoy the luxury; I collapsed on the bed contemplating the future, and fell asleep.

The following day, the police raided the cleaner's shop, steaming through windows and doors, but no-one was there. Franny had left only minutes earlier. The entire contents, right down to the three Tefal-coated pots and pans, one clothes horse and one ironing-board, were seized and stored as evidence in the event of my capture.

We moved into the mews house and established ourselves. The Captain did my running for me, although I also used 'Elegant Head' Bill, who really did have an elegant head and was a dead ringer for Alain Delon. He was another strange character but he loved the whole scene, which was in effect being my batman, going up to Harrods with a shopping list and buying all our essential delicacies.

Those next six months were a really crazy time. We had a standing order at Christopher's in Jermyn Street for a dozen bottles of Veuve Clicquot Rosé and a dozen bottles of anything else which the resident Master of Wine would suggest. God knows if we ever drank it all. I created my first work of art – a collage as big as a door made of wine labels, bits of cork, silver foil from champagne bottles and photographs of Lamborghinis, Ferraris and Porsches. I called it 'The Good Life'. I rarely ventured outside. My weight had ballooned to sixteen stone and I arranged to buy a set of weights and a rowing machine. I spent my days working out, reading, watching television and drinking.

Franny had one night out a week, usually squired by either Elegant Head Bill or the Captain. They went for a meal or perhaps to the pictures.

As the months passed, we learned what had happened to Paddy after Mickey and his partner had shopped him. He was remanded in custody until the trial and then acquitted of all charges relating to the Train. A free man, he was obviously set on revenge: he wanted his money and he wanted the men who had set him up. He knew a few heavies and they moved into action, immediately targeting Chad, who wasn't a particularly good runner. Violence had always frightened the life out of Chad. He explained that he had nothing to do with the sting. He'd simply introduced Mickey because he had a flat and could look after Paddy.

He was probably telling the truth, but matters weren't helped by another incident. Chad had the cottage down at Folkestone and he had briefly looked after Paddy in the days after the Train. Paddy had buried three grand in the garden – it was mad money so that if the rest was lost, he had a stash to call upon.

After Paddy was nicked and remanded in custody, Chad was short of money and probably assumed that Paddy would be convicted and jailed for a long stretch. So he dug up the three grand and spent it. On the surface this sounds like a minor misdemeanour, but given the long-term relationship between them, it was very serious. They were very close and had done major work together. When Paddy was acquitted and found the money gone, he accused Chad of stealing it.

Years later, Chad said to me, 'I didn't steal it, Bruce, I took it. We'd been pals for years, he knows that I wouldn't have taken it unless I needed it. I would have given it back somewhere along the line.'

Paddy accepted the situation stoically, with a few reservations as to Chad's motive; but their relationship was irreparably damaged and they never spoke to each other again.

Mickey and his partner were also chased down and found at a relative's house in Bath. I could imagine they were plenty scared when the heavies arrived at the door. Mickey said he would get Paddy the money. He left the house with a suitcase, saying, 'Follow me and I'll take you to where it is.'

They followed him and he drove into a police station. Sitting outside, waiting, they wondered what on earth he was pulling. Mickey never did emerge. When they returned the next day, his car had gone and from that day onwards he was never seen again.

His partner died about a week later. Of natural causes, of course, although Mickey was the one who was apparently very ill. Paddy went down to the funeral, obviously hoping that Mickey would show up, or that he'd find some clue about the whereabouts of his money. Nothing came of it but because of his connections with Billy Hill it was rumoured that Mickey might have escaped to Tangier. In truth, he could have gone anywhere. He was a worldly guy with ninety grand to spend – £1 million pounds in today's money – it's not hard with that sort of dough to move to Australia or to buy yourself a nice yacht and sail the Caribbean.

Paddy got over losing the money – even though he'd lost more than most good thieves steal in a lifetime. What with the forty grand that was stolen from Ivy and the cash from the Train, he had every right to be bitter.

My sense of being imprisoned in my own home grew gradually worse. Franny and I got on well enough but being constantly together, living in each other's pockets, wasn't healthy. Most nights, Bill or the Captain would stay and have something to eat and occasionally Harry would slip round very circumspectly because, obviously, he was on the Flying Squad's hit list for surveillance.

One night he stayed with us and went out next morning to discover that his car had been stolen from two streets away. Of course, he reported it to the police but gave a totally different location. As bad luck would have it, the car had been driven into a river and they had nicked the geezer responsible as he was dragged from the water. He told them where he had nicked the car from, and it didn't match up to Harry's account. The police didn't say anything but they must have been suspicious. Knowing Harry was linked to me, they decided to keep following him, figuring that sooner or later he would lead them to their prey.

The isolation also began to affect Franny, because it kept her from her family and friends. Of our entire circle, only Harry knew we were still in the country. The rest assumed we had fled abroad.

'There's no reason why you can't go out,' I told Franny. 'You have top-class wigs and stuff to wear. You just have to be careful.'

A few nights later, she was out with Elegant in the Rib Room at the Carlton Tower and excused herself to go to the ladies' room. She was standing in front of a mirror when in walked her sister Barbara. Franny was longing to say 'hello' because they hadn't seen each other since the robbery. Her disguise was so good that her own sister didn't recognize her.

But by far the most difficult separation was from Nick, who was not yet two years old. We both desperately wished we could see him and give him a cuddle. There were days when I even contemplated asking Harry to get him in the pram and walk him down a road somewhere, so we could watch him from a distance and see he was OK. How could he understand what had happened to his parents?

30

By 10 December 1963, eleven members of the gang had been arrested: Roger, Charlie, Biggsy, Jim Hussey, Lennie Field, Brian Field, Tom Wisbey, Gordon, Bob Welch, Paddy and Roy – plus a chap called Bill Boal whom I didn't know.

Of the others, I had heard little. Harry was in contact with Buster's friends, and knew he was safe, 'dwelling the box' (*biding his time*) until he could make his move. The occasional whisper indicated that he was working on some sort of deal to enable him to come forward with a plea that he had only been an accessory after the fact.

Flossy had no previous convictions and stayed well out of contact with the group. A shadowy figure, nobody knew exactly where he lived – or even what his real name was. All we knew was that he was one hundred per cent, and was sure to last out the hullaballoo. The last report of him said that he was in a safe house, banged up with two gorgeous girls and enough champagne to sink a battleship.

Jimmy White had disappeared after we'd had a chance meeting in Park House, Edgware Road. A furnished flat available for short-term lets, it was well used for assignations both covert and romantic, but was on the Old Bill's list. I paid it a flying visit – an in and out job – and on my way out I bumped into Jimmy. He bore no resemblance to his wanted photo, which was probably an old one from the nick. He had his wife's poodle, Gigi, tucked inside his overcoat, with just the face peeking out. We exchanged a few hurried words, mine principally being a warning that Park House wasn't the place to be seen.

'I'm only here for the night,' he said. 'I'm moving on tomorrow. If you need to find me, contact Mary.' Then he moved swiftly on to the pavement and was gone.

Of the others, only Frank Munroe and Alf Thomas were at large, discounting Peter, Biggsy's train-driver pal. It remained a mystery why he hadn't been nicked, considering that Biggsy was collared. Frank was a dynamo with the South Coast firm and had plenty of help. Word filtered through that he was OK – sweating it out but confident that he'd make it. Alf Thomas was another wild card. He had proved a very reliable worker on the Train after putting in so much time on the Weybridge caper. I felt sure that he would evade capture.

It was clear to me that failing to clean up the farm was one mistake. Allowing myself to be seen by Mr Rixon, the farm's previous owner, and his next-door neighbour was another. Even so, I was confident that there was very little incriminating evidence that could link us with the events of 8 August.

What no-one considered was Tommy Butler's ambition and his willingness to circumvent the system. I had always had the utmost respect and admiration for Butler. He was a true professional, as dedicated to his work as I was to mine. His mission in life was to catch crooks by whatever means were necessary; he had a job to do and didn't shirk it. To him, the end justified the means.

Tommy Butler did what he had to do. Perhaps he was ordered to do it by the inner cabal of the Yard responding to their political masters. We were considered to have directly challenged the Establishment, and this impertinence had to be slapped down and crushed dramatically.

From my safe house in Kensington I watched developments unfold with alarming speed and reacted in disbelief to some of the revelations emerging from the Yard. I expected irregularities – these are commonplace, but they are normally corrected by a fair trial. This time it was different. The Flying Squad was determined to make sure that nobody slipped through the net – not even the innocent.

On 20 January 1964, the trial began before Mr Justice Edmund Davies in the Aylesbury District Council Chamber, which had been turned into a courtroom for the purpose. It had the advantage of being close to the scene of the crime and investigation but, more importantly for the police, it made the chances of jury nobbling more remote than if it had been heard at the Old Bailey.

What took place over the next nine weeks was one of the most celebrated trials in British legal history. If Vietnam was the first 'television war', then the Train was the first 'television crime'. The thrust of the prosecution case rested on forensic evidence and a number of casual clues that we were alleged to have left at the scene of the crime and Leatherslade Farm. Much of the evidence was disputed at the trial.

A typical example involved Dr Ian Holden of the Metropolitan Police Laboratory at New Scotland Yard, who testified that on 26 August he had discovered evidence implicating Gordon Goody in the robbery. Gordon had friends who ran a pub, the Windmill, in Upper Ground, Blackfriars. He stayed there frequently and had done for years, with his own room and a change of clothing. After his arrest in the Leicester hotel where he had been mistaken for me and later reluctantly released, the police searched first his room at the Windmill and then the whole pub. Among articles removed were a pair of shoes – brown, suede, Tru-form, size tens with criss-crossed rubber patterned soles. The resident managers, Mrs Alexander and her husband, both claimed that the shoes were pristinely clean when the police took them away. They were, however, found by the police to bear traces of yellow and khaki paint. These were compared with samples of paint taken from a tin of yellow paint which had been found at the farm and proved to be similar but not identical.

Holden next examined the khaki paint from the shoes and khaki paint from the Land-Rover and these proved to be identical. Similarly, he found the yellow-painted lorry to have identical paint to the tin, but only similar to that on the shoes.

Further examination of the two Land-Rovers resulted in the discovery of minute traces of khaki and yellow paint on the pedals. Both paints were identical to those found on the shoes, although it was impossible to confirm that the same shoes had put the paint on the pedals. Finally, at the farm, Dr Holden found traces of yellow paint that had been spilt, mixed into the gravel with mineral content. When analysed, a sample of this was found to be identical to the shoes and the pedals. He had successfully established a link between the shoes, the wearer of the shoes and Leatherslade Farm.

This was the only evidence to convict Gordon. It didn't matter that the defence had its own equally eminent scientist who challenged Dr Holden's testimony. The two equally expert witnesses created a stalemate and the jury was left to decide. That they ultimately chose to convict Gordon may well have been influenced by disclosures that the man in the dock had been charged with, and acquitted of, the Airport Robbery. The prosecution emphasized this point repeatedly and the implication of course was: make sure you don't acquit him of this one!

Counsel for Gordon hinted at tainted evidence and in his summing-up to the jury Judge Davies referred to these suggestions, saying, 'There can be misguided people amongst police and detective forces as there can be in the law, in industry, anywhere . . . We will examine the full implications of the evidence before we come to so ugly a conclusion or give room to so ugly a suspicion.'

Fifteen years later, Piers Paul Reid commented upon the defence case in *The Train Robbers*, 'In the case of Gordon Goody, the discovery of the two distinct paints on the sole of his shoes was little short of a miracle. Here was a man who was known to work with Bruce Reynolds and Charlie Wilson, had walked out of two trials for the Airport Robbery, had humiliated the forensic experts by exposing their failure to notice the forged link in the chain, and had boasted in advance that he was about to take part in something big.'

Nevertheless, this almost-new pair of shoes blemished by paint got Gordon a prison sentence of thirty years.

I still find this difficult to fathom. Gordon Goody was a real professional; he'd been at it all his life. He would systematically destroy his clothing and shoes after each robbery – we all did, it was elementary. Here was a man who spent £80 for a top Savile Row suit and the only time he would be seen in a pair of brown, suede, rubber-soled shoes would be while working. They were cheap and could be thrown away afterwards. Why did he keep such incriminating evidence around him? Thrift perhaps? Someone who had just received £150,000 for his whack was unlikely to be concerned about keeping a ten-pound pair of shoes.

Paint from the Land-Rover was also used to convict Gordon. Jimmy and I had stolen the light blue vehicle from the West End and delivered it to Gordon at his lock-up garage. It was his job to paint it. However, Gordon – always careful – decided it was in his own best interests to get someone else to do it.

Although this amounted to a breach of security – allowing someone else to be privy to part of the plot – Gordon never went near the garage and the newly painted Land-Rover. It was collected by Jimmy and driven to Leatherslade Farm. I don't remember Gordon ever driving any of the vehicles, but the prosecution used paint samples found on the pedals of a Land-Rover to link him with the crime.

In his summing-up, Judge Davies asked the jury to consider the defence suggestions of a fit-up. He put it to the jury that if a policeman, detective or scientific officer like Dr Holden were to be a party to such a plot 'would they not [take care] to see that there could be no possible room for doubt that the paint alleged to be found in various places at Leatherslade Farm ... and the paint alleged to have been found on Mr Goody's shoes was indubitably the same; no point in perpetrating the plot otherwise, is there?'

It was a rhetorical question.

There were probably fewer than two hundred criminals operating in the British Isles who were capable of pulling off the Train Robbery. Yet we were apparently so appallingly amateurish that we left a string of clues behind us at Leatherslade Farm that would have embarrassed a twelve-year-old shoplifter. The most damaging of these were finger and palm prints, which from a legal point of view were considered incontrovertible and sacrosanct.

The prosecution produced a flood of incriminating smudges. This was their list:

ROY JAMES – print on plate, print on Johnson's First Aid Travel Kit.

CHARLIE WILSON – print on kitchen window-sill, drum of salt, Johnson's First Aid Travel Kit.

RONALD BIGGS – print on Monopoly box lid, Heinz Tomato Ketchup bottle, Pyrex plate.

BUSTER EDWARDS – prints on Barclays Bank wrapper, Pwllheli Branch, left-hand print on green (khaki) Land-Rover.

JAMES HUSSEY – print right palm on Austin lorry tailboard.

THOMAS WISBEY – left palm print on chrome handrail of the bathroom at farm.

ROBERT WELCH – left and right palm print on can of Pipkin ale.

JAMES WHITE – a palm mark on a post-robbery-dated copy of the *Oxford Times*, found hidden in a mailbag.

BRUCE REYNOLDS – prints on two Monopoly tokens and a Heinz Tomato Ketchup bottle.

Now that's quite a lot of fingerprints to leave behind, especially considering that Detective Inspector Gerald Lambourne, a print specialist, called us 'highly skilled, top echelon criminals'.

It is also surprising considering that we systematically cleaned the farm for hours before we left. I supervised the operation, and it was still going on when I left. Every wall, door, bench, chair, table, mirror, tap, window-sill, stair railing and kitchen implement was wiped clean.

Lambourne admitted that there was: 'strong evidence that the occupants [of the farm] themselves had tried to wash away traces of fingerprints, using two large sponges we found in the kitchen. In fairness to them they were at a disadvantage: they could not see their prints, but we could.' The implication was obvious – they were cleverer than us.

It was also remarkable how the prints managed to connect almost everyone to the farm and the vehicles used in the robbery. The only exception was Paddy, whose prints were found on a Monopoly set at the farm. His barrister argued that there was no evidence as to when the prints were left. Paddy could have innocently been playing Monopoly weeks earlier and had nothing to do with the robbery. Because these prints were the only evidence offered by police, Paddy was acquitted.

Several of the others tried a similar defence, but there were no more loose ends – as the fingerprint evidence emerged it directly and very neatly linked people to the farm.

But every such victory has a victim – sometimes more than one. In this case it was Bill Boal, who was arrested with Roger Cordrey and charged with conspiracy to rob and receiving. He was sentenced to 24 years. Bill Boal was an innocent man. The Establishment sent him to prison, where he subsequently died, leaving behind a widow and children. If the train driver Jack Mills was the victim of our crime, then Bill Boal was a victim of the judicial process. And while we, the Great Train Robbers, accepted responsibility for injuring Jack Mills, I have yet to hear of anyone accepting responsibility for what was done to Bill Boal.

He was caught with Roger Cordrey, who had £80,000 stolen from the train, but that is all. There was no evidence to convict him of robbery or conspiracy to rob, until the police arranged a minute examination of his clothes which had been removed from him in a police cell. A small brass knob was found in the inner lining of an inside pocket. This knob was said to have traces of yellow paint which proved to be the same as paint found at the farm.

When Dr Holden made a methodical search of Boal's home, which included spectrograph examination of paint samples, there was nothing that compared with the paint on the knob. Therefore, it must have come from the farm. How? Boal had never been to the farm in his life. I knew that; so did all the others.

Bill Boal's defence counsel did not suggest the paint had been planted but Judge Davies asked the jury to consider whether 'any reliability can be placed on the yellow paint which Dr Holden says he found on the knob?' The defence said no, the Crown said yes – the jury, unfortunately, took the latter view.

I read with disbelief the reports of his trial and conviction. If the innocent were being convicted, what chance did the guilty have? Tommy Butler was doing the job that society expected of him.

On 15 April the sentences were due to be delivered. Mr Justice Edmund Davies prefaced his judgement with the words: '[This is] a crime which in its impudence and enormity is the first of its kind in this country. I propose to do all in my power to ensure that it is the last of its kind; for your outrageous conduct constitutes an intolerable menace to the well-being of society. Let us clear out of the way any romantic notions of daredevilry. This is nothing less than a sordid crime of violence inspired by vast greed . . . To deal with this case leniently would be a positively evil thing.'

Chas, Wisbey, Biggsy, Hussey, Welch, Roy and Gordon were sentenced to thirty years. Boal, twenty-four years. Roger, twenty years. Brian Field and Lenny Field, five years. John Wheater, three years.

I was with Franny at Albert Mews watching the six o'clock news on the television. It gave maximum coverage to the sentences, with a potted history of the robbery and the saga that had followed.

At first I couldn't believe it. How could they do this? These sentences would throw the whole system out of kilter: at a stroke, they'd rendered their tariffs ineffectual. What sentences could they now award to the truly savage and horrendous crimes – forty years? Fifty years? A hundred years? These were American-style sentences but this wasn't America; the prison system wasn't equipped for it, nor were the police, and nor, come to that, was most of society.

'This is insanity!' I said to Franny. 'They've created a monster that will haunt them for ever.'

I'd expected the sentences to match the crime, the tariff being ten to fifteen years for similar crimes. But the Train was unique; there was no precedent. The 1948 London Airport raid, known as the Battle of Heathrow, was perhaps in the same category but the maximum sentence handed out there was a twelve.

The sentences were Draconian, but the old-boy network ensured that the black sheep from their own class remained removed from the hard core, which meant that the lawyers Brian Field and John Wheater got minimum sentences – five years and three years respectively. It put the whole joke into perspective, for without their information and complicity there could not have been a Great Train Robbery.

I regretted what had happened to Mills, but I believe it was exaggerated out of all proportion. Little did we know that for the next thirty years debate would rage over which of us coshed the driver. When Piers Paul Reid wrote his book, the publishers wanted the name of the perpetrator before they would do a deal. Buster, being Buster, said, 'OK, I done it.' Of course, it wasn't Buster. He was nowhere near Mills. The man that did it was one of the three who got away.

Although I wasn't there, I do know that it wasn't planned. The last thing we wanted was to injure the train driver. By the same token, none of us was overly concerned about what happened. When I saw Mills with Bob and Charlie he had a cut on his head but seemed totally all right. No-one took any particular notice: he'd just had a whack and that was it.

In truth, the person responsible was the pal of Jimmy's we had recruited for the Weybridge job when we thought we might need some muscle. He was a big strong guy and we needed that. I don't blame him, although the veterans of the firm would probably have subdued Mills differently. After all, if you've got three guys all weighing sixteen stone on top of you, you can't move very far – it's as simple as that.

Ten years after the event, ex-Detective Chief Superintendent Frank Williams said in his book *No Fixed Address: The Great Train Robbers on the Run*, published in 1973, 'At least three men who were directly involved are still at liberty and enjoying to the full their share of the money stolen and the profits from the way they invested it. One of them is the man responsible for the attack on the train driver.

'The train driver's assailant is not some phantom figure lurking in the criminal underworld, I traced him, identified him and took him to Scotland Yard where, with Tommy Butler, I questioned him. We were certain of our facts but he could not be charged because of lack of evidence suitable for presentation in a court; he had left no fingerprints or identifiable marks anywhere.

'None of those arrested informed on him although he had completely disobeyed instructions and used violence during the robbery.'

There is no doubt that the authorities used the attack on Mills to brand the Great Train Robbers as brutal, murderous gangsters, who had to be hunted down and punished severely, scotching perceptions that we were in any way glamorous figures who had pulled off a filmscript plot.

Mills was awarded compensation of £250 by the Post Office and returned to work on less onerous duties. For the record, when he died of leukaemia seven years later, aged sixty-four, the coroner felt impelled to add that it had nothing to do with the bang on the head. Yet the belief persisted that it did.

I have always felt the injury was almost the only weapon available to the Establishment in its battle for public support after a year of setbacks and scandals – Kim Philby, John Profumo, Peter Rachman, and then Harold Macmillan's decision not to lead the Tories into the next election.

It was as if we'd coshed the Establishment and not the train driver.

If Tommy Butler was the number-one headhunter, then my head was as necessary to him as John the Baptist's had been to Salome. We were both living out our roles, the hunter and the hunted. I thought of his moves as he thought of mine. He was never very far away and at times he felt so close that I could smell his breath and taste the prison porridge in my mouth.

As the sentences were handed down, I realized that I couldn't stay in Britain. Although Franny and I were quite happy in the mews house, the frustration of being unable to walk the streets and hold our baby son had become intolerable.

One night Franny came home with Harry and they found the house wrecked. Drunk and tormented, I had gone completely off my head, smashing a Hoover and going from room to room breaking things until I collapsed in a heap on the bed. The fear of arrest was only part of the problem. The fear of what fellow thieves might be plotting was much bigger. The underworld's immediate reaction was inevitable: everyone was looking for a piece of the action. It's always the same when a big touch goes off. Every hustler, thief and entrepreneur is looking to get in: every one of them is thinking, How can I get my hands on a bit of it?

I knew, because I'd done the same myself. A consignment of bullion is stolen, you listen to the gossip and find out who is rumoured to be responsible. If you know the firm then you leave it out; if you don't know them then you look at the possibilities of stealing it from them. If you can't steal it, then you look for the opportunity to handle it for them, taking a percentage for your trouble. Hustlers and entrepreneurs do their presentations on how the 'parcel' is to be sold, moved or exchanged – the ploy is to separate the parcel from its present owners.

With a robbery like the 'Train' the main drawback of these activities was that the whole of the underworld was in a state of chaos because the Old Bill was charging around like a bull in a china shop. Everyone who was anyone was getting turned over and most were petrified that they would be wrongly linked with the crime and fitted up.

After a major coup, criminal activity goes on the back burner; everyone holds his breath until the police have moved on. The only exceptions in this case were the diehards who recognized that this was precisely the time to do a bit of IPO (*impersonating a police officer*) work. Targets holding ready money would be approached by crims with false police identities and spun a yarn about 'We are looking for Great Train Robbery money, we believe you might be holding some, we are required to search your premises.' Naturally the target would protest his innocence, but the premises would be searched and if money was found it would be confiscated 'pending further enquiries'. A receipt would be issued and off would go the IPO mob with their spoils – another nice little earner!

A few cases of this were reported after the Train – not all of them involving crims. Strong rumour had it that genuine policemen were involved in some raids. You had to take your hat off to them: in an open market, anything goes.

Sometimes the attempts to get a slice of the action were more sinister. I heard that while Charlie, Gordon and the others were in custody, awaiting trial, one of the wives was approached by a man who asked her for £5,000 to nobble one of the jurors. This unsubtle attempt at extortion brought home to the guys just how vulnerable their women would be while they were in jail.

Charlie decided to nip this in the bud and arranged for the wife to meet the would-be extortionist at a house in Clapham.

When he arrived, the man was greeted by a few of Wilson's boys equipped with a mallet and six-inch nails. They intended to nail him to a tree on Clapham Common but he broke loose and ran down the road into a shop. They followed him, caught him at the rear of the premises and voiced their concerns, leaving him bleeding and unconscious with broken bones.

When the sentences were handed down by Mr Justice Edmund Davies, I knew that it was time to leave Britain. I couldn't live like a caged animal any longer. We had to get out and create a new life for ourselves. I began considering what countries didn't have extradition treaties with Britain. Initially, I liked the sound of South Africa, particularly because it was English-speaking. But through a close friend I was introduced to an American who suggested a better alternative – Mexico.

A meeting was arranged in March, shrouded in secrecy. Harry picked him up at eight o'clock in the evening, made him lie on the back seat with a blanket over his head and brought him to the mews. From our first introduction, I realized this guy was almost a caricature of a typical American. He was overweight and quite arrogant, but he almost genuflected in my presence, as if he thought I was Lucky Luciano.

He had many friends in Mexico, he said, including senior politicians, and had been to school with the Present of Mexico's son.

'Yeah, I can arrange things for you in Mexico. No problem.'

After he'd left, I turned to Franny.

'I guess it's Mexico then,' she said before I even opened my mouth.

31

Number-one priority was to get a false passport. This, in fact, had been arranged before the Train, but the heat generated by the robbery had made it necessary to get another. My first new identity was to be that of an old acquaintance, a boxer whom Paddy and I had taken on several youthful jaunts.

Larry was a big guy who fancied being a crim until one fraught evening with us in South London that finished in a high-speed police chase. It was one of those nights when nothing went right. We had picked up a ringer at Clapham and Larry was sitting in the back seat, all expansive, saying, 'Fucking hell, this is good – just like the movies, innit?'

When we got to the plot, creeping through a back garden, the dogs started barking, lights went on and we spied a police patrol car coming down the street. Paddy and I started running. We were fit, we were used to it; for us, this was part of every night's entertainment.

We got to the far side of the Kingston bypass and could see the police cars patrolling the streets, looking for us. Further up the road we found a garage with an Austin A90 Atlantic – a pretty fast car for the time. We pushed it down on to the road, got it started and took off just as the alarm was raised by someone putting their head out of a window.

Coming past Hook roundabout, the police were waiting for us. Paddy lost control completely. We had two police cars behind us as the Austin slewed across the road sideways and folded around a large overhead lighting standard. Before the car had finished bending, Paddy and I were out and running. We didn't think about Larry. Vaguely, behind us, I could hear him in the distance, shouting, 'Wait for me! Wait for me!'

Poor Larry suffered that night. We were leaping garden fences, diving over hedges and crawling through bushes. It didn't matter what we confronted, Larry was in it. He bounced off trees, slipped into ornamental fish ponds and tripped over dogs. Dripping wet and puffing, he cried, 'I can't run any more. That's it.'

It was half-past four in the morning. We hadn't broken into anywhere, we hadn't pocketed any loot. All we'd done was be chased all night. When we finally got back to Clapham, aboard an Austin Seven we nicked, Larry was shattered.

'We'll have more luck tonight,' I said to him.

'Yeah, sure, tonight,' he replied weakly. He never came out with us again.

Larry now resurfaced. For a few quid he let me use his identity and the documentation was arranged bearing his name but my photograph. Unfortunately, a few days after the Train, the police visited him. 'I panicked and burnt it,' he said.

Another had to be arranged. Harry did the business with a lovely character called 'Two Moon' Tom, a guy who liked a drink and had done a bit of cabbing and some film work as an extra. He was never going to travel abroad and arranged for me to take his identity. A series of photographs was taken where I had my head shaved and looked like Martin Borman's brother-in-law. My new identity was Keith Clement Miller and my occupation was listed as 'writer'. Because Miller wasn't married, however, there had to be a separate identity for Franny. She became Angela Green and so completely did we become these new 'people' that I never called her Franny or Frances again. Even to this day, I still call her Angela – a name she loves.

Now the big question was, how to get out the country? We looked at various alternatives, some of them totally outlandish. I had the idea of buying a Cadillac and having a compartment built in the large boot, big enough for me to hide inside. Then I suggested, 'You know, I'll get some diving equipment – I'll go underwater across the Channel!'

Far more practical was the discovery of an accredited pilot who was happy to fly me out of Britain in a light plane for ten grand. 'I can take you to Ostend,' he said. 'The way I go in there are no customs. You won't have any problems.'

Harry volunteered to do a dry run. They left on a Saturday morning in a small, three-seater Cessna. The entire flight was hampered by electric storms which buffeted the plane and terrified Harry, who had never flown in something so small. He told me afterwards, 'Don't eat any breakfast and there's no problem whatsoever.'

My finances also had to be rearranged. Without ever having to see the money, Fred did some international money-broking via a character called Herman the German, who organized a Swiss bank account. It cost me ten per cent.

That final week couldn't pass quickly enough. Angela spent her time endlessly sorting out my clothes, as much to kill time as anything else. 'You won't need heavy suits,' she'd say one day, only to replace them the next with, 'You'd better have something warm just in case – the guidebook said it's cold at night at this time of the year.' Then the day after that she'd arrange a mixture of the two.

I didn't care; all that mattered was that it took her mind off what was going to happen, which principally was that we were parting. Shirts were washed and ironed, only to be done again without being worn; she wanted perfection, she wanted to be sure she'd done everything she could to make this part of the caper a success. How it went could determine our future prospects in a foreign country.

We discussed Nick. Angela missed him dreadfully – we both did – but we also knew that the police would be watching him. Because the Flying Squad wanted me, not Angela, once I was gone she could surrender herself to Butler at the Yard and then be reunited with Nick. But what could she expect? Would he be vindictive towards her, aware that I'd flown the coop?

Angela didn't care. She was so excited about being reunited with her baby and her family that she was willing to tackle Butler. She might be losing her husband, though only temporarily we hoped, but she was regaining her son.

We went over the plan time and again, trying to protect ourselves in every way. I was Britain's most wanted man – every newspaper, police bulletin board, TV station and customs post displayed my photograph. Most people assumed I was already overseas and the supposed sightings of me ranged from Rio to Bangkok.

On my last night in England, Angela and I had a quiet meal in the mews house, drinking wine and talking about our future. The plan was for her to join me in a month or so. She would bring Nick and we would start a new life together.

Early on a June morning, Harry picked me up and we drove to Elstree. The pilot was waiting at the timbered gate of the airfield and silhouetted against the trees was a tiny plane. As we took off, bumping along the grass, I pictured in my mind the images of old Resistance films where fliers on the escape route back to England took off from deserted fields for Channel crossing. As the plane banked, I looked down and saw Harry waving. I felt a lump in my throat, and wondered if and when I would see my best pal again. Come to that, would I ever see England again?

Leaving filled me with deep sadness. England was my home. I had grown up on the streets of London, kicking balls in the parks, eating fish and chips on a Friday night, graduating to shopping at Harrods and lunch at the Compleat Angler in Marlow, watching the Thames go by, a pint of beer in my hand.

It wasn't a direct flight. We had to put down at Gatwick to refuel and lodge a flight plan. I didn't get out of the plane and the pilot soon returned, giving me a thumbs-up to say everything was OK. We took off again, turning east across Sussex. I tried to pick out the towns as we soared above the patchwork quilt of fields sewn together by hedgerows, and then we hit the English Channel.

As we landed at Ostend, the pilot shook my hand. 'Well, here we are. You walk through that gate, I have to go over there.' He pointed to a rundown cluster of buildings and hangars.

I walked through and emerged into a car park where Harry had arranged for the Captain to pick me up. Looking round, I could see no-one. The Captain was normally very reliable. Just as I began to worry, a figure stepped out from behind a brand-new Mercedes, wearing a white trench coat and looking every inch the man from Interpol. The Captain was on one of his fantasy trips.

We drove into Brussels, where I was due to pick up the flight to Mexico on the following day. With the bulk of the money safely in Switzerland, I was carrying my movers money of three or four grand in a shoulder-bag.

Harry joined us that night, having flown over on a scheduled flight. After being cooped up for so long I wante to go and celebrate the fact that I could walk the streets an go into a bar or a restaurant or a nightclub. For once I did listen to Harry's advice. My darker side took over and, ro drunk, I had a row with the owner of a club and had t restrained from thumping him. In my stupor, I took ag him for being German and wanted to refight the whole The poor man pleaded with me, 'I'm Belgian, not a Ger

Harry took me back to the hotel and went to get me another bottle. When he got back, the Captain said, 'He's gone.'

'Well, couldn't you stop him?'

God knows where I went; just mooching around, going from bar to bar. Luckily I didn't get into any further trouble and eventually found my hotel again. Harry was furious and made sure I was firmly escorted on to the Sabena flight to Mexico a few hours later. As I reached the immigration control counter, I handed my passport to a surly-looking officer with bushy eyebrows and a disbelieving twist to his mouth. He flicked through the pages, each pristinely blank – no entry stamp for Belgium, or exit from England. I smiled when he looked up at me and checked the photograph of the Nazi fugitive. Then he reached below the counter. I'm fucked, I thought. I was positive he was about to pull a gun or press an alarm button.

Bang! Bang! The stamp thudded into the passport and he thrust it back to me.

I passed into the transit lounge and sat down. Almost at once, my name was called over the Tannoy. 'Would Mr K. C. Miller please report to the Sabena desk.'

My heart began racing. I was trying to think, What had I missed? What check-in procedure was this? Were the Old Bill waiting for me? Were they playing some perverse game of cat and mouse, letting me get so far towards freedom, only to withdraw it when it was within my grasp? But there was nowhere to run. If I was nicked, I was nicked, and that's the way it was meant to be.

Retracing my footsteps, I was greeted by a smiling receptionist who said, 'Mr Miller? Mr K. C. Miller?'

'Yes.'

'Can I see your passport, ticket and boarding pass, please?'

I wondered even more what this was all about as I passed them over.

She thumbed through the documents while I played close attention to her body language. She appeared to be without guile, so I nonchalantly allowed my gaze to wander. There was nothing or nobody in the vicinity that appeared to pose a threat. She took my nonchalance for boredom and quickly said, 'I'm terribly sorry to have bothered you, sir – but as a First Class passenger you should have been issued with our hospitality pack.'

With that, she handed over a handsome travel bag laden with slippers, cologne and various other freebies. I gave her the biggest smile of thanks she had probably ever received and turned away.

As the jet took off, I ordered myself a Scotch – a heart starter. But even then, the drama hadn't finished. We were due to refuel in Toronto but a problem with the engines grounded the plane there and we had to disembark.

'We apologize for the inconvenience,' the captain said. 'Due to technical difficulties, this flight will not continue today. Those passengers travelling on to Mexico will be accommodated in a hotel overnight.'

I wasn't happy about this. It meant that I had to go through Canadian customs – another opportunity for questions to be raised about how I got into Belgium. Like, where was my exit stamp for England?

As it turned out, the check was cursory to say the least, and I spent a relatively peaceful night in a drab airport hotel. My principal worry the next morning was trying to get my shoes on. They were new, from Harrods, and my feet had swollen during the flight so I could barely walk in the bloody things.

And so it was that at seven o'clock on the evening of 6 June 1964, I walked down eighteen silver aircraft steps and set a socked foot down on Mexican soil.

32

I took the big Chrysler taxi from the airport knowing full well that the driver would rip me off. So what? He had to keep himself in tortillas, and I was happy to pay over the odds. I had plenty of money, I believed in redistribution, and I knew that it would look good at the Hilton – sort of help me establish my credentials.

I tried a few phrases of halting Spanish, and to my amazement he appeared to understand. Unfortunately, I couldn't understand a word of his replies.

It was about a ten-mile drive from the airport to the hotel on Paseo de la Reforma and he managed to make it last over half an hour. We drove through the sort of wasteland that surrounds most airports, then hit the light industrial sector and shanty towns. As we approached the centre of town, we were welcomed by broad, tree-lined avenues. It wasn't the Mexico that I'd envisaged, but what can any taxi ride from the airport tell you? Only the same old story, that some people are richer than others, and a few are even richer than those. What I saw, however, I liked. The real Mexico could wait.

I booked into the Hilton and spent the first two days sleeping and mooching around. Finally I bought a street map and starting walking. It was something my dad had taught me, years earlier. We would go for long walks and he'd point out landmarks. 'See that church, there,' he'd say, 'and the clock-tower behind it?' Later he'd say to me, 'Now, you show me the way back home.'

Within a few days, I'd worn out my Harrods shoes and knew my way around the centre of the city. For longer trips, I used a wonderful cab driver I'd discovered who'd been a captain in the Mexican army and drove a big old Chevvie.

'Is it a good army?' I asked him one day.

'Yes, beautiful on parade.'

He then told me that Mexico had at one time had the most honest president in the world. 'Why is that, then?' I asked.

'Some people no liked him. They put a bomb in his car. It blew his arm off.'

'How does that make him more honest?'

'Señor, now when the money ees on the table, he can scoop with only one arm!'

On my fourth night, I woke up and thought the whole room was turning round. Bruce, you arsehole, drunk again! Then I realized it wasn't me. A massive earthquake was shaking the entire building, sending it pitching from side to side. There were screams and shouts from the corridors as people tried to escape. For a split-second the old thief resurfaced and I thought I could slip into their empty rooms and lift a few goodies. Then I thought, Hold on a minute, what do you wanna do that for? You got all the money you need. I piled downstairs and stood with the crowd on the pavement staring at the large crack running down one side of the hotel.

The next day I rented a car and drove five hours to Acapulco. I took off early in brilliant sunshine to avoid the chaos of the morning traffic. After a year off the road I didn't fancy my chances against the tens of thousands of Mexicans who each saw themselves as contenders for the Formula One crown. I'd driven through Paris in the hairy days before the Peripherique, but these 'muchachos' were something else. You had to match them at their own game, which wasn't easy for gringos driving rented cars. The chances of contact with another vehicle were high, and so, therefore, were the chances of contact with la policia. Not too clever in the circs.

Acapulco was a surprisingly small place. The old town was disappointing at first; I'd been expecting another Riviera but the glitz of Cannes wasn't there. However, the ambience of the local life and the beaches more than compensated. I couldn't wait to get into that blue Pacific Ocean.

Lying on the beach, I forget how powerful the sun could be and soon looked like a six-foot chilli pepper. I went shopping for lightweight clothes and decided to go native, picking up all Mexican gear. Only a few days afterwards did I find out that I was wearing the typical uniform of a restaurateur – a floral shirt with embroidery across the chest and white cotton trousers.

The Hilton was ten minutes' walk from town and as I came home that first night, half pissed, two guys slipped from behind the palm trees, one of them brandishing a knife. 'Give us your money!'

Being half drunk, I slung them my wallet. 'There's me money. Now fuck off!'

The blade flashed silver in front of my eyes and blood oozed from a nick in my chest. It could have been worse. Normally I carried quite a bit of cash, but this time I lost only three quid and my Omega watch. Fucking hell, that's lovely, I thought, reading an imaginary headline in my mind: GREAT TRAIN ROBBER FLEES TO ACAPULCO, IS ROBBED ON FIRST NIGHT.

From then on I was more careful, arranging to buy a gun which I kept in the car for security until that, too, was stolen.

* * *

The second stage of the escape plan was now put in motion. In early July, Angela walked into New Scotland Yard, accompanied by her solicitor, and asked to see Tommy Butler.

Angela was taken to an interview room and questioned for five hours. Butler tried to bully her into revealing where I was hiding but Angela stayed calm. She was frightened – half expecting to find that he was a super-human monster who could read her mind, but she discovered that he was an ordinary human being.

'We're going to hold you for a week,' Tommy threatened.

Angela showed him her toilet bag with her toothbrush. 'I've come prepared.'

Tommy smiled, shook his head. 'You've been well trained, haven't you?'

Finally he told her that she was free to go.

'By the way,' said Tommy, 'your son has been in hospital. He's OK now, but it was a close-run thing.'

He wasn't lying. Nicky had apparently got hold of some pills and swallowed them like sweets. They managed to pump his stomach just in time.

Mother and son were now free to be reunited for the first time in ten months. Angela barely recognized the two-year-old, who was now chattering away. At Mary and Rene's suggestion, she took Nick to the South of France for a couple of weeks, hoping to get back into his world. The holiday was a farce because everywhere they went – on the beach, having dinner, in the park – there were undercover policemen watching them from the bushes. When it was pretty obvious that I wasn't silly enough to meet up with them there, the police finally backed off, hoping to get me later.

The reunion wasn't very successful. Nick was so used to Mary and Rene looking after him that Angela was almost a stranger. They didn't get on at all, which was emotionally hard on Angela.

I hadn't any set date for them to join me in Mexico; that was all being worked out. In the meantime, I enjoyed my rediscovered freedom and met some interesting characters. One of them was a Frenchman and ex-Foreign Legionnaire, who was propping up the bar in the Congo, a club in the foothills behind Acapulco. It was probably the most horrible place I'd ever been in my life, which was why I loved it and went there a lot.

I made an even better friend when I went to a tailor, assuming that Mexico City was something like Hong Kong and I could have a suit made up in a day. The proprietor was in his mid-thirties, of medium height and build. He looked Jewish and could have been from anywhere in middle Europe. His English was excellent, and we soon fell into conversation. He introduced himself as 'Joe', and finally asked the inevitable. 'And what are you doing in Mexico?'

'I'm a writer,' I said. 'I'm looking for a bit of colour and I was thinking of settling here. I like the sun.'

I ordered a couple of suits and told Joe I would call back and pick them up in a few days.

My tourist visa to Mexico was only valid for 28 days, in which time I had to find a solicitor and arrange the immigration papers to get permanent residency. Joe introduced me to a solicitor who was willing to handle the application. At the same time, I contacted my American friend who claimed to have gone to school with the President of Mexico's son. He arranged to fly down for a week. It was his job to introduce me to the people that mattered in Mexico City. It took me no time at all to discover that, although he had been at school with the President's son, they were six years old at the time. My Mr Fix-it was next to useless, but in typical American style he was very adept at blundering into other people's conversations and introducing himself, even when the intrusion was blatantly unwelcome. With my English reserve, I found this very embarrassing. I was the sort of guy that wouldn't speak to somebody on a plane unless they spoke to me first.

My circle of friends expanded rapidly, however – all chosen with a view to my future comfort and security. I was shown around a new housing development, attached to a golf course, by the architect, a Texan called Roberto Engelking, who looked like he'd come straight from riding on the range. He wore cowboy boots with high heels, which he propped on his desk as he opened a bottle of Jack Daniel's Green Label and poured me a slug. We kept drinking and at some time during the afternoon I heard myself agreeing to buy an American car which would be fetched down to Tijuana. I mistakenly thought that when my status changed from tourist to *imigrado* I would be allowed to own a car in Mexico City. The arrangements were made and two weeks later I caught a plane to Tijuana.

I'd read all about the infamous border town which the Americans call the arsehole of the world. Every vice you can think of was there in abundance. Twenty million people crossed the border every year, making it the world's most visited town, and it catered to the lowest common denominator. Its roots went back to the days of Prohibition, and young Americans could drink in the bars there at the age of eighteen, as opposed to twenty-one back home. From what I saw, however, you could get a drink there at the age of six, as long as you had the money. And if dirty ladies weren't your bag, then there was the gambling, horse racing, fronton (*jai alai*) and any sort of card game.

A young American delivered the Thunderbird and was handsomely rewarded. I planned to stay the Friday night and then drive back because I was expecting an important call from Angela or Harry on the Sunday. Unfortunately, what I didn't realize was that Tijuana was effectively no longer in Mexico. It was a free port. I had stupidly left my safe country just as my 28-day tourist visa expired. I needed a new one and the immigration office was closed for the weekend.

I had to get back to Mexico City. I knew that if Angela called and I wasn't there she'd fear the worst. On Saturday morning I decided to sneak back across and pointed the Thunderbird along rocky dirt tracks and headed into the desert. It was stinking hot, but the air-conditioning worked a treat and as long as the car didn't break down I wasn't in danger. A hundred miles further on, out of the heat haze a border post appeared which wasn't marked on my road map. I pulled out a wad of money, expecting to be able to lubricate my way through.

'No, get the fuck back,' was the gift of the guard's reaction. He pointed towards Tijuana.

I booked into the four-star comfort of a Travelodge motel and rang up my architect friend to explain the situation. In typical Yank style, he said, 'Hey, no problem. I got a friend, a big politico, he'll help you out.'

After another phone call I found this 'friend', who arranged for me to meet him at a private golf club on the outskirts of the city. He arrived in a convoy of two limousines, filled with flunkies who opened the door and doffed their caps as he stepped into the heat of the morning. This man looked every inch a big shot. Over lunch, he snapped his fingers, summoning more wine, food and finally a telephone. 'Well, Mr Miller. You have no problem. I am ringing my friend the judge.'

They spoke and when he put down the receiver, he said, 'If you go and see him at half-past two he'll sort it all out for you.'

I made a mental note to organize a gift for my saviour. He wasn't the type of geezer you would slip fifty pesos to, but perhaps a gold Dunhill lighter might be the ticket.

After lunch, I met the judge. If only Britain had legal officers like this man. He immediately told me that he owned three brothels in Tijuana and was hoping to expand. I was welcome to sample the merchandise. While we drank through the afternoon, he sent someone out to get the official papers and approved a new visa.

'You could have problems crossing the border by road,' said the judge.

'Yeah, they already turned me back at one spot,' I said.

'They're all looking for money.'

'No, I tried that.'

The judge raised his eyebrows. 'Maybe he'd had a bad morning.'

I could see that the judge was also looking for an angle – a subtle method of being rewarded for his services. Finally he said, 'Maybe it would be better if I brought your car down to Mexico City. I could do with a trip down there and my wife could come as well.'

'An excellent idea,' I said. 'But look, you'd better have some money for expenses.' I have him a thousand dollars. It was all part of the game.

Angela was fine and planned to join me within a fortnight. In the meantime, I had to arrange an apartment. I mentioned it to Joe when he delivered my suits.

'I can help there,' he said. 'I know people with flats and apartments. One of my customers is the President of Mexico's son.'

I thought, I've heard this one before! Joe must have read my mind. 'No, no,' he said. 'Not the President's first son. He's been married twice and this is his second wife's son – a very nice man, a captain in the Mexican air force. He's a pilot and has various properties.'

I was taken to see a magnificent penthouse on Insurgentes Sur. Although it had lost some of its bloom, it was still palatial, with an ornamental pool, a sunken black marble bath big enough to fit a dozen brazen nymphettes, and spectacular views from huge plate-glass windows. I arranged a lease on the same day that my Mexican papers were approved and I was given residency status. As part of the deal, I had to lodge six grand in a bank account that couldn't be touched.

Angela was contacting me almost once a week, normally from a telephone at London Airport. Finally, in late July 1964, I told her that it was safe to join me. Again, Harry made the arrangements. Three separate groups flew to Northern Ireland – Angela and Nick, Mary and Rene, and Harry and his wife. Then they motored down into the Republic to Shannon, making sure they weren't followed or traced.

Angela and Nick were put on a flight to Mexico. Their new identities were Angela and Kevin Green. Because 'Kevin' was supposed to be a boy of four and Nick was only two years old, Angela tried to compensate by dressing him in long trousers and a hat.

I was excited about seeing them and spent a hundred quid on flowers, filling the apartment, and a similar amount on toys for Nick. Waiting at the airport, I was dying for a drink, but didn't want to be drunk when they arrived. The flight was delayed and Nick had apparently thrown tantrums throughout. When Angela walked through the gate, holding his hand, she looked absolutely shattered – but lovelier than ever.

'This is your dad,' she said.

'Hello, Daddy,' said Nick, but I could see that he didn't know me from Adam.

In the Thunderbird, Angela tried to tell me everything that had happened in a jumble of anecdotes and stories.

'What's it like? What have you been doing?' she asked.

I drove into the underground garage, put a key in the lift and pressed for the penthouse. The doors opened directly into the living-room and she was completely overwhelmed. There were panoramic views of Mexico City and Popocatepetl volcano. When Nick saw his own personal mountain of presents he thought it was Christmas. 'Look at that! Look at this!' he cried, running across the cool white marble floors and exploring. Eventually, he flaked out amongst the model cars, soldier dolls and building sets.

Finally Angela broke down. 'It's been terrible, just terrible,' she said. 'I haven't been able to get to grips with Nick at all. Maybe he's been spoilt, or wants to punish me for leaving him.'

A week later we drove down to Acapulco. As far as Angela and I were concerned, everything was marvellous; Nick was the only flaw. We were staying at the Hilton, on the beach, and he was terrified of the water. Walking along the sand, if the wash came within a hundred yards of him, he started screaming. Later we discovered that he had once been knocked over by a wave while paddling.

Every day was a battle with him. He threw tantrums and screaming fits, followed by sullen silences. It was so awful that I thought he'd be happier back home with Mary. Finally, I snapped when he put on a performance in a restaurant. We got into the car, drove up into the hills behind Acapulco and I said, 'Let him cry.'

Nick cried for about two hours.

'I'm not taking any notice, Nick. We both love you but we have to stop this.'

He tried everything – the outrageous screams, the muffled sobbing, the pathetic whimpering, occasionally looking up to see if we were taking any notice. Finally he had cried himself to exhaustion and I said, 'Have you finished now?'

'Yes.'

'Good. We love you, Nick – more than anything in the world – but things are different now. If you're a good boy, we'll have lots of fun and everything will be fine.'

We never had a problem again. Obviously, like all kids, he used to play up a little bit, but it was never unreasonable. It was wonderful being with him every day – not many fathers can do that – and I tried to make up for the time we had been separated. Within a week he was swimming in the pool and paddling in the sea – his fear had gone.

For the first few months we familiarized ourselves with our new home. It wasn't a holiday; this was our future. We could never go back to Britain. I'd go kite flying with Nick and take him to the funfair; or we'd take day trips into the countryside. We booked him into an exclusive nursery school, mainly for American kids, which was situated in one of the oldest parts of Mexico City, San Angel. It cost a lot but was good because it helped him settle and make friends. Angela dropped him off there each morning and I picked him up.

We went out most nights, often to the cinema. It was a curious anomaly that in a country robbed blind by its politicians, every cinema was restricted as to how much it could charge patrons. Everybody in Mexico could afford to go because the prices were pegged to peasant wages. I also went to the boxing, often in the rougher areas which were awash with sweat and tequila fumes. Once they knew I was English not a *yanqui*, it was OK. I wouldn't be in there five minutes before someone said, 'Hey, *Ingles*, you want one beer?'

Joe turned out to be an absolute diamond of a guy, which was humbling to me because I'd always been a little bit 'yiddified', the term at the time for being anti-semitic. There was no reason for my prejudice, although I remembered my old man being that way. He used to do impressions of 'sheenies', and claim that it was the Jews who started wars. Joe was part of the 20,000-strong Sephardic Jewish community, whose ways seemed archaic to me. They rarely mixed with outsiders but Joe took me into his family. He had six brothers, two of whom were accountants and another a doctor.

Joe was a very good businessman and among his wealthy clientele were the people who owned the Aztec stadium and also several breweries. Although I could not be one of them, they knew me, and between them could solve any problem that surfaced. Through him, I began considering my business options. By this time, my whack from the robbery had dwindled to £90,000 and we were spending £400 a month. I needed to do something if the money was to last.

Every year Joe would get lists from all the politicos, detailing the gifts they wanted to send to everyone from their chauffeur, or secretary, to the Minister of the Interior. At the bottom end of the scale would be a Parker fountain pen for the minions and at the top end would be a Ford Galaxy. Joe supplied all these things and took a commission. He was buying gold lighters from a Dunhill agent, but said to me one day, 'This guy has no idea. I'd quite like to take that over.'

I started thinking. In any third world country you can make packets by starting up industries or importing products which simply aren't available. Of course, it is rigorously controlled, but if you grease the right palms and keep the politicos on-side, the opportunities are endless.

Joe said, 'We could look into the possibility of importing Dunhill soaps and fragrances into Mexico. Better still, why not make them here?'

The wheels were put in motion and we began interviewing people and looking at factories which could make the glassware for us and the moulds for the soap. We bought the Dunhill agency off the incumbent and then flew to New York to meet senior Dunhill representatives. The parent company, Dunhill London, wasn't doing fragrances then but they were big business in America.

The chairman was a very nice guy – a former lieutenant-commander in the Navy. He approved the idea but during discussions I realized that I was totally out of my depth. I didn't have a mind like Joe's that could instantly work out the odds and percentages.

From time to time, they turned to me and asked, 'What do you think, KC?'

'Well, you know, I'm not a businessman . . .' I'd mumble. But the more I protested, the more they thought I was a canny Englishman. After all, I was living the good life in Mexico. I had to have made my money somewhere.

The deal went through and we started setting up the factories. In the meantime, we imported the soaps and fragrances. The products were launched in Mexico City at an extravagant party attended by all the movers and shakers. We even invited the equivalent of a consul from the British Embassy. He chatted away to me, totally oblivious to the fact that I was Britain's most wanted criminal.

From Joe's point of view, I exactly fitted the bill. Who better to sell the Dunhill range than an 'English gentleman' who could give the produce the necessary social cachet?

33

Each morning, when Angela dropped Nick to school, I was up, shaved and on my way to the office in one of our two cars. My friendly traffic policeman would take the keys and put the car in a parking lot opposite Joe's store.

Often I'd have breakfast at Sanborn's, an American-style restaurant, and saunter through town, picking up the airmail editions of *The Times* and the *Daily Telegraph* to read how Chelsea were doing in the Cup. Hardly a day went by when there wasn't some mention of the Train.

The Press were still reporting sightings of me everywhere from Bangkok to Birmingham. Apparently I had undergone plastic surgery and was a 'master of disguise'. Photographs were mocked up showing my 'many faces' – with a beard, without a beard, with glasses, without glasses. I had supposedly been sighted having dinners in Buenos Aires and Rio, as well as being seen in Kuala Lumpur and Tibet. When some wag scrawled 'Bruce Reynolds Slept Here' on the wall of a deserted French army hut in the Sahara, the police went scurrying to investigate.

On one such morning in August 1964, I flicked open the papers, leaned back on a park bench with my feet in the sun and glanced incredulously at the headlines. 'JAIL BUSTERS FREE TRAIN ROBBER – THEY KNOCK OUT GUARD, OPEN CELL, GIVE PRISONERS NEW SUIT.' 'ANNIVERSARY ESCAPE WITH THE HELP OF JAIL BUSTERS.' Charlie Wilson had been sprung from Winson Green prison in Birmingham, less than a year after being sentenced. Nice one, Chas!

Charlie's success filled me with pride. We'd finessed the Establishment yet again; they had thought it was all over, the dust had settled, but now the storm was raging again. The Press took it up, hounding the Home Secretary, the prison authorities and the police. They wanted blood. How could a notorious criminal serving what amounted to a double life sentence for robbery escape from saturation security in a maximum-security prison?

I knew how. Charlie, along with a few others, had made provision. The plan went a long way back and was rooted deeply in friendship and loyalty. A mutual pact had been established that in the event of one going to prison the others would ensure his escape. To my eyes these virtues of friendship and loyalty shone like a beacon when compared to the back-biting, the corruption and the stench of hypocrisy that encompassed the Establishment – and that included the media.

The *News of the World* came up with their 'exclusive' story of the escape – how a group of mercenaries, all ex-Special Forces, had been given the contract for the escape. How they had trained in an old chateau in France, replicating the obstacles – the scaling of the high perimeter wall, the surreptitious entry into the main prison with keys, the capture and containment of the screw who guarded Charlie's door, the hurried getaway through the prison before scaling the wall to freedom. A specially converted petrol tanker was waiting for them and when Charlie slipped inside, the hatches were bolted down, and away they went.

What bollocks! It was a great story but bore little relationship to the truth. Charlie's three rescuers were all friends, headed by an old pal, a Special Forces veteran of the Korean War, and also of the Airport raid and the Irish Mail. He was truly one of our own. His two companions were experienced crims, and both had army backgrounds.

After Charlie was sprung, he was driven to London by car and installed in a Knightsbridge flat till March the following year. A passport in the name of Alloway was arranged, and in April, bearded, bespectacled and be-rucksacked, Charlie caught the ferry to Calais as a hitchhiker. From there he was driven to the South of France where a villa had been prepared at Ramatuelle, just outside St Tropez. With typical panache, Charlie the fugitive became an eccentric, ginger-bearded giant who water-ski'd all day behind his newly purchased Riva speedboat.

Of course, Charlie wasn't the only member of the firm still on the run. Buster, too, was ducking and diving. In February '65, I had a call from Harry, saying that Buster was looking to get out of Britain. 'He wants to know if he can come to Mexico,' he said. 'If it's not all right, then say so, he understands. He'll go somewhere else.'

Obviously, Buster didn't want to cramp my style. I discussed it with Angela, weighing up the consequences, for and against. Angela had never met Buster's wife, June, but she knew they had a daughter, Nicolette, who was about the same age as Nick. I'd met June and found her a very pleasant woman and, of course, Buster was basically one of nature's nice guys. He was so laid back I couldn't remember ever hearing him utter a sharp word. It would be nice, too, to have friends from home; people with whom we could go out and explore Mexico.

On the negative side, there was the security risk. Angela and I had been very careful to cover our tracks and make sure nobody knew where we'd gone except Harry, Mary and Rene. We didn't write letters home, or telephone. Even though there was no extradition treaty between Britain and Mexico, I didn't want Tommy Butler and the boys from the Flying Squad camping on my doorstep waiting for me to make a mistake.

'So what do you think?' I asked Angela.

'It would be good for Nick,' she said.

'And good for you?'

'Yes, why not.'

I told Harry the news and a month later we received details of the travel arrangements. I booked Jack and Pauline Ryan, and their daughter Kate, into a suite at the Isobel, the best hotel in Mexico City, and we all went to the airport to meet them.

Harry had already warned me about Buster's plastic surgery, afraid that I wouldn't recognize him. No such worries. When he appeared at the gate, holding his daughter, I knew him at once, even though he had lost weight and had a new chin that would have put Tommy Trinder's in the shade. We embraced and had a great laugh about his face job.

It was a nice reunion, full of jokes and stories and tinged with Buster's sense of relief.

Over dinner that night he explained his movements since the robbery. For the first three months he had stayed at Wraysbury near Staines before slipping across the Channel to Antwerp on a Belgian freighter. A German couple who had handled all the arrangements were at the dockside to greet him. They drove him to Cologne, where he was introduced to Hanne Schmidt, an elegant woman of aristocratic bearing. She had once looked after the German business interests of Otto Skorzeny, the famous commando who had rescued Mussolini and become a personal favourite of Hitler.

'What can I do for you?' she asked Buster, in a brisk, no-nonsense manner.

Buster reeled off his list of priorities: 'Plastic surgery, passports, a Swiss bank account, and passages to Mexico for myself and my family.'

'Consider it done,' he was told.

At the first clinic, the surgeon was told that Buster was a 'friend of the Party', and no questions were asked. However, the day before the operation Buster was told that alternative arrangements would have to be made. The surgeon's wife, who owned the clinic, had refused to co-operate.

The second clinic was clearly a backstreet establishment. After two operations Hanne Schmidt collected Buster and drove him to Düsseldorf, where he was placed in a flat in the care of a woman called Annaliese von Lutzberg, the widow of a Prussian aristocrat who'd been killed in the war. She was apparently a friend of Hanne's mother.

The first operations were unsuccessful and Buster had to return to the clinic for further treatment. Meanwhile, he divided his time between Annaliese and Hanne Schmidt. Both German ladies were enthralled by his accounts of the train robbery and were genuinely disappointed when the time came for him to leave.

He was reunited with June and Nicolette at Düsseldorf airport and with their new identities they caught the Sabena flight to Mexico City.

* * *

I put my business aspirations on hold for a month and helped the 'Ryans' settle in to their new life. Their flat was about ten minutes' walk from ours and five minutes from one of the main bull rings. There were several nightclubs close by, along with a big Argentinian restaurant, La Mansion, which did great meat.

June had never been abroad and she looked at everything with a mixture of distrust and nervousness. She was, however, a lovely lady with a very pleasant disposition. She and Buster had been sweethearts since their teens and it showed. They were always concerned about each other, and equally so about their daughter.

As I'd hoped, Angela and June got on well, taking the kids off to school, the swimming-pool or the ice-skating rink; going shopping, drinking tea in the cafés. They came from almost identical South London backgrounds, although Angela had been abroad often and had acquired that veneer of know-how, whereas June was lost and struggling to find her way. Angela tried to help, telling her about accepted practice and helping her with the language, but because she was much younger than June there were occasional signs of resentment.

I was living and spending with no regard for the future. Buster, it turned out, had been far wiser with his investments – including putting £10,000 in a Spanish property deal suggested by Hanne Schmidt. The first dividend was $9,000 and was delivered personally by Hanna, who arrived in Mexico with a French friend, the daughter of an important arms manufacturer. Buster and I met them for lunch at Delmonico's and I was suitably impressed. Both had that *bon ton* about them, and the class was obvious.

'Would you be prepared to be involved in the arms business?' Hanne asked. 'There are opportunities in Argentina – the Peronistas need weapons.'

She was remarkably well informed on the political situation in the Argentine, talking of Juan Peron and the late Eva as if they were very good friends.

'It doesn't do anything for me, I'm afraid,' I said. 'I want to stay in Mexico.'

Hanne said nothing for several moments and then uttered a statement that almost amounted to an order. 'We want you to take Panama,' she said.

Now that was a great idea. My old cell-mate Max had once exhorted me to think big. 'You've got to sack a city,' he said, but this was stealing a country. Suddenly, I could see myself as the liberator of Panama. But the conversation drifted and as lunch drew to a close there was no more talk of armed insurrection or gun-running. I never saw Hanne Schmidt again.

The next morning, Buster and I were doing the rounds of the hotels when we picked up the English papers for 8 June. Loitering in one hotel foyer, Buster's subtle gasp of surprise made me look up. 'Fucking hell!' he whispered. 'Biggsy had it away from Wandsworth!'

If Charlie's escape had been audacious then Ronnie's was downright cheeky. Using a home-made rope ladder, he lowered himself over the wall into a specially constructed turret on a lorry that was parked outside. Two getaway cars waited near by. I later learned that Biggsy went first to Paris, where a plastic surgeon changed his features, and then to Adelaide and Melbourne in Australia, where he became Terry Cook, pommie carpenter.

The escape turned up the heat again. International newspapers and television carried the story, rehashing details of the robbery and the endless speculation of where we might all be. This was a crime that just wouldn't lie down and die.

There was always the risk that someone would recognize me in Mexico, which attracted a fair number of British tourists, particularly to Acapulco, which was a haven for the well-to-do from Europe and America. During the Acapulco Film Festival, Angela and I went to a live charity performance starring Trini Lopez and found ourselves surrounded by British visitors. Sipping a glass of champagne afterwards, I spotted Samantha Eggar sitting near by. Samantha was best known for *The Collector*, a film with Terence Stamp from the book by John Fowles.

'There's Samantha Eggar. I've got to have a word with her,' I said to Angela.

I steamed over. 'Do you remember me? From the Star, Belgravia – I met you with Kim.'

Samantha was the cousin of Dandy Kim Caborne-Water-field, who would occasionally fetch her in to the bar, showing her off as if to say, 'Look what I've got.' She was only seventeen at the time and had gorgeous auburn hair and the best bum I'd ever seen in my life.

'Of course,' she said, only vaguely recognizing me.

We began chatting away like old friends and I found myself asking her to lunch for the following day.

'Sure, I'd love to,' she said, giving me a stunning smile.

'OK, I'll be there, with my wife and my son.'

By next morning I'd sobered up and thought: Hold on, it's all right meeting someone when you're drunk but in the cold light of day what questions will she ask? Would she put two and two together and recognize me?

It wasn't worth the risk and Samantha lunched alone.

I had a similar experience a year later when Michael Caine was in Mexico making a film. I had met him once before in the early sixties at a new club called the Establishment in London. Harry and I were there with Terry Maidment, an old friend, who had worked as a steward on the cross-Atlantic liners before getting into films as an extra. Terry was a good-looking guy, being groomed for possible stardom. He bore a striking physical resemblance to Albert Finney and would often play his stand-in. They eventually became great friends.

Terry also knew Michael Caine and Terry Stamp, up-and-comers on the verge of achieving greatness. As we brushed shoulders at the bar he introduced us. Caine and I had several mutual acquaintances including Stanley Baker, who was a friend of Albert Dimes and whom I had met several times in the Italian café in Frith Street that seemed to be the hub of Albert's activities. Tall and straight-backed, Caine had just been on television playing an off-the-wall character and I was very impressed. I especially liked the fact that we both wore horn-rimmed glasses and a lot of people commented on how much I looked like him.

We didn't chat long. I told him I thought that he could go a long way and then spent the rest of the evening drinking and chatting up girls. The class barriers were falling, the working-class was on the move – Michael Caine was proof of that.

In Acapulco I ran into Caine again at an Italian restaurant called Dino's, not far from the Hilton. He had recently played Harry Palmer in *The Ipcress File* – a big box-office hit. Just as Angela and I were leaving and walking to the Cadillac, Caine got out of a cab with a beautiful girl on his arm. Off the top of my head, I yelled, 'Oi, Harry, how ya going?'

'All right,' he yelled back, smiling.

'You don't remember me, do you?'

'Sure I do – I just can't place the name.'

'Not to worry. Enjoy your meal, Harry.'

I got into the car and suddenly realized what a stupid thing I had done. Suppose he had recognized me?

My only other serious brush with detection was again triggered by alcohol.

I got nicked for a traffic offence while driving home drunk one night. The accepted practice was to slip the arresting officers a fistful of pesos and everything was sweet, but I had the misfortune to get a by-the-book copper who figured I was an upstart Yank driving a flash car. At the time there were only about six Cadillacs in Mexico City.

Drunkenly, I said, 'Here's your money, boys,' and virtually threw it at them.

Then this copper says. 'Who do you think you are? Bloody gringo, *yanqui*.'

I tried to explain that I was English, not American, but it was too late. I said to his mate, 'Won't he take the money?'

'No. Offer him a thousand dollars and he will not accept it.'

I started to worry. People disappeared all the time in Mexican prisons – normally not foreigners but I wasn't in a position to start calling in the British Foreign Office and asking them to rescue me. Not that it would have mattered. When Angela rang the Embassy, using my false name, she was told it was entirely my problem.

I was in a police cell for six hours, surrounded by a handful of locals who could have stepped straight out of a spaghetti Western.

In broken Spanish, I asked one of them what the food was like in prison.

'Ees OK.'

'So what do you get for breakfast?'

'Beans.'

'And do you get lunch?'

'Si.'

'What is it?'

'Beans.'

'So what's for dinner then?'

He shrugged. 'Beans.'

Thank God for Joe. He knew the governor of the prison and, after Angela's phone call, he went round and delivered a bottle of Dunhill aftershave. I was a free man again.

Within a month of their arrival, it was obvious that Buster and June weren't happy in Mexico. They were looking at it differently from Angela and me. For us, our new life was for ever. We would always live in Mexico, or perhaps somewhere else, but never go back to England. Buster and June never crossed that important mental hurdle. Their homesickness set in when they realized that my plans didn't include any possibility of our returning home. June couldn't accept this. To her, Mexico was just an interlude until she could return home to her family and London.

I discovered this when Buster casually mentioned the possibility of eventually doing a deal and returning to the UK. Surprised, I said to him, 'Is that your ultimate plan?'

'Yeah. We'll kill a couple of years and then I think we'll go back. I can say that I only played a small part in the robbery – maybe I can do a deal and get a lesser sentence. Maybe I could get away with a five. I could live with that.'

'Surely you're not serious,' I said.

Buster shrugged his shoulders. 'We've got to go home, Bruce. You know how June is – she's worried about her family, her mum and dad; and she's concerned about Nicolette and her future here, about our future here, too. Let's face it, the dough's running out and we've got nothing coming in. I don't know how long we can last.'

I could see that Buster wasn't happy but couldn't accept that going back to England was the answer.

'Listen, mate, you've gotta do what you've gotta do. But if June's unhappy now, it's not going to get any better if you get nicked. Think of the kid. Think of yourself! Do you fancy doing a thirty? Fucking hell!'

'It won't be that long,' he said. 'I reckon I can still do a deal, perhaps work the accessory-after-the-fact label. The climate's changed, witnesses have died. I think they'll play.'

'Sounds like you've made your decision,' I said. 'There's not much I can say. It's your life – your decision. I can see Tom (*Butler*) and Frank (*Williams*) doing a deal, but whether they'll stand for the accessory story, well, I don't know about that. I hope so. Fucking good luck, mate: a jack's alive (*five*), you could be out in three.'

Buster tried to explain himself, but the reasons were obvious. June was unhappy and Buster loved her too much to let it continue.

I was still upset, though. I had imagined Buster and I would be business partners as well as friends. Our futures would be linked together. June never really gave Mexico a chance. Buster would quite happily have stayed, but the pressure was too great. Later I discovered that June had been sending letters to her mother, a major breach of security, but I didn't say anything. Not even my father knew where we were. Matters were further complicated when I had a call from Harry.

'You heard about Charlie?'

'Yeah. He's away. Where is he?'

'Montreal.'

'Canada?'

'Yeah. He wants to come down for a visit.'

'At this rate, we'll all be here,' I joked.

I barely recognized Charlie when I met him at the airport. He had always been big, over six foot and powerfully built, having worked as a butcher lugging carcasses around a market, but he turned up with a fantastic tan, ginger hair and a dyed ginger beard. He wore small wire-rimmed glasses, which looked incongruous, and I thought, My God – what have you done to yourself?

It was great to see him – my old pal from school days when we used to sit in the Anderson shelter smoking Woodbines and discussing the mysteries of women. Who would have thought that thirty years later we would be sitting in Mexico City, he an escaped convict and me on the run?

'Harry told me that Buster'd had plastic surgery,' he said one night. 'I was interested in it myself, until I found out it cost twenty grand. "Fuck twenty grand," I said to Harry. "I'll get Joey to hit me in the face with a shovel and then go to St Thomas's and let them sort it out." '

Charlie stayed about six weeks, bunking down with Buster and investigating the possibilities of moving down permanently. Unfortunately, he wasn't enamoured of Mexico. 'You've got to come up to Canada,' he said.

His wife Pat and their three daughters were still in England, but Charlie was confident that he could make a new life for them in Canada. He wanted them to grow up somewhere with a familiar culture and language. Mexico, he felt, was too foreign.

We took him down to Acapulco, Buster at the wheel of his new Mercedes and me in the Caddy. We had a great time, especially when Harry turned up to complete the picture. We spent Christmas and New Year together in Mexico City, toasting absent friends and wondering, with the proverbial lumps in our throats, what 1966 was going to bring.

Charlie returned to Montreal in early January. Buster was relieved. Aside from getting underfoot, Charlie had taken a fancy to a young Mexican maid – not the done thing – and she'd been found walking around the house in Charlie's shoes, thinking he was God.

Although it was sad to see him leave, I arranged to return the visit and to examine the benefits of Montreal.

Three weeks later, Charlie met me at the airport, along with his then girlfriend, an attractive nurse. Charlie always seemed to have a mistress or two simmering on the back burner, but somehow always managed to hold his marriage together. This one was very pleasant with a good sense of humour, although seeing them together, all lovey-dovey, I worried that they were too familiar. When we got back to Charlie's rented house, a modern place in a leafy street, I took him aside. 'You haven't told her anything about yourself?' I asked.

'No, course not, I wouldn't do that.'

A little later, we were having a beer and talking about women, when Charlie said, 'You know, it's a coincidence, but my girl's been having an affair with the Montreal Chief of Police.'

'Are you crazy?' I exploded.

'No, it's OK, Bruce – really. He doesn't know who I am. Although it's funny, he said to her one night, "I know who your boyfriend is. He's Ronald Edwards, the English geezer, isn't he?"'

My jaw dropped.

'I mean, who the fuck is Ronald Edwards?' said Charlie, laughing.

'I'll tell you who he is,' I said. 'It's fucking Buster!'

Very few people knew Buster's surname, let alone his proper Christian name. Charlie had only ever known him as Buster.

'Christ! What am I gonna do?' he asked.

'Well, I don't think I fancy staying here with you, Charlie,' I said, heading for my suitcase and a timetable of flights. I was shaken. I'd been sweet for over a year but suddenly I felt the resurgence of fear. My rich life had glossed over the stark reality – perhaps I'd become complacent – but all that was shattered. That afternoon I caught a plane to Mexico. As I said goodbye to Charlie, I told him, 'Move house, Chas. Lose the girl and for fuck's sake be more careful.'

He took my advice and bought a piece of land in a place called Rigaud, on a lake about twenty miles outside Montreal. Pat and the girls joined him and he settled down, building a house and slowly becoming part of the small community. He was on the local curling team, playing alongside the village policeman, and a stalwart supporter of the local school, which the girls were attending.

In April of that year, while having breakfast with Buster in Sanborn's and reading the papers, we learned the sickening news that Jimmy White had been nicked. We were both choked. Jimmy and his wife Claire were such a close couple, with a young son, Stephen, who was around about the same age as Nick and Nicolette. I looked at Buster and his eyes told me that he'd read the same scenario: it could be us; how would we cope?

The Establishment had struck back but, even so, Buster was more determined than ever to do a deal and go home. If the dominoes were going to fall, it was better to do the deal now

on his own terms rather than get nicked and be at their mercy
– for thirty years.

Jimmy's trial was in June and he was sentenced to eighteen
years, giving Buster further encouragement to try a trade-off.

The new media barrage repeatedly focused on the fugitives
still at large. I couldn't help wondering how Charlie would
fare in Canada. At least we were resident in a country without
an extradition treaty with Great Britain; it gave us an edge that
poor Charlie lacked.

It was sad seeing Buster and June off at the airport. It was
Friday 16 September, and they were going home to face the
music. Buster had been in contact with a pal who had acted
as a go-between with Detective Superintendent Frank Williams, who was working with Tommy Butler. Indications
suggested that it was now a favourable time, though there
were no guarantees that Buster would get a lesser sentence.
However, the term of five years predominated throughout the
dialogue and Frank Williams was known as an honourable
man.

Buster's pal called Frank to say that Buster was ready to
give himself up. He could be found at his pal's place. Frank
came in person to arrest him, and accepted his story that he'd
gone with Jimmy White to clear up the farm for the sum of
£10,000. Buster denied taking any part in the robbery.

The two-day trial at Nottingham Assizes on 8 and 9
December 1966 found Buster guilty of conspiracy to rob, and
robbery. He was sentenced to twelve years on the first count
and fifteen years on the second, the two sentences to run
concurrently. It was a far cry from the five years that had been
hoped for, but at least it was half what the others had got, and
three years less than Jimmy White. All in all, Buster didn't do
so badly. Any vague thoughts that Angela and I might one day
return, however, were wiped out by the sentence. What was
the point? Even so, the whole atmosphere of our life in
Mexico was tarnished by what happened to Buster. I began
drinking more heavily – and the dark side of my character
was always susceptible to booze.

Money was slipping away. That was the problem with
Mexico. The cost of living was cheap, but five per cent of the

country owned all the wealth. I was trying to keep up with that five per cent and it was costing me a fortune.

Angela and I still had our good times. I took her to Las Vegas, where Joe had *carte blanche* at three or four casinos because he was a big player. He had a twenty-grand credit limit at each of them and could raise a hundred grand no worries at all.

I once said to him, 'Couldn't you build it up to fifty or a hundred grand or maybe half a million, and then say fuck 'em?'

'No, I don't want to say fuck 'em,' he said. 'These people are in the Mafia.' I could see his point.

When Angela and I were there we discovered that Sinatra and Sammy Davies were performing a one-off show at the Sands. Through a contact of Joe's, we managed to get a table and Angela got all dolled up in a green silk dress that I'd bought her from Saks in Fifth Avenue. When we arrived, we were shown to a table right at the back. I summoned a member of the staff and said, 'I want another table.'

'I'm sorry, sir, this is the only one available.'

'Fetch me the manager.'

The manager came over and I handed him a hundred dollars.

'I expect you would like a better table, sir?' he said, issuing commands and staying at my shoulder until we were comfortably seated directly beneath the stage.

That's where we were when 'old Blue Eyes' sauntered out, pointed down to Angela, blew her a kiss and said, 'I see we've got the Green Hornet here tonight.'

Angela spent the rest of the evening on a cloud. Frank Sinatra had spoken to her; she couldn't believe it.

But for every good night, there was a bad one – as if a penalty had to be paid. Only a few weeks later, in Mexico City, we were driving home half drunk after a night out and Angela said something that made me snap. I don't remember what it was, but the result was a slap that she didn't deserve. Her nose started to bleed, staining her face and dress. I didn't know what made me do it. The drink? Resentment? Who knows? I cried afterwards, trying to say I was sorry.

I knew then that we couldn't continue the way we were living. That night, as I hugged her and tried to soothe away her pain, we talked about our future and decided that it was time to leave Mexico. We had to find another country to call home.

34

Loading up the Cadillac, we set off for Canada, hoping it offered better prospects and a reasonable life. Although I'd visited Charlie in Montreal, Angela didn't know what to expect. Nor did we know if we could obtain the necessary papers, afford a house or find a job.

Joe was disappointed but he could sympathize with my financial position. I was on a roller-coaster and there was no way of getting off without totally changing my lifestyle.

Having freighted all our possessions and said our goodbyes, we drove out of Mexico City on 6 December 1966, singing songs to keep Nick amused and planning a leisurely trip north, sightseeing and enjoying the open road. Each day we drove maybe six hours and then pulled up at one of the big restaurant chains for lunch. At night we found a motel with a swimming-pool. It was always Nick's job to go and get the bucket of ice from the ice machine for the cans of Dr Pepper he liked and for his parents' nightly constitutionals, a glass of Jack Daniel's for me and a vodka for Angela.

We chose a route through parts of America steeped in legend – places that I remembered from films and the books I'd read. Sometimes these were well out of our way, like Missouri, where the James boys robbed banks and blazed away in shoot-outs. We went to Tombstone and saw the OK Corral, a place that barely seemed big enough to hold its own history.

In Chicago we ate in the VIP room of the Playboy Club because Joe had special gold-card membership, and a week later, on 23 December, we crossed the Canadian border and arrived at Charlie's lakeside house in Rigaud, outside Montreal.

Christmas was wonderful. After two and a half years of relentless sun, we revelled in the snow, tobogganing, walking on a frozen river, snapping icicles off the caves to cool the festive champagne. The Wilsons were a very happy family. Chas idolized his wife, Pat, and their three daughters. His family life was, and always had been, sacrosanct. Sure he played around, but never to the detriment of his wife and family. In all respects he was a great father and a good husband.

Charlie had been financially secure to start with. His money was invested with an old friend that he had been partners with for years. They had many legitimate businesses together – betting shops, restaurants, and an interest in a chain of provincial newspapers. On the face of it he had no worries, but things changed. Chas discovered that his friend had been investing wildly in speculative schemes, and his holdings were down to a cash value of about £30,000. Chas thought he'd been fucked – and without a kiss. He was very peeved.

My funds, too, were running out – I had about £30,000–£40,000 left – and we discussed the possibility of pulling off a few coups. We had new identities, no past records and a whole new country to rob. We began to investigate getting back into the game. I was quite excited about the whole idea of pulling off a big *coup* in Canada. A contact of Charlie's knew the movements of several money shipments which contained Canadian dollars that had been spent in New York and were being shipped back to Montreal. Two security men would pick up half a dozen sacks of money at the airport.

We staked out the pick-up and saw the mailbags unloaded and put into an estate car before being driven to central Montreal. The only security was that no-one was supposed to know what they were carrying. They were in plain clothes and travelling in an unmarked vehicle. The problem, however, was that the car had an extra guard inside and the route from the airport was along the busy main street. When they arrived at the headquarters, the sacks were carried through swinging doors and down a fifty-yard corridor to another set of swinging doors. As soon as they entered the corridor a padlock was put on the door to make sure nobody could follow them.

It was possible, we decided, to hold them up at gun-point as they entered the corridor, take the bags and lock them in afterwards. We'd be away and the coup would be totally bloodless. In the end, we messed around with the details for too long and the coup died a death.

My confidence was further battered when Angela and I crossed back into the US to organize new documents for the Cadillac, which still carried Texan plates. *En route* from Albany USA we were required to stop. Two immigration officers glanced at our passports and requested that we step inside. There were two other officers in attendance. It was about nine o'clock at night.

They wanted to know what we were doing, where we were staying and why I'd been a resident in Mexico. Obviously, we didn't smell right. Suddenly I began worrying about what Charlie had been up to. Were we putting ourselves at risk?

One of the officers was clearly aggravated by something. Some sixth sense seemed to be telling him that all was not right with the people in front of him. He was doing his best to draw out what should have been a perfunctory check, since all our papers were in order. His companion was either playing the other half of the good-guy routine or was genuinely amused at his colleague's zeal.

'Where have you been?'

'To Albany, New York state.'

'And what for, may I ask?'

'To change the Texas plates on my Cadillac for New York plates.'

'And why would you be doing that?'

'Because I have plans to sell the car in New York.'

A long, drawn-out 'um', then: 'I see from your passport that you've been living in Mexico.'

'Yes, we are residents there,' I said, nodding to include Angela.

He was still holding our passports, re-examining the pages one by one, a performance that seemed to give him much satisfaction.

'And just what do you do in Mexico, Mr Miller?'

'I am with Dunhill International. We're expanding our operations in Latin America.'

'Oh, I see.' The name of Dunhill clearly carried some weight with him.

'Do you have all your car documents with you?'

'Yes, they're in my briefcase.'

He opened it and began scrutinizing various pieces of paper before passing them to his fellow officer. All the documents underlined my legitimacy – letterheads from Bank de Nacional de Mexico, Dunhill New York, Dunhill London, Diner's Club de Mexico, driving licences, our residential papers for Mexico.

The official took the documents, rummaged around for a few minutes, then handed them back to me. Finally, his tone changed and an attempt at *bonhomie* was introduced into the dialogue as he stamped our passports before wishing us – although it was late at night – to have a nice day.

Arriving back at Charlie's I told him that Montreal didn't suit us and we wanted to check out Vancouver on the west coast. Leaving the Cadillac, we caught the Canadian Pacific Railway over the Rockies. The journey took three days and the only view from the window was snow, snow and more snow. I remember getting out in Calgary, standing on the platform and the wind going right through me. One minute I was warm and the next minute I was so cold I couldn't speak.

Vancouver was one of the nicest places I'd ever seen. It was like Los Angeles without the slums, all very nicely laid out and modern. We were staying in a hotel with self-catering facilities not far from the harbour. After years of craving adventure and living for the moment, I wanted to settle down and lead a normal life. I wanted a home, a job, Nick in school and a few quid in the bank.

We didn't waste any time. I set about house-hunting and looking at schools for Nick, as well as investigating changing my status from tourist to immigrant. The last task seemed straightforward enough. It said quite clearly on all the forms that, if you produced the necessary funds to show you were not going to be a burden to the state, then immigration was a formality.

Still worried about my brush with the customs officers, I decided to make our application in entirely new names. This involved flying to Brussels in Belgium as Keith Miller, Angela Green and Kevin Green. A week later we flew back again, this time as the Firth family. I had shaved off my moustache to complete the new look. As we came back through passport control, Nick whispered to me, 'Who am I now, Daddy? Am I Colin today or Kevin?'

'You're Colin Firth. Remember that. You're Colin Firth.'

'OK,' he said. Nick never had any real problems with his multiple identities. We always called him Nico, or Chico as a diminutive, and told curious questioners that it was his nickname.

When we reached the immigration desk, I handed over the passports and felt Nick tugging at my shirt sleeve.

'Daddy,' he said, 'why have you shaved off your moustache?'

I smiled weakly at the officer as he waved us through.

I put three grand in a bank account and lodged our migrant application. Everything in our lives was then provisional. I provisionally became a trainee salesman for a real estate agent, provisionally enrolled Nick in a school and provisionally put a deposit down on a house, a modern ranch-style place which was owned by a seafaring tug captain.

My only concern was that as the Firth family we didn't have any background. We had no references from England or documentation establishing our existence. When we tried to get a mortgage for the house, I realized for the first time what was meant by the term Global Village. The bank manager asked, 'What's your former address in England? We have to check your credit rating.'

There was the rub. The Firths did exist in England, but not with a credit rating. Eventually, I did a deal with the tug captain and took out a private mortgage with him. I paid $2,000 deposit on the house and agreed to pay off the balance at a certain amount per month.

When we shook hands on the deal, I realized that it was a major step for me, because at last we were going to be able to lead what was considered a normal life. A mortgage, a job, school fees to pay – we were going to be an ordinary family. It would be a far more modest existence than in Mexico because we didn't have the money and we no longer had to 'keep up with the Rodriguezes'. Even our new car matched our more modest aspirations: a sensible four-door Oldsmobile.

Still, our new life was dependent on the immigration people approving our application. After a month nothing had happened so I went downtown to the immigration office and sat waiting in reception with similar would-be migrants. I got into conversation with a couple of Australians and New Zealanders and discovered that their papers had been sorted out within two weeks and work permits arranged. In my case it was, 'Well, we're not quite sure yet.'

I continued going down once a week and hearing the usual, 'Nothing's come through yet, Mr Firth.'

Finally I said, 'I'd like to see someone in authority. I'm not happy with this, I'm a British subject and I don't think I'm getting the treatment that I deserve.'

I was hoping an aggressive stance might trigger some action, but their whole attitude was ambivalent. Eventually someone of higher authority was summoned and I voiced my complaint to him. It fell on deaf ears. This isn't right, I thought. Why are they treating me differently? Yet there couldn't be anything radically wrong otherwise there would be police involved or immigration investigators.

Finally, I said, 'Well, if there's nothing sorted out by next week, I'll consider withdrawing the application.'

'That's your privilege,' I was told.

Angela was upset. All her hopes were hinging on the house and the prospect of getting settled rather than moving around.

'Listen, love,' I said, 'I don't like the look of it at all – there's definitely something not quite right.'

As always, she understood. 'If you don't think it's right, we can't stay.' Like me, Angela felt that our freedom was the most important thing. To risk losing it was unthinkable. We decided to leave virtually immediately, even though it meant forfeiting the deposit on the house.

Before leaving, I phoned the immigration department and said that I was no longer in a position to stay in Vancouver because of their time-wasting. I was going to Montreal and if anything came through I would be staying at the Holiday Inn. This wasn't the case, but I knew that I could send someone along to see if there were any letters and to check if the police were waiting.

We stayed with Charlie and his family. Chas was still trying to convince me to stay in Montreal but it wasn't good for security for us to be seen together and I didn't trust his contacts. We were stateless and homeless, low on money and trying to decide what to do next. I didn't care about extradition treaties with Britain any more. I just wanted to be settled and financially secure.

'Let's go back to Europe,' I said to Angela. 'We both love the South of France.'

'Are you sure it's safe?'

'We just have to be careful. The heat is off. They won't give up looking, especially Tommy Butler, but they won't be looking as hard.'

35

In early 1967 we flew to Nice, where I ceased being Firth and became Miller again because I had a credit card in that name with the Diner's Club of Mexico. We drove down to St Maxime and booked into a little hotel for a week until an estate agent came up with a small bungalow for us called Trois Pigeons. It was about three hundred yards outside St Maxime on the St Tropez road, and right on the seafront. We settled in there for the summer while I considered the next move.

I didn't fancy Australia: Biggsy was there. So, too, were lots of other crims who were wanted for questioning over various things. I certainly didn't want to be scooped up in any net placed for them. Then I remembered a former screw, an ex-Navy man who had been round the world, telling me about the best place he had ever visited.

'Without a doubt, New Zealand,' he said. 'It's a lovely place to live.'

'A bit wet, isn't it?'

'No, it's beautiful, you should go there.'

I started giving this some serious thought. Having had my fill of the high life in Mexico, I would be happy settling down somewhere quiet. I didn't know what I'd do for a living, but apparently everyone in the Antipodes did quite well for themselves.

The first priority was to get more money. The Swiss bank account was almost empty and we were surviving on the Diner's Club card, which I knew would be paid by Joe in Mexico. I wasn't concerned because I had money invested with him. My mind started drifting back to all the old plots that Chad and I had considered a decade earlier. It was as if time had stood still. I also thought about something the Ulsterman had told Gordon and Buster before the Train: 'When you've done this, there's another one you can do in Leeds. It involves a van with a driver, his mate and a security guy. You're looking at three million.'

Our first visitor that summer was Harry, who had set up in the textile business and was doing very well. He was happy to be out of the game. He'd been at it since his pre-teens and the adventurous side of it had palled years before. Once he had found the alternative, there was no going back. He explained to me what a relief it was to sleep at night without the fear of the early morning call from the heavy mob.

While we were sipping wine at a beach-side café, I asked him about Brian Field, our only contact with the Ulsterman. 'If he's home from prison, will you see if you can find out where he is?'

Little Freddy also came over and I visited him in Monte Carlo.

'It looks like I'm gonna have to come home and get to work again,' I said. 'Is there anything buzzing?'

'Bits and pieces. There's one down in Wales which looks very good.'

The work involved the removal of platinum mesh from ICI at a plant near Cardiff. Apparently it was worth a couple of hundred grand. I was interested but still unsure about whether to risk going back to Britain. I'd been out of the game for nearly four years. Freedom is infectious.

We were enjoying our summer, lying in the sun and strolling five minutes to a beach-side restaurant. Nick was at a great age and we would leave Angela on the beach and go back to the villa to watch the Tour de France on television. At times it was like a grand reunion. Charlie came over from Canada and stayed a week.

The Captain also visited, pretending this time that he was Captain Scott, a wealthy playboy, and frequenting one of the private clubs that ran speed boat trips from St Tropez across the bay to St Maxime. One night he was lauding it up, dancing with other men's wives and hob-nobbing, when a party of wealthy revellers sent across a bottle of champagne. Not to be outdone, the Captain sent back six bottles, as much as to say, 'Anything you can do I can do better.' It was all on his credit card, which of course he never paid.

Before leaving New York I'd bought a Mustang and arranged to have it shipped to Ostend. It was an absolute brute of a car which did 135 mph flat out on straight road but was hopeless around the bends. I discovered this, first-hand, a month later when I had an argument with Angela one night and took off driving towards St Tropez, fifteen minutes away. I vaguely remembered drinking double vodkas as fast as they could serve them at the club and the next thing I knew I was sitting in the Mustang in a field several feet below a main roundabout. Apparently I had ploughed into a concrete bridgement which supported the road and gone over a ten-foot drop on to the field below. The abutment to the support had steel reinforcing rods sticking out of it and one of them had gone completely through the windscreen and embedded itself in the passenger seat. Anyone sitting there would have been impaled.

From being totally drunk I was stone-cold sober, and I realized the police would arrive within minutes. I left the car, climbed on to the road and hitched a lift home, uninjured but obviously shaken. The next morning at half-past six, I phoned the nearest police station, got on my bicycle and started riding back to the car. I punished myself, sweating pure vodka and cursing my stupidity.

The gendarmerie already had the details of the accident. They sent a breakdown truck to retrieve the car and parked it at a local garage. The old French mechanic wandered outside.

'No problem,' he said, a great big hammer in his hand. 'We fix.'

'No, I don't think so. It's a write off.'

'No, monsieur. I fix good.' I didn't want the car fixed good. I didn't want the car full stop. It was fully insured through the American dealer – oddly enough with the same company that paid our rewards for the Train – so I rang the insurance office in Nice and they sent down a valuer. Within a fortnight I received a cheque for five thousand dollars.

This time I really had learned my lesson – no more sports cars. I took Angela and Nick to Germany and we bought a very sensible four-door saloon, a 250 Mercedes. I talked to Angela about the future. 'We need to raise some cash,' I said. 'Then we can decide where to go next.'

'So what are you saying?' she asked dubiously.

'I'm going back to England. Not for long – three months maximum. I can get in, do the business and get out.'

'What about Nick and me?'

'You could stay here.'

'No. I want to come too.' How could I say no to her? She had been away from home for so many years.

Before leaving England I had given the lease on the mews house to the Captain and the furniture to Elegant Head. I think the Captain bought the furniture and moved in, settling very nicely until a month later he lost the lot in a card game with some moody Polish count who lived in Earls Court. Eventually, the Captain got the house for us for a month. Angela and Nick would stay there while I was working.

She went back first with Nick, taking a normal scheduled flight to Heathrow. I met the Captain in Paris. We had decided to fly into Shannon in Ireland, go through passport control and rent a car for the drive across the border to Belfast. From there we could get on the shuttle and enter England without having to go through passport control.

Collecting his Alfa Romeo from the airport car park, we headed into town along the familiar road. The drive brought back all the old feelings of home; I'd never realized how much I'd missed the place.

Albert Mews was not so much a prison this time, yet it wasn't quite as safe as I'd have liked, either. The Count started sniffing around, figuring that Angela was a woman on her own with Nick and might crave companionship. He would visit the house and I had to hide in the loft while Angela got rid of him.

'Don't you ever go out, dear?' he asked. 'You should go out, I know a nice little place near by.'

I was still trying to get in touch with Brian Field, and discovered that someone had been waiting for him on the day he was released from prison – a character called Scotch Jack Buggy, who'd just done eight or nine years for shooting someone at Club Pigalle. Buggy was a heavy and I knew his opening line: 'I know you got money from the Train, give me some or else.' I don't know what happened to Brian but I'm sure it was no picnic. He probably got roughed up, maybe tortured; whatever the case, he went to ground.

Not long afterwards Scotch Jack got into an argument with someone at the Bridge Club in Mount Street. His opponent was holding something far better than a bridge hand – a Luger 9mm – and Scotch Jack got what was coming to him. Rather unusually in the circumstances, that wasn't the last of him. Two off-duty policemen, deep-sea fishing off the coast of Dover, hooked a bundle and reeled it in. They landed what was left of Scotch Jack. Franny Daniels, one of Billy Hill's old companions, was charged with the murder and acquitted.

With no sign of Brian Field, I went to see Little Freddy about the job in Wales. It seemed straightforward enough. The firm had one key to the strong room where the platinum was kept, but needed another.

'Can you get a key made up?' asked Fred. 'If we do it at the right time, there's £200,000 worth of platinum there.'

I made contact with the firm and then spoke to Harry. Although he was out of the game he was still good for advice. Even so, I had to be careful. Harry had been under observation for years because he was known to be my closest friend. At one stage he was sitting in his MG reading a letter from me, sent via a third party, when a policeman came along and snatched it through the car window. Harry's wife had the presence of mind to snatch it back and he planted his foot down and sped off. He immediately got in touch with his solicitor, fearing the police would strike back. There were no reprisals. The Met were happy to keep clocking his car, noting its location and assuming that they were narrowing down the area where I was likely to be hiding.

I also sought the advice of Roller Reg, who was living in a small mews house in Kensington. Although I hadn't seen him in four or five years, I didn't telephone first. I hooted up from the car and saw the upstairs curtain waver. Reg waved down. He opened the door as if it was only a day since I'd seen him, saying, 'Hello, Bruce, how you doing? Cup of tea?'

As we shared a brew, I told him the situation. 'Basically, I ain't got too much money, Reg. I've got a couple of bits of work to go on, I don't know if you're interested?'

'Yeah, but I'm working with another guy now.'

'Do I know him?'

'No, but he's all right.'

It turned out that Reg wasn't the man for the ICI job, so I contacted Rick, an excellent key man, who had put me up for a few days after the Train. His response wasn't helpful: 'Look, Bruce, I'd love to help but obviously I don't want to be seen anywhere with you.'

'That's understandable, that's my protection as well,' I said.

On Fred's instigation I went down to Cardiff and met the two contacts, Bill and Ben, who both worked there in some minor managerial position. They explained that platinum mesh was used as a catalyst in the production of certain chemicals; after prolonged usage it lost its efficiency through erosion, which ensured that a regular supply was needed. Bill and Ben knew when the stock was replenished, where it was stored and the location of the strongroom. What was more, they had an impression of the strongroom's key.

I stayed overnight before Ben took me on a guided tour outside the works, pointing out the relevant buildings whilst I identified them on the map that they had provided. The processing plant was a vast sprawl of enormous tubes and pipes, like something from a space-age fantasy. Parts of the complex worked 24 hours a day, which meant that movement at night would not be out of the ordinary. Security was prominent at the main gate, but the inner security was haphazard – the roving guards spent most of the night playing cards, with the occasional stroll to the main gate to justify their existence.

The strongroom building was central to the administration block but adjacent to warehousing and storage facilities so we could park a truck there without raising comment. The most likely escape route was through normally locked access gates on the perimeter, to which Bill and Ben had the key. They also had a lock-up five miles away which would be convenient for a changeover. They seemed to have thought of everything.

When I asked about the strongroom key, they confidently produced the impression set in cuttlefish. How did they know about that? Amateurs normally used a bar of soap like they'd seen it done on telly. These guys were definitely in the know. 'You're quite confident about this?' Bill asked. 'You can get the key cut?'

'No problem, I've got the best key man in London,' I said, thinking of Rick but wishing Jimmy White was available. 'Which of you is going to try the key for size?'

'We'll both be trying it,' they answered in unison, with the eagerness of those with larceny in their hearts.

'See you in a week then.' On the long drive home, I was happy and optimistic. The impression of the key was in my briefcase. It was going to open the door to freedom again. New Zealand here we come!

I met up with Rick, gave him the cuttlefish and filled him in on the plan. He was enthusiastic and I arranged to pick him up at Cardiff airport in a week's time, when the key would be ready. We met as arranged with Bill and Ben. They were impressed, regarding the key as if it was the Holy Grail.

'We'll try it in the next few days and then we'll be in touch,' said Bill.

I refrained from asking, 'Why not tomorrow?' That was their business; only they knew when they could gain access without arousing suspicion.

Fred called later that week. His cryptic message indicated that our male couldn't make it with his female and suggested that further stimulation might be necessary if we wanted to ensure a fruitful coupling. I agreed to go down to Cardiff again with Rick. Frankly I was amazed; Rick was a master craftsman who'd fitted up quite a few banks in his time. There was no way that he'd lose his touch. All the same, I knew the tolerances on security locks were very tight. I'd seen Jimmy take off a couple of 'thou' from a key with a file and emery cloth to make it work; perhaps that was all this one needed.

Rick agreed when I picked him up at the airport. He asked Bill and Ben what degree of turn the key had achieved. Then he gently went to work with his files. 'That'll do it. It's OK now,' he said, passing the key back to Bill. Ben smiled before reaching out and holding it admiringly in his hand. 'Great! If it's OK, then the next delivery should be ours!' he said, smiling pointedly at Bill.

'All of ours,' I corrected him, taking exception to his proprietorial air. He needed reminding that we were part of it too.

I waited all week but the expected call didn't materialize. I was puzzled; there should have been a yes or no from Wales via Fred. Then I had a surprise visit from Harry. 'Bad news, Bruce,' he said.

Driving back from the airport to his flat in Wimbledon, Rick had been surrounded by twenty or thirty policemen – all armed – and dragged into a van. He was roughed up at the station and interrogated for hours before they charged him with the armed robbery of a big jeweller's in Knightsbridge which had been knocked off by six or seven guys with shotguns. Rick wouldn't have gone near a job like that. He didn't touch guns. He was a key man.

'You know this ain't my fucking game,' he told the police. 'I don't hold people up in daylight.'

'Sorry, sunshine, you're nicked,' said the detective.

Eventually Rick had to pay £1,500 for the charges to be dropped, and as he was leaving the station one of the officers said to him, 'You know what it's all about, don't you?'

'What do you mean?'

'You're seeing the other fella, and we know you're seeing the other fella. Well, you know your own business but my advice to you is to leave him out.'

Harry recounted the whole story to me and then said, 'You know what the answer is, Bruce, don't you?'

'Of course I know the bloody answer – they know I'm back.'

Rick's pull signified the end of our working partnership, because he would be under constant surveillance. I couldn't blame him; he had to look after himself. He had stared down the barrel at fourteen years on the Moor for something that he hadn't done and would never dream of doing.

The next day Fred rang me up. The tone of his voice was congratulatory. 'I see you've been busy – nice one, mate.'

'Busy?' I said. 'I've been waiting for a call all week. Where have you been?'

Fred's voice changed suddenly. 'You mean you haven't been out, you haven't been busy?'

'No, I told you. I've been waiting for a call from you or the Flowerpot Men.'

'Then get the *Telegraph*, page three. Only a snippet but it's worth a quarter of a mil to someone.'

'Are you saying what I think you're saying?' There was a sick, sinking feeling in the pit of my stomach.

'Yes I am. Our thoughts are meshed together.'

'And Angela's a platinum blonde?'

'Yes indeed.'

'Fucking hell! I don't understand it, do you?'

'No I don't. They definitely think it's you.'

I put down the receiver, lost in the maze of thought. What the fuck had happened? My mind went into overdrive, and it kept throwing up a single thought: Those Welsh bastards! Forget Bill and Ben the Flowerpot Men – what about Bill and Ben the Platinum Mesh Men!

It was the first in a series of setbacks. Ever since returning to England I had been hunted and at times I couldn't tell whether the hounds were in front of or behind me.

On another job for Little Freddy, this one in Pontypridd, the owner of a slaughterhouse apparently kept a large stash in the safe. I had a look but eventually turned down the work because his elderly mother rarely left the house and she would have had to be tied up and kept quiet.

A week later I heard from Fred. 'Did you hear about the slaughterhouse coup? Someone went in the other night, steamed in three-handed. The mother said to 'em: "Don't hurt me, boys, don't hurt me; the money's upstairs under the bed!" They got ten grand.'

'What about the safe?' I asked.

'That's the priceless part. The old bird knew the money was in the safe, so she directs them to a bit of money under the mattress and they left thinking they got the main prize.'

'Bloody amateurs,' I laughed.

'Yeah, but, Bruce – Old Bill think you done it. So does the contact who stuck the work up!'

'Well, it's not me,' I said furiously. 'It's my fucking reputation on the line and I don't make mistakes and my people always get paid.'

Everything I touched was turning to stone. Tommy Butler was getting closer by the day and lady luck was changing sides like a cheap whore. Keep running, Bruce, I told myself. Funk it.

Another piece of work surfaced. Again, the information came from Rolly, Fred's man in Wales. The target this time was the owner of a wholesale ice-cream business run in conjunction with restaurants, cafés and amusement arcades all over the principality, although the head office was in Porthcawl. He was a big punter who boasted about his distrust of banks and how he had large amounts of cash that he couldn't declare without a swingeing investigation from the tax man. He even confided that he never kept his money at home, but was more than satisfied with a locked safe in the strongroom at head office, all belled up above a seafront restaurant and amusement arcade. I fancied solving his tax worries by taking the cash off his hands.

The Captain drove me there with Jump-on Jim, an old friend who had been a successful businessman, with interests in escort agencies, ticket agencies, photographic and office supplies – all flourishing, but never providing quite enough dosh for Jimmy's needs. Jump-on wanted to be dining at the Ritz and dancing at Annabel's every night, and with a different lady on each arm.

It wasn't safe to park a car all night, so we unloaded the equipment – two oxygen bottles, two propane bottles, bolt-cutters, jemmies, torches and black-out material – and arranged for the Captain to return the next morning at six-thirty precisely. Despite the alarms, the place was so big I was confident that we could make a clean entry. Coming to a double-doored gate with a wicker door that led into the yard, I demonstrated my prowess by leaping up and over and dropping to the other side. I was just about to open the wicker door when Jim pushed it and strolled through. 'Always check the door first,' he said, giving me a grin.

After crossing the yard, we found a door on the fire escape and began drilling several holes. Finally I realized that the whole structure was metal reinforced from behind. We decided to try another route and I began drilling through a barred ground-floor window, showing Jump-on the best technique. Suddenly, I looked up and he was peering at me from inside.

'How did you fucking get in there?'

'There's a door open round the side,' he said smiling.

Christ, what a cock-up, I thought, bundling the gear inside.

We passed through various open doors *en route* to the second floor, home of the strongroom. I couldn't understand why all the doors were open; they all had alarm points attached, but these were useless unless the door was closed.

The entrance to the second floor was locked. As we broke it down and entered, I suddenly saw – too late – that the door was alarmed.

'We've set the alarm off, mate,' I said.

There was little use running. The Captain wasn't due back until six-thirty and if we tried to flee, we were easy targets on the street. We were stranded and there was little option but to get up on the roof and wait – funking that the alarm wasn't switched on. It was a blind, million-to-one chance, but our only hope.

From the roof we watched the main road that led into town, looking for police vehicles, and waiting for the inevitable. It was a nightmare. The gale-force wind coming in off the sea was peppered with rain and salt spray. We were cold and wet and very scared. I could see the headline: 'TRAIN ROBBER CAUGHT ON WELSH ROOFTOP.' Ah well, I comforted myself, they could hardly give me more than thirty years.

My thoughts turned to Angela and Nick, and what would become of them. It was too awful to contemplate. There are no atheists in a foxhole, and I was kneeling and praying: 'Get me out of this one, God, and I promise I'll never do it again.' A familiar enough litany, but by the end of another fifteen minutes I knew that it had been answered.

'Looks sweet,' I said. 'The alarm can't have gone off.'

'Thank God for that,' Jim said.

As we made our way back towards the second floor, it dawned on me why nothing had happened. With the constant battering that the building got from the sea winds, the alarm would have been set off every hour or so. The owners had probably switched it off, relying on the visible presence of a system to protect them.

We got into the strongroom by knocking out the brickwork over the door. Dropping through, I found the safe, an older-type Chatwood Milner, surrounded by bags of silver. To me that meant that the safe was chockablock with notes, with no room for coins. Jimmy masked the opening above the door to black out flashlight from the oxy/propane torch, whilst I prepared the equipment. I was cutting well, with about six inches to go, when I ran out of oxygen.

Our strength was ebbing and we made hard work of manhandling the heavy bottle up and through the gap in the brickwork. I'd just got going again when Jim whispered, 'I can hear people on the ground floor!'

I looked at my watch. It was five forty-five. Could we still do it? I thought that we could. I began cutting again, but this time Jim's warning was more urgent. 'They're moving about up here, mate. Cleaners, I think. We've got to get out, and get out now!'

'Give me another ten minutes.' 'Fuck ten minutes! We'll be fucking nicked by then.'

Reluctantly, I had to admit defeat. I'd done all I could; it just wasn't meant to be. Maybe the Supreme Being was punishing me for my broken promise. After one last, loving, lingering look at the safe, I turned away. So near and yet so far.

Jim had packed the silver in a holdall and we clambered through the gap over the door. As we dropped to the floor and brushed debris from our clothes, two lady cleaners walked past us with buckets and mops in their hands.

'Gas Board,' I remarked in what I fondly imagined was the language of the leek, before walking briskly on.

We got out of the building, into the yard, and through the wicker door. We were out, but not safe. The Captain wasn't due for half an hour.

The streets were deserted, and if the cleaners raised the alarm we were bound to be nicked. Trying to look purposeful, we walked up the main street. Jim spotted a newsagent's and we ducked inside. Miraculously they sold cups of tea, and we stood sipping and looking nonchalant for as long as we could before taking to the street again. For the first time in his life the Captain was five minutes early. We jumped into the car and breathed huge sighs of relief as he drove fast towards the comparative safety of Cardiff.

Three times unlucky, I said to myself. The ICI plant, the slaughterhouse and now this. I was going to have to think again.

36

Tommy Butler and the boys from the Flying Squad made sure that I knew they were close behind. Friends and former associates were regularly tailed or pulled in for questioning. It was only a matter of time before one of them cracked under the threats of dubious charges against them.

Most policemen would have relaxed years ago, assuming that eventually I would make a mistake, but not Butler. He was relentless – as if taking it personally. Anyone would have thought I'd stolen his beloved mother's life savings from under her pillow instead of cash from the nation's largest banks.

We learned much later that Butler placed saturation surveillance on Charlie's partner Don. They logged his trip to France and placed it in the 'movement of associates' file, but luckily they didn't follow him to Nice, where he met Charlie and they joined Harry and me for dinner. It would have been a nasty interruption of one of those meals you never forget – lobsters and sea bass, Dom Pérignon and more Dom Pérignon. We finally left the table at about four the next morning.

Don was eventually followed to Montreal, and Butler called in the Mounties to conduct surveillance. At Rigaud, Don was photographed with Charlie and his family. Even so, the Mounties didn't move in. They were waiting to see who else might turn up – in particular, yours truly.

Then it was time for Tommy Butler's moment of glory. He flew to Montreal and collected a task force of fifty Mounties.

They knocked on Charlie's door at eight o'clock in the morning, just as he was about to take his three daughters to school. Chas opened the door, saw Tom and his armed retinue and must have known the game was up.

'Hello, Charlie,' said Tom.

'Fucking hell, Tom,' replied Chas. 'You'd better come in. Not that lot though.'

'Thanks. You look well, Charlie.'

'And you, guv. Cup of tea?'

We couldn't stay in Albert Mews any longer than a second month so the Captain found us a place at Newdigate, just outside Dorking. It was Japanese-style, built on the side of a lake, and owned by Peter Asher, Jane Asher's brother. Peter was one half of Peter & Gordon, the singing duo, and he filled the place with pop stars and showbusiness types, including the Beatles. I thought, Nothing puts fame into perspective like using the same bath and porcelain throne as the likes of Paul, John, George and Ringo – and Jane!

We moved in a few weeks before Christmas, quickly becoming friends with the caretakers, a nice couple with two children about Nick's age. We looked like a wealthy middle-class family, above suspicion, although I did have one hell of a scare when the wife told Angela that her father had at one time owned Leatherslade Farm. I didn't know how it came up in conversation but it was an astonishing coincidence.

Early in the New Year, the Captain organized another move, this time to a mews flat just off Exhibition Road. There was a little school for Nick round the corner in Chelsea, where he was enrolled as Nicholas East. Almost six years old, he was a good kid and didn't question being given a new name. I simply said, 'Nick, you're so and so today. That's your new name. He got lost at Richmond swimming-pool one day and there was an announcement over the public-address system. 'We have found a fair-haired boy dressed in a blue T-shirt and shorts who doesn't know his name.'

Angela recognized the description and collected him. 'I did know my name, Mum,' he explained, 'But I didn't know whether it was safe to tell them or not.' Nick obviously knew far more than I gave him credit for. He was watching television and overhearing snippets of conversation – I'd forgotten that all kids are great eavesdroppers.

About six weeks after moving to the flat, the Captain arrived looking flustered.

'There's something seriously wrong,' he said. 'It's my bank manager. You know the guy, he's always been on our side, giving out loans to all the right people and copping the necessary for his help. He is in a terrible state. He says to me, "What have you been up to, Alan? The police have been in. They were asking questions about you."'

'Did he say what it was about?' I asked. 'Did they give him any indication?'

'No, none at all,' said the Captain.

'Right, we got to think about this one. Can we talk to him direct?'

'No.'

'What about Jump-on?'

'Yeah, he knows him. He could go.'

I called Jump-on and he agreed to see the bank manager. Back he came with the details.

'The police went in real heavy, asking about the Captain. They said, "Do you know anything about BR?" So he says, "What do you mean, British Rail?" And the copper says, "Nearly right."'

'Fuck me!' I said.

Jump-on shook his head. 'Looks as if they definitely got a connection between the Captain and you, Bruce.'

'And if they're looking into the Captain, they're eventually going to run through his bank statements and see how he's been paying money to different estate agents. Then the agents are gonna tell them the addresses and we'll have fifty coppers arriving for breakfast. We're moving.'

I reasoned that it was probably safer to live a good way outside London and drove down to Torquay. I looked for a house to rent and eventually settled on Villa Cap Martin, a square, white house on a hilltop in Braddons Hill Road East, with panoramic views of the town, sea and palm-tree-lined coast. It reminded me very much of the Riviera.

The house was owned by Jane, a widow in her thirties who lived next door with her widowed mother, Mrs Anne Sofrini.

Jane had two children, a girl and boy aged eight and four. Her father had owned the 'Boulogne', a well-known restaurant in London's West End, before moving to Torquay and opening restaurants there, playing host to all the locals who mattered. We were to spend a lot of time with them over the next few weeks, being introduced to their friends and slowly being enveloped in a cloak of respectability.

Our children all went to the local Catholic school and we took turns dropping them off and picking them up. Everything was comfortable and secure except for the money, which was running out quickly. Whereas once we bought a case of champagne every week, it was now a single bottle of vodka, sipped sparingly. I was going up to town two or three days a week, staying with Jump-on in a flat just off the King's Road. My transport was a Mark-2 Lotus Cortina which I'd nicked when it had about 1,500 miles on the clock. I changed the plates and arranged cover notes, insurance and my driving licence in the name of Miller.

One particular night Angela and I went to a restaurant in Kingsbridge which had been advertised as being exceptionally good. In a drunken state, she said to me, 'Can I drive the Lotus home?'

Angela was a very good driver, but all her experience behind the wheel was with automatics rather than a manual gear shift. Even so, I agreed. Coming out of Coombe, she lost control and we finished up in a ditch beside the road. The front suspension was damaged and it took more than a week for a garage to get the parts. I decided against using it so freely in the future; I would keep it parked in London as a working ringer. In the meantime, I arranged for Angela to have driving lessons.

Both of us were using international licences which weren't really valid if we were living in Britain. Angela's instructor convinced me to have a couple of refreshers and retake my test. With the lessons duly completed, I took my test at Newton Abbot. The test instructor got into the passenger seat and started making polite conversation as I eased my foot off the clutch and pulled away.

'I used to be in the Flying Squad before I retired,' he said. I nearly drove us off the road.

'Yeah, I had thirty years with them. Now I do this to make a few quid on the side. What's your line of business, Mr Miller?'

'Antiques,' I said, keeping my eyes fixed on the road.

He chatted on and finally told me that I had passed. 'You seemed a bit nervous at first,' he said, 'but that could have been me. Instructors often make people nervous.' If only he'd known.

We had been in Torquay for about a month when Angela woke one night with cramps that almost doubled her over in pain. A local GP referred her to Royal Marsden Hospital to be screened for possible cervical cancer.

'Whatever you do, don't come up here,' she said to me on the telephone. 'Don't take the risk.'

But life didn't really mean a lot to me if Angela wasn't there. We'd been together so long and shared so much that I couldn't stay away from the hospital. I left Nick with Jane next door and drove to London. I sat with her for an hour, holding her hand. We didn't say much; both of us realized that if cancer was diagnosed we faced a dilemma. I wasn't in a position to care for Nick on my own. I was on the run and trying to raise money. I couldn't take him along for the ride. Frightened, I found myself praying again and making promises to God that I couldn't keep.

'Don't come up again,' said Angela. 'Even if it's serious, don't come back.'

That night a woman in a nearby bed asked Angela, 'Is your husband on the Force?'

'No. Why?'

'My husband is a policeman. He was up here last night and he thought he recognized him.'

Thankfully, the medical news was good and Angela was discharged and allowed to come home. The following weekend, by way of celebration, we set off on a curious pilgrimage. It was almost exactly five years since the Great Train Robbery and I took Angela and Nick to visit the scene of the crime. We lunched first at Henley and then drove to Cheddington where the train was stopped. Gazing up at Bridego Bridge, I was amazed at how little the scene had changed. Somehow I expected it to be different; I expected it to bear some remnant of evidence that this was where the largest robbery in history had unfolded. But there was nothing to record the event.

Standing in the sunshine, staring at the strip of railway line, I explained exactly how the train was stopped, separated and then relieved of its contents. The magic of that night was still with me, even if the money had gone.

Growing more and more frustrated, I spent most of each week in London trying to arrange jobs. I was driving a Mini Cooper, bought in Twickenham for £900 cash and registered in Angela's name. Normally I arranged to meet Jump-on, using a special code that involved an underground map which was marked with our own sequence of names for each of the stations and landmarks. When I said, 'I'll see you at Sloane Square,' it meant that I'd see him at Camden Town, or if I said, 'I'll meet you at Lancaster Gate,' it meant Baker Street.

One particular night, I rang Jimmy and said, 'I'm coming up into town. I'll see you in the Potter's about half-past eight.' The Potter's was a pub on King's Road, but Jimmy knew I meant that I would see him at Sloane Square tube. We met, had a drink and I crashed at his flat. Meanwhile, Harry just happened to be in the Potter's that night at nine o'clock. The police surrounded the place, and steamed in looking for me. The only explanation was that Jimmy's phone had been wired. If so, the police could also have noted the Cooper occasionally parked in his street. They were getting too close for comfort.

Rather than risk staying with friends, I arranged to rent a bedsit in Kew – a fleapit, but it was only for a few nights a week while I looked at various bits of work with Roller Reg. Nothing was going right for me – even the smallest things – but I persevered and prayed my luck would change. I even looked at Weybridge again, going down at two o'clock in the morning to watch the money train arrive. I staked out the Post Office for several nights, using a vacant cottage overlooking the car park, but I couldn't see any way to beat the security.

In all this period, I only had one touch. It was a bit of work in Macclesfield that had been on the books for almost a decade. According to the source, there was fifty grand in readies hidden in the home of a businessman. Rick, the key man, had looked at it previously but the house was always occupied and he wasn't inclined to tie people up. It wasn't his game. Another problem was finding the money. Even if the information was correct, you would have to convince one of the hostages to reveal its location. For a percentage thief, it wasn't good value but I was getting desperate. I needed money to leave the country and establish a new life in New Zealand.

I drove up with Roller Reg and his partner in an old Post Office van we'd nicked. We arrived at about half-past ten in the morning, planning to do the old 'Parcel at the door' routine, but the house was empty. I went through a back window and within five minutes I'd found a parcel under a mattress that contained almost exactly twenty grand. We probably should have spent more time looking but it was a nice, clean job and I had enough from my third share to pay the bills.

Six weeks later, early in November, I was stopped by a policeman in Torquay for having parked too close to a pedestrian crossing. It was only a minor misdemeanour, but he demanded my licence, insurance and car registration documents. When I explained that I didn't have them with me, he told me to produce them at the local police station within 24 hours.

I wasn't particularly worried. All the papers were in order and the car was properly owned and maintained. Even so, there was a slight chance that somebody would recognize me at the station. By the same token, if I didn't go down, they would be even more suspicious. Confidence was the key, I decided. I would act totally naturally.

The next afternoon I picked Nick and the kids up from school and dropped them home. Then I said, 'I gotta go to the police station. Do you want to come?'

Nick started crying. 'Don't go, Dad, please don't go!'

'It's all right. There's nothing to worry about.'

'No, Dad, don't, please!'

'It's all right, really.'

When I got to the station, Nick stood beside me as I handed over the documents. It was a routine check and we were thanked for our co-operation. Outside, I said to Nick, 'See, I told you so. You didn't have to worry. Everything is fine.'

That night I drove to London to meet Roller Reg. We had a bit of work arranged, knocking over a house in Kent. The owners were away so we had all night to strip the place, taking up the carpets and floorboards, looking for a safe. After four hours we had found nothing except the consolation prize of a case of champagne each. 'With Christmas being so close, it's quite handy,' I said, trying to hide my disappointment. 'At least we won't be thirsty.'

It was late when we left the house.

'You're not going home now, are you?' said Reg. 'You're gonna be on the road with that in the back.' He motioned towards the case of champagne.

'What's a case of champagne? I got all my credentials, I don't mind a pull.'

Bombing happily along the road, I stopped on the bypass just outside Exeter and called Angela. 'Run a bath, love, I'll be home in an hour.'

It was about twelve forty-five when I saw a white police car parked off the side of the road on a hillside near Barton. I had never seen one around there before, but thinking no more of it, I drove on to Torquay, pulled into the garage and slid into a nice warm bath with a glass of champagne snugly in my hand.

It was about two o'clock when I hit the sack, snuggling up close to Angela and contemplating our future in New Zealand. She wrapped her arms around me, clinging tightly as if frightened of letting me go.

At twenty to seven the next morning I woke to the sound of Nick's voice.

'Doorbell, Dad!'

'It's probably Jane from next door,' I yelled. 'Can you answer it?'

I heard voices at the door and the pounding of feet up the stairs. The bedroom door burst open and a dozen policemen piled through, diving on to the bed and pinning me down.

Angela screamed, absolutely terrified, and Nick huddled in the corner, too frightened to cry.

Then I saw Tommy Butler in the doorway. He looked older and greyer than I remembered. The years had not been gentle.

'Long time no see, Bruce,' he said. 'But I've got you at last.'

I looked at him and smiled. '*C'est la vie*, Tom.'

37

There was no escape this time. For a split second I contemplated diving through the bedroom window, which would have brought me out on to the lawn, thirty feet below, but the place was surrounded and the game was up.

'Have a look under the pillow,' said Tom, who obviously believed everything he read in the papers. One of the tabloids had run a headline saying, '**HE'LL NEVER BE TAKEN ALIVE.**'

They kept us in the bedroom while the house was searched and eventually I was allowed to get dressed. Surrounded by officers, I wanted to talk to Nick – to explain to him what had happened. He was hugging Angela, sobbing his heart out.

'Listen, Mr Butler, is there any chance that I could have a word with me boy?'

'Yeah.'

'In the other room, in private?'

He gave me a look that said, 'You've got to be joking.'

So I went over to Nick and knelt down beside him. 'Look, I'm sorry, son. Your dad's been a naughty boy and has got to go away.'

'When will you be coming back?' he asked, wiping his eyes with his sleeve.

'I don't know. But just remember one thing. I love you. I will always love you.'

Angela was in a terrible state. Her whole world had crashed around her and she knew that I wasn't going to be around to hold things together. We had only a few thousand pounds left – how would she survive? How would she look after Nick?

On the way to the Aylesbury police station, the Flying Squad boys were slagging me. They were ecstatic and already boasting. 'We nearly had you in Wales, Bruce.'

'Yeah? But you didn't, did ya?' I mocked.

I was in the back seat and, as we drove towards Aylesbury, the whole horror of prison life flashed through my mind; the beatings, drudgery, isolation and pointless routine. I wasn't handcuffed, and for a fraction of a second I considered throwing myself over the seat, grabbing the steering wheel and turning us into the path of an oncoming lorry. That would be the end of it, I thought.

Butler had an odd sense of humour. When we got to Aylesbury police station, the driver pulled into a space marked 'Probation'. Butler looked at him and said, 'What are you doing? Fucking probation? Park somewhere else.'

They were waiting when we arrived, a phalanx of officers lining the path to the station's entrance. Without handcuffs, they couldn't identify who was the Train Robber until Tom placed a proprietorial arm around my shoulders, signifying to the whole world that I was his. To the victor the spoils. I didn't begrudge him his victory; he'd earned it. I'd had my day and now it was his.

A top jolly introduced himself to Butler before showing us to an interview room. He called for tea and attempted to make himself part of the action. Tom wasn't having any of that; this was his triumph – he didn't want the uniformed branch of a provincial police force nicking his kudos. The jolly was shown to the door and then Tom told the rest of the Flying Squad boys that perhaps they'd better lose themselves for a while as well. They were clearly disappointed; they'd hoped to be in at the kill, but Tom didn't seem to want them being privy to our dialogue.

'Now then, Bruce,' he said when we were alone.

'Yes, Tom,' I answered. It was a stratagem on my part. Apart from the moment in my bedroom, when hunter and hunted met for the first time, I had been careful to refer to him either as Mr Butler or guv'nor. He was clearly appreciative of such niceties, but now I was making it plain that we were on equal terms, regardless of my position.

He was a bit taken aback, almost as if he resented the familiarity, but he had more important matters to contend with. 'Now then, Bruce. First off, you know that you've got to go away – that's the way it is. Second, I'm retiring. I've got a nice little job lined up at Midland Bank in the New Year – head of security, and I don't want you fucking it up. I want this over and done with.'

Tom leaned closer, putting his hands flat on the table. 'Let me tell you, if you're going to plead not guilty, you've got no chance. I've got too much evidence against you. I've got all the receipts for the equipment found at the farm.'

I raised an eyebrow. We both knew bloody well that I'd burned every last one of them. 'Yes, all the receipts,' he said. 'As well as fingerprints.'

'I know about the fucking prints. What a joke!'

Tommy smiled. 'And then there's your lifestyle and movements. You can't win, Bruce. Now listen to me, you have to decide how we do this. You don't want to see Angela in the nick and your son in care, do you? There's going to be no-one to look after them – they'll all be in the nick – your family and friends, Harry, Mary, Rene, the Captain . . . Then there's your old man. Think of him, he's a highly respected man in the unions – this will destroy him. You don't want that, do you? Ask yourself, "What chance have I got?" Then tell yourself, "No chance whatsoever." '

We spent hours playing a cat-and-mouse game. Tommy told me about the times he was close to nicking me – at least once in France and also when I hid behind the sofa in Croydon and pretended to be Angela's illicit lover.

Then he asked, 'What were you doing renting cars in Birmingham a few months back? What were you doing up there?'

'That's for you to find out, isn't it, Tom?'

'And you were fucking about down at Weybridge, weren't you?'

'I've been fucking about everywhere, Tom, you know that!'

'You wouldn't have got much you know.'

'No? You wanna put a figure on it?'

'I don't think you'd have got more than fifty grand.'

How the hell would he know? I thought. It was GPO money. I'd seen the bags coming off the train and why would the police be guarding it like the crown jewels if there was only fifty grand?

'So we know you've been active – reports from Wales and the Midlands indicate that you've been bang at it. That's going to look great in front of the judge, on top of the Train. You're going to look a real menace – a threat to society. Who knows what he might give you? It's a showcase trial, Bruce, it could be a showcase sentence. Look at George Blake . . .

'You know the score, Bruce. You've challenged the Establishment and we can't allow that. Examples have to be made, we've got to discourage the others. We're not playing cops and robbers any more; we both know that. This is about maintaining faith in the system.

'You've had a good run, Bruce, but it's over. You've lost. Go gracefully, it's your only chance. You're a bright boy, you'll salvage something out of it.'

'Can you give me any help, Tom?' I asked.

'I'll be saying that you co-operated as much as anyone can in the circumstances. That's all I can say.'

'But what about the Train? Can you put me down as playing a minor role?'

'No, Bruce, because it would make me look foolish. I've been going to the South of France every year, thanks to you. Nice little paid holidays, all put down to the investigation. I can't suddenly say, "Reynolds was only the messenger boy." We can't have another Buster, can we? Justice must be seen to be done.'

'I understand, Tom, but there are still ways to minimize my role – or at least not exaggerate it. If I plead guilty, think of all the aggravation that I'm saving the court – the witnesses won't have to be called; how many are there . . . a hundred or so? And how long was the big trial? Ten or twelve weeks? I can save everyone a lot of time and money, or I can make it last as long as that, if not longer.'

'Bruce, don't take that route,' said Tom. 'I know how you're feeling – you think that everything is against you, that the cards are stacked . . . well they are. You're thinking, Fuck it, fight it and go down with all guns blazing. Well, Bruce, that's bollocks! Everyone loses and the one that loses the most is you. Take my advice, keep the casualties down, plead guilty.'

'What about parole? Can you give me any help there?'

'Parole isn't part of the process yet, but rest assured that if and when it does come in, you'll be considered the same as anyone.'

'But you can give me an edge – you can provide the background when it does come in, can't you?'

'Yes, I can – and I will. I'm not an unreasonable man, you should know that by now.'

I looked at Tom for a long time, giving him the cold appraisal. I was thinking, Can I trust him? He was probably thinking the same thing. There was no reason to doubt him. He was on his final case, his final triumphal coup; he'd nicked me and I'd go to prison. He was right: I'd lost, and I had to accept it.

'OK, Tom, you've got a deal. I plead guilty to the Train, conspiracy and all that, and none of my family or friends get any aggro, no charges, nothing. Is that it?'

'That's it, Bruce. You've got my word on it.'

He offered his hand and with a strong grip sealed the moment.

There was almost a sense of theatre about it, shaped in my mind by countless Saturday-morning Westerns; the sheriff had got his man. *Mano a mano*, this was a different Butler. It was his last hurrah before retirement, and he could afford to let the human side emerge, perhaps for the first time.

'I suppose I'd better call the others in, they're a bit unhappy at being left out,' he said, gesturing at the silhouettes visible behind the glass-panelled door.

He reached for the door handle, but then paused, turned to me and said, 'You'd have made a good cop, Bruce.'

I smiled. 'Yeah, Tom, and you'd have made a good thief.'

I think he liked that.

I knew that Tommy Butler would make sure the evidence was conclusive. That was how the system worked.

It is odd the way society views police corruption. For years it simply did not exist in the public's mind. Policemen were brave, upstanding and trustworthy. No-one would ever doubt the word of an officer. By the early seventies, however, this attitude was changing and Sir Robert Mark, who took over as Metropolitan Police Commissioner, promised to do away with corruption within the force. His philosophy seemed to be: 'A good police force is one that catches more criminals than it employs.'

Tommy Butler was one of the detectives who had thrived under the old system. He cut corners, bent rules, garnished the truth – whatever it took to secure a conviction. According to Butler, when Charlie was first arrested he had uttered the immortal words, 'You won't make it stick without the poppy.' Oddly enough, this phrase crops up several times in Butler's earlier cases. Apparently crims couldn't help uttering it every time Tom burst through the door. I have no idea where he got it from. It certainly wasn't part of Charlie's vocabulary nor any of the group's. If anything, it sounded like a relic from Edgar Wallace's *The Squealer*. Perhaps detective fiction was Butler's source.

Much later Biggsy told me a good story about his arrest and interview in 1963. Tommy had advised him to make a full statement about his part in the crime and the roles of the other robbers. Of course, Ronnie had refused to co-operate.

'It doesn't really matter, Ron,' Tommy Butler said. 'We've probably got enough on you and most of the others already. What we haven't got, we can make up.'

Despite this, I always rated Tommy Butler as an honourable detective. He didn't sell his soul to criminals for money; or take bribes. In the rough and tumble world of the fifties and sixties, he simply took shortcuts which he saw as legitimate.

After more tea at Aylesbury police headquarters, we started the paperwork – statements, queries, dialogue. It was all standard procedure. The police were in good spirits.

Already my mind had switched to limiting the damage. For Angela's and Nick's sake, I had to avoid a long sentence. Perhaps if I made some attempt at restitution, the judge would look at me more favourably? Unfortunately, the only money left from the Train was the five grand in Mexico which was in the name of K. C. Miller. I provided the details.

To further enhance my chances, I stressed in my statement that crime didn't pay. 'It has only brought misery to my wife and young son who could suffer the after-effects for a long time to come,' I said.

After the questioning was over, I was escorted to the charge room and formally charged with robbing the train and conspiracy to rob the train. The time of reckoning had begun.

Under heavy escort with a police convoy, I was transferred to Linslade Magistrate's Court, and lodged there overnight in readiness for my first appearance in court the next morning. I had a police officer with me all night who was a local with very little experience. He asked me to sign his warrant card – 'This is for me son, you know.'

During the evening, the chief constable came in to see me. 'Pleased to meet you, Mr Reynolds,' he said, shaking my hand. 'Is everything all right?'

'Yeah.'

'Well, look after him,' he said to the constable. And to me: 'I wish you all the best of luck.'

I was being treated like an equal. That was the hypocrisy of the whole thing. If I'd just been nicked for breaking into someone's house, they would have treated me like dirt. But because I was Bruce Reynolds, the Train Robber, I was respected.

When I appeared in court the next day, eleven plain-clothes detectives filled the two rows of public seats and another line of detectives stood in front of the public gallery. After a five-minute hearing I was remanded in custody until the trial.

I was transferred to Leicester, which had a maximum security wing. For reasons known only to the authorities, I was separated from the other prisoners on remand and kept on my own except for exercise periods. The governor was quite friendly, however, and allowed certain privileges, including half a bottle of wine a day, along with the food parcels brought in by Angela, and my nightly cigar.

He came round one evening and sniffed the smoke appreciatively. 'Nice cigar, Bruce?'

'Yeah, take one.'

'Well, thank you very much,' he beamed.

Although some of the others in the firm had received thirty-year sentences, I was still hopeful that common sense would prevail. My solicitor was more circumspect.

'We don't know what's going to happen. They're really looking for a scapegoat. You could get thirty-five.' The longest I had ever been inside was three and a half. Even ten years seemed unbelievably long.

'How the fuck do you do ten years?' I had once asked a long-timer.

'It's a funny thing, Bruce, but you lose yourself,' he replied. 'For the first couple of years you are conscious of the time, then there seems to be a middle period where you don't know it goes and then you start counting again when there are two years to go.'

Typically, there was a lot of black humour floating around in the exercise yard. Somebody reminded me of the classic where the judge gives a guy twenty years and the crim says, 'I can't do it, my Lord.'

The judge replies, 'Well, try and do as much as you can!'

Someone else told me a story about Ian Barry, who had been nicked with Ronnie Kray and got life with a minimum of twenty years.

'You got twenty, Ian,' he'd been asked, 'how are you doing it?'

He answered, 'I do five years at a time.'

My brief was Cyril Salmon, a barrister who was the scion of a distinguished legal family that included a Law Lord with the curious name of Lord Salmon of Sandwich. His role wasn't demanding. I pleaded guilty and relied on Cyril to poetically plead mitigation. Through the legal grapevine I heard that there was difficulty finding a judge who would preside over my case because most had already allowed themselves to be quoted by the media.

I knew more or less how it would go. Justice Davies, the original judge, had doled out thirty-year sentences, obviously having been directed from above. Later, when Jimmy White was sentenced, the new judge hadn't got the message and announced privately, 'It goes against my principles to give anyone more than eighteen years for anything. That's my ceiling.' Of course, this made the original sentences look a bit ludicrous. Then came Buster who was named all the way through as being one of the main protagonists. He received fifteen years. Little wonder that the others were sitting in their cells awaiting the outcome of my trial, hoping that if I received a lesser sentence they would have good grounds for appeal.

There was very little evidence given, due to my plea of guilty. When Tommy Butler was called to the stand, he was asked what position I held in the firm. 'Somewhere near the top,' he answered.

Cyril Salmon was quite brilliant in his summing-up. He gave such a glowing account of my good character and qualities as a husband and father that I began to wonder, Who is he talking about?

This charade continued when the judge complimented him on his brilliant plea of mitigation and said the whole court had been thankful for the way he had presented these matters. This sounded promising. Then I realized that he was just giving him a boost, knowing that nothing was going to alter what was coming.

On 14 January 1969, the sentence was handed down at Buckingham Assizes, Aylesbury.

As Angela sobbed in the public gallery, Mr Justice Thomson said: 'The fact that you avoided arrest for five years and, presumably, during that time were able to enjoy the fruits of your crime, does not, in my view, constitute any reason for passing upon you any less sentence now than you would have received then, even though it is no doubt true that your enjoyment of these fruits was associated with the fear of ultimate arrest.'

He concluded with the words I had been dreading. 'Bruce Richard Reynolds, I sentence you to twenty-five years' imprisonment.'

One of the newspapers reported that 'Reynolds stumbled from the dock'. I don't remember it that way. I was expecting the sentence, although I had hoped it would be twenty. Such harsh sentences were ludicrous when you considered the crime. The traitor George Blake was responsible for revealing the identities of dozens of British agents to the Soviets which resulted in upwards of forty people being killed, and he was given forty-two years. When you start giving people thirty years for robbery with the minimum of violence involved, what do you give people who do really bad things?

I wasn't alone in my condemnation. Within a year of the original sentences being handed down, a committee including politicians from both Houses had been formed to press for a reduction in the penalties for the Train. It petitioned the Home Office, arguing that the sentence did not fit the crime.

Sir Robert Mark, the Commissioner of the Met, said in 1972, 'I know only too well that there are a number of criminals active in London who are far more violent. It is only logical to wonder why . . . the Great Train Robbers should be regarded as qualifying for harsher treatment.'

38

They allowed me to see Angela for half an hour in the courthouse before taking me away. She hadn't slept for three weeks before the trial and had lost twenty-one pounds in weight. Totally shell-shocked, I put my arms around her and she began to cry. We were both trying to be brave, bolstering ourselves, but we knew that the adventure was over and it was the end of our life together. The future couldn't be contemplated.

While on the run we had talked about capture. I had told Angela that if it ever happened we should make a complete break, no pretence, nothing, the end. I couldn't face the mental torture of infidelity; I'd suffered enough with Rita, I couldn't go through that again without losing my sanity.

But holding Angela in my arms, feeling her sob against my chest, I knew I couldn't let go of her. Angela needed me now more than ever. She was on her own with Nick. She needed to feel that I was with her; even if I was in prison. In truth, I needed her just as much. I needed someone to motivate me, to give some sort of purpose to the years locked away. In between hugs and kisses and tears were the endearments and the promises. We'd been through so much together, we kidded ourselves that we'd get through this, too – together.

Parole was being discussed in the corridors of power; it was suggested that prisoners could be out after serving a third of their sentence. If granted, I could be home in eight years and four months. I seized on this, holding it out to Angela as a candle of hope. 'Listen, love, with parole it's only eight years,' I said. 'That's not so long, is it?'

'Of course not,' she said, putting on a brave face. 'It's just a few years out of our lives.'

'And it will go quickly. Look at Steak, he did a ten, he's home now.'

'I know, I know. We'll do it, you'll see. I'll be good.'

'You're always good, sweetheart. The best.'

'I've got Nick to take care of and as he gets older he'll keep me company.'

'I'm going to miss seeing him grow up,' I said sadly.

'No you won't. I'll bring him to see you; and we'll write.'

'We're not going to let this destroy us; plenty of relationships have survived after years in prison. You have to have faith.'

'Have faith in me,' she said.

There was no talk of a possible escape. We both knew what life on the run had been like even with bundles of money. What would it be like without any?

Finally, Blackie, the special watch officer, told us that our time was up.

'Not yet,' Angela cried.

'Sorry, Mrs Reynolds, but you've already had longer than allowed.'

Angela was holding me tightly. She didn't want to let go, and the tears began to flow. 'Come on,' I whispered in her ear. 'Chin up, babe, don't let the side down. Show them how brave you are.'

She nodded and loosened her grip.

I looked at Blackie, gestured towards Angela, and said, 'Tell her about parole, chief. I could be home in eight, isn't that right?'

'Yeah, if he behaves himself he could be home in eight or thereabouts. It's up to him.'

'There. You see – it's not the end of the world, we've got a future.'

She wiped her eyes before presenting her face for a goodbye kiss.

'I love you,' she whispered.

'I love you too,' I said, my throat so tight I could hardly utter the words. As we had our last embrace I tried to will my strength into her. The moment was so charged that the tears broke through again.

'Give Nick a big hug and a kiss from me,' I said, and then she was led out of the cell, sobbing.

For all our brave words, the truth would prove to be cruel. I had no control over the future; no other option but to see it through to the end.

The police had treated Angela well after my arrest and there was no animosity. They even let her keep five hundred quid of the money that I arranged to return. Jane and her mother were also very helpful and didn't turn Angela and Nick out of the house in Torquay. Jane actually expressed her regret and told journalists that she thought I was a nice man.

I was so grateful that I wrote her a letter. 'First of all I would like to apologize for any inconvenience I have caused and I know there has been plenty,' I said. 'Secondly, thank you so much for being so kind to Angela. It was a terrible shock to her but thank God she does seem to be bearing up with it now. You and all the kind friends in Torquay have helped her tremendously with your sympathy. In a way this has been a relief for me. We have been running for five years and, apart from Angela, Nick had to have roots. We thought we had found it at Cap Martin. However, it was not to be.'

The first night of my incarceration, the doctor and the governor visited my cell. 'How do you feel about your sentence?' the doctor asked.

'Not too happy.'

'You don't feel suicidal? You don't want anything?'

'What do you mean? Do I want anything to help me end it all, is that what you're asking?' He just laughed.

I think it was Lord Mountbatten who was the first to say that you should put all your rotten eggs in one basket. This was the whole idea behind the maximum-security wings. They were envisaged as some sort of Alcatraz where all the very worst criminals could be locked away and forgotten. Of course, one of the first things that happened was that Wally Probyn, John McVicar and Joe Martin escaped from such a wing in Durham in 1968 making the authorities look decidedly foolish.

My own position wasn't helped by the Chief Constable of Durham, Tommy Muir, who had been reported as suggesting that nuclear weapons might be used to spring the Great Train Robbers from jail. He said we should all be shot, even offering to do it himself. Of course, the Press had a field day and Tommy tried to backtrack, claiming he shouldn't have said 'shoot' but 'give them hemlock'.

This sense of hysteria spread and one senior member of staff told me that he entirely agreed with the Chief Constable. 'I can only wish the fucking Home Office would give me the order – I'd line you up against the wall and shoot you tomorrow.'

Although the regime was designed to be harsh, the maximum-security wing at Durham was unlike any other I had experienced. For one thing, there was greater freedom, with cell doors open during the day and only locked at night. I threw myself into the chores, mainly to keep my sanity but also because it would look good on my record if I wanted to get transferred from the security wing and eventually seek parole. That was my priority, and to that end I became a model con.

There were only about eight of us on the wing. Although I had no long-time friends among the inmates, I knew a few by reputation – people like Ronnie Kray, Charlie Richardson and Roy Hall. I bumped into them most days while working out in the weights room and in the exercise yard, an enormous open-air cage. Above us, in an isolated series of cells, was a wing holding characters like Ian Brady, the Moors murderer. We had no contact with him, which was for his safety not ours.

In many ways Durham began to resemble the Ronnie Barker comedy *Porridge*. When we complained to the governor about the quality of the food, he asked, 'Well, could you cook for yourselves, if I was to give you the provisions?'

'Sure,' we said.

He started by giving us basic supplies and arranging for the principal officer cook to come in two nights a week to give us cookery lessons. Eight of us would crowd into a little cell with a cooker at one end, while we were taught basic food preparation and how to make soups and sauces.

The prison officer in charge of all the food was elevated, by inmates, to the rank of Chief, an affectionate barrow-boy term. He would normally relax in a seat getting his shoulders massaged while we cooked up steaks and stews with the best cuts of meat and other ingredients. The secret of success was to keep the Chief happy. One of the Lambrianou brothers, the notorious henchmen of the Krays, was in Durham and it was his role to engage the prison officer in light-hearted banter, particularly about golf and soccer, the Chief's twin passions.

'Good ground, St Andrew's, Chiefie,' Lambrianou would say.

'What do you know about St Andrew's?'

'I played golf there.'

'You haven't played golf anywhere, you're just a fucking southern wanker.'

'I have, and I've played at Wembley.'

This little ritual was repeated time and again and, of course, the Chief loved it. These were the nation's leading criminals and he had them pandering to his every whim. Lovely! It was only a matter of time, however, before one of the heavy screws tried to stir things up. He got hold of the Chief and bullied him. 'What's your game then? Why are these bastards getting steak every other day? And cakes? They got a year's supply of bleedin' Weetabix!' Weetabix was normally only a Sunday treat but we had boxes and boxes, thanks to the Chief.

'What's it got to do with you?' says the Chief.

'I don't like to see them rats eating this food. They're not entitled to it.'

'All right,' he said, 'come and have a look tomorrow.'

The next day the Chief arrived with food fit for a king. The other screw nearly exploded when he saw us tucking into plateloads of steak and fresh strawberries – far better fare than was being served up in the prison officers' mess. The more they leant on Chiefie, the more extravagant our supplies became, until finally he was hauled before the governor.

'Why are they having peaches and cream and stuff like that?' he was asked.

'Here's my budget,' said the Chief, handing over details of his spending. 'All that they get is what is allowed under Regulation so-and-so and so-and-so.'

That was the end of the argument.

Jimmy Green, an ace assistant governor, was quite an innovative prison officer with strong ideas about education and expanding the mind. Aside from adding to the library, he started fetching in lecturers from Durham University, and their talks became, I suppose, the highlight of the week. We touched on various topics and also had group readings of Shakespeare's plays. I was sure that reforms such as this helped a lot of prisoners, not least John McVicar, who went from being Public Enemy Number One to eventually getting a postgraduate degree in sociology and fashioning a successful career as an author and freelance journalist writing for *Esquire*, the *New Statesman* and the *Guardian*.

Meanwhile, I started going to the workshop, where a civilian blacksmith was teaching us a trade. We built a fifty-foot balcony rail of ironwork to go round the church in the nick and also a big sign that was presented to the prettiest village in County Durham to swing on the village green.

In my first two years at Durham I had very little trouble. The only hiccup occurred when the Home Office introduced a new visiting system whereby no-one could visit Category A, maximum-security prisoners, unless they were immediate family, and even then they had to have their photographs taken and presented to the Home Office. A lot of the inmates angrily asked, 'Why should my family have their photographs taken? They haven't done anything wrong.'

A delegation came to see me, wanting to know what we should do. 'Well, as far as I'm concerned, we do nothing,' I said. 'The only person likely to visit me is Angela and my boy. They've probably got fifty thousand photographs of her already, so I'm not worried about one more.'

'That's not the point.'

'Look, it might not be the point but I can't get worked up over this.'

Then someone suggested a hunger strike.

'Fucking bollocks! If you go on fucking hunger strike, you're only harming yourselves. It's been used over and over again, no-one ever wins out of it.'

Finally I suggested an alternative. 'What about psychological warfare?'

'What do you mean?'

'They're used to routine. Each day we do the same things, we lift weights at a certain time, we watch TV at a certain time. Just start mixing it up with something a bit different.' I explained that, at a given signal during the day, everyone should run down to the ground-floor dining room and huddle together for a few minutes before dispersing. Similarly, in the exercise yard, we could suddenly huddle together in the centre, thirty yards from the wire, so they couldn't hear what we were saying.

'It will drive them crazy,' I said. 'They'll be really worried that something is going down but won't know for sure.'

Some of them liked the idea but others complained that they would probably decide to split us all up. The argument went round in circles and eventually they decided on a hunger strike. I told them I wasn't interested, which created a degree of antagonism. The first night of the hunger strike, they were all locked up. I was down in the kitchen, eating a big steak, and I thought, Poor bastards, as the smell wafted up into their cells. After five days only the hard core stayed with it and most of them had small stashes of provisions hidden away. The whole exercise was pointless and eventually folded, but afterwards a few of them gave me the cold shoulder for not having participated. I didn't care. It was very important for me for the future, because I had shown the authorities that I wasn't a person who could be dragged into anything.

Angela and Nick visited me every few weeks during the first year. It was a long, tiring journey on the train from London and Angela would arrive looking hollow-eyed and washed out.

Since the trial they had been living in Queens Road, Weybridge. She had bought the three-roomed flat with the money from her story that had been published in the German magazine *Stern* and then serialized in the *Sunday Mirror*.

Nick was going to the local school. He was seven years old now and knew the whole story of the Train. There had been a lot of television coverage and Angela had to answer his numerous questions. Sometimes he saved a question for me. My problem was to couch the answers in such a way that he didn't regard my exploits as heroic, yet neither would he think of them as beyond the pale.

'What I did was wrong,' I explained. 'I was young, and when you're young you sometimes make mistakes. These mistakes have cost me my freedom, and separation from you and Mum.'

Visits at Durham were very congenial, set in a large room with tables and chairs. As the total complement of our wing was eight prisoners, we usually staggered our visits so that in practice we had the room to ourselves. There would be two screws in attendance, but the surveillance was usually discreet. Tea and biscuits were served as our visitors arrived. I'd embrace Nick first, to let him see that he was my priority, then Angela. Then we'd settle down with our tea and exchange our news. I tried to have some present ready for Nick – usually a model kit that I'd spent hours making up. The only problem I had was with a German Tiger tank that worked by remote control. The authorities were dubious because of the electronics, which they surmised could be used somehow to jam the security systems.

Angela and Nick would talk about their lives – each anecdote unfolding through two different pairs of eyes, the worldly and the innocent. I'd allot a time for Angela and a time for Nick before we had a final get-together.

Always I was optimistic, concentrating on the positive – our hopes for the future, better conditions, miracles that might happen to bring me home sooner.

Angela would talk about the flat, her work and our friends. Nick told me about school and his friends. I'd been writing to him every week since I was captured and he would send back a drawing and, later, when he mastered his writing, he would send letters. Sometimes he brought me his artwork from school, including a picture that he painted of me with the caption, 'The World's Best Dad'.

As Nick grew older, he sent me postcards with his letters. They'd be from the National War Museum or the Tate Gallery, any place that he visited. Usually I'd write something relevant to the picture which I'd crib from an encyclopedia or a dictionary of art. I knew that a lot of it would pass over his head, but it was all a form of communication between us. I always remembered, as adults rarely do, how much my dad's weekly letter, with its postal order for sixpence and the copy of the *Knockout* comic, had meant to me when I'd been evacuated during the war.

Angela's and Nick's visits kept me alive. I counted the days between them and the hours leading up to their arrival. Then, all too quickly, the time had gone and they were going home. Afterwards, I would lie in my cell and think of all the things that I wished I'd said but didn't have the time.

Towards the end of the first year, I knew that Angela and I were drifting apart. Struggling to cope on her own, Angela began to resent what had happened. We fought and the visits became awkward, painful meetings. Afterwards, I sat in my cell, more depressed than I could ever remember.

The Senior Medical Officer, an ex-Navy man, spoke to Angela because he could sense my torment. She didn't want to explain the situation but eventually he asked her, 'Is there someone else in the picture?'

'No, not really,' she said, which of course was no answer at all.

Afterwards, I pleaded with the doctor for help because I was on the verge of stringing myself up. If someone could have given me a pill to end it all, I would have happily swallowed it. Angela represented my future. She was the only reason I kept going because I wanted to be with her. If she gave up on me, I had no reason to live.

I was given a sedative each night. It numbed the pain but after a month I said to the doctor, 'I've gotta come off of this, I'd sooner feel pain than feel this absolute nothingness that's around me.'

Things with Angela didn't improve. In truth, it turned into a form of guerilla warfare – we couldn't fuck, so the alternative was to fight, even though every harsh word and recrimination pulled us a little further apart. I was trying to defend the indefensible. I had no right to ask her to wait for me, but I fought just the same. I would write pleading letters, threatening letters, smaltzy letters, anything to trigger a response. 'Remember when . . .?' 'How can you do this to me?' 'Think of the child.'

In February 1971 I received a visit from my dad that plunged my spirits even lower. Amy, my stepmother, had died at the relatively early age of 57. Dad was distraught. He had been due for retirement shortly and they had made all sorts of plans for the future. Her death was a replay of his early life, when my mother had passed away just when life was beginning to look rosy. Now he'd lost his second partner in life, after 33 years together.

I wasn't allowed to go to the funeral because I was a Category A prisoner, but my thoughts were very much with my poor dad on the day.

When the news arrived that I was being moved to Chelmsford in Essex, I became more hopeful about patching things up with Angela. It would be easier for her and Nick to visit. And although it was another maximum-security wing, I was told that I wouldn't be there long. Maybe I could save my marriage after all.

The transfer from Durham involved a high-speed dash across country with three cars in front of the two prison vans and motor cycle outriders. I was handed over to the chief prison officer, who said, 'I'm Lloydy, how you doing, Bruce? We know all about you – a scholar and a gentleman.'

I knew a few of the other cons. Charlie Kray was there for the first few weeks before being transferred to Albany, on the Isle of Wight, and I ran and spotted weights with Eddie Richardson, Charlie's younger brother.

Angela still visited, although primarily to bring Nick. Still I was optimistic – most people who'd gone to Chelmsford were soon transferred out of the security wing.

'I will get parole, look, I'm on my way,' I told her. 'Only another six years and I'm eligible. It's only five Christmases.'

The conditions at Chelmsford were very good. The governor had been a submarine captain and I think he had seen Guy Gibson in The Dam Busters a few too many times because he had this old black Labrador that he used to walk through the wing, saying, 'Hello, boys. Everything all right?'

His regime was fairly loose. We were allowed extra visits during the week and relatives could fetch in a meal. Eddie Richardson's wife would turn up with a sirloin of beef and the governor would have to say, 'It's not meant to be like this you know, lads!'

It was a good system which unwittingly allowed young prisoners to learn that they could lead a normal life without being thieves. They would listen to the screws talking about their boats and cars and going to Spain on holiday. Young cons who had never been out of the country realized that, for all their criminal enterprises, the screws had better cars and lifestyles than they had.

The facilities included a large sports field and workshops, although our endeavours seemed entirely pointless when they had us making formica seats for old people to put in the bath so they could get in and out more easily. The idea was good but the design was hopeless.

The only aggravation at Chelmsford arose when news filtered through that Durham was closing and they had to find places for the Section 43s – guys like Ian Brady. The normal prison population was outraged, particularly when our regular PO told us that the Cannock Chase murderer, who had apparently killed two little girls, was joining us. 'There's no way we can stand for that,' said Terry Millman, one of the younger, hot-headed cons. 'I'm telling you, if he comes in here, I'll hit him right on the chin.'

'The governor's got to do what the Home Office orders,' said the PO.

'Well, fetch the governor in and I'll tell him.'

Old Griffiths the governor arrived, his Labrador slobbering on his shoes. 'I understand your concerns but my hands are tied. It's up to you. You got it good here. Don't rock the boat.'

This rather ambiguous response pleased many people. When Griffiths left, the deputy governor wanted to say a few words.

'I understand that there's a certain amount of dissatisfaction that other prisoners are coming in whom you don't feel that you should mix with. May I remind you, you are all convicts and you will all do as you're told.'

'Like fuck we will,' said Millman. 'Send the cunt in and you'll see what happens.'

'You'll be nicked for assault.'

'Lovely. Take a few years' remission, I got plenty – I got ten years for you to play around with.' The deputy governor walked out.

A few days later, the child murderer arrived and was shown around Chelmsford. He could obviously sense he wasn't welcome. He was flanked by two screws when Millman walked straight up to him and hit him right on the chin.

'That's enough, Terry,' they said, dragging the geezer out and into a cell.

Obviously, Terry was nicked, which didn't mean anything. The next day, Griffiths came down and announced that the Home Office had rethought the transfer and the child killer would not be staying. Sanity had prevailed.

Soon it was mooted that all the security wings were to be closed – an embarrassing political climb-down. My move from Durham had been part of the early planning and in Chelmsford they also began to whittle the numbers down, transferring people to other prisons. I was one of the last to leave, along with a guy called Hussein, who was doing life for the kidnapping and murder of Mrs McKay, wife of the managing director of the *News of the World*. It got to the point where we were the last two on the wing. Naturally, both of us were hopeful that we were going to be transferred out of maximum security.

Hussein was called up first by the governor.

'I'm going to Leicester,' he said to me when he returned, rightly disappointed. Leicester had the worst ratings of them all, particularly since an attempted mass escape. The atmosphere was so bad that screws virtually stood outside the cell doors, watching every bodily function.

Leicester, I thought, thank goodness for that. If he's going there, I must be going somewhere else.

The next day I was called in to see the governor after a night as the only prisoner on the wing. His exact words were, 'Well, Bruce, *der Tag*.'

'Where is it then?' I asked.

'Leicester. Don't be too upset, I don't think you'll be there long.'

'I fucking hope not,' I said bitterly.

I spent an unpleasant twelve months or so there, desperate all the time to leave. The crunch finally came during a visit by inspecting magistrates with a senior officer from the Government. The form was that they would knock, push open the cell door and say, 'All right?' and you were supposed to respond, 'Yes, sir, all right.'

Only this time I was thinking, No, I'm not all right. What about the geezer who was stabbed this morning, and the other who was smashed over the head with a mug? How much longer have I got to live like this?

So when the door opened, I said, 'No, I am fucking not all right!'

'What? What?' spluttered a magistrate.

'I said, I am not all right. Do you want me to kill someone? You put me with murderers, is that what you want to make me – a murderer?'

It obviously had the desired effect because within two days a screw whispered to me, 'I think you'll be on your way soon, but don't say anything to anyone.'

'Any idea where?'

'Well, I got an idea, but I can't tell you for obvious reasons.'

I fancied Ley Hill, a much easier nick with a good cricket team that had its own blazer. Unfortunately, it was not to be. After two years in Durham, a year in Chelmsford and a year at Leicester, I was transferred to Parkhurst on the Isle of Wight. At least I was out of maximum security and in with the main prison population. It was going to be difficult being an ordinary con but I had a reputation – I was a face. Go to any prison and all the plum jobs are held by faces, whether it be in the library or in reception. It's the faces that the screws can rely on to get the job done, without fuss or trouble.

The strength of my reputation was soon apparent. 'Hello, Bruce, you don't know me, I'm Gibbsy,' said my cell-mate next door. I knew precisely who he was – he'd been nicked with an old pal of mine, Dixie. The two of them were shot by the police in a get-up at Bournemouth.

'All your mates are here,' he said. 'Peter so and so and Freddy so and so . . .' He was reciting names to me of people I'd never heard of.

I played along. 'Oh yeah? Yeah? Well, that's great.'

Then it dawned on me what was happening. I'd done it myself years earlier with Alfie Hines, the celebrated safebreaker. I met him once but I'd tell people he was a pal of mine because it gave me stature. All these guys I didn't know were using my name because they wanted credibility.

Out in the exercise yard, I met one of my admirers. 'Hello, I'm Peter – you remember me?'

'Yeah,' I said.

Course I didn't remember him, but I could see immediately that he was a big guy who had some authority. I wasn't going to embarrass him – quite the opposite, I wanted his help. We chatted like long-lost friends.

Peter invited me to meet Bill. 'Bill? Who's Bill?'

'You know, Liverpool Bill? He more or less runs the nick.'

'Oh him,' I said. 'Yeah, I know Bill, my old mate Bill.'

This slippery operator was another who made great claims to being a pal of mine, so come Monday, out on exercise, I went through the charade all over again.

'Hello, Bill, how you going?'

'Bruce! Long time no see.'

'Yeah, too long.'

Soon we were best mates, running together and going for walks. I got to know about his family and the ins and outs of his relationship with his wife. Billy used to infuriate me because I wanted him to say how badly he thought Angela was behaving, but he never would. He'd say, 'Don't worry, you'll see it's all different. She don't mean what she's saying –'

'Don't be ridiculous! Don't you understand? She's playing around . . .'

Bill would never agree. Maybe it was his way of handling the separation from his wife.

Charlie Wilson was also in Parkhurst, although still in the maximum-security wing. The governor and the chief pulled me one day during exercise and said, 'How do you fancy seeing him?'

'Great!'

We had our visit in the 'nonce' wing, compartmentalized and secure. Chas looked very fit, smiling and cheerful as usual. He was freighted up with goodies like Mars bars and Cadbury's chocolate – a luxury for me now that I was on normal location.

'I miss the privileges of the security wing,' I said, 'but I'm thankful to be out. The atmosphere was too claustrophobic for me in there.'

Chas didn't smoke and was surprised to see that I had succumbed to the addiction.

'A legacy of my aggro with Angela,' I explained.

'I was sorry to hear about that, Bruce,' he said. 'I count myself lucky that my relationship with Pat is as strong as ever.'

The future with parole on the books was looking promising, and we projected our chances. The yardstick would be how Roger Cordrey and the innocent Bill Boal would fare; they would be the first ones to be eligible. We were both hopeful; we could get our heads around eight years four months and in Charlie's case ten years. It was a lot easier to handle than sixteen years eight or twelve years.

We swapped stories about our arrests. 'I'm still not sure about my partner Don,' he said. 'I reckon some deal was struck that saw me nicked.'

'Tom Butler told me they'd followed Don to Canada.'

'There's more to it than that, I'm certain. But we'll never know the truth.'

All too soon, it was time to go. I reminded him that the last time we had met and parted had been in St Maxime.

'Lobsters and Dom,' he said. 'A bit of an evening, that one!'

It wasn't easy to say goodbye to such an old friend.

My main ambition was to get a job in the library but I couldn't expect such a plum job so soon. Instead they put me into the light textile shop, making curtains. I had never used a sewing-machine in my life and was effing and blinding, breaking needles left, right and centre, but eventually I got the hang of it.

After six weeks a vacancy came up on the cutting table and Bill recommended me for the job. It was a top position in the shop, paying more money with the added responsibility.

It was two years before a job came up in the library. It wasn't a particularly good library and my tasks really only involved going to A wing, collecting their library books and taking them to the G wing and taking the books from G wing to B wing, and so on. At least it gave me the run of the nick and somehow I made it a full-time job, along with being on the film committee.

I had been inside for almost seven years and my marriage to Angela was basically over. There seemed to be nothing left betwen us and when she wrote it was only in response to questions about Nick. I looked vainly for signs of affection, but her letters no longer ended with love and kisses. It was just 'Best wishes'.

Sometimes there'd be a little glimpse of what we had once had, but it was obvious that Angela now had her own life. What did I have to offer but promises and dreams?

Normally she visited with Nick, but one day I saw her on her own and asked, 'Do you think that we have any possible chance?'

'No, Bruce, I don't think so. But I don't really know.'

'Then I think the best thing to do is to get a divorce,' I said, half hoping she would cry and say no, no, no, but she was silent. 'I'll get the divorce. If you apply it's not gonna look so good for me on a parole application. They'll think I'm gonna get the hump and come out and kill the lover. It's better if it comes from me.'

'All right,' she said.

I wrote to my solicitor. He was slow to reply and I worried about whether I could go through with it. Then, two months later, out of the blue, Smithy, my assistant governor, called me down and said, 'Sign this.'

'What is it?'

'Divorce papers.'

I was so shocked I didn't know what to say. Then I looked at the documents and saw that Angela had changed her name by deed poll. She wanted me to sign for the divorce in the name of Conway.

'I won't do it,' I said to Smithy. 'I'm not Conway.'

'Yes you are.'

'If I'm Conway, I shouldn't be in here. Bruce Reynolds is in here, not Conway.'

I eventually signed, surprised that Angela had gone through with it. I was surprised, too, about the mix-up in names. It was only much later that I learned that when Angela had changed her name by deed poll, the solicitor had inadvertently changed the whole family's.

That evening at exercise, I lay down on the grass feeling very sorry for myself. I knew the divorce was inevitable. Angela and I had been twisting the knife in each other – it couldn't have continued. At least I wouldn't worry so much about her. Life would go on. There were plenty more women, I told myself. Perhaps not like Angela but what right did I have to find true love twice in a lifetime?

39

After three and a half years on the island I was told that I was transferring to Maidstone. I was elated. The Kent prison had a good reputation, with a first-class gym and a swimming-pool. But when I arrived I was disappointed. Petty regulations, like having to wear a tie at the weekly film, spoiled the atmosphere.

I found myself in a modern wing with many familiar faces from Parkhurst, one of whom was Muldoon, a good artist who painted my portrait sitting in the canteen. Many of the other inmates were drug dealers and pot was surprisingly easy to get. I had smoked one or two joints before, but suddenly it was so readily available and the regime was so relaxed that I started using it regularly to deaden the senses and help time pass more quickly.

Harry began visiting now that I was no longer a Category A prisoner. Until then, because of his previous convictions, he hadn't been allowed into a maximum-security wing. In spite of this, he still fetched Nick along each month and waited outside for the visiting hour to finish. I never forgot his kindness.

Nick was six when I went away and thanks to Harry and Angela my relationship with him managed to survive. By the time he had won a scholarship to Emmanuel School in Wandsworth, he was fourteen and able to travel to Maidstone on his own.

Visits were held in a large hall that was laid out like a cafeteria, with tables spread liberally around. Refreshments were served from a bar by the local Women's Guild. The families gathered around the tea urns and plates of sandwiches; it was a real social occasion. Table hopping was as prevalent as in the old days at the Astor.

I was always proud of Nick; he was very personable and enthusiastic, able to meet people on any level and communicate. We had a lot in common, not the least being our looks. When pals in the nick met him they would say, 'Fucking hell, Bruce, he's a ringer for you.' My reply would always be, 'Thank God for that.'

I'd observed all his stages, the crazes and interests. When he became keen on music, I bought a guitar for him from a fellow con – the Baron, a well-known bank robber – and he had guitar lessons at school until he found rugby. He loved that until he decided, after a particularly severe mauling, that it was a bloody stupid game. Then he found his niche. Always a good swimmer, he made the school's water polo team, captaining it on many occasions.

He was progressing well at school. All his reports were good, with the proviso that he could do much better if he applied himself. What he liked he was good at; what he didn't, he waffled through. I'd always encouraged him to read, and I maintained his enthusiasm by sending him books that I thought he might like – children's classics like *Treasure Island* at first, and then weightier novels like *Catch 22*. Angela told me that he was always reading late into the night with the aid of his torch underneath the bedclothes.

After books, we talked about films, comparing notes on the plot and the actors, or how the film compared with the book. Inevitably films could take us down memory lane and a lot of our dialogue would begin, 'Do you remember when . . .?'

Nick reminded me of when I'd taken him to see *Jungle Book* at Ascot and afterwards we had a rowing-boat out on the Thames for the rest of the day. I'd shown him how to row, and told him how my dad had taken me on the Serpentine for my first lesson. Always eager to hear of my childhood, he was very fond of my dad. The feeling was mutual. I wondered if Dad felt he was partly responsible for my fate – just as I wondered if Nick would be affected by my separation from him. I had many moments travelling the guilt road. It was painful to think about all the time that I'd lost with Nick. I only had myself to blame, but realizing and accepting this didn't make it any easier. I told myself that I would make it up to him and we made plans for the future – one of them was to ride down to the South of France on our bikes. We had the route all mapped out in our letters.

Because he was using another name, his schoolfriends were unlikely to be aware of his father's history, but I told him:

'Nick, if anyone asks about why I'm not around, you tell them that I work for the Government in security.'

Well, I wasn't lying.

Another welcome visitor was Joe, my old business partner from Mexico. He came to see me once a year on his annual buying trips to Europe for jewellery and glass for the store. He and his partner Moyses stayed in London and had a chauffeur-driven Mercedes to bring them to the prison.

'Did you have any idea who I was when I was in Mexico?' I asked him.

'No. But I knew there was something wrong. I figured you left England because of tax problems – something like that.'

Joe didn't think any the less of me, perhaps because of the sort of moral climate in which he lived. He was supportive and would say things like, 'Bruce, when you get out, you gotta come back to Mexico.'

'What do you want a con like me for, Joe?'

'Because you're honest.'

Not many people would say that. Having lost Angela and then missed seeing Nick grow up, at least I was wanted in Mexico.

Maidstone proved to be quite progressive. There were weekly meetings, loosely called discussion groups, with all sorts of guest speakers, including the then Archbishop of Canterbury. He impressed me a lot.

We also had a female welfare officer in the wing, a nice lady with two very attractive daughters. It was amazing how suddenly the cons would brush their teeth a dozen times, comb their hair and clean their fingernails before seeing her. I would have been right there with them, but after eight years inside my confidence was shattered and I thought, What would she want with the likes of me?

It sounds pitiful, but the years at Maidstone were probably the happiest years in my life. All I was doing, basically, was running, swimming and playing badminton. The food was good and, getting back from the gym at eight o'clock most nights, we'd sit in a pal's cell and smoke a few pipes. Sometimes I'd almost crawl to my cell, collapsing with laughter. The screws would come along, push the door open and say, 'It's a bit heavy in here, innit?'

After not seeing Angela in almost two years, she turned up with Nick on a visiting day in 1977. Her brother Jimmy, the youngest in the family, had died. Having already lost her mother and father and having no contact with Rita, Angela was terribly upset.

For the first hour it was difficult between us, but when it came time to say goodbye I gave her a kiss and suddenly she didn't want to go. Afterwards I said to my mate Frank, 'You won't believe this, Frank, after all these years when at times I wanted to kill her – and planned to kill her when I got out – nothing's changed between us in spite of it all. I still love her and I think she loves me.'

'What you gonna do?' he asked.

'There's nothing I can do at the moment. She knows where I am and if she really wants to do anything, I'm here. I think she's complicated her life with another relationship. I'll just have to wait and see.'

I missed female companionship. At times, I would have done anything to spend time with a woman. Normally, I tried to work out my frustration by throwing myself into exercise but it wasn't helped when Harry would come and see me and happily chat away about his different conquests.

Sensing my needs, Harry eventually fetched down one or two interesting ladies who didn't mind having their bodies fondled over the tea and Wagon Wheels in the course of a visit. These total strangers, dolled up in nice dresses and make-up, would be sitting opposite me across a wooden table, making small talk, while my hands were sliding along their thighs and beyond.

Maidstone wasn't as sexually barren as other places. Because of the weekly classes and lectures there were women coming backwards and forwards, which did wonders for morale as well as personal hygiene. In the old days at the Hate Factory, you would step out of your cell each morning and be almost bowled over by the smell of shit and perspiration. The nearest woman was the typist in the governor's office and you only saw her when trouble loomed.

Of course we all took solace in the embrace of the five-fingered widow. We'd wank over girlie magazines, swapping them between us and with the screws. What else was a young man to do?

Years later, I came across a girl who said to me, 'You've been in prison, haven't you?'

'Yeah,' I said. 'How can you tell?'

'They're all a bit fucking kinky when they've been in prison,' she smiled.

Of course there is homosexuality in gaols. It doesn't go on to the extent that many people believe but it does happen. Conditions were ripe for it in Borstal because of the extra freedom and the fact that many inmates, aged between sixteen and twenty-one, were still experimenting with their sexuality. At the adult prisons there was less opportunity, although in the old days in Wandsworth you got the professional trollops, blokes with names like Trixie or Angel, who used to use the bindings of books to rouge up their lips and then parade through the exercise yard, pirouetting and shaking their tails.

It reminded me of being fourteen years old and having my dad tell me that there were 'some funny men' around and I should steer clear of them.

Oddly enough, there was nothing feminine at all about some of the gaolhouse queens. Trixie was a fifteen-stone ex-Scots Guardsman and he would always burst out laughing when describing his activities. 'They get the biggest surprise of their life with me,' he'd say, "cos after they've done it to me, I do it to them!'

40

I was eligible for parole after I'd done a third of my sentence – eight years and four months – but I didn't really expect it to be approved, even though all the others, except for Charlie, were out of prison.

When it was refused the assistant governor said I was a 'certainty' for it next time. Surprisingly, I wasn't too disappointed. What was there for me on the outside anyway? It seemed like a mythical place; reality existed inside, where I had everything I wanted. I was in terrific shape physically, and mentally I was OK; I had golden oldies under the bed and if I got fed up with my 'girls' I could always borrow Frank's or someone else's. I didn't yearn for the West End clubs or the restaurants of Piccadilly or the pubs of Paddington and Chelsea. I was happy in gaol. It was my home.

In April 1978 I was offered day release to acclimatize to the outside world, working during the day and reporting back to the prison each night, to prove to the authorities that I was totally reformed and could take my place in society. Effectively it meant that I was being released six months early.

To start the ball rolling, I was given five days' 'home leave'. I came out with only one thing on my mind. After ten years without a woman, I wanted to melt into the arms of some lovely and enjoy the carnal pleasures denied me for so long.

Harry picked me up from Maidstone. He was waiting outside the gates in his old Hillman Hunter. It wasn't quite what I had envisaged in my dreams of birds and booze. I wanted to be picked up in a Ferrari by some long-legged blonde who would dive between my legs before the car had shifted out of second gear.

Harry sensed my disappointment. 'Don't worry, Bruce. Max has booked a club and a few young ladies. We got you a suite at the White House hotel.'

I saw a few people during the afternoon, including Mary and Rene. It was almost unreal sitting in their living-room, sipping a Scotch as if nothing had changed and we'd seen each other every weekend for the past decade. I was in a daze, being led by others who were determined to celebrate my homecoming.

Max had booked us a table at a Hungarian club in Soho where a band of middle-aged gypsies played appalling violin music. My first inclination was to run but I couldn't disappoint them. My date for the evening was a stunning brunette from North London who had very kissable, bee-stung lips that were always pouted in readiness. Legless, I took her back to the White House and ordered another bottle of champagne. We were lying on the bed, sipping from tall glasses and playing touchy-feely. That was the last thing I remember. I woke up next morning and there was a note on the pillow that said: 'Sorry, luv, I couldn't wake you!'

Ten years! I'd been without a woman for ten years and I get pissed and fall asleep when this lovely was ready, willing and able!

I was peeved. I caught up with Harry. 'What was with the Hungarian place?'

'Well,' he said, 'Max knows what a lunatic you are. We wanted you in a closed environment so that if you went berserk, we could shut the doors and straighten the people up . . .'

'Go berserk?'

Suddenly, it all became clear. Harry wasn't sure how I was going to react, particularly about Angela. He thought I might do something stupid.

'Get me a car,' I said angrily.

'I'll drive you, mate.'

'No. I don't want you to drive me, I want to drive myself. I don't want you looking at what I'm doing. I've had people looking at me for ten years. I've had people examining how many times a night I shit and piss. I don't want you looking at me. You get me a car or I'll get me own car.'

I didn't try to see Angela but I wanted to find Nick. Early in the morning, I went down to Emmanuel School, hoping to see him arrive at school. Nick was surprised and we embraced. The last time I had hugged him in freedom had been nearly ten years earlier when he was barely six years old. He was a young man now; I had missed his childhood and couldn't take up the reins as if nothing had happened. Our relationship would from now on be more fraternal.

Over the next few days I was happy to catch up with acquaintances. I went to see Gordon, who had a wholesale potato business and fish stalls. He couldn't do enough for me and we seemed closer than ever because we'd both been through the system. He understood my sense of loss and how alien the world seemed. A decade of my life had gone. When I went into prison, Woodstock was still fresh in the memory, men had just landed on the moon, there were hippies, flower children and anti-Vietnam demonstrations, and Harold Wilson was Prime Minister.

The years from '69 to '78 had been filled with historic events, but it had little effect on my life, insulated safe within prison walls. What had I missed? Some of it was a relief: platform shoes, flared trousers, kipper ties, disco music.

I'd read about terrorism but had never felt threatened by it. Now, sitting on the tube, I became acutely aware of the warning signs about packages left on seats. All the time I had been in prison, the people of London had been in the front line. Now I, too, was a vulnerable citizen, and it was scary. This aspect of violence had escalated worldwide while I'd been away. Black groups were seeking bloody independence from their colonial masters; political factions were moving towards the gun. Every country had its IRA, Angry Brigade, Red Brigade, Baader-Meinhof, Frelimo or ANC. Had the world changed or was it that we were suddenly so much better informed?

I was dressing as I'd dressed in 1969 – suits and ties, most formal. The casual look was in – jeans, trainers and T-shirts, the pop stars' legacy. A stroll around my favourite London showed that the exclusivity of the West End had gone. In its place, seemingly populated by an influx of foreign shopkeepers, traders and entrepreneurs, was a shabbiness that to my eyes reduced everything to the lowest common denominator. Fast-food outlets created tons of rubbish with an efficiency that created the illusion that that was their business. Only the hallowed few stood firm, standing for what had once been the pride of London; Bond Street and my favourite, Jermyn Street, still went through the motions, but with an attitude that suggested that they knew that their time had gone.

I had missed the Olympic games of '72 and '76, in Munich and Montreal. When I went away Rod Laver had just won Wimbledon. Now the new champion was Bjorn Borg. It was still tennis, but almost a new game. The same advances had been made in motor racing. New cars, new drivers, new rules, almost a new event. The new champ was Mario Andretti, an American of all people coming to Europe to usurp the title. And though I didn't take much notice at the time, the sports pages were announcing that we had a potentially great cricketer in a young 22-year-old called Ian Botham.

I was the proverbial fish out of water. My clothes were the same, but who was I?

Gordon had somehow adapted. Out had gone Savile Row and in had come the Marlboro Man. In truth, he looked more like the Marlboro Man than the real version. He was also into smoking pot, which made him a lot nicer all round. He gave me a nice bit of smoke. Sadly though, the alcohol, the drugs and the sense of disenchantment all mingled and made me feel even more isolated and depressed.

With only one day left of my freedom, I still hadn't got laid. It was coming out of my ears like a teenage tearaway but nothing was going right. People were trying to help, saying they would get so and so, or invite a friend of a friend. Finally I said, 'How about Mandy?'

This was one of the girls that Harry had brought down to Maidstone during visiting hours – a natural blonde who looked great in black stockings. Apparently, Harry used her a lot in the course of transactions in the textile business.

Alone togther in the hotel suite, Mandy smiled coyly. We were both drunk and stoned and all I can really remember is that she had her rump in the air and I was vaguely doing something with my hands and in the midst of passion she was saying, 'I've really got to have my brake pads adjusted on my left-side front wheel.'

We went through the entire night and I couldn't get an erection. At eight o'clock Harry was due to pick me up and take me to the station; it was his job to make sure I got back to Maidstone nick on time. I knew Harry would be early, he always was.

Mandy and I still hadn't made it and I was getting desperate. It was a question of killing someone if I didn't purge my frustration. Finally I got going and was just nearing paradise when there was a knock, knock, knock on the door.

It was Harry with a big smile on his face, 'Hello, hello, nice night?'

'Come back in half an hour,' I said, slamming the door.

'You'll be late,' he shouted.

'I don't fucking care. Come back in half an hour or don't come back at all.'

He left and I got back to business. Finally, the deed was done but I was in a terrible state when Harry returned. I smoked a joint in silence as he drove me to the station and put me on the train. He gave me a pair of dark glasses and a hat to wear because he figured the Press would be waiting for me back at the nick, wanting a photograph for the morning editions.

I knocked on the prison gates, totally zonked out of my head. The gate screw shouted, 'What do you want?'

'It's me. I wanna come inside.'

I took off the hat, stepped over the threshold and said to them, 'Fucking parole, leave me out. I can't handle living out there.'

Three months later, my day release started and I moved into a hotel at Wormwood Scrubs. The Press had been waiting for my departure but the governor managed to slip me out the back entrance.

A woman prison officer showed me around Scrubs hostel and explained the ground rules, telling me what time I had to be back each evening, the cleaning roster and food situation. All I could think was, What am I doing here? I'd be better off at Maidstone.

I was allowed home for the weekend and spent it at Harry's, sleeping in his son's room.

It was the beginning of the worst six months of my life. Nothing seemed real any more. Even Harry had changed after a decade and we no longer had much in common. With no wife, no home and no job, I felt more alone than at any other time in my life. I walked the streets at night and seriously thought about going back inside.

Gordon rescued me and took me under his wing. He introduced me to his girlfriend who lived in Chessington. 'She'd do you,' he said. 'She's got her own house for the children and is separated from her old man.' Gordon was planning a move to Spain and obviously wanted to make sure Janine was looked after. It was a case of killing two birds with one stone.

'You can come over any time and stay the night,' she told me when we went over, and I thought she was nice, although physically not my type.

I visited her again a few weeks later, this time on my own. She had about six friends round and they were sitting in the garden, surrounded by their children. I felt uncomfortable at first but they were all friendly and young. One in particular looked very much like Angela and I was quite attracted to her but unfortunately it wasn't reciprocated.

As each weekend ended, I grew fonder of Janine. She was very bright and had a tremendous sense of humour. An affair began, and since her ex was prone to dropping in – especially when he'd had a drink – much of it was carried out in other people's front rooms. We had a portable air mattress that we used to take with us and Janine would leave her daughter with friends.

I was still lonely and unhappy but it's amazing how having a woman interested in you does wonders for your motivation.

The hostel was situated outside the prison itself. Formerly the gate house or lodge, it was run by the principal officer, with a woman civil servant to handle the administrative side. Designed as a halfway house between prison and freedom for long-term prisoners reaching the end of their sentences, it was intended to integrate them gradually into society under some form of control. On the successful completion of, generally, six months, they passed on to the control of their parole or probation officer for their period of parole.

During the week, I went to work in the morning and returned in the evening by ten-thirty. Infringement of the rules could lead to being returned to prison.

My stint ended in October 1978 and control was passed on to my first parole officer. One of the conditions of my release was that I find a job. That was what the parole board would want to hear when I came up before them. Obviously, given my record, it wasn't going to be easy. I was forty-seven years old and my last proper employment was drilling washers at seventeen.

Harry and Max arranged for me to work for a friend of theirs who was also in the textile business. He had a shop about four doors away in Great Titchfield Street, so most of the time I spent with them. I told my parole officer that I was staying at my father's address in Dagenham. Dad had retired in 1974, three years after Amy died. He had transferred his activities from Trade Union work to the Labour Party and local politics, becoming a local councillor. He had written and visited me in prison and also kept in contact with Angela and Nick, although he diplomatically remained aloof from our domestic problems and divorce. He only commented once, when he said to me, 'Bruce, what can you expect?'

A friend of a friend was importing pine furniture from Swaziland and offered me work. He wanted me to go to Amsterdam for the weekend, which in theory breached my parole. At the very least I should have contacted my parole officer first.

When I did contact him, he was astonished.

'How could you get to Amsterdam?'

'I've got a passport.'

'How did you get a passport?'

'When I was in prison. I wrote and applied.'

He was astonished and took a few seconds to recover his cool. 'Well, you shouldn't have gone. You're under my jurisdiction.'

He was pretty pissed off, but I tried to explain.

'Look, I've been offered work. It's a good job but it means I'm gonna have to travel.'

'No, no, no, you can't do that.'

'I haven't got the job then.'

'You can get another one.'

'You're so out of touch. Where have you been all your life? For guys like me, jobs don't drop off the trees. You say no to this and you put me out on the street. I've got no recourse but to go back to the old game.'

'Well, that's up to you, isn't it? If you want to go back to prison . . .'

'That's the point. I *want* to go back to fucking prison! It's fucking better than being out here dealing with bastards like you.'

'I'll make your comments known to the parole board.'

He didn't have the chance – I phoned them first. I explained the situation and was given a new parole officer based in London instead of Dagenham. Quentin Crewe was a great guy, who sadly died a few years later when still a relatively young man.

He wasn't an idiot, and basically said, 'Do what you want to do. If you want to go to Africa, it's up to you. There's no way anyone can stop you. There's nothing laid down in any regulations, as long as you tell me what you're doing.'

So from then on I did just that. I would call him at his office in Kensington High Street and he would say, 'Listen, Bruce, you're sailing a bit close to the wind, aren't you, seeing all these old pals?'

'Who else can I see?' I told him. 'With my past history, I'm not likely to be hob-nobbing with bishops and captains of industry.'

I was still working part-time in the textile business, wanting to stay close to Max and Harry, but they had a major falling out. Things had apparently been going wrong for ages and they decided to end the partnership. These were two of my closest friends; I was deeply hurt and felt even more alienated. It also left me in a difficult position. My time at the hostel was almost over and I had to find a flat. I had bought a few clothes when I first came home, but decided against getting a car. I felt so depressed I might have put a hose on the exhaust pipe and ended it all.

I rented a tiny one-bedroom place in Harrowby Street near the National Sporting Club off the Edgware Road. It was owned by a rich friend of Max's – a character who started building his fortune at the age of eight by swimming under the barges on the Thames and securing tarpaulins held between his teeth. Now, at seventy-six, he looked twenty years younger and would go to church tea dances and chat up old ladies over tea and sandwiches.

I spent my first Christmas alone in the flat, getting stoned and watching television. I hated everyone but most of all I hated myself.

Eventually, thanks to Glen, an old mate who had a portfolio of properties that he'd just sold for three mil, I moved to another flat in Wandsworth Bridge Road. Glen was in the process of leaving the country as a tax exile, but he gave me some money and asked me to look into getting him a parcel delivery franchise from City Link. I bought a little Peugeot as a runabout and started my research.

On the face of it, the Croydon area franchise seemed quite a good proposition and Glen said, 'If you're interested in it, Bruce, I'll put the money up.'

To get a list of all the businesses in the area I had to go to Westminster Library and nick a directory. I took it back to someone's office, duplicated every page, and then returned it. I got maps of the various areas enlarged, and went into it as professionally as I could. But what my researches really boiled down to was that the whole business was built on the co-operation of British Rail. If there were any problems with the trains, you'd have done your money.

Glen had his accountant come down and go over the figures. I was going to be drawing a salary of thirteen grand, but I felt duty bound to point out that I didn't consider it a good risk to lay out eighty grand on a franchise when overnight British Rail could turn around and say, 'Sorry, chum, we're not going to carry your parcels any more.' Glen was in a hurry; he was on his way to Spain and the project got shelved. 'Never mind,' he said, 'we'll see what else we can do.'

Scratching about, I got talking to Joe and we tried to see if there was something for me in America or Mexico. I felt like I was floundering in the deep end of a pool where my feet couldn't quite touch the bottom.

Frank Munroe, who was one of the three who'd got away with the Train, had been working as a film stunt man for a while and then moved into waste paper collection. He had found quite a nice niche and expanded into scrap metal, becoming a major player in the steel business, recycling big girders. Frank had some help from Glen setting himself up and together they arranged to find me a job. If Chad had been a big influence in my life, then I had similarly affected Frank.

'Yeah, I can help you, Bruce,' he said, 'if you're willing to do anything and you're not still in the game. I'm out of it now. I got a good business and I don't want to be involved with anyone who could cause me problems.'

My wages were basically token expenses – about fifty quid a week, although there were quite a few unofficial bonuses when loads were cut up and sold. The fact that Frank didn't want anything to do with outright criminality didn't mean he was shy of doing dubious business deals. Old habits die hard.

He would send me up to Scotland to organize loading a boat with scrap iron, or tell me to look at a demolition site to see if it was worth bidding on the scrap. Slowly I picked up information, although he gave gave me the smaller jobs and would often undermine me. I accepted it because it was a different world from the one I left in 1968. This was the way Frank did business.

After a while I realized that I couldn't stay working for Frank. There were slack periods and he was never going to give me any major responsibility. Then a steel strike squeezed the market and Frank took me out to dinner. Over a glass of wine he said, 'Things are difficult, Bruce.'

I knew what was coming.

'If you wanna stay with the firm, the most I can offer you is working the computer. If you want to do a course, I can make you a clerk in the office.'

He tried to be very diplomatic but I knew he wanted me to leave. I'd just paid the deposit on a brand-new 2-litre Capri Ghia and the firm was paying the instalments.

'I'll keep up the payments for the car, don't worry about that,' said Frank. 'If you crack it some time in the future, you might like to put something back.'

It was the pay-off.

41

By the early eighties, I was still living in Wandsworth Bridge Road, above the betting shop and beside a Chinese restaurant. Janine was still in the picture and Nick would drop by occasionally. He was in his second year in the Navy, having trained in *Raleigh* and *Collingwood* stations. He was on HMS *Hermes* during the Falklands War and up until October '82.

Nick was still a keen cyclist, riding at club meetings and charity races, and had a fixture at Battersea Park one weekend. Angela went along to watch. I was stoned out of my box on the Sunday afternoon, rolling around the bed with Janine, when there was a knock on the door. It was Nick. He'd come from the park. 'Mum's over the road with Auntie Barbara,' he said.

'Really? Ask her up.'

'Um, well, she wants you to ask her.'

I went down and found Angela sitting in her car, obviously nervous.

'Hello,' I said.

'Hi.'

'You're looking well.'

'Thanks.'

'You want to come up?'

'No. Really we have to go.'

'Just for a few minutes,' I said. 'Have a cup of tea.'

Angela gave me a weak smile. Her freckled Irish face was still as pretty as ever but I could see the care-worn creases of age and loneliness.

Nick got a Chinese take-away from the place next door and we sat in the small living-room. Angela and Janine were sizing each other up. Janine knew all about what had happened between us; she'd heard my stories when I was drunk, stoned or depressed. In many ways she had helped me see Angela's position, giving me a woman's point of view.

They stayed for a few hours, and when Angela left she said, 'Maybe I'll see you again sometime.' Of course this created a problem with Janine. She didn't want my ex-wife on the scene. From my point of view, I was suddenly all twisted up inside again – drawn this way and that. I still loved Angela and wanted to be with her, but I didn't want to be hurt again and nor did I want to hurt her.

Janine was frightened of her ex-husband, a lunatic when he'd had a few, who had beaten her heavily and would still occasionally threaten to come looking for her. I knew there was a danger and contemplated getting a weapon for protection. One evening at Janine's flat he came in through the window with a carving knife. He blindly lunged at the bed, stabbing at the bedclothes. It turned out that she'd known he was coming. She was trying to start trouble between us, perhaps hoping that I would get him out of the way for ever.

I remembered her asking me, 'Bruce, have you ever killed anyone?'

'No, I haven't.'

'Really? Come on, you can tell me. I bet you have.'

She probably didn't want me to kill her ex, but she certainly wanted him frightened or locked away. I knew none of this when the knife was slicing open the covers. I was spinning and curling in to a ball, trying to avoid the blade. He cut my arm quite badly, covering the sheets with blood. Meanwhile, Janine had picked up her daughter and run next door for help.

Her ex-old man ran when he saw the blood, probably thinking he'd finished me for good. I got up and got dressed as best I could, trying to stem the flow. Before leaving the flat I picked up the carving knife from the floor, took it to the sink and washed off his prints.

Two policemen were outside, talking to the neighbour who had raised the alarm. They didn't see me so I kept walking, with blood oozing through my coat, and got to my car parked further along the street. Starting it very gingerly, I drove round the corner into Dancer Road and up to the Fulham Road. At the top, a police car flagged me down.

'What's that blood on your arm?' an officer asked.

'I fell over.'

'We've just had a call about a stabbing in Mimosa Street.'

'No. I just fell over.' At the time I was thinking, How bad am I hurt? Am I bleeding to death? Then I remembered the three joints in my jacket. As they asked me questions, I slipped the joints from my pocket and dropped them, kicking them into the curb.

A cab screeched to a halt; the driver leaned out. 'I got a customer with a gun,' he said, motioning to the back. The policemen dived in, dragging this guy out and spreadeagling him on the pavement.

'Finished with me?' I asked.

'Yeah, go on.'

Growing light-headed, I couldn't focus my thoughts. I kept thinking in terms of having done something criminal. I couldn't go to hospital; a doctor would report me. What could I do? I drove to Battersea Park and sat in the car, slipping in and out of consciousness. When my head cleared, I went to find Gordon, who had been flitting backwards and forwards from Spain, having yet to make the final move. He bathed the wound, which was about an inch deep, and gave me clean clothes. The next day he took me to Roehampton Hospital and I told them I'd fallen on a glass.

It turned out that Gordon knew my attacker. 'You gotta look at it from his point of view,' he said. 'I mean you was with his ex-old woman in his bed, and his kid in the next room. You know you can understand the emotions of it – especially with a bit of booze in you.'

I bore no grudge – that's why I wiped the prints off the knife. The poor bastard was having a hard time and missing his daughter. Apparently, he was full of remorse afterwards when his daughter asked him, 'Why did you stab Bruce, Daddy?'

I continued seeing Janine, although I knew she had another lover. I think it was just the two of us, but with Janine you could never be sure.

About a month later I was having a drink with Dave, a former workmate from the steel works and an aspiring Hell's Angel. We got nicely sauced before driving home and on the way I was nearly sliced in half by a madman who was obviously even more pissed. I gave chase, trying to corner the guy before he killed someone.

Eventually he pulled into a garage at Hammersmith and ran into the office. I ran after him, clumped him one, and told the manager to call the police. 'What's it all about?' he said.

'This geezer's fucking drunk out of his head.'

'You ain't doing too bad yourself.'

'Well, this geezer will end up killing someone.'

When the police arrived, the senior cozzer asked for my name and address. I didn't know if he recognized me but he gave me a very meaningful look and told me to lose myself while they dealt with the drunk. Gladly, I thought. I went outside, but I couldn't find Dave and the car. Obviously, he'd seen the police arrive and driven off, thinking he was doing me a favour. When I got home to Wandsworth Bridge Road at one o'clock in the morning, there was still no sign of the car. This meant I had no keys for the flat and it was virtually impossible to break in. Maybe Dave took the car home, I thought, walking round to his place in Chelsea. No sign of it there.

Finally, with no place to sleep, I went to Janine's, knocking on her door at three in the morning. Her new lover answered. 'I'm in a bit of trouble,' I said.

'Well, don't fetch your troubles round here.'

My first inclination was to whack him one. Then Janine called out, 'What's up?'

'I'm in a bit of trouble,' I said.

'OK, you can sleep on the sofa.' For the next two hours I lay there, watching the ceiling vibrate and listening to the bedroom performance being put on for my benefit. When I couldn't stand it any more I got up and left. Jumping in the back of a cab, I told the driver, 'I've locked myself out. I need a place to hang out. Is there an all-night café?'

He took me to a place just off the Fulham Road where I ordered roast beef and coffee and sat alone, feeling sorry for myself. At the far end of the café were three men and I recognized one of them as the guy who had stabbed me. Depressed and angry, I contemplated the knife lying in my roast beef and gravy. It would be so easy to plunge it into his back when he wasn't looking. I could call it revenge. They would put me back inside: send me home. Common sense prevailed and I slipped out of the café without him seeing me.

I split up with Janine soon afterwards and began spending more time with Angela. After a few phone calls, I asked her down to Portsmouth for the weekend to see Nick. We couldn't find him on the Saturday, so I suggested we get a hotel for the night and try again the next day.

'There's no way I'm going all the way back, and all the way down again,' I said. 'How do you feel about that?'

'All right,' she said, smiling. The old magic was there. After making love, we started talking about the future. She still wasn't sure but I was prepared to wait.

We found Nick on Sunday and then drove back that afternoon. The holiday traffic was heavy and we decided to stay the night at Dorking and spend the next day walking around Epsom. It was nice to be together. We had shared so much – the highs and the lows – but after so long apart it was a process of falling back in love with each other.

I didn't put pressure on Angela. It was up to her. Our reconciliation was a slow, emotional rediscovery, taken one day at a time. Eventually she moved into the flat in Wandsworth Bridge Road but after a month she baled out, still unsure of what she wanted.

Nick had a regular girlfriend when he was at home on leave. He visited me quite often and became friendly with the guy upstairs, who worked for Richard Branson. One day, I met him on the stairs and he said, 'It's Richard's birthday. He's having a party – why don't you and Nick come down?'

'Yeah lovely, I'll have some of that.'

Branson had a place in the country near Oxford. I wasn't sure how strong our invitation was, so I took a copy of Piers Paul Reid's book on the Train as a present and wrote inside, 'Happy Birthday, Richard. Best Wishes, Bruce Reynolds.'

When we arrived, our names weren't on the guest list, so I told some flunky, 'Give Richard the book and we'll wait.'

Branson appeared at the door and shook my hand. 'Quite a surprise,' he said. 'Come inside. You're going to upstage me at my own birthday party.'

It was a marvellous do. When you have that sort of money, you can afford live bands, three marquees, go-karts, mini aeroplanes and hot air balloons. Nick disappeared and re-emerged with a stunning girl who was only fourteen but looked like a *Vogue* model. Joan Collins was in the swimming-pool. She could somehow swim, talk, sip champagne and never smudge her lipstick. I bumped into Mick Jagger at the bar and asked him how he got into his jeans without making his voice break. He laughed and told me to keep my hands off the silverware.

Nick's new friend introduced me to her mother, a very nice woman, and we got on famously. They lived on a houseboat at Little Venice, not far from where Branson had his own floating *pied-à-terre*. Nick eventually became a regular at the houseboat and was treated like an adopted son. Through him, I got to know the entire family and spent many happy summer hours in their local, the Warwick Castle.

One night, sitting in the pub, Angela tried to explain to me what was wrong and why she couldn't make a decision about us. Obviously there was still something between us, but she was scared.

'Look at it this way, Ange,' I said. 'What have we got to lose? We'll never know unless we try again.'

42

It's odd how your life turns out. When I first got out of prison, I actually thought of ending it all. I couldn't see a future. More than anyone else, it was Gordon who saved me from these self-destructive impulses. He was an unlikely counsellor, having only been out of prison himself for eighteen months, but he showed me that it was possible to rebuild a life.

My boyhood friend Charlie was the last to be released. When Gordon went to Spain it was logical that I would see more of Chas but in many ways we had drifted apart. The others I saw periodically, all except for Biggsy, who had become an author, pop star, playboy and professional exile in Rio.

Most of them had gone straight, or at least discovered that as businessmen they could be legitimately bent. Tommy Wisbey owned a pub. Bobby Welch had a gambling club. Big Jim Hussey was in Warren Street, dealing in cars. Roger Cordrey had a flower shop. Jimmy White ran his own painting and decorating business. Buster had a flower stall at Waterloo Station. Roy James was in Hatton Garden, designing and manufacturing jewellery. Gordon had bought property and a bar in Spain, thinking that it was safer to stay out of the country. Charlie had an interest in the wholesale greengrocery business, though he, too, thought it would be advisable to live abroad and was making plans accordingly.

Occasionally, I was approached by criminals who wanted to use my expertise or advice. One firm was contemplating a similar coup to the Airport and offered me a half-a-million-pound whack. They planned to hit a Brinks van at the Lufthansa loading bay, which wasn't going to be easy because El Al was next door and the Israelis were a security nightmare because of the threat of Arab terrorism.

Although it would have been a fitting epitaph to my career, I had no desire to risk my freedom again. I realized that I wasn't interested in crime. I had done everything I had ever set out to do. I had climbed Everest. There were no bigger mountains to conquer.

In reality, I was an old crook who was virtually living on handouts from other old crooks. One of them was Terry Nash, the Stoppo King – the complimentary title awarded to him on account of the amount of 'stoppos' or escapes, usually of the hectic kind, he used to have in his youth. He had become quite big in the greengrocery and florist game; branching out, he had just bought a restaurant-cum-club in South Kensington.

He offered me a job – nothing really specific, but basically I would run errands and help him renovate and manage the club. If someone wanted a sandwich, I made a sandwich; if someone wanted a large vodka, they got a large vodka. I was also going to the markets for him, buying groceries and flowers. I wasn't proud of being a cleaner and humping boxes around but I no longer cared about the illusion of being a big shot. Maybe I lost it in the nick. The people who counted knew who I was, and that was all that mattered.

I was also helping my pal Barry, another club owner in the East End. It wasn't Aspinall's, that was for sure, but every week there was a big poker game and people would play for as much as ten grand.

Angela and I were living in Streatham. It was humble but comfortable, with just enough money to feed ourselves and buy the weekly bottle of vodka. For the first time in a long time I was happy again. Fate hadn't forgotten me, however.

Angela suffered a nervous breakdown. I found her one day, rocking back and forth, staring out the window. 'There's no-one around,' she said. 'What's happened to everyone? You're not telling me. You're not telling me what's going on.'

Nick was at home on leave but between us we couldn't convince Angela to seek help. Slowly she became more ill. Finally she went into hospital for two weeks and I was floundering again, not knowing what direction to go in. Perhaps Angela could see that circumstances were driving me back to my old ways. I was mixing with bad company because it was all I knew.

The doctor recommended she be taken to the Maudsley, the psychiatric hospital. Angela was furious. She accused me of locking her up and took off her wedding and engagement rings and threw them away. After several days she was transferred to another institution, an old Victorian hospital in Tooting Bec. 'What am I doing in here?' she cried. 'When am I going home? You don't know what it's like in here.'

Don't know what it's like? I knew exactly what she was going through.

When Angela came home, we had even less money and some strange things began happening. Initially, I dismissed them as paranoia. A lady friend of ours called at the house and her car was broken into in busy Streatham High Road. The back window was smashed and her briefcase taken. On her next visit, she was stopped and searched by police outside our place. They found a gram and a half of dope and she was fined £25.

Then I noticed a van parked opposite which sat there all day. There was no-one in the front, but you couldn't see into the back. Could it be the police sniffing around? I didn't know why I was suspicious. Perhaps because I was seeing Barry and mixing with lots of dubious people at the club.

Several weeks later, I went to a party thrown by Zorba the Greek, who had apparently hit the big-time after a drug-smuggling run from India. His place in Crouch End looked like a Turkish harem, with mirrors on the walls and pillows strewn around the floor. He had crates of champagne and wine, along with attractive side-dishes piled high with Charlie (*coke*). He was big-time and wanted everyone to see it.

Getting home at nine o'clock on Saturday morning, I slept most of the day. On Sunday morning, Angela wanted to put some flowers on her brother's grave. I was driving Barry's wife's car, a Capri, but I knew he wouldn't mind if I took a run down to Mitcham cemetery. Parking up, Angela took two carrier bags and a trowel from the boot and we spent half an hour tidying and planting flowers around Jimmy's grave. Mary was also buried near by, so we visited her plot.

Getting back to the Capri, we discovered the side window had been smashed and Angela's handbag was missing. I couldn't believe it. Something didn't feel right. Our door keys were in the handbag, along with a tiny amount of dope. Perhaps it was a routine burglary, I couldn't be sure.

We broke into the house through the service hatch which had been boarded up at the front and I reported the theft to the police. Three days later I had a call from Herne Hill Police Station. 'Your wife's bag has been found – would you like to come and pick it up?'

Of course, I was dubious because of the dope. There was only a tiny amount, but it was still a risk. 'Thanks very much,' I said. 'Where did you find it?'

'In the front garden of a house in Herne Hill.'

Angela went to collect the bag and nothing was missing. The dope was still there, wrapped in plastic. I was now truly worried. It wasn't the work of a casual thief. Nobody takes a risk stealing a handbag and then throws it away intact.

Suddenly, the pieces started falling into place. I mapped out the scenario. The police thought they had a coup. They must have followed the Capri from the Greek's house, knowing he was a drug smuggler. Obviously, they couldn't trace the car registration because Barry had only just bought the Capri for his wife and the papers hadn't passed through the DVLC in Swansea. They tailed the car to my block of flats and waited outside – not knowing that I was driving.

I could just imagine them sitting outside throughout the Saturday.

'How long we gonna wait?' they'd have been asking themselves.

'Give it till Sunday.'

Then they see Angela and me put the carrier bags into the car, along with the trowel and they're sure we are going to a drop-off. They follow us down to the cemetery, watching while we tend the graves. Finally, curiosity gets the better of them and they break into the car to learn our identities.

I dropped the Capri back to Barry and explained what had happened. He didn't seem overly concerned but Barry had one of those minds that could blank things out he didn't want to know about. A week later, I was at the club and one of the regulars asked me if I was going home via Canning Town. 'If you go past the Duke's Head, can you give this to Tim?' He gave me a package.

I wasn't worried because I knew Tim and I had dropped off packages before, never knowing what was in them. Ignorance is no excuse, of course, but I didn't even consider saying no. On my way home I stopped in at the Duke's Head and Tim jumped into the car. I gave him the package, he put it away and got into his van. As I pulled away, I saw them: two carloads of plain-clothed policemen.

What do they want? I thought. Am I being nicked? Nothing happened but I drove back to Barry's club and told him that the heat was definitely on Tim.

'Don't jump to conclusions, Bruce. Let's wait and see,' he said.

Two days later, at five o'clock in the morning, there was a knock at our door. The flat had a security entrance so nobody could get in from the street. Angela looked through the spyhole in the door and saw a distraught woman.

'What do you want?'

'I must speak to you, please open the door, I must speak to you, it's very important, it's a matter of life and death.'

'Well I can't at the moment, I'm not dressed . . .' Angela said.

'Please, please open the door.'

'Listen, just tell me what you want?'

'When you go shopping this morning will you . . .?'

'It's five o'clock in the morning!' Angela shouted. 'Why are you waking me to talk about shopping?'

The woman left but gave Angela her flat number. I didn't like the sound of it but sent Angela to confront her. When she came back she looked worried. 'What's wrong?' I said.

'I can't be sure, but I don't think the woman in the flat is the same woman who was outside the door.'

Now I knew something was wrong, but couldn't figure it out. Nothing made sense. Two days later there was another knock on the door. 'Your water tap's leaking into our flat below,' said the voice.

I opened the door and the police came charging inside, along with sniffer dogs. There were about ten of them and they immediately got heavy.

'All right, you in here. She goes in there,' one of them said, motioning Angela into the bedroom.

'You can't do that, she's not very well,' I said.

'Fucking do as you're told.'

I didn't want a row, knowing I couldn't win, but I was angry. Eventually the officer in charge calmed me down and allowed Angela to stay with me.

'Right. Where is it?' he said.

'Where's what?'

'You know what.'

'We got nothing here,' I said. 'Rip the place to pieces.'

They did just that. The wallpaper, carpets, beds, cupboards — everything was stripped, dismantled and broken up. The most they found was eight grams of weed.

Now it all fell into place. They had been following Tim, and when they nicked him they found the parcel, which I now assumed was drugs. Automatically, they jumped to the conclusion that I had given it to him and that I was a major dealer. Apparently there was a lot of speed being manufactured and the Mr Big was living somewhere in South London. They assumed it was me, and hence the heavy-handedness. The only thing they could find to attach any importance to were some plastic bags.

'What are these?'

'Jiffy bags.'

'Oh yes, and what do you use them for?'

'Like it says on the packet – for storing things in the fridge.'

'Is that all?'

'Yes, that's all.' Of course, the drug squad was disappointed at having failed to catch their man. They thought they were smashing a major amphetamine factory but instead had just shown their hand to the real criminals, who would hear about the raid and shut up shop. They charged me with possession and began threatening to link me with Tim and include 'intent to supply'.

'What have you got to say about that?'

'Nothing,' I said. 'I've got nothing to say about anything.'

I made bail after a week, desperate to get home because I was worried about Angela. I was almost certain she'd go to pieces.

It was nearly a year before the case came to court. I pleaded not guilty for the first time in my life, because I was innocent of the charge. I also told them, 'If you think I'm involved in drugs, just have a look at my bank accounts. I've no money, I don't have a car, and I haven't had a holiday for five years.'

All to no avail. To them it was a simple equation: ex-Train Robber, he must be guilty.

Two days into the trial, a woman reporter, whose court reporting made me wonder if she had been given her job on the shape of her arse, wrote a story that was headlined: 'MAJOR DRUG RING BUST TRAIN ROBBER INVOLVED.' The trial wasn't even over and I'd been convicted in print.

The next day, the judge offered me a retrial because of the story but I weighed up the pros and cons. A couple of the jury had smiled at Angela and more or less intimated that things were going my way. Similarly, I would seem more confident of my innocence if I continued with the trial.

So much for the theory!

Towards the end, my counsel said, 'Bruce, it doesn't look very good. You should brace yourself for a bit of time.'

OK, I thought, at worst it would be eighteen months and I'll be home in a year. I should have kept my legs crossed. The judge had the wind up. 'I see no other recourse but to send you to prison for three years.'

Angela collapsed outside the court and Rene took her home. I was in a daze. How could they expect a guy who'd spent twenty years in the nick to be changed by another spell inside? It was ludicrous and a total waste of time and money.

43

I was 54 years old and back in the Hate Factory. I left behind a woman with a broken heart who was fighting to maintain her sanity. When Angela collapsed again, I wasn't there for her. Nor was Nick, who had been sent to the Falklands for his second tour, this time on the HMS *Southampton* as part of the fleet left behind to clean up and do routine patrols.

Wandsworth Prison had changed, although it was still dirty, scruffy and short-staffed. The discipline was quite lax because there were so few screws but it meant we were locked up for 23 hours a day, which can become a personal torture. We only got out for half an hour's exercise in the morning and half an hour in the afternoon.

On my first day, I was approached by a young guy, barely in his twenties, who asked, 'Are you Bruce?'

'Yeah.'

'The Bruce? The Train Robber?'

'Yeah.'

'My dad knows you.'

'Does he? What's his name?'

When he told me I drew a deep breath. I didn't know his dad personally, although I'd heard the name and knew he got life for a heavy bit of work in which someone had died. Here was the syndrome continuing – like father, like son, I thought. Thank God Nick was in the Navy. Thank God he didn't finish up like his dad.

Initially I couldn't get a job. The stabbing incident at Wandsworth was still a black mark and screws never forget. Eventually, Ronnie Leslie, who had helped spring Biggsy from Wandsworth, organized a place for me in the laundry. It was heaven because I was out of my cell and doing something, even if it was just taking sheets from the washing-machines and feeding them through an enormous roller.

The old boys' network was as strong as ever and I bumped into screws and assistant governors that I'd met years earlier. If not old friends, they were certainly friendly faces. A surprising number were ex-Navy men who were thrilled to hear that Nick was serving in the Falklands. Through these salty old boys, I lobbied for a move from Wandsworth to Spring Hill, an open prison which I reckoned would be nicer for Angela when she visited. She had seen enough locks, bars and bolts to last her a lifetime.

They were taking a chance sending me there. It was like an army camp, with no walls or ditches or moats. We slept in dormitories that looked out across an enormous expanse of fields in which we could run or go for walks on Sundays. We were even allowed to use the swimming-pool at the local public school, Stowe.

Next door was Grendon Underwood, which was really more of a mental prison, and although the two institutions were separate there was a degree of co-operation. The deputy governor was an old chum, Major Smith from Parkhurst.

'Good heavens, Bruce, I didn't expect to see you again. What went wrong?'

I explained and he seemed genuinely sorry.

Visits were allowed every two weeks and lasted two hours, after a one-hour train journey from Marylebone to Aylesbury. Yes, Aylesbury: it appeared there was no shaking off the past.

As befits an open prison, the visits at Spring Hill were very relaxed. They were held in a building which also doubled as the cinema and television room. It was spacious, there were facilities to purchase refreshments, and the staff kept themselves to themselves. The general ambience was encouraging to visitors – especially children. No electric grilled doors here or forbidding grey walls.

'Things might have been different between us on the long sentence if you'd been in these conditions,' Angela said.

It was certainly a far cry from the days at Chelmsford where I'd go to my cell after a visit and wave a white hanky from the window in final farewell to my two loved ones. They'd drive to a car park outside the prison and wave from there in response; it was a gut-wrenching experience for all of us. Thank God those days were over; this wasn't the end of the world, at the worst I'd be home in two years – with luck, eighteen months. We could handle that – or so we thought.

Angela and I could sit holding hands, with the occasional restrained kiss, talking about the past and our plans for the future.

I told Angela that I'd done a lot of soul-searching since I'd been away. I saw this separation as the final test for both of us. We had found each other again under difficult circumstances and been torn apart. Now we didn't know if another absence was going to destroy everything again.

'Things are going to be different,' I said, and of that I was determined. They had to be; I'd had enough of prisons, and so had Angela. The time had come for me to hang up my gloves. I was no longer the man I used to be, and Angela, too, had changed. Time had produced a different perspective for both of us. With my notoriety I was always going to be in the frame; I had to get away from my past and stay away.

I'd had my fill of prison culture. The stories sound the same after twenty-odd years; the big touches, the cars they were going to buy, the holidays they were going to take. It was like an echo from the past. Yet I knew that for every thousand cons who boasted about their futures, probably only five would reach anywhere near their expectations. Even that handful would finish up in prison again.

However, what scared me most about my stay at Spring Hill was that I was quite happy there. I wasn't supposed to be happy in prison. I was supposed to want to get out. What had I become? I was running, swimming, eating wheatgerm in my porridge each morning, lunching on coleslaw from the kitchen – all simple things. If I was happy with such basic pleasures, why couldn't I be happy living the same life outside – only more so because I would be with Angela?

The date was announced for my parole hearing, but Angela had another breakdown. She went into hospital and then discharged herself so that nobody knew where she'd gone. There were stories about her having withdrawn money out of the bank – difficult, I reasoned, considering we didn't have any – and that the police had been alerted. I was getting phone calls from concerned friends, via the governor. Nobody knew where she'd gone. I was sick with worry and praying for compassionate early release to look after her.

I never found out where Angela went. She disappeared for six days and then went back to hospital of her own volition. When they transferred her to Warlingham, just outside Croydon, she began phoning at odd times during the day and night. The governor finally told me, 'We can't keep taking the calls like this, Bruce. It's obviously not doing either of you any good.'

From one day to the next, I couldn't predict Angela's state of mind. Her mood swings were violent and irrational. She would scream at me one day, or sob inconsolably the next. Her severe depression had first started in 1977 following the death of her brother Jimmy. She took an overdose and landed up in hospital: the diagnosis was that it had been induced by an accumulation of stress and general despair. She was eventually diagnosed as suffering from manic depression.

Mrs McNair Kay, the prison welfare officer, took me to see Angela at Warlingham. She was a very experienced social worker, compassionate, clearcut and very much aware of the dangers of Angela's condition and that she could lose reality for ever if she was locked up in a mental hospital. We left

Spring Hill at 8.30 a.m. for the three-hour drive and I sat in the Metro, dressed in civilian clothes, wondering what I would say to Angela. My parole hearing was due in a month and I wanted her home; I wanted to look after her.

Warlingham was set in landscaped gardens, a relatively modern hospital yet showing scars of neglect from cuts from the National Health Service. We went into a ward and spoke to a doctor about Angela's condition before I was allowed to see her.

Angela knew that I was there and came into the ward. She was looking well, appeared rational and was overjoyed to see me. The four of us had a bit of a chat before Angela and I were allowed to go to her room on our own. Angela told me that she was fighting to get the section lifted and be discharged. 'I feel that I'm being obstructed rather than helped,' she said.

I'd heard what the doctor had said, and I knew from past experience that Angela did not totally comprehend her condition. At the same time, however, I didn't have total confidence in her treatment, and I didn't want her to think I was siding with the opposition.

A fellow patient came into Angela's room and interrupted our conversation. Angela reacted violently, totally out of character. Initially I was surprised, but then I realized what was happening. The hospital was just another institution. As in prison, it was vital to maintain your own integrity; you had to establish that you couldn't be fucked around. Angela was rationally defending herself and her position.

Mrs McNair Kay took us to lunch in a local pub and the three of us talked through the problems. There were no answers, just hope for the future. As I kissed Angela goodbye, I reflected sadly that I was going back to an institution, leaving behind Angela in another. Would we ever escape these places?

The drive back was long, dreary and silent. We had exhausted our conversation. Mrs McNair Kay knew it wasn't going to be easy for us but we both agreed it had been a good day. We'd bolstered Angela and shown her that she wasn't on her own. For better or for worse, she still had me.

* * *

After being released in March 1985, I devoted all my time to getting Angela well again. We still had the flat in Streatham and I did the shopping each morning and organized her diet and exercise. I was right into raw vegetables and the power of healthy living to cure all manner of ills.

Although I tried to keep it from Angela, we were struggling financially, living from week to week. When an old friend came to me and offered me a bit of work, I was tempted. The coup was for two hundred grand and my whack would be fifty. I could really have used the money. It would have been our pension and seen us through to the end. I thought about it long and hard. Angela had just received ten grand from the sale of a flat she had owned with her former boyfriend; it wasn't big money but enough for me to decide that this coup wasn't worth the risk. I might have wanted more money, but I didn't need it. I was looking at my life from a totally different perspective. I was happy with my lot. Angela was on the mend and we were closer than we had been for years. Why jeopardize it? Why risk spending another fifteen years inside?

Life was pretty simple. We didn't need a lot. Fresh veggies from the greengrocer; a bottle of wine on special occasions; a walk through the park on the weekend. We didn't need a car or restaurant meals or holidays. Only occasionally would I show my face in the clubs and meet up with old friends. Once a month I'd go to fights with Barry, who had good connections in the fight game. These outings were good for my ego because I was treated in much the same way as an old champion. Instead of saying, 'This is so and so, the former middleweight champion,' the young fighters were told, 'This is Bruce Reynolds, the Great Train Robber.'

I would look at these starry-eyed hopefuls and remember what I was like at eighteen – full of ambition and desire, addicted to adrenalin. Who were *they* trying to impress?

In the spring of 1986, I stood outside a chapel in Dagenham for another funeral.

There had been a cremation and a short, succinct chapel service, the spoken eulogies reinforced by hundreds of floral tributes and the many people of all classes who'd congregated to pay their last respects. The occasion was all that my dad would have wanted.

Mac, my half-brother, had rung me up telling me that Dad had collapsed at home and had been taken into hospital. We went over immediately. The look on Mac's face told us the worst. Dad was lying unconscious, breathing shallowly through his open, toothless mouth. He looked so vulnerable, yet at peace.

The doctors said that he'd had a stroke. They didn't expect him to regain consciousness, but if he did there was a strong possibility that he'd be brain damaged. We were aghast. We couldn't imagine the old man as a cabbage; he'd have hated it; independence of spirit was everything to him.

There was nothing that anybody could do. Five days of waiting saw no change; we sat and talked and hoped amongst ourselves at his bedside, but the shallow breathing told its own story. I was at home when Mac phoned to say that Dad had died without regaining consciousness.

'I hope you understand,' I said, 'but I'm happy that he went that way. He was seventy-seven, he had lived a full life and he was active to the end. He died without suffering – what more can anyone ask?'

Now the old man was having a great send-off. Mac had done him proud; I played a secondary part in the proceedings. Mac was the new head of the family, if not in age or seniority, then certainly in terms of responsibility. He and his wife Wendy had looked after Dad ever since Amy died in 1971. They had seen him through the lot, in sickness and in health. Living near by, they'd been his family while I was in prison, and, sad to say, when I'd been out. Mac had been everything that I had not, the dutiful son and responsible parent. I owed a lot to him.

I shook hands with the Lady Mayoress and other local dignitaries. Their eyes betrayed their curiosity, the flicker of excitement at shaking hands with notoriety, the flatness of disappointment when they realized that I wasn't Bruce Reynolds the Train Robber, I was just the son of Thomas Reynolds bidding him the last farewell, wishing him well on his journey into the unknown.

* * *

The Great Train Robbery had gone from the front page into English folklore. Periodically, there were stories recapping the events or Biggsy would surface with some new publicity stunt. Although he had played only a small part in the robbery, he had become the best-known member of the firm because of his playboy antics and the botched attempts to bring him back.

For many years there had been talk of making a film about the robbery and several projects started and then faltered. Then in about 1984, I heard about another production, this one called *Buster* and centred on Buster Edwards, who had become a lovable landmark at Waterloo Station, where he sold flowers.

I didn't hear any more about the project for two years, apparently due to financial problems, but then I was told that Phil Collins had agreed to play the lead role and pre-production was up and running. With such a bankable name, there were no longer any problems with money but it did create a problem with credibility. Everybody knew Phil Collins – it took a huge leap of the imagination to pretend he was a Great Train Robber.

The making of *Buster* opened all sorts of doors. There wasn't much money involved but I was asked to be a consultant, particularly for the scenes in Mexico. I met the producer, Norma Heyman, at a dinner party at her house in Chelsea. Among those sitting round the table were David Green, the director, and Bobbie Keach, a former professional footballer and great friend of Terry Venables and Bobby Moore. Elizabeth Taylor arrived late and I was thrilled about meeting her in the flesh. Under all the make-up and jewels, she was still a beautiful woman. Ironically, Liz had been a target of ours for years. While waiting for her to arrive, I joked to Norma: 'I could always tell her how we nearly stole her jewellery while she was staying at Englefield Green.'

I was shown the original script, which I didn't like particularly. As it turned out, the final version was only mildly more appealing. There was so much artistic licence I could barely recognize myself, let alone some of the other characters. There was a scene in the original script – thankfully cut from the final version – where Buster and I purportedly robbed a bank in Mexico while our wives were fighting on the pavement outside to create a diversion. Fantasy, of course.

The actual robbery scenes were done very well. I went up to watch the filming near the Railway Museum in York. There was a single stretch of line normally used by one of the small steam trains for excursions, and they laid another fifty yards of track alongside it. For added authenticity, the museum had provided an English Electric Diesel. For the scenery shots, they had found a place that looked a lot like Bridego Bridge, and after some paint and bits of cardboard were added it looked virtually identical.

I met Larry Lamb, who played my part, and we developed a good friendship. I still see him now and then. At Shepperton Studios, I also met one of my lifelong heroes, Anthony Quayle – star of *Ice Cold in Alex* and *The Guns of Navarone* and, in real life, of behind-the-lines operations with Force 266, the Albanian section of SOE. He was a big man, and his handshake was steel firm.

'How do you feel about your activities portrayed on film?' he said.

'Probably the same as you did when you filmed *Guns of Navarone*,' I said.

Quayle raised a quizzical eyebrow.

'I am aware of your work with SOE,' I said.

He looked at me steadily for a moment and then a wry grin crossed his face. 'It's all an illusion, you know,' he said. Then he used a quote that I recognized from Brecht's *Galileo*: 'Unhappy the land that has need of heroes.'

I smiled back. I knew what he meant. I had seen the photograph of him on an Albanian hillside, bearded and binoculared, one hand on his hip at right angles, the other firmly on his walking stick that was thrust deep into the snow, his pistol holster slung low on his left, the sub machine-gun prominently displayed, butt end down in the snow. Oh yes, I knew where he had been. Sure it was all an illusion, but while it lasted it was as real as life itself.

When the film was finally released, I was very disappointed. The final shot was of Buster being interviewed outside his flower stall at Waterloo. In the original script I had seen, the caption had come up: 'Bruce Reynolds came back to

England, was arrested and sentenced to twenty-five years in jail.'

But now there was nothing. As far as the audience was concerned, they would walk out of the cinema believing I was probably dead or still in prison.

Years later, people still asked me, 'Why didn't they say what happened to you?'

Buster did quite well at the box-office, although there was a great deal of hypocrisy surrounding the launch. Only a few commentators picked up on the fact that Phil Collins was portraying a Train Robber as being a lovable rogue.

If the film had a positive effect on me, it was that it triggered my interest in writing. Having spent a lifetime reading books – after all, I had plenty of spare time – I starting jotting down bits and pieces and gathering my thoughts. I was toying with the idea of putting the record straight; of telling it from the inside. In many ways I wanted to help people understand how a bright kid from a reasonably loving home had finished up as one of Britain's most notorious thieves.

And there was one person in particular that I wanted to explain it all to.

The son of Thomas Richard Reynolds and Dorothy Margaret (née Keen), born in London on 7 September 1931, at Charing Cross Hospital in the Strand.

EPILOGUE

As the clock chimed midnight on 24 April 1990, I opened a bottle of Dom and poured two glasses. Champagne was a rarity in our lives but it was Angela's 47th birthday – a good enough reason to celebrate.

At six the next morning, I was roused by a phone call from Frank, my old running pal from Maidstone nick, who was now living in Spain.

'Have you heard the news?' he asked.

'Heard what?'

'Chas is dead. He's been shot at the villa in Marbella.'

I was too shocked to reply. It seemed unbelievable. Charlie Wilson, my childhood friend and accomplice; a kindred spirit with so much *joie de vivre* that nothing could cool his incredible sense of fun and his winning smile.

'What happened?' I mumbled, barely listening to the words.

'It was a professional hit,' said Frank. 'Pat was in the house but she's OK. I don't know the details.'

'A hit? On Chas? Who the fuck would want him dead?'

'I know, I know. None of us can understand it.'

I held the phone in silence, trying to fathom the enormity of the news. Frank could sense my distress. 'I just thought you oughta know, Bruce. I'm sorry. I know you were tight.'

When Frank said goodbye, I cradled the telephone for several minutes until Angela brought me a cup of tea and gently prised the handset from my fingers.

The morning papers were decorated with headlines about the killing. There was all the familiar hype, the post-mortems on the Train Robbery, the wild speculation about gangland vendettas and drug dealing. The hacks were clutching at straws and out-doing each other with catchy labels. Chas was the 'Silent Man', 'the King', 'the Brains', 'the Treasurer'. Then he became 'an Aristocrat of Crime', 'Mr Big of the Costa Drug Runners', 'the Commander in Chief of Crime', even a 'Cockney Robin Hood' – how Charlie would have loved that one.

Slowly the true story began to emerge.

23 April had been Pat and Charlie's 35th wedding anniversary and they had invited friends around for drinks by the pool. They had moved to the Costa del Sol six years earlier, wanting to enjoy the good life in the sun. Working alongside local labourers, Chas had turned a pokey little bungalow into a luxury hacienda, importing pink marble from Portugal and creating ornate balconies. He was proud of the place and jokingly called it 'Chequers'.

The last guests had left by late afternoon and Chas was in the kitchen slicing tomatoes and cucumbers for a salad when the doorbell rang. Pat answered it and there was a young man standing outside wearing a grey track suit and a baseball cap. He was a Londoner, Pat could tell from his accent, and he asked to see Charlie.

Charlie must have recognized the name because he came to the door straightaway and invited the young man inside. Pat disappeared into the house, knowing better than to hang around while Charlie was discussing business. The two men walked across the patio to the barbecue Charlie had built into the back wall, where they stood talking for a few minutes. Pat heard raised voices, then two loud bangs.

The end was quick. Charlie was kicked, very hard, and as he doubled over he was punched in the face, breaking his nose. Then the attacker took out a revolver from under his track suit and fired at point-blank range. One shot went into Charlie's neck, severing his carotid artery; a second went into his mouth and out through the back of his head.

Bobo, the family's Alsatian-husky cross, must have gone to his master's rescue because he received a kick in the chest which broke his front leg and put him out of action. He was put down later that day.

Pat rushed into the garden and found Charlie staggering towards the pool with blood spurting from his neck. She told the police later that he seemed to be pointing, with a shaking finger, towards the back wall, trying to tell her something.

During the following days, there was wild speculation about the execution. The Spanish police were convinced that Charlie was involved in drug smuggling – the usual motive for murders along the Costa. Pat was adamant that Charlie was not into drugs and I agreed with her – although no-one will probably ever know the truth. He was anti-drugs, a non-smoker, who rarely drank and was happy living out his remaining years untroubled in the sun.

Sure he knew drug-runners – we all did – but he didn't mix with them. He and Pat rarely went out, preferring to stay home and watch television beamed in to the big satellite dish in the garden. They never openly socialized with the criminal fraternity in Marbella.

Charlie didn't want any aggro. After his release in 1979, he had plenty of it. Twice he was charged with VAT fraud and both trials failed to come up with a guilty verdict. He was also charged with conspiracy to rob from a security van, but the case was dropped when the police officers involved were investigated for corruption. Afterwards he knew that they would never leave him alone – so he retired to Spain.

The funeral was on 10 May, at Streatham cemetery in south London. The rain just stopped in time. Five limousines led the convoy of fifty cars. On the roof rack of the front limo was a huge floral display spelling out the name 'CHAS'.

Angela, Nick and I arrived in time to see the cortège pass. Pat was in the front car, rocking with sobs. Daughters Cheryl, Tracy and Leander held on to their mother, tears chasing down their cheeks.

I remember the Christmas we spent with them in Canada. Charlie had been bustling about, joking, playing with the kids, carving the joint, washing-up; there was nothing he wouldn't do for his family and friends. One evening we had twelve screaming kids packed into his big old Cadillac, taking them to a Christmas carol service at the local community centre.

'What would their parents make of it if they knew who we were?' I joked.

Charlie laughed and shook his head.

Now he was on his last ride. Our roots went back forty years. We'd been the triumvirate, Chas, Buster and I – the fugitives that the whole world had been looking for. We had played the game and given them a good run.

The media were out in force – drugs and death are good stimulants for circulation. With so many photographers and cameramen jostling for position outside the chapel, we had difficulty getting past them.

Then I heard the familiar strains of 'My Way' – Charlie's signature tune – and I couldn't help but smile. It summed up his personality and his life. As the final notes faded, the Minister, Revd Kevin Parkes from nearby St Anne's, began the service, 'I am the Resurrection . . .'

I left before the final song. I wanted to avoid the reporters waiting outside, and went unrecognized until I saw Roy James and we embraced. He had put on some weight since our last meeting and, like me, was struggling to comprehend what had happened.

A reporter thrust a microphone between us.

'Are you Roy James?' he asked.

'No,' said Roy. 'You've made a mistake.'

'Come on! You're Roy James.' Other journalists had arrived.

Finally Roy shrugged and nodded his head. 'Charlie was one of the best,' he said, before turning to leave. I had already slipped away.

Briefly, I found Jimmy White – always a problem because he'd lost none of his ability to blend into the background. We exchanged condolences with a handshake and then he, too, was gone.

The crowd parted to let Pat and her daughters through to the graveside. Pat was supported by Norman Radford, Charlie's cousin. I felt choked when I saw her. She had been through so much in her life, like all the Train Robbers' wives – the years of absent husbands, the endless round of prison visits, struggling to cope on their own. What a relief it must have been for Pat when Chas finally came home and they retired to Marbella. She must have felt that it was all over. Now she had every right to cry.

The mahogany coffin, polished like a mirror, was lowered in the ground as the dozens of wreaths were stacked up on each side.

I found Buster, moist-eyed and with his hair gone snow white. He had left his flower business under the station bridge at Waterloo to walk behind the coffin.

Beside him was Bob Welch, struggling on crutches. A cartilage operation had gone wrong in prison and he's spent the rest of his life trying operation after operation to get it right. It was sad because Bob had been a great footballer in his youth.

Pat was led to the graveside, a single red rose crushed in her hand.

'We are entrusting our brother Charlie to His keeping,' said Revd Parkes and then Pat kissed the rose and let it fall on the coffin.

After the family, Bob hobbled to the grave, reached down for some earth and let it trickle to the bottom. Then came Buster, unable to look. Finally, it was my turn.

I crumbled earth between my fingers, looked down and uttered my own epitaph to Charlie.

'He never left anyone behind.'

You couldn't say more than that.

Charlie's was just one of many funerals I was to attend over the next handful of years.

On Tuesday 30 November 1994, Buster Edwards was found dead by his brother in a lock-up garage near his flower stall at London's Waterloo station. He had hanged himself from a steel girder after going on a drinking binge. He was 62.

I didn't know how someone could get in the state of mind to do what Buster did. He was said to have had money problems after a drop in business at the stall he had run since his release from prison in 1975, but in truth Buster had been unhappy for some time. He had hated going straight. We had both been criminals more for the hell of it – the excitement – than the rewards. Perhaps it was like what happens when a footballer or mountaineer comes to the end of their career. They live their entire life on the edge, but what happens when it's all over, when you have to stop? It was very hard for both of us when we quit. When we came out of jail we were old men, and too well known. We knew we had to stop for our families' sakes. But you never stop missing the buzz.

Outside his little Victorian terrace home in Walworth a few days later, the funeral cortège of more than twenty cars began its slow journey through the south London streets on which Buster had learned his trade. At the head was his wife, June, whose floral tribute bore a lyric from 'Two Hearts', the theme song from the film *Buster*.

Bob Welch was also there, but not Jim Hussey or Tommy Wisbey, who were both serving time for cocaine trafficking. Roy James was also absent, having just been jailed for six years after a shooting incident in which his ex-wife and father-in-law were wounded.

At Waterloo the procession paused, then we continued the rest of the eight-mile journey to Streatham.

About a hundred mourners filed into the chapel of the South London Crematorium under a cold sky the colour of slate.

Friends and relatives could not believe that the Buster they knew might wish to take his own life, but, in a newspaper interview I'd read shortly before his death, he may have given us all a clue. 'I know I'm lucky to have got the chance to have this stall and be my own boss, but it's so dreary compared with the life I used to lead. It wasn't even the money. I had been on jobs that hadn't netted me a penny but, oh, does the adrenalin flow. My main excitement here is sorting out the fights between the winos.'

As I left the crematorium, the grey clouds parted for a brief moment and I looked up at the patch of blue sky. 'Do us a favour, will you, mate?' I muttered. 'Say hello to Charlie for me.'

Less than two months later, my dearest friend, Harry, who'd taken part in what was at the time the largest postwar robbery but was never caught, made his final escape. One of the best-known faces in the London underworld in the 1950s and 1960s, Harry fell to his death from a window in Brentford on 15 January 1995 after suffering from depression. Ten days later, he was being cremated to the strains of Charlie Parker.

In 1952, Harry had taken part in the Eastcastle Street mailbag robbery in which £287,000 was stolen from a Post Office van on its way across the West End from Paddington Station. The crime was regarded so seriously by the Establishment that Sir Winston Churchill, then prime minister, required daily updates on the investigation, and the postmaster-general, Earl de la Warr, had to explain to Parliament what had gone wrong. A £25,000 reward was offered for information leading to recovery of the money, a thousand officers took part in searches and dozens of London's villains were rounded up, but Harry and the others were never caught.

Police regarded it as the first of a new era of 'project' crime, in which meticulous planning was used, as opposed to the old-fashioned smash-and-grab. Rehearsals had been carried out in roads outside London under the pretext that a crime movie was being shot.

After that, Harry was involved in most of the major crimes of the time and, although he was not much older than me, he was very much my mentor. 'Lucky' Harry never got caught. In fact, he only ever served a short sentence for a matter unrelated to the many robberies he took part in. On the day of the Great Train Robbery in 1963, he happened to be in Cannes with a family of French-Iranian millionaires. Somebody, I can't imagine who, must have tipped him off that something major was about to happen and an alibi might be advisable.

Soon afterwards, married and with a family, Harry decided to quit crime completely. He went into the textile business and lived a respectable life in west London.

I had visited Harry at least once a week ever since I came out of prison, and I knew he'd been profoundly affected by Buster's death. Another close friend and work associate of ours, Rick Withers, had also died recently, compounding his depression.

It was my honour to deliver Harry's eulogy on that miserable, windswept morning, and I told the packed chapel, 'We were partners and friends for over forty-five years. He was always there, his loyalty unquestionable. During the years of my absence he took over the role of surrogate father to Nick, my son, who loved him like he loved me.

'Harry was responsible for Nick's development and growth. My son is as much a part of Harry as he is of me. Our relationship could not have developed without his help. Neither could it have been maintained. Uncle Harry will be sorely missed by Nick.

'He'd had a good life, rich and fulfilling, justifying his name of Lucky Harry. I remember that I'd been fishing for marlin in the Bay of Acapulco for three days without a bite. Harry came out with me and got a bite – fought and landed a fourteen-foot marlin. He was so proud. He thought he was Ernest Hemingway that day. Maybe he was.

'Sadly, in his last years, his luck was diminished by his illness. He'd been a young champ, and now he was an old champ who couldn't make the final count. The Harry who died last week wasn't the Harry we knew and loved, the Harry who never gave up the struggle.'

His last letter to me, written three weeks earlier, amply demonstrated this:

'Hello Mate and Angie – I hope I did not punish you too much on the phone . . . but I will desist . . . and punish you in the flesh when we meet. I feel I will make the struggle to survive, as I know there is no other way and maybe in the end it will be for the best. Maybe Jung might have said . . . life is the struggle . . . and the struggle is life . . . Lots of love, Harry.'

On 5 June 1997, George 'Taters' Chatham, the man known as the Thief of the Century, and reckoned to have stolen as much as £30 million over the years but then gambled it all away, died penniless in a nursing home in Battersea. His wife and daughter had predeceased him.

Just two months later, I was at another funeral, this time of Roy James, Great Train Robber, racing car driver, silversmith and one-time Queens Park Rangers trialist. Roy had become the fifth and youngest of the Great Train Robbers to die.

Whilst in prison, Roy had kept himself fit and, with remission for good behaviour, was released on 15 August 1975, having served just over a third of his thirty-year sentence. He was immediately back in the gym, determined to work his way back into motor racing. Within weeks, however, Roy had broken his leg in a crash while testing at Silverstone. 'I went through Abbey Corner with 9,200 r.p.m. on the clock,' he told *Autosport*. 'The times were coming down nicely and I'd have had a decent position on the grid for the British Grand Prix Atlantic race. After twelve years it felt good and I was elated. I can't wait to have a go again. Time is not on my side. I can't afford to miss a day.'

Roy even spoke of hoping to be in Formula One within two years, but time had indeed run out on him. Roy's age, those twelve years away from the track, technical developments in his absence and a lack of money all contributed to him fading from the scene.

Roy wound up back at the Old Bailey. In 1984, along with Charlie Wilson and six others, he was accused of a £2.4 million VAT fraud. Customs and Excise alleged that the eight had melted down gold coins into gold bars, smuggled them into the UK, then sold them, pocketing the VAT. Roy was acquitted, while Charlie eventually paid over £400,000 to Customs to avoid a retrial.

Roy returned to silversmithing in Hatton Garden. In February 1982 he married a woman thirty years his junior.

The marriage soon broke down, buckling under the strain of the huge age gap. There were arguments over custody of the children, which was eventually awarded to Roy, and a settlement of £150,000 which Roy was supposed to pay but never did.

In May 1993, his ex-wife and her father were returning the children to Roy after a day's outing. Roy drew a gun and shot the man three times; luckily he wasn't killed, but was extensively scarred and later partially lost the use of one arm. 'He told me he was so angry he felt like putting both hands around my neck and strangling the life out of me,' Roy's ex-wife told the jury at the Old Bailey when he denied the attempted murder of her father.

In his defence, Roy claimed he had been depressed by the death of his mother, financial problems and the break-up of his marriage. He had, he said, suffered an 'out-of-body experience'. He could recall seeing himself holding the gun, but not firing more than one shot.

Sentencing him to six years in prison, Judge Geoffrey Grigson told Roy, 'I take into account that since 1964 you have not been convicted of any criminal offence and have made a new life for yourself and have devoted yourself to your family . . .'

In the autumn of 1996, Roy underwent triple bypass surgery and was released from prison early in 1997. He died on 21 August after another heart attack.

I couldn't believe it. He had been the youngest and fittest of us all.

Our French-crewed plane took off on its 8,400-mile journey from an airfield in southern England at 3.09 p.m. on Friday 4 May 2001. The fourteen-seater Dassault Falcon 900 executive jet first headed for Cape Verde Island, off the west coast of Africa. After refuelling, it carried on to Rio.

The Sun had initiated the retrieval mission and were liaising closely with the police over the operation. We knew that Scotland Yard would have a team of detectives on hand when Ronnie returned.

As well as the two reporters, my son Nick was also on the flight. He would help Ronnie's son, Michael, cope with his departure. Over the years, I had watched with immense pride as Nick's list of achievements grew longer, and many was the time I'd muttered my gratitude to the fates for stopping him from following in my criminal footsteps.

When he left the Royal Navy after the Falklands Conflict, Nick had pursued his interests in music and art, playing the harmonica with the band Octopus and getting to number 33 in the charts. He is now playing with Alabama 3, who did the theme music for *The Sopranos*, and who were a main stage act at the Glastonbury festival 2002 alongside the likes of Coldplay, Rod Stewart and the Stereophonics. He was also a talented sculptor, and among other works had done bronze castings of Andy McNab's head and Buzz Aldrin's foot. His critically acclaimed exhibition, *Cons To Icons*, had been a London sell-out.

I looked around me. Everybody on the plane was rather more casually dressed than I was. I was wearing the same blue discharge blazer I'd worn when I left Maidstone prison in 1978. It symbolised my re-entry into British society, just as Ronnie had to do now.

It was a hot, sunny, dusty morning. We stopped at a roadside bar for a large neat tequila just before what was sure to be an emotional meeting at lunchtime on Saturday, twelve hours after the jet touched down. I needed Mexican courage to face up to the emotional impact of seeing Ron. I was still apprehensive because I was the person who'd seduced him into being in the gang. I didn't want to get him into another mess.

I'd last seen him in September 2000 when I flew to Rio as the guest of a computer game company Ronnie was involved with, and had thought then that I'd never see him again. It had been hard to disguise my shock when I saw Ronnie again. He was a shadow of the legend who had evaded British justice for 35 years. A second stroke had robbed him of his speech and left him partially paralysed – and since then he'd had a third. Yet for all that, his eyes had an amazing range of expression and he gave a thumbs up, a smile or a frown to convey his viewpoint.

Soon after my return to the UK he'd written me a letter. 'I can't keep running any longer,' he said. Struck dumb by the strokes, he had scribbled out his thoughts on a pad. 'I am a sick man. My last wish is to walk into a Margate pub as an Englishman and buy a pint of bitter. I hope I live long enough to be able to do that.'

I agreed with him wholeheartedly. I felt he should come home for the simple reason that nobody should die in a foreign field. In the words of John Steinbeck, no man should be buried in alien soil.

I saw Ronnie's son Michael in London several weeks later. I'd sent Ron a reply to his letter saying that if he came home it would be his last great adventure. I told him, 'This is a tough one. Only you can decide.'

It wasn't long afterwards that Ron organised for an e-mail to be sent to Scotland Yard, asking for a passport. The message read: 'I would like to give myself up to you. What I need is passport documentation to travel back to Britain. I am prepared to be arrested at the gate when I arrive at Heathrow Airport and submit myself to the due process of the law.' He signed off, 'Ronald Arthur Biggs, Rio de Janeiro, 2 May 2001.' And in a final gesture that his return plan was genuine, he even included a thumbprint which would be matched with the Great Train Robbery records still held at the Yard.

Ironically, the emergency passport that the consulate rushed through for him was the first Ronnie had ever had. He'd spent years on the run after going over the wall at Wandsworth Prison, through Belgium, France, Australia, Tahiti, Panama, Bolivia, Barbados and Brazil, but he had never travelled under his own name before.

There were tears in our eyes when we met at the palatial home of a friend where Ronnie was spending his last few days in Brazil. Embracing him, I said, 'I'm sorry I got you into this mess in the first place.'

The response I got from Ron was every bit as tearful and emotional as mine. There had always been warmth in our souls for each other that was hard to describe.

I told him he was showing tremendous courage to go home and face the music. None of us knew what the authorities intended to do with him. We just hoped they'd be fair to him;

maybe some sort of amnesty or immediate parole in view of his advanced ill health.

The following morning, Monday 7 May, Ronnie was finally on his way to Britain after 13,068 days on the run. Our plane took off from Rio de Janeiro airport at 9.18 p.m. British time amid scenes of pandemonium.

We'd driven as a group in a minibus, and there was an unexpected drama when the vehicle had to be diverted because of a gunfight between rival drug gangs in a shanty town on the route to the airport. Then all hell broke loose as we finally arrived at Terminal Two, where our executive jet was waiting. More than a hundred journalists from all round the world besieged us, and in the end security staff ordered the driver to leave for the sake of public safety. We parked up under a palm tree a mile away while the situation was assessed, then a British Consular official phoned to call the minibus to Terminal One. We were smuggled into the building, then ushered secretly into Terminal Two.

Tears filled Ronnie's eyes as he took one last look at Brazil. Soon afterwards the jet roared into the sky above Sugarloaf Mountain and headed over the Atlantic for the thirteen-hour journey home.

In the cargo hold were Ronnie's three cases, crammed with his most cherished possessions. One contained books full of newspaper cuttings about the robbery and his life on the run. Another was full of jazz CDs by Ella Fitzgerald, Mel Torme and Memphis Slim. Also jammed in was an eight-inch crystal model of a diesel locomotive, given to him by his ex-wife, Charmian. Michael looked at me and said, 'His whole life is packed up in those three suitcases.'

I looked at Ron. He'd been unable to resist a joke as he tucked into his last breakfast in Rio – porridge. He'd put down his spoon and held up his hands, pretending to grasp prison bars. Then he reached for his pad and pen. Dabbing a handkerchief to his face as he wrote, he explained he did not want to be a burden any more to his son and his young family. Michael had spent the last eighteen months caring for his father after his third stroke. Ronnie added, 'He is a very good son to me. He can't go on with his own life while carrying me.'

* * *

Ronald Arthur Biggs was arrested the moment he was helped down the aircraft steps and his feet touched British soil. He was whisked away for an appearance before a magistrate in Hammersmith, then taken to Belmarsh prison in Kent, where he still is. I visit him as often as I am allowed, and every time I see him I am reminded that our lives have been bound together by Fate. When I look at his frail frame I see my own mortality. *C'est la vie!*

INDEX